Son of the pioneering ethnobotanist Jessie Williamson, Tom Williamson was born in Malawi and educated at schools in Africa and England. After gaining degrees in geology at Brasenose College, Oxford and geochemistry at the University of Leeds, Williamson worked as an exploration geologist for the gold and copper industries in Africa. Then he worked for a period at the Science Museum, London, producing in 1977 what was probably the world's first popular exhibition on climate change.

Later Williamson returned to the metals field. Working for a UN agency, Williamson monitored the global tin industry, writing reports for governments. While making these studies of placer tin mining, in Brazil and elsewhere, Williamson also became interested in the placer mining of another more valuable metal, gold.

It is the latter precious metal that, according to the missing science revealed in *Probe*, ET prospecting and mining bots may have focused on, when exploiting the placer metal resources of Earth and other earthlike planets.

PROBE
Alien-free Edition

Tom Williamson

Published in 2022 by SilverWood Books

SilverWood Books Ltd
14 Small Street, Bristol, BS1 1DE, United Kingdom
www.silverwoodbooks.co.uk

Copyright © Tom Williamson 2022
Image copyrights credited throughout

Cover picture: enhanced digital sky image DSC02012, exposure time 1/640 second, acquired at 1326 local time on 30 April 2013 by Dr Rob Hartland from his home in the Perth Hills, Western Australia with a Sony DSC Cyber-shot DSC RX 100 compact camera. One interpretation of this image would be that it represents a giant high-aspect-ratio tube-like mother probe. Courtesy: Dr Rob Hartland, wispyclouds.net

The right of Tom Williamson to be identified as the author of this work has been asserted in accordance with the Copyright, Designs and Patents Act 1988 Sections 77 and 78.

All rights reserved. No part of this publication may be reproduced, stored in a retrieval system, or transmitted in any form or by any means, electronic, mechanical, photocopying, recording or otherwise, without prior permission of the copyright holder.

ISBN 978-1-80042-123-3 (paperback)
ISBN 978-1-80042-124-0 (ebook)

British Library Cataloguing in Publication Data
A CIP catalogue record for this book is
available from the British Library

Page design and typesetting by SilverWood Books

Contents

	Acknowledgements	7
1	Authentic Alien Artifact?	9
2	The McDonald Conjecture	16
3	Aliens – or not?	46
4	Probe Theory Evolves	64
5	Did World War II attract Probes?	72
6	Project Identification	83
7	Searching for Gold?	88
8	The Faraday Effect	111
9	Like Baxter's Angelia	124
10	Kirtland	142
11	Bentwaters and Whiteman	154
12	Beam Forward	163
13	The French Connection	175
14	The Dalnegorsk Events	189
15	Scientists Start Work	208
16	Artificial Life	226
17	Molybdenum and Gold	239
18	Von Neumann Machines	246

19	The Collierville Bots	275
20	Growing Probes	289
21	Science not UFOlogy	296

Appendices

1	The 1976/77 US Navy 'fence'	308
2	US Secret Satellite Detection of 'Fast-Walkers', 1988	310
3	The Hartland Digital Images	311
4	US Congress attending to UFOs	314
5	The Wargo hypothesis	317
6	War of Words	321
	Science and General References	323
	UFOlogy References	337
	Index	340

Acknowledgements

Many people and organisations have helped me to complete this book. The magic of Google Translate has made possible the provisional account, presented in Chapters 14, 15 and 16, of the science carried out in the 1990s by teams of accredited experts in Russia and the Ukraine that later went missing.

To adequately convey the scale of the missing science and its context, multiple images, including leaked laboratory photographs and images of anomalous activity, were needed. To organise the printing of a book with so many images is a significant challenge. So, I would like to thank Helen Hart and her colleagues at SilverWood Books for working hard to produce this book with its 94 black and white figures and eight colour plates.

Last, but not least, I thank my wife, Sara Swee Yong, for her never-failing support during this long project.

1

Authentic Alien Artifact?

On 26 March 2012, the National Atomic Testing Museum in Las Vegas opened an exhibition, *Area 51: Myth or Reality*, dealing with the notoriously secretive Area 51 military base on the southern shore of Groom Lake, Nevada. The base has been long connected with the testing of experimental aircraft and weapons systems. Given the vast popular interest in UFOs, it's not surprising that the base also became a focus for claims about UFO activity. Not only have witnesses reported strange lights in the sky; there have also been claims that crashed alien spacecraft have been studied there and the information used to design advanced US military projects – so-called reverse engineering. There have even been rumours that the remains of the humanoid crew of an alien spacecraft that allegedly crashed at Roswell, New Mexico, in 1947, have been studied in Area 51.

You don't need to be a genius to see that government officials trying to maintain secrecy about so-called Black Projects might have encouraged rumours about UFO activity at Area 51. But stories about aliens and UFOs also make for great entertainment. So, it's also not surprising that the curators of the National Atomic Testing Museum sought to exploit this rich vein of modern folklore in their Area 51 exhibit.

But one of the most provocative items in the exhibition wasn't connected with Area 51. In a display area accompanied by the sign *Authentic Alien Artifact* was a vial containing small fragments (Fig 1). The sign stated "On Jan. 29 1986, a UFO crashed in Dalnegorsk, located in the Soviet Union. The crash is referred to as the Roswell incident of the Soviet Union. There were numerous witnesses to the crash with most

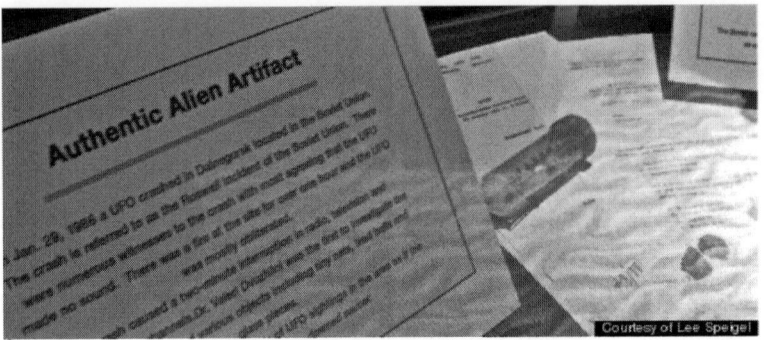

Fig 1. The Authentic Alien Artifact display, as it appeared in the National Atomic Testing Museum's 2012 exhibition Area 51:Myth or Reality. *[National Atomic Testing Museum, Las Vegas]*

agreeing that the UFO made no sound. There was a fire at the site for over one hour and the UFO was mostly obliterated."

The exhibit went on to state that the crash caused a two-minute interruption in radio and television. "Dr Valeri Dvuzhilni was the first to investigate," the text continued. "He collected various objects including 'tiny nets' and 'lead balls.'"

The display stated: "Three Soviet academic centers and 11 research institutes analyzed the objects from this UFO crash. The distance between atoms is different from ordinary iron. Radar cannot be reflected from the material." The Museum's display added "Elements in the material may disappear and new ones appear after heating. One piece disappeared completely in front of four witnesses. The core of the material is composed of a substance with anti-gravitational properties."

Many visitors were impressed. But scientists were perplexed. Given the Museum's links with the Smithsonian Institution in Washington, one would expect a high scientific standard from the display. Yet much of the information in the exhibit seemed to have come from the world of pseudoscience.

For a start, take the ideas implicit in the notion "Roswell incident of the Soviet Union". There are excellent reasons to disbelieve claims that an alien spacecraft crashed at Roswell, New Mexico in 1947. First, the stories are anthropomorphic. The grey humanoid aliens that many UFOlogists believe to have piloted the craft strongly resemble the extraterrestrial beings featured in the pre-World War I science fiction novels of the British writer H.G.Wells. Real aliens wouldn't look like that.

Second, if scientists really had studied the remains of Roswell aliens and their craft, it would have been impossible to contain the ensuing scientific knowledge. The insights resulting from an understanding of alien biology and technology would have leaked out and galvanized scientists worldwide. That simply didn't happen.

So comparisons with the alleged Roswell incident did nothing to dispel the aura of pseudoscience hanging over the Museum's Dalnegorsk exhibit. Moreover, other claims made in the display lacked scientific plausibility. Pieces of material don't simply disappear – after all, the fragments of Dalnegorsk material have stayed obstinately in their vial ever since the exhibit opened. And what, outside pseudoscience, is "a substance with anti-gravitational properties"?

One man who could perhaps shed light on all this is the veteran American investigative journalist, George Knapp. Based in Las Vegas, Knapp travelled to Dalnegorsk in the 1990s and interviewed Valeri Dvuzhilni for a TV program. Later, Dvuzhilni came to the USA and gave Knapp the material displayed by the Museum.

In an interview with HuffPost journalist Lee Speigel (HuffPost Weird News, 1 August 2012), Knapp amplified the Las Vegas Museum's description of the Dalnegorsk material. Knapp said:

"Valeri Dvuzhilni of the Academy of Sciences was first to arrive on the scene two days later. He collected samples of strange metallic mesh scattered at the site, and samples of rocks and vegetation which had been scorched in the crash."

"Samples were later analyzed by several Russian scientific institutes. In the days after the crash, hundreds of witnesses saw other UFO-type craft flying in and around Height 611 [the peak where the 'UFO' was seen], as if searching for the crash site."

All very interesting, if true. But far from being a member of the Soviet or Russian Academy of Sciences, in 1986 Dvuzhilni was a humble Dalnegorsk biology teacher.[1] And, in 2012, Dvuzhilni wasn't merely the area's leading UFOlogist, he was also a crucial contributor to the Dalnegorsk economy. Following problems resulting from increased awareness of the environmental costs of the polluting local metal smelters, the town's city fathers embraced UFO tourism as enthusiastically as their counterparts in Roswell, New Mexico. Dvuzhilni was the star, giving talks to parties of tourists visiting Height 611.

But before dismissing Valery Dvuzhilni as just another of those pseudoscientists who have cashed in on stories about incidents like the alleged Roswell crash, we should check the Museum's claim that scientists from *fourteen* academic centers and institutes have studied the Dalnegorsk material. In view of the dubious nature of some of the other statements made in the display, scientists may have regarded this statement with scepticism.

At first I too was doubtful. But then I did some research using Google Translate. The results were surprising – the Museum is correct. At taxpayers' expense a great deal of costly, high-quality scientific research has been done on the Height 611 remains, starting with a comprehensive study at Tomsk Polytechnical University (TPU). This was and remains a highly regarded academic institute, comparable with Caltech, MIT and Imperial College, London. Research here was followed by work at many other universities and institutes, as will be discussed in Chapter 15.

And Valery Dvuzhilni was the man who sparked off this wave of scientific research, by sending a package including some of the remains from the Height 611 event to scientists at TPU. Dvuzhilni tried to follow this university-level research while it lasted and in recent years has done his best to promote continued scientific study of the Height 611 material.

So why haven't the Russian and Ukrainian scientists published their findings in peer-reviewed journals? Never before in the history of science, surely, have so many accredited science teams done so much costly work on such an important subject with so little impact on the global scientific community.

To explain such a spectacular failure to publish, we need to pinpoint an equally powerful obstacle to scientific publication. One such roadblock has indeed been identified. It's been called 'the UFO taboo'.[2]

One account of this taboo comes from social scientists. Alexander Wendt, of Ohio State University, and Raymond Duvall, of the University of Minnesota, have applied the thinking of French philosophers like Michel Foucault and Jacques Derrida to the subject.[3]

Wendt and Duvall grasped the essence of the problem clearly. Scientists have never investigated UFOs properly because they assume that none are of ET origin. Yet how could scientists know this without investigating them? Indeed, as Wendt and Duvall point out, the Fermi Paradox – Where are all the ETs? – *obliges* scientists to study reports of this kind. Yet not only do they ignore such reports, they often ridicule those who do report or study them.

So Wendt and Duvall have correctly identified a 'UFO taboo' and drawn attention to its irrational nature. But the rest of their analysis is flawed.

As implied by the title of their paper, *Sovereignty and the UFO*, Wendt and Duvall argue that governments have imposed the taboo, scientists merely echo the thinking of their political masters. But that's not true. Today several governments, including France, Chile and Argentina, maintain ongoing scientific investigations into reports of anomalous aerial objects. Others, such as Belgium and Brazil, have authorised their air forces to mount investigations when appropriate.

So it's primarily the world's scientific community that maintains the UFO taboo. Although this global embargo reflects the global nature of science, its precise shape varies from country to country. In Chapters 14 and 15 we'll look further at the way it may have operated in the Soviet Union, and later Russia, when scientists there were studying the Height 611 remains.

In view of the scientists' UFO taboo, one might have expected the National Atomic Testing Museum in Las Vegas to collaborate with the science media in maintaining an information blackout about the 29 January 1986 Height 611 event and its study at so many Russian and Ukrainian universities and institutes. But evidently several factors specific to Las Vegas came into play. Not least, as we've seen, local journalist George Knapp possessed some actual physical remains from the Height 611 event, given to him by Valery Dvuzhilni. When then Museum

Fig 2. Allan Palmer, Director of the National Atomic Testing Museum, Las Vegas examines a fragment of the remains from the 1986 Height 611 high-temperature event. [National Atomic Testing Museum, Las Vegas]

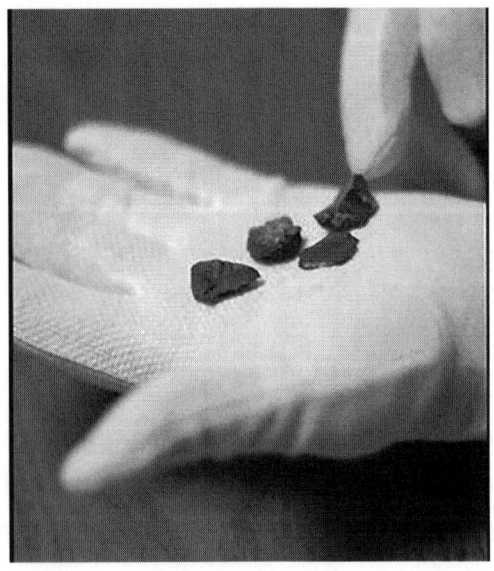

Fig 3. Remains from the 1986 Height 611 high-temperature event in Allan Palmer's hand. [National Atomic Testing Museum, Las Vegas]

Director Allan Palmer and his curators planned the 2012 Area 51 display, the opportunity to display some of these remains as a highlight of the exhibition must have seemed too good to pass up.

Unfortunately, with the UFO taboo in place – not to mention the language barrier – it was evidently impossible for the curators to find scientific specialists to check that the display material was correct. Generally scientists are only too happy to assist curators with this kind of work, as I know from my own experience many years ago as a junior curator at the UK's national Science Museum in London. That this wasn't done at Las Vegas – and pseudoscience broke through – wasn't so much the fault of the curators, as a sad consequence of the scientists' UFO taboo.

Endnotes

1 Google Translate from: http://anomalia.kulichki.ru/text6/176.htm Document downloaded 25 November 2012.

2 Hynek 1968, p.5.

3 Wendt and Duvall 2008.

2

The McDonald Conjecture

Imagine that one of the world's leading atmospheric physicists, a member of the US National Academy of Sciences, who was well known for his publications on cloud physics, weather modification and micrometeorology, had presented solid data supporting the conjecture that some witness reports of anomalous objects might have been stimulated by activities of ET probes. Imagine that this energetic scientist's data and arguments found such favour with his colleagues that the American Institute of Aeronautics and Astronautics (AIAA) set up a subcommittee specially to investigate this possibility. Imagine further that he even persuaded the US Congress to set up a series of hearings on the subject. He raised the question with President Johnson himself, so effectively that the President set up a special high-level scientific commission that later reported (secretly) in the scientist's favour. The physicist, whose name was James McDonald, even presented his ET probe conjecture to the relevant United Nations committee in New York.

I suspect that if you related all this to the average scientist working in astronomy and space science today, they would doubt that it had ever happened. When working at the Science Museum, London, when we mounted an exhibition on space exploration in the late 1970s, I can't recall McDonald's work ever being discussed.

Clearly, only a near-genius could have changed scientific opinion so much within a few years. And only one of the strangest taboos in the history of science could have obscured McDonald's pioneering work from twenty-first century scientists.

Fig 4. James McDonald [Swords, 2014]

Born in Duluth, Minnesota, on 7 May 1920 to an Irish-American family, James Edward McDonald earned his PhD in physics at the University of Iowa. Specialising in cloud physics, he became a leading US atmospheric physicist. He joined the University of Arizona in 1954, eventually serving as Professor in the Department of Meteorology and Senior Physicist in the Institute of Atmospheric Physics, which he had helped to establish. A member of the National Academy of Sciences from 1965, he served on the Academy's Panel on Weather and Climate Modification.

McDonald met his future wife, Betsy Hunt, while serving as an aerology instructor with the US Navy during World War II. The couple had six children and lived in a large rambling house on the outskirts of Tucson. Both widely read and highly sociable, the couple enjoyed many activities, particularly hiking in the semi desert mountain ranges surrounding Tucson.

McDonald impressed his Tucson colleagues from the start. Here's a tribute from Benjamin Herman, a later Director of the Institute of Atmospheric Physics, who was Mac's first graduate student:

"McDonald was the most thorough scientific researcher I have ever known. When he started on a problem and researched it, by the time he was finished he probably knew more than every expert in the world on that problem."

"In my opinion, McDonald was the closest thing to a genius, if he wasn't a genius, that I ever saw... The guy's insight was unbelievable; he would just run circles round us mortals here."[1]

Not only a scientific genius or near genius, Mac had outstanding personal skills. He was an expert interviewer of eyewitnesses and could quickly establish a rapport with people at all levels, whether they were top scientists, military figures or ordinary folk.

What set McDonald on this unique track to challenge scientific opinion? In 1954, together with four meteorologists, he saw an unexplained silver object hovering over the Santa Rita Mountains, south of Tucson.[2] He checked astronomical explanations, balloons and so on. Then he wrote to the Air Force, who were unable to identify the object.

Though McDonald never made much of his own unexplained sighting, he naturally became interested in local UFO reports in the Tucson area. He investigated hundreds of cases in his spare time. After careful investigation, he could identify about 98 per cent of the cases, but about two per cent remained unexplained, hinting at the existence of a phenomenon not yet studied by science.

In 1966 McDonald decided to go public with his view that unexplained UFO reports presented a huge challenge to science. If anyone could change scientific opinion on this question, he could, McDonald thought. And the time seemed ripe for making such an attempt.

In March 1966 a wave of UFO sightings had aroused the local press in Michigan, and the Air Force's Blue Book consultant, Allen Hynek, had prompted much ridicule by talking of "swamp gas". In response to pressure from his angry Michigan constituents, Representative Gerald Ford (later President Ford) had raised the question of UFOs in Congress – and the competence of the Air Force to investigate them. There was now a mood to fund an independent study of the problem, and McDonald saw an opportunity to play a role.

He moved swiftly. The repeated sightings in Michigan suggested the possibility of studying UFOs under controlled conditions, like other well-established scientific phenomena. So he approached NASA's Al Eggers. McDonald proposed that a team of scientists, equipped with precision cameras, spectroscopes, magnetometers and other monitoring equipment, be established. When repeated UFO sightings took place in a particular area, as had just happened in Michigan, the mobile team could be rushed in to collect scientific data. Eggers liked the idea.[3]

But to set up such a team would take time and money. McDonald knew that there was a pile of relevant data in the Air Force's Project Blue Book files. So, exploiting the current dissatisfaction with Project Blue Book and taking advantage of longstanding rivalry between the US Navy and the US Air Force, McDonald secured funding from the Office for Naval Research for a study of the cases in the Blue Book files – officially the grant was for work in cloud physics.

The files were then held at Wright-Patterson Air Force Base at Dayton, Ohio, and during the next few years, McDonald examined hundreds of Blue Book cases. Because the bulk of these came from officers at Air Force bases, obvious misidentified phenomena, such as apparitions of the planet Venus, were generally excluded, and McDonald found that many of the cases were of great scientific interest.

But studying the Blue Book files was also a frustrating task. McDonald was shocked at the incompetence and lack of scientific knowledge of the Blue Book staff. Even its scientific consultant, astronomer Allen Hynek, had made egregious errors in his anxiety to please his Air Force paymasters by incorrectly identifying puzzling UFO phenomena, McDonald found.

McDonald identified two key incidents in the Blue Book files where the Air Force had failed in this way. One had happened near Red Bluff, California in 1960, the other in Portage County, Ohio in 1966.

In the first case, at about 2300 local time on August 13 1960, on a back road south of Red Bluff, California, two Highway Patrolmen saw ahead of them what they took to be an aircraft about to crash. They stopped their car and jumped out, ready to help. They were surprised to hear no noise and astonished to see that, instead of crashing, the long

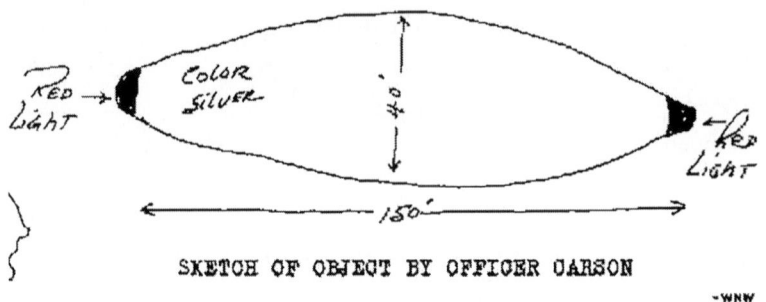

Fig 5. Red Bluff, California, 13 August 1960. Sketch by California State Highway Patrolman Charles Carson of the anomalous object witnessed by Patrolman Stanley Scott and himself at about 2300 local time on the night of 13 August 1960. [http://4.bp.blogspot.com]

metallic-looking object reversed its steep descent, climbed to a height of several hundred feet and hovered.

In a report to his Area Commander[4] one of the officers, Charles Carson, noted:

"At this time, it was clearly visible to both of us and clearly not an aircraft of any design familiar to us. It was surrounded by a glow, making the round or oblong object visible. At each end or each side of the object, there were definite red lights (Fig 5). At times about five white lights were visible between the red lights. As we watched, the object moved again and performed aerial feats that were actually unbelievable."

Then the object moved silently towards them, sweeping the area with a huge red light as it did so. The officers tried to radio the nearest dispatcher for help but strong interference prevented them from doing so.

The object then moved slowly to the east, the officers followed and saw another similar object join it, both objects emitting red beams from time to time. In the end, after more than two hours of observation – and a confirmation that the Red Bluff Air Force radar station had tracked the object – the officers saw both objects disappear below the eastern horizon.

James McDonald interviewed Charles Carson in 1966 and talked with other witnesses who had reported seeing the first object from various other local viewing points. Carson told him that the first object was "within easy pistol range" when it first moved towards them and the police officers were debating whether to fire when it stopped. Professor Michael Swords, formerly of Western Michigan University, who made a much later study of McDonald's unpublished interview notes, revealed that Carson had told McDonald of the first object "its beam seemed to extend out into the air, and then to end in some curious manner that [I] do not understand then or now."[5] McDonald evidently thought it unwise to mention Carson's seemingly crazy observation of a truncated light beam at the time.

How did Blue Book explain this close-up observation of what appeared to be a large, high-technology surveillance device, emitting red beams and surrounded by a glowing mass of air? "Refraction of the planet Mars and the two bright stars Aldebaran and Betelgeuse" was the verdict. When an astronomer pointed out that neither of the stars was even above the horizon at the time, Blue Book changed the explanation to read "Mars and Capella".

Naturally McDonald was outraged by these explanations and was even more upset when Donald Menzel, a Harvard astronomer who had written books claiming UFOs were a myth, supported them. McDonald commented, "If Menzel and Blue Book think California Highway Patrolmen draw their .44s in uneasiness over looking at a refracted image of Capella, then I cannot share their readiness to so easily discredit and discount reliable witnesses".[6]

Reliable police witnesses were also involved in the incident that took place on 17 April 1966 in Portage County, Ohio. Indeed, more than any other incident in the Blue Book files, this was the one that convinced McDonald that he had to give priority to the UFO problem.

The incident started at about 0500 local time when two police officers were investigating a stolen car. They noticed a bright light approaching them. As it got closer and reached a point about 100 feet above them, they saw that it came from an oval object about 45 feet across. It brightly illuminated the ground and then moved away down the road towards the east, tilting forward in such a way that the light beam illuminated the ground to its rear (Fig 6).

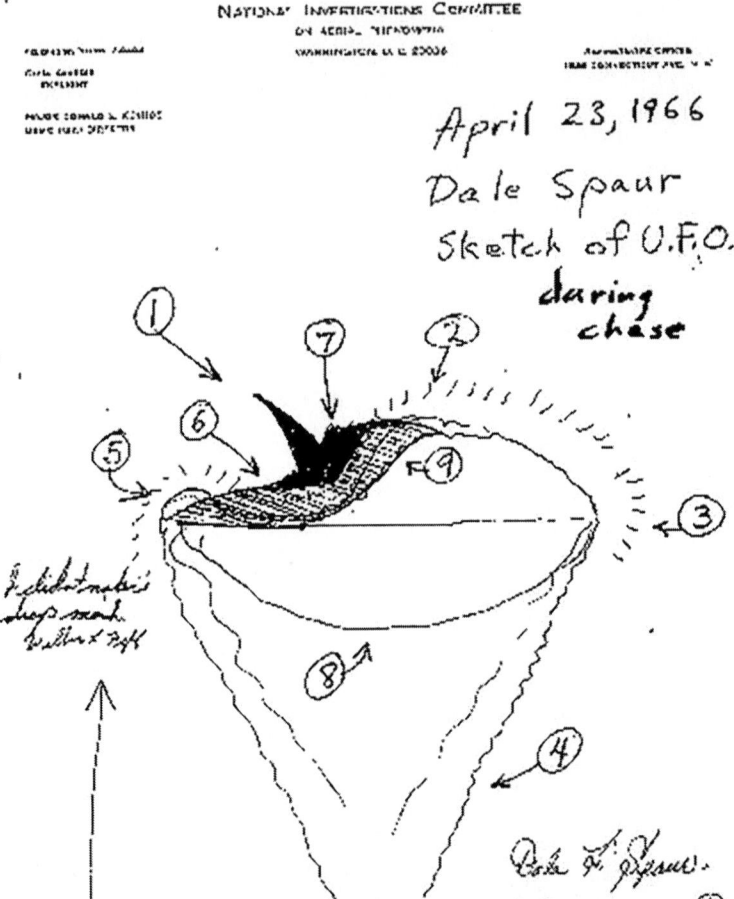

Fig 6. Portage County Ohio police chase, 17 April 1966. Patrolman Dale Spaur's sketch of the object that Patrolman Wilbur Neff and himself observed for several minutes. 1. Projection. 2. Dome-shaped top. 3. Glowing front (leading edge). 4. Cone-shaped light underneath. 5. Glowing tip of trailing edge. 6. Metallic surface. 7. Sharp drop-off (Officer Neff remembers a more rounded shape). 8. Rounded 'undercarriage'. 9. Line separating metallic from self-illuminated. [http://www.nicap.org/images/raven7.gif]

Instructed by their radio operator to chase it, the two officers followed it to the southeast along Route 224 through Mahoning County. As the dawn light increased, the officers saw the object in silhouette and noticed that it began to take on a metallic appearance. Other police officers joined in the chase, which, after more than thirty minutes of pursuit, led across the state boundary into Pennsylvania.

How did Blue Book explain this one? Major (later Lt. Col.) Hector Quintanilla, the Blue Book boss from 1963 until its closure in 1969, concluded in an April 22 1966 press statement that the officers had first chased an Echo communications satellite and then, as the light increased, the planet Venus.

Though Venus (and the Moon) was indeed in the eastern pre-dawn sky at the time, and many witnesses have mistaken Venus for a UFO, in this case Quintanilla's explanations were absurd. The official Blue Book scientific consultant, Allen Hynek, rejected them[7] as did William Powers, Hynek's astronomical colleague at Northwestern University. Ohio Congressman William Stanton was so concerned at Quintanilla's mishandling of the case that he raised it with US Air Force authorities at the highest levels.

In July 1966, having mastered details of the Portage County case, including the input by Hynek, Powers, journalists and independent UFO investigators, McDonald confronted Quintanilla face-to-face in the Blue Book office at Dayton, Ohio. He told the major that he'd given his boss, Colonel Louis DeGoes, a file of information that conclusively proved that the object chased by the officers could not have been an Echo satellite or Venus. "What do you propose to do about that?" McDonald asked. "I'll change it to 'unidentified'," Quintanilla replied.[8]

He never did.

After a further year of intensive study of US government UFO report files, witness interviewing and networking with his contacts among the US scientific elite, McDonald was ready to present his findings at the highest national and international levels.

In the US, McDonald raised the UFO problem with President Lyndon Johnson.[9] He lobbied the President so persistently, that "to get McDonald off my back" Johnson set up an informal UFO study, administered by Vice President Hubert Humphrey's advisor for aeronautical and aerospace affairs, Frank Rand. Briefed twice by McDonald, the Rand study group included General James T. Stewart, who was director of the Office of Space Systems, legendary University of Michigan astronomer, Hazel Losh, and Arthur Lundahl, of the National Photographic Interpretation Center. The conclusions of this study group were secret, but Professor Michael Swords, formerly of Western Michigan University, who saw a draft of Rand's unpublished memoirs, has stated that President Johnson's study group concluded that the UFO phenomena probably involved advanced ET technology.[10]

Internationally, United Nations Secretary General U Thant now reportedly considered the UFO problem to be one of the most serious challenges facing the United Nations. Unfortunately, the recent outbreak of war in the Middle East prevented U Thant from attending in person when McDonald addressed the UN's Outer Space Affairs Committee on 7 June 1967.[11] McDonald expressed his ideas not only to the UN committee but, in a later letter directly to U Thant, outlined his theory that credibly reported low-level sightings of machine-like objects – cases like Red Bluff, California, in 1960 and Portage County, Ohio, in 1966 – suggested the possibility of ET probes of some kind.

And such cases weren't confined to the USA. Father William Gill, an Anglican missionary in Boianai, New Guinea, had reported spectacular close-up sightings in June 1959 of a machine-like object by himself and his flock. There were many other credible UFO reports from Australasia, including an incident at Westall High School near Melbourne in April 1966 that McDonald was keen to investigate. Fortunately, his work on atmospheric physics for the Office of Naval Research would take him to New Zealand and Australia in June 1966. So, after getting the Navy's approval for doing some UFO research there in his spare time, he was able to use his interviewing and investigative skills to see how well his ET probe hypothesis fitted these Southern Hemisphere UFO cases.

Having returned from New Guinea, William Gill now lived near Melbourne and after talking to him McDonald was impressed with his testimony. McDonald was particularly interested in Gill's account of the glow or "sparkling halo" that apparently traced the main object's periphery – as in the Red Bluff and Portage County reports. The glow intensified when the object moved, Gill told McDonald.[12]

McDonald spent the next two years like a whirlwind of energy, fitting his UFO research and talks in with his many other scientific activities.

One important group of experts keen to hear McDonald speak were members of the American Institute of Aeronautics and Astronautics (AIAA). After these meetings, McDonald would often stay on and chat with the members, sometimes gleaning information that led to valuable information suppressed by the Air Force.

For example, after talking to members of the Chicago section of the AIAA on 26 September 1968, McDonald learned of a mid-1950s UFO chase by two F-86B jets out of Castle Air Force Base, California. He later conducted a telephone interview with one of the pilots, Al Akins, who now worked for United Airlines.

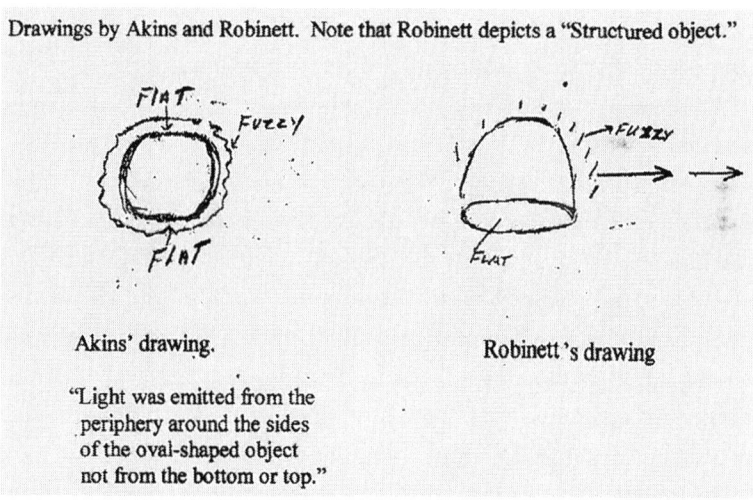

Drawings by Akins and Robinett. Note that Robinett depicts a "Structured object."

Akins' drawing.

"Light was emitted from the periphery around the sides of the oval-shaped object not from the bottom or top."

Robinett's drawing

Fig 7. Sketches in completed Air Force questionnaire of luminous anomalous object chased by two F-86B pilots, Alvin Akins and Jerry Robinett, out of Castle AFB, California between 2320 and 2340 PST on 7 October 1956. Left: sketch by Lt. Alvin Akins. Right: sketch by Lt. Jerry Robinett. [Gross 2003 p 40]

McDonald elicited key facts from Akins. After receiving ground reports of a strange pulsating light, the Castle AFB tower had vectored the two aircraft towards the luminous object. The tower visually confirmed the object and both pilots got a good look at it before it whipped out of sight. To Akins, it had appeared football-like in side view but round in plan form. Though not detected by ground radar, the pilots reported transient returns from their airborne nose radars and were puzzled by the curious way in which the echoes disappeared almost immediately. McDonald, tongue in cheek, suggested the possibility of alien ECM (electronic counter-measures).

What particularly interested McDonald was Akins' revelation that after their UFO chase the two pilots were debriefed by highly knowledgeable USAF officers – not from Project Blue Book – who told them never to make any statements about the chase. Could there be a secret system, McDonald wondered, in which competent (as opposed to Blue Book) investigators hushed up UFO intercept pilots after they'd had a good sighting?[13,14]

It later turned out that the investigators who debriefed the two pilots in 1956 were from the 4602nd Air Intelligence Service Squadron (AISS), a group that conducted field investigations for Blue Book during the mid-1950s. Lieutenant Akins' account and witness sketch in the questionnaire add detail to the account he gave McDonald in 1968.

Akins stated that the chase took place between 2320 and 2340 local time on 7 October 1956. He confirmed the strange nature of the airborne radar detection that he later reported to McDonald and stated that the object had a fuzzy surround, "very bright like burning phosphorous (sic), shimmering and changing in intensity".[15] When the object rose into the clouds it did so "nearly instantaneously", Akins wrote. He concluded that the object "showed evidence of intelligent control and construction, something foreign to our culture possibly".[16] In his questionnaire, Lieutenant Jerry Robinett confirmed Lieutenant Akins's testimony of the object's acceleration, great speed, fuzzy appearance and emission of bright white light. He estimated it to have been about 100-120 feet high and 50-60 feet in diameter, in profile "looking like the dome of an observatory" (Fig 7). Robinett added, "from the limited amount of observations I made I would say it was a planned and constructed object."

Wow. How could the Air Force publicly acknowledge such close-up descriptions by its own pilots of these hi-tech objects, apparently surrounded by plasma coronas, that were evidently operating freely in US airspace? Of course it couldn't. And because the two F-86B pilots could be ordered to remain silent, as Akins told McDonald in 1968, the Air Force could deploy its only option, the Big Lie.

So Lt-Colonel Lee Lambert, commanding officer of the 456th Fighter Interceptor Squadron, to which the two pilots belonged, told journalists that his pilots had "found nothing".[17]

Not being able to command civilians to silence, Lambert added that the civilian reports that had led to the F-86 chase might have been caused by "migratory birds with phosphorescent glow reflected against the cloud formation."[18]

No comment. It's interesting to speculate how James McDonald, with his scientific stature and contacts extending to Presidential and UN Secretary-General level might have exploited this certain evidence of US Air Force lying had such information been available to him in 1968.

What did encourage McDonald in 1968 was that in February of that year a remarkable new incident strengthened his hypothesis that ET probes might be surveying our planet. At Redlands, California, on the evening of 4 February, at 1920 local time, at least twenty witnesses saw a large object, round in plan, apparently about 50-60 feet in diameter, move slowly over the town towards the northeast at an estimated height of about 300 feet. Witnesses observed a row of eight to ten lights on top of the object, alternating in color and "something resembling flames" below its lower surface. Witnesses reported that after travelling about a mile, the object stopped, hovered briefly, jerked forward, hovered again, then shot straight upward and hovered again. Finally, after about five minutes, the object shot off to the northwest.

What made the Redlands case exceptional was that a team of scientists from Redlands University immediately investigated it.[19,20] The team included the chemist Reinhold Krantz, Director of the University's

Fig 8. Left to right: James McDonald, University of Arizona, Philip Seff, Judson Sanderson and John Brownfield, all from the University of Redlands, California. The Redlands professors investigated a multiple-witness sighting at Redlands on 4 February 1968 and sent their report to the Condon Committee.
[http://2.bp.blogspot.com]

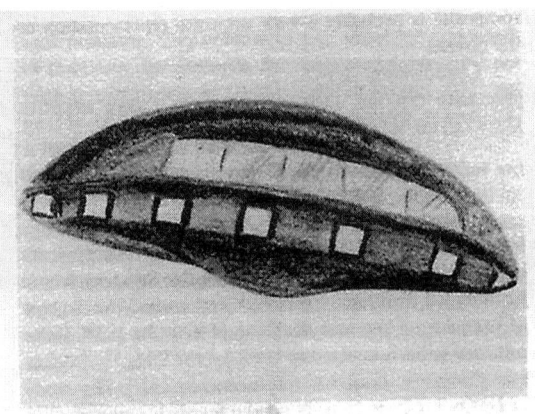

Artist: John Brownfield. APRO.

Fig 9. John Brownfield, University of Redlands, based this interpretation of the 4 February 1968 Redlands object on many eyewitness descriptions.
[http://www.nicap.org/images/ar-680204draw.jpg]

Science Division, geology professor Philip Seff, mathematics professor Judson Sanderson and art instructor, John Brownfield (Fig 8). After working from the descriptions of many witnesses, Brownfield produced a composite sketch of the 'thing' (Fig 9).

McDonald was delighted. Following his example, university scientists were at last braving ridicule and investigating UFO reports. And his campaigning was continuing to change the attitudes of key scientific figures. For instance astronomer Thornton Page, of Wesleyan University, one of the five members of the Robertson Panel, organised by the CIA, that in 1953 had recommended the official debunking of UFO reports, had come round to the view that UFOs might present a serious challenge to science. "To tell the truth, Jim," Page said to McDonald at a dinner on 26 January, 1968, following one of McDonald's scientific presentations, "Until you entered the field publicly, I thought it [the study of UFO reports] was a fringe subject, misidentifications, mass hysteria. You've changed all that."[21]

Another important new McDonald ally was SETI pioneer and radio astronomer Frank Drake. Drake had the advantage over both Page and McDonald that when serving as an electronics officer on the heavy cruiser USS Albany in the North Atlantic, he had witnessed an anomalous object emerge from the water. He'd told the story to Carl Sagan who had in turn told it to McDonald[22] (Fig 11, Note 22). Such an experience was guaranteed to make Drake a supporter of McDonald's campaign for well-funded UFO research and in May 1967 Drake expressed his views in a letter to the National Academy of Sciences.

"I feel that it is clear that a thorough and broad investigation of UFOs is called for. The evidence is overwhelming that there is a real physical and not solely psychological UFO phenomenon. In view of the peculiarity of the phenomenon, and the broad public interest in it, there is justification for the expenditure of considerable funds to elucidate it."[23]

McDonald's campaigning for a Congressional Hearing on UFOs was going well, too. The *Symposium on Unidentified Flying Objects* finally took place on 29 July 1968 before the House Committee on Science and Astronautics. About a dozen Congress members attended together with

Fig 10. Frank Drake. [Swords 2014]

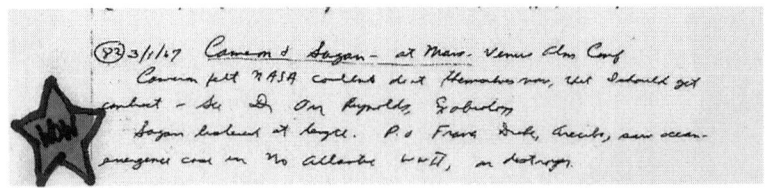

Fig 11. Handwritten note by James McDonald published by Michael Swords in 2014. My reading of McDonald's second sentence is: 'Sagan listened at length. P.O. Frank Drake, Arecibo, saw ocean emergence case in No Atlantic WWII, on destroyer.' Michael Swords added the WOW. [Swords 2014]

a dozen journalists, but the discussion was confined to panelists and Committee members.

Allen Hynek, the only scientist in the world who'd had official responsibility for interpreting UFO reports over a period of many years, opened proceedings with an excellent presentation. Wisely he said nothing about the 'occupant' cases that he would later consider so important.

At first, he'd regarded the UFO subject as "rank nonsense", he told the assembled Congress members. He only became involved because the Air Force asked him to do so twenty years earlier.

But over the years, as he studied case after case in the Project Blue Book files, Hynek had to acknowledge that some reports by reliable witnesses constituted a serious challenge to science. For example, many such witnesses had reported brightly illuminated objects hovering a few hundred feet over their cars; at the same time their car motors stopped, headlights dimmed or failed and car radios stopped playing. These functions returned after the unidentified objects had disappeared, Hynek told the Congress assembly.[24,25]

Intriguing phenomena like this ought to be studied by scientists, Hynek said. But "there appears to be a scientific taboo on even the passive tabulation of UFO reports." There was no mechanism, for example "for the publication of a paper on reported occurrences of electromagnetic phenomena in UFO encounters."

Clearly no serious work could be done until the taboo was lifted, Hynek said. But until the taboo was lifted, no serious scientific work could be done.

The position was even worse than that, Hynek told the House Committee. Because scientists couldn't find papers discussing unexplained UFO sightings in respected science journals, any knowledge they had was likely to be based on the sensationalised, inaccurate accounts found in pulp magazines and paperbacks. Such accounts were likely to provoke "mental nausea," Hynek said, and scientists, therefore, tended to relegate the whole UFO subject to the trash heap.

Hynek concluded by noting, as UN Secretary General U Thant had already done, that the UFO problem was a global one and he, therefore, recommended a properly funded in-depth scientific study of UFOs at the national and international level. He suggested that the US Congress should establish a UFO Scientific Board of Inquiry, while internationally the US should cooperate with the UN in setting up a clearinghouse for the exchange of UFO information.

James McDonald spoke next.[26] Privately he thought that Allen Hynek's record as a debunker for the US Air Force had been a major factor in engendering scientists' dismissive attitude to the UFO problem. But publicly, he could ill afford to criticise a scientist whose 'official' analysis of the UFO problem and recommendations for future action now corresponded closely with his own. So he praised Hynek for his insights into witness psychology and largely agreed with the astronomer's proposals for future scientific research though emphasising that a pluralistic approach was needed – involving NASA for example – and that only the best scientists would be capable of tackling the problem.

At the Congress Hearing, McDonald made clear that his intensive study of high-quality witness reports, for example, the hovering, car-stopping cases studied by Hynek, suggested that in default of reasonable alternative explanations, scientists should consider the extraterrestrial surveillance conjecture.

Most people, then as now, interpreted 'extraterrestrial' to mean extra-terrestrial humanoids – humanlike beings with humanlike agendas. But why, then, hadn't 'they' made contact with humans? McDonald pointed out that this question, put to him time and time again, was silly. It was "a homocentric fallacy of the most obvious nature." Then McDonald said:

> "If we were under surveillance from some advanced technology sufficiently advanced to do what we cannot do in the sense of interstellar travel, then, as Arthur Clarke has put it quite well, quoted in *Time* magazine the last week, we have an odd situation. Arthur Clarke points out that any sufficiently advanced technology would be indistinguishable from magic. How well that applies to UFO sightings. You have a feeling you are dealing with some very high-technology devices of an entirely real nature which defy explanation in terms of present-day science. To say that we could anticipate the values, reasons, motivations, and so on, of any such system that has the capability of getting here from somewhere else is fallacious."

But if it was naive to expect high-technology devices incorporating some kind of AI to 'make contact,' such devices might be programmed to respond to simple Morse-type visual signals. Responding to a question from a Committee member, McDonald stated that he had a file of such 'light response' cases. Effortlessly quoting a mass of detail from memory, he referred to two returns of flashlight signals in 1967, one at Shamokin, PA and the other at Newton, NH. And in Australia, McDonald recalled, he'd talked with some kangaroo hunters. Out hunting, a disc had come over and one hunter had said "give them Morse." The flash came back faithfully, McDonald said, and the hunters left in a hurry.

Another important speaker at the Congress Hearing was Robert Baker. Baker was a brilliant young scientist then at UCLA and a prominent member of the AIAA. One of Baker's specialties was the use of radar and other data to determine orbital characteristics of missiles, spacecraft, and other objects in the near-earth environment. Crucially he had top secret security clearance and therefore had access to information about US military detection of what he called "anomalistic observational phenomena" (AOP) in space, events that ET probe theory predicted, but about which McDonald, who had no security clearances, had no information.

Baker made several key points.[27] First, the inbuilt selectivity of existing systems would prevent them from detecting anomalies of the kind reported by human witnesses as UFOs. Nevertheless, Baker intriguingly stated, there was one partially classified space surveillance system that had generated anomalistic alarms, all so far unexplained.

Baker believed that a research program should be set up to detect AOP in the near-earth environment and that a mobile task force be set up to respond quickly to reported anomalous incidents. This might include phased-array radars, with new control systems that would need to be devised to enable the detection of erratic motion. Optical cameras, including spectrographic equipment, could be slaved to the radar systems.

Baker's notion of a mobile AOP task force resonated with McDonald, because he had already suggested a similar, though much simpler, idea to NASA's Al Eggers.

Baker's ideas for detection of possible ET probes in near-earth space were fine in principle. But the huge practical problem, not fully spelt out by Baker in his Congress presentation, was the militarisation of near-earth space. Baker worried that a procession of fireballs (large meteoroids) in near polar orbit might be mistaken for a Soviet ballistic missile attack on the USA. If fireballs could be confused with Soviet ballistic missiles, so could ET probes. Any system sophisticated enough to detect possible incoming or outgoing ET probes – and any resulting detections – would therefore be bound to remain top secret. This requirement for military secrecy remains to this day probably the single biggest obstacle to the testing of ET probe theory.

Yet another important speaker at the Congress Symposium was the astronomer Carl Sagan.[28] Sagan had read McDonald's article *UFOs: Greatest Scientific Problem of Our Times?* presented before the annual meeting of the American Society of Newspaper Editors on 22 April 1967.[29] In May 1967 Sagan wrote to McDonald congratulating him on the piece.[30] He urged McDonald to write the piece up in a form "suited for some scientific journal" and foresaw no difficulty in publishing it.

In his letter Sagan made points some of which he would reiterate at the Symposium.

> "What concerns me is the variety and frequency of objects which are on your list of unidentifieds. Why should there be huge numbers of extraterrestrial spacecraft investigating the Earth? Why such a great variety of spacecraft and why us? What's so special about the Earth."

Sagan's points contradicted widely publicised remarks he had made at the spring meeting of the American Astronautical Society in 1966. There he'd said that spacemen "may have visited Earth thousands of times in the past few billions of years".[31] Compared with Sagan's postulated thousands of visits, in his ASNE piece McDonald had listed only eighteen cases (including Portage County at Number One and Red Bluff at Number Four). And as for special reasons for studying the Earth, even in 1968, long before the important 2003 suggestion by NASA historian Steven Dick that 'postbiological' ET civilisations might have sound reasons for studying Earth (see Chapter 4), the Fermi Paradox provided sufficient reason for humans to expect visits from ET.

Since Carl Sagan, like Thornton Page and Frank Drake, had a high opinion of McDonald's abilities, and since Sagan himself had not studied the Blue Book files, why, unlike Page and Drake, did Sagan now distance his position from those of Hynek and McDonald, the two scientists who *had* studied the Blue Book data?

A six-letter word. Condon.

Following the Michigan swamp gas fracas in 1966, James McDonald, with his relevant expertise and high reputation, had seemed the most likely scientist to undertake an enquiry into the UFO problem, perhaps a one-man project under the auspices of the US National Academy of Sciences.

But in the end, instead of the independent enquiry that an increasing number of US scientists were now hoping for, and instead of McDonald playing a major role in it, it somehow emerged that the Air Force would mount an enquiry into its own conduct. It cajoled Edward Condon, illustrious physicist, grand old man of US Science, a scientist who viewed UFO reports more with amusement than interest, to head an enquiry into the problem, funded, of course, by itself. This study at the University of Colorado became known as the Colorado Project.

Published in October 1968, the Condon Report's Executive Summary included the key statement:

> "Our general conclusion is that nothing has come from the study of UFOs in the past 21 years that has added to scientific knowledge. Careful consideration of the record as it is available to us leads us to conclude that further extensive study of UFOs probably cannot be justified in the expectation that science will be advanced thereby."[32]

By the time of the July Congress hearings, Edward Condon's negative conclusions were already known or rumoured. Indeed, at the Congress Symposium, Representative Ryan had repeatedly tried to raise the question of the objectivity of the Condon Committee's reported conclusions. In deciding the stance to adopt in his Congress presentation, Sagan, a young scientist who had to consider his future career, would certainly have borne Condon's rumoured conclusions in mind.

How on earth could Edward Condon's study of the Blue Book

data have led him to write an Executive Summary so completely at odds with the conclusions of Hynek and McDonald, the two chief accredited experts, in their presentations at the Congress Symposium? The short answer is as disquieting as it is astonishing. Neither Condon nor any other members of his team (apart from Allen Hynek, who himself contributed to the Condon Report) had made an intensive study of the Blue Book files. And Condon excluded McDonald's three key cases, Red Bluff 1960, Portage County 1966, and Redlands 1968 on grounds that don't stand up to scientific scrutiny.

Despite these defects, and despite unprecedented internecine strife amongst the members of the Colorado Committee,[33] as they studied the UFO data more closely, members of the Committee moved away from the pervasive scientific scepticism towards the broad position shared by Hynek, McDonald, Page and Drake, namely that high-quality UFO reports constituted an important challenge to science. After studying minutes of the successive meetings of the Colorado Committee, Michael Swords, of Western Michigan University, concluded that at least eleven of the top fifteen Committee staff members broadly agreed with this position, and disagreed with Condon's Executive Summary.[34]

The views of the Committee members are reflected in the actual contents of the Report. Despite the scandalous refusal to discuss the key McDonald cases, the contents of the Report broadly support McDonald's position rather than Condon's. Allen Hynek and Thornton Page agreed that Condon's Executive Summary was not supported by the contents of the lengthy Report.[35] Has such a thing ever happened before? Even in politics, in which biased reports supporting pre-determined conclusions are common, it is rare to find such a blatant example of a free-floating Executive Summary. In science, it may be unparalleled. Professors Alexander Wendt and Raymond Duvall, viewing the Condon Report from the vantage of academics outside the power structure of US science,[36] characterised it as a 'show trial'.

Professor Michael Swords' research in the archives of the Colorado Project in the American Philosophical Library, Philadelphia, has thrown light on the pressures that Condon's Air Force paymasters put on him during the period before he wrote his Executive Summary. For example, in a January 1967 letter to Robert Low, a very competent University of Colorado administrator, who was a friend and admirer of Condon, the Air Force's Colonel Robert Hippler explained precisely what outcome the Air Force wanted from the Report. He made it clear that the Air Force wanted to close down the now embarrassing Project Blue Book and that the Colorado Project should, therefore, be able to come to an anti-ET conclusion. If Condon and his team needed further time to make such a "proper recommendation," then an extension beyond 1968 could be arranged, Hippler wrote.[37]

So Condon's free-floating Executive Summary perfectly matched the Air Force's requirements. But that doesn't mean that Condon was a stooge. Like the majority of elite US scientists, who obtained their information on UFOs from popular culture because there were no scientific papers on the subject, Condon sincerely believed UFOs were a nonsense problem. And he was too old and too grand to change his mind.

But there are clues to suggest that, despite being a tough guy, Condon had to work himself up to write a summary so at odds with the views of his Committee colleagues. Instead of immersing himself in the UFO data and puzzling about challenging cases, he ignored the advice of his colleagues and attended a conference of fringe UFOlogists at New York City, held in 22-23 June, 1967.[38] The society of nutters, who claimed to have had dealings with space aliens, might give him the extra emotional drive needed to make no concessions at all to the increasing number of his colleagues who were moving towards the Hynek-Page-Drake-McDonald position.

However Condon worked himself up to it, or justified it to himself, the dark deed was finally done. McDonald naturally objected in the strongest terms. In June 1969, after receiving a letter from Condon criticising his own views, McDonald wrote back, enclosing summaries of recent talks in which he had criticised Condon's Report, observing "Your conclusions do not at all seem to be supported by the Report's contents... In giving the Academy such a Report, I believe you did science a direct disservice. That the Academy processes could lead to endorsement is disturbing."[39]

As McDonald forecast, the NAS did indeed endorse Condon's

Report. 'Disturbing' is too mild an adjective to characterise the endorsement by such an august body of a self-contradictory report. Did the eleven NAS panelists – who had not themselves studied the Blue Book data and had no expertise in the relevant discipline of atmospheric physics – endorse the Report itself or its contradictory Executive Summary?

And if Condon needed to indulge himself in irrelevant talk about space aliens in order to reach the mood to write his summary, the NAS panel evidently also needed to invoke aliens in order to endorse it. In their review of the Condon Report in *Icarus*[40] – the issue in which James McDonald published his damning review of the Report[41] – the eleven NAS panelists wrote "the least likely explanation of UFOs is the hypothesis of extra-terrestrial visitations by intelligent beings." Yet McDonald's ET probe hypothesis, as put forward consistently for several years and made clear in his statements to the Congress Committee,[42] proposed "surveillance from some advanced technology" not "visitations by intelligent beings." Either the NAS panelists genuinely failed to understand the hypothesis they were rejecting, or they purposely distorted McDonald's conjecture in order to secure a cheap dismissal of it.

How might we expect US scientists to respond to all of this? Given the effectiveness of McDonald's campaigning, we might predict strong resistance to Condon's conclusions in the short term. The long-term response would largely depend on how effectively McDonald continued his campaigning.

Developments did indeed conform to this pattern. An AAAS UFO symposium had been mooted for several years. Having pleaded in vain to Vice-President Spiro Agnew to stop the conference, Condon next wrote to the Chairman of the AAAS, Walter Orr Roberts. Condon would agree to the meeting if a fair discussion could be arranged. "But from personal knowledge of the UFO buffs, I know it [a fair discussion] cannot. These people in varying degrees insist that visitors are coming to Earth from other civilizations. Some insist that this is known to our government and that the truth is being deliberately held back from the public. After careful study I conclude that there is no scientifically valid evidence in support of either proposition".[43]

It's difficult to believe that an eminent scientist could put forward such a ludicrous argument. Over the years, the US government had spent a great deal of money collecting high-quality UFO reports. The purpose of the AAAS meeting was to provide a forum in which the government's scientific consultant, Allen Hynek and other scientists could discuss this evidence and its implications for future scientific research. Far from giving a platform to 'UFO buffs' the scientists speaking at the conference would demonstrate the scientific approach to the UFO problem and expose the nutters for the crazies that they were.

Orr Roberts therefore rejected Condon's request and the AAAS UFO conference went ahead in late December 1969. The proceedings were later published, under the title *UFOS: A Scientific Debate* (1974), edited by Carl Sagan and Thornton Page, the organisers of the conference, a work that remains one of the best introductions to this field of research.[44] Even the popular science magazine *New Scientist*, not known for its coverage of UFO evidence, was impressed with the book.

Now that Condon had done his worst, McDonald seemed to have decided that he need no longer refrain from criticising what he saw as Allen Hynek's role in establishing the scientific tradition of UFO debunking. If science was truly in default, as indicated by the title of McDonald's own AAAS conference paper, then Hynek had to take a large share of the blame. Naturally, McDonald didn't name Hynek as culprit, but when he referred to "so slight a total amount of scientific competence in two decades of Air Force supported investigations" there was no doubt that Hynek was the man he had in mind. Hynek's persistent debunking, McDonald believed, had been chiefly responsible for the widespread scientific view that the Air Force had applied the best scientific brains to the UFO problem and found little of interest.

But the US Air Force was not, after all, a scientific organisation. More serious, from a scientific point of view, McDonald pointed out, were the failings of the Condon Report. Having already privately taken Condon to task for his free-floating Executive Summary, McDonald now stressed that Condon had addressed only a "tiny fraction of the really puzzling UFO reports" (it excluded top cases like Red Bluff, Portage County and Redlands). But even after that elimination process, thirty of the ninety cases specifically addressed remained unexplained. With so high a proportion of unexplained cases, how could Condon reasonably conclude that "further extensive study of UFOs probably cannot be justified in the expectation that science will be advanced thereby"?

McDonald then highlighted the challenges posed by some of these unexplained cases, including the complex 1956 Lakenheath-Bentwaters, UK, radar-visual incident and the important 1957 incident at Kirtland AFB, New Mexico (see Chapter 10). To explain such puzzling cases, suggesting the involvement of "intelligent control" or "some broadly cybernetic equivalent thereof", as a working hypothesis James McDonald proposed "the hypothesis that something in the nature of extraterrestrial devices engaged in something in the nature of surveillance lies at the heart of the UFO problem."

McDonald always chose his words carefully and the words "something in the nature of" are crucial. For unlike SETI people, UFOlogists and the eleven NAS panelists, who all apparently thought that ET meant intelligent beings like us, McDonald understood the folly of trying to imprison ET within narrow anthropomorphic concepts.

Apart from the holding of the key AAAS meeting, another important short-term victory for McDonald and Hynek over Condon lay in the attitude of the important AIAA (American Institute of Aeronautics and Astronautics). Unlike Condon himself and unlike the NAS panel that had endorsed his Report, the members of the AIAA had technical expertise relevant to the UFO problem.

In August 1967 James McDonald had presented his analysis of the UFO problem to an enthusiastic group of AIAA scientists and engineers in Washington. In that year, two AIAA Technical Committees, one concerned with the atmospheric environment and the other with space physics and atmospheric physics, jointly appointed a UFO Subcommittee. The AIAA UFO Subcommittee members soon appreciated the complex nature of the UFO problem and set themselves the task of finding out whether a scientific problem truly existed. Their work was, therefore, parallel to that of the Condon Committee.

And indeed, their conclusions, published in November 1970,[45] were remarkably close to those of the Condon Committee members who had moved away from Condon's own "nonsense problem" assessment towards the Hynek-McDonald-Page-Drake position that UFOs presented a significant challenge to science. Echoing McDonald's words in his June 1969 letter to Condon, the AIAA UFO Subcommittee stated that "The UFO Subcommittee did not find a basis in the report for his [Condon's] prediction that nothing of scientific value will come of further studies." The AIAA assessment continued, "In fact, the Subcommittee finds that the opposite conclusion could have been drawn from its [the Condon Report's] content, namely, that a phenomenon with such a high ratio of unexplained cases (about 30%) should arouse sufficient scientific curiosity to continue its study." Finally "The Subcommittee sees the only promising approach as a continuing, moderate-level effort with emphasis on improved data collection by objective means and on high-quality scientific analysis."

Apart from the UFO puzzle, James McDonald continued to concern himself with many other scientific problems linked with the atmosphere. In 1970 the most politically pressing of these were the potential problems posed by fleets of SSTs (supersonic transports) operating in the stratosphere.

Some years earlier Boeing Corporation had won a contract with the US government to develop a prototype SST. But the extra cloudiness caused by condensation trails of fleets of SSTs might have damaging climatic effects. Moreover there might be damage to the UV-shielding ozone layer. The NAS Panel on Weather and Climate Modification, of which McDonald had been a member since 1965, had the task of examining such questions.

Congress decided to hold hearings in March 1971 about whether or not they should cancel government contracts for SSTs. As the NAS's chief expert on this problem, in 1970, McDonald decided to focus full time on SST issues, putting the UFO problem temporarily on the backburner. Although he concluded after intense investigation that SSTs wouldn't cause climate-damaging cloudiness, he found that they might indeed irretrievably damage the ozone shield, likely leading to increases in incidence of skin cancer.

By November 1970, McDonald believed the new evidence of

likely SST links with skin cancer required urgent action by Congress, even before the March 1971 hearings, and informed the NAS panel accordingly. But the panel was reluctant to move quickly, and, impatient as ever, McDonald decided to testify at the March hearings as an independent scientist. He therefore now became a vulnerable target for the politicians representing commercial interests angling for government cash for SST development.

On 2 March 1971, at the invitation of Illinois Representative Sidney Yates, James McDonald appeared before a subcommittee of the House Appropriations Committee conducting the SST hearings. One pro-SST politician on the subcommittee who intended to damage McDonald's credibility was Representative Silvio Conte, of Massachusetts.

Conte planned his attack carefully. In his appended written statement for the 1968 Congress Symposium,[46] in one paragraph of an 85-page document, McDonald had acknowledged the existence of 'occupant' reports. Conte put together a collection of quotes from this paragraph and read them out to the Committee, giving the impression that McDonald attached far more importance to such reports than he in fact did.

Unfair to Mac, of course, but politics is a dirty game. Having thus prepared his ground, Conte then pounced:

> "A man who comes here and tells me that the SST flying in the stratosphere is going to cause thousands of skin cancers has to back up his theory that there are little men flying around in the sky"[47]

The hearing room broke down in laughter.

In the end McDonald and his allies won the argument on SSTs and Congress killed the mooted contract with Boeing. But his public ridicule at the Congress SST hearing, together with the recent knowledge that he would not get hoped-for funding for UFO research from the NSF (National Science Foundation) had a depressing effect on McDonald.

Then, towards the end of March 1971, problems with his marriage to Betsy that had been simmering for some time came to a head. While

Mac had been away from home so much, particularly in recent months as a result of his involvement with the urgent SST issues, she had been having an affair with a younger man. She now wanted a divorce and before Mac left for a government SST meeting scheduled to start on 18 March, she told him that she would write him a letter explaining her problems and give it to him on his return.

That she did. Already depressed, Betsy's letter asking for a divorce may have been the critical factor that took Mac into full clinical depression. He immediately planned suicide.

Nevertheless, he remained rational. He knew that the Institute of Atmospheric Physics would look after his research papers in atmospheric physics, but what about his UFO work? He hoped that his UFO papers would be archived at the University of Arizona Library, but who could carry on his UFO research and complete the UFO book that he'd been planning?

He knew it would require "someone of roughly my background and concerns",[48] but how many scientists fitted that bill? Certainly not Allen Hynek, with whom he had parted company on bad terms after meeting at a radar meteorology conference at Tucson on 17 November 1970, at which McDonald had presented a key paper.[49]

Before dawn on 9 April 1971 he wrote a short note to Betsy and shot himself in the head. But he only managed to blind himself. Never one to fail in a project, even if it was his own suicide, Mac bided his time and tried again on 12 June.

By this time, although his IAP colleagues didn't know it, Mac had recovered some sight. He called a taxi from his IAP office in Tucson, bought a 0.38 revolver from a pawn shop, had the taxi man drive him to a cross roads in the desert, walked over a mile to the Canyon del Oro, an old dry wash that he knew, and shot himself again.

Police found his body around midday on 13 June.[50]

Endnotes

1 Druffel 2003, p.14–15.
2 Druffel 2003, p.19–20.
3 ibid. p.47.
4 Hynek 1978, p.93.
5 Swords *et al.* 2012, p.297.
6 McDonald 1967b, p.18.
7 Hynek 1972, p.100–108.
8 Druffel 2003, p.144.
9 Swords et al. 2012, p.308.
10 ibid. p.309.
11 Druffel 2003, p.168.
12 ibid. p.181.
13 Gross 2003a, p.37.
14 ibid. p.36.
15 ibid. p.38.
16 ibid. p.38.
17 ibid. p.37.
18 ibid. p.37.
19 Hynek 1972, p.262.
20 McDonald 1968b.
21 Druffel 2003, p.270.
22 Swords 2014.
23 ibid.
24 Hynek 1968.
25 Hynek 1969.
26 McDonald 1968b.
27 Baker 1968.
28 Sagan 1968.

29 McDonald 1967b.

30 Druffel 2003, p.554.

31 Swords 2006, p.546.

32 Condon and Gillmor 1968.

33 Dick 2001, p.15.

34 Swords *et al.* 2012, p.330.

35 Page 1969.

36 Wendt and Duvall 2008, p.626.

37 Swords *et al.* 2012, p.331.

38 Swords *et al.* 2012, p.320.

39 Druffel 2003 Appendix 16-B, p.574.

40 Clemence *et al.* 1969.

41 McDonald 1969a.

42 McDonald 1968b.

43 Druffel 2003, p.431.

44 Sagan and Page (Ed.) 1974.

45 Kuettner, J.P. *et al.* 1970, p.49.

46 McDonald 1968b.

47 Druffel 2003, p.503.

48 Druffel 2003, p.513.

49 McDonald 1970.

50 Druffel 2003, p.519.

3

Aliens – or not?

After James McDonald's death, apart from debunker Donald Menzel, Allen Hynek was the only scientist of standing who was an acknowledged expert on 'the UFO problem'. Many years of work as the US Air Force's official scientific consultant had given the astronomer a certain status. In the post-McDonald era, with many elite US scientists reverting to their pre-McDonald views that UFOs were a nonsense problem, the pressure was on Hynek to show that, on the contrary, certain high-quality UFO reports presented a challenge to science.

Hitherto, Hynek had been reticent about his theories, merely stating that his prolonged study of Blue Book cases had led him to part company with Donald Menzel and agree with McDonald that some cases, such as Red Bluff 1960, Portage County 1966, and Redlands 1968 constituted a serious scientific puzzle. But, after the closure of Blue Book and the loss of his post as consultant to the Air Force, Hynek decided to 'come out' and make public his working hypotheses. This he did in his 1972 book *The UFO Experience*.[1]

I was shocked to read it. Hynek is good at applying scientific analysis to case histories, and it was this quality that led him to appreciate the scientific challenge of the more puzzling Blue Book cases. But when it came to forming general hypotheses, he fell headlong into the very trap that McDonald had warned against in his 1968 presentation to Congress – anthropomorphism.

In *The UFO Experience*, Hynek commends two works, *The Humanoids*,[2] a work written by Charles Bowen, the editor of the now defunct British UFO magazine *Flying Saucer Review*, and *Passport to*

Magonia,[3] written by Hynek's friend, French scientist Jacques Vallée. These books talk about aliens of all kinds: tall Nordics, alarming giants and hairy, bellicose dwarfs. Some aliens speak French or Spanish well, others don't. Some wear diving suits or helmets, some don't. Some make friendly gestures to humans, others show hostility. Some aliens steal things from farmers, for example, rabbits, dogs, fertilisers. And so on.

Today, as a result of the work of cognitive scientists like Pascal Boyer,[4] we know how human minds work as hyperactive agent-detection (HAD) systems. Our minds are quick to interpret clues such as unusual movements as signs of agents that may be plotting against us. Such systems would have had survival value in the past. Better respond to a hundred imaginary bogeys than fall victim to a hungry predator. One might well suspect that such systems have operated in witnesses' minds to create the aliens of Bowen and Vallée.

But in the 1970s insights of this kind weren't yet available. So we can understand how Hynek, never as clear-sighted as McDonald and now surrounded by UFOlogists rather than scientists, moved from being the leading UFO debunker towards the popular view that humanoid aliens were visiting Earth. Despite the fact that the overwhelming majority of UFO witnesses reported no aliens, no doubt the humanoids were there, perhaps operating the spacecraft controls or hatching their bizarre abduction schemes.

The really shocking thing about Hynek's *The UFO Experience* though, is not so much the astronomer's newfound belief in aliens, but the revelation of his participation in the unscientific practice of persuading UFO eyewitnesses to undergo so-called 'hypnotic regression'. Given that witnesses already face ridicule from sceptics, to persuade these vulnerable people to endure sessions with quacks would seem to raise questions about Hynek's own sanity. We can see the full horror of Hynek's approach in his account of the celebrated Barney and Betty Hill sighting, near Indian Head, New Hampshire on the night of 19/20 September 1961.[5]

Driving back to their home in New Hampshire after a vacation in Canada, the Hills saw a strange light in the sky moving erratically in the vicinity of the gibbous Moon and the planet Jupiter. They stopped to observe it with binoculars and then observed it flashing multicolored lights. After they resumed their journey, Betty still observed the lights, which continued to move erratically, and gave the impression of spinning. Finally, the lights descended and hovered directly in front of them, reminding Barney Hill of a huge pancake.

Having stopped the car again about one mile south of Indian Head, Barney stepped outside and examined the apparition with binoculars. He later reported having seen what appeared like a double row of illuminated rectangular windows with a red light at each end. The apparition appeared to be about sixty to eighty feet in diameter and about three hundred feet away. Barney later claimed to have seen what looked like a group of humanoid figures inside the craft, moving about with the precision of "German officers." As the craft tilted downwards, Barney had the impression that one of these entities – the 'leader' in Fig 12 – was communicating a frightening message to him.

(xx.)

(xx.) Fuller, John. *The Interrupted Journey*. p.28.

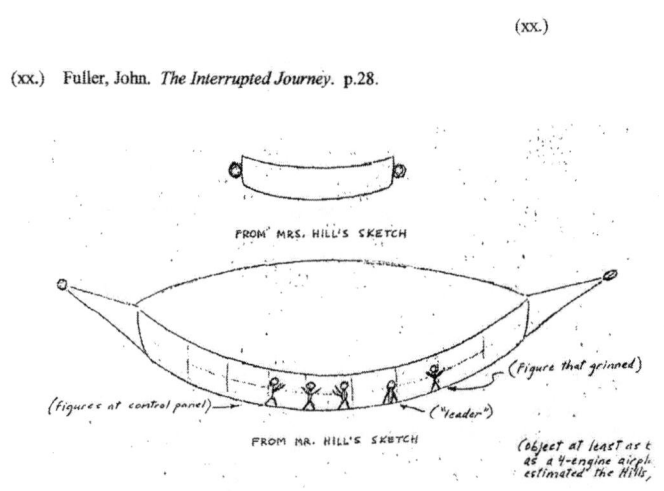

Fig 12. On 20 September 1961 Betty and Barney Hill made separate sketches of the apparition they claimed to have seen the previous night near Indian Head, New Hampshire. Above: From Betty Hill's sketch. Below: From Barney Hill's sketch.
[Fuller 1966 p 28]

Scared out of his wits by what he had seen, and fearing capture by the aliens, Barney ran back to the car. He then drove away at high speed and the couple heard a series of beeping sounds. They arrived home in Portsmouth, New Hampshire at about dawn.

When the couple awoke after some sleep, Barney made the sensible suggestion that the pair should go into separate rooms and each make drawings of the apparition they'd seen. This they did (Fig 12). Betty later reported their encounter to the US Air Force and the Blue Book team subsequently investigated it.

Although not initially involved, Allen Hynek later took a strong interest in the case. In *The UFO Experience* Hynek devoted seven pages to the incident.[6] In his book Hynek focused on a hypnosis session involving the Hills, hypnotist Dr Benjamin Simon and himself. Simon had already elicited many stories from the couple in previous hypnosis sessions, including one in which humanoids examined Barney Hill's genitals. Hynek was more interested in details of the alleged landing of the object and, in response to his questioning, a hypnotised Betty Hill told him that the craft's rim was "a little bit above the ground" and "there was a ramp that came down."[7]

Of course the aliens would need a ramp in order to clamber down from their flying saucer. Hynek's naïve endorsement of 'hypnotic regression' led to Betty Hill's famous hypnotically revealed 'star map' being taken far more seriously than it should have been. Based on the view of space from the Zeta Reticuli star system, about forty light years away, from where the aliens had allegedly come, Betty's 'star map' allowed Carl Sagan and others to demonstrate the folly of Hynekian UFOlogy (Wikipedia: Barney and Betty Hill).

Apart from silly stories 'revealed' by hypnosis, is there any evidence that the Hills encountered aliens at all? Compare the Hills' Indian Head drawings, shown in Fig 12, with those prepared by witnesses, or artists acting on their behalf, depicting what was reported in six other 1960s 'close encounters' – Figs 5, 6, 9, 13, 14, 15. All seven reported objects were in the same apparent size range, all presented the same broad shape to the witnesses. Four of the apparitions, Red Bluff (Fig 5), Indian Head

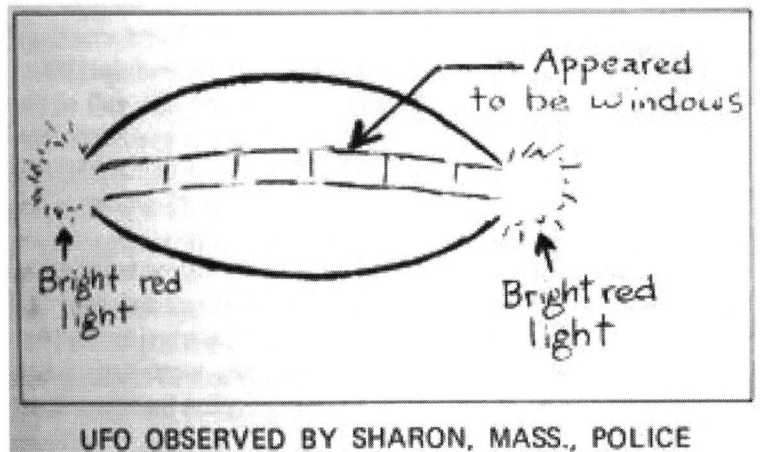

Fig 13. Sharon MS, 20 April 1966. On the early morning of 20 April 1966, Sergeant Bernard Coffey and Officer Frederick Jones of the Sharon police reported viewing this anomalous object. Sergeant Coffey reported 'I viewed a red light in front and a red light to the rear that remained on (not flashing) and a wide section of white light extending from red light to red light and appeared to be inside lights. I concentrated on trying to see inside of the object for any figures or movements but failed to detect any signs of life or figures.' [http://www.nicap.org/newlook/section_IV.htm]

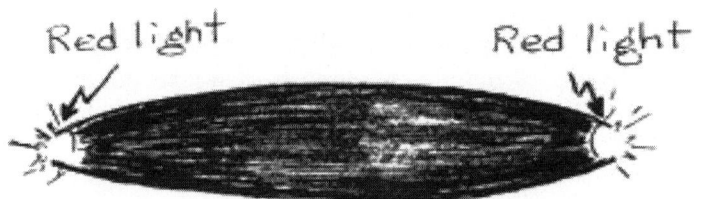

Fig 14. Bellingham MS, 19 April 1966. At about 2200 local time on the evening of 19 April 1966, Mrs. Peggy Kudla of Bellingham MS, several miles west southwest from Sharon, 'saw a narrow oval or cigar-shaped object of very large apparent size, at first tipped at an angle. At each end was a bright red light, steady at first but blinking later as the UFO moved away.' The UFO appeared to be at an altitude of about 200 feet and at its closest point was estimated to be about 300 feet away.' [http://www.nicap.org/newlook/section_IV.htm]

(Fig 12), Sharon (Fig 13) and Bellingham (Fig 14), had a red light at each end. Four of them, Redlands (Fig 9), Indian Head, Sharon and Odessa (Fig 15), presented features that witnesses interpreted as illuminated rectangular panels or windows.

But only Barney Hill saw aliens. Even Betty Hill saw none and her sketch of the Indian Head object (Fig 12) shows only a band of light apparently emerging from the periphery of a thick tilted disc, with red lights at each end.

Once we look at all these sketches together, and assume that they do indeed depict real objects, the common features suggest that they may have been surveillance devices of a particular class. The illuminated rectangular panels may have served both to illuminate the scene and collect reflected photons.

But it's easy to see how the mind's agent-detection systems could have interpreted these bright luminous panels as windows and the dark vertical bands between them as erect human figures – like soldiers on

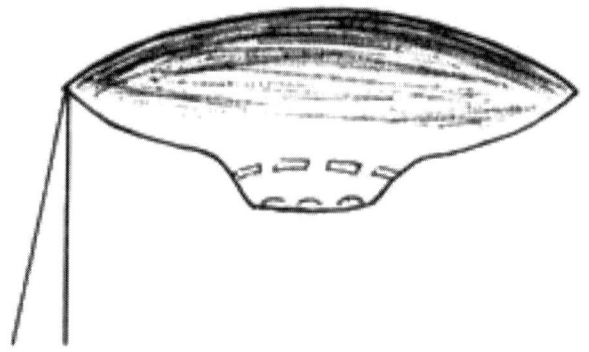

Fig 15. Odessa Delaware, 9 February 1967. At about 2045 local time on 9 February 1967, driving south towards Odessa, Mr. and Mrs. Donald Guseman saw two lights ahead, a green light on the left and a red one on the right. They approached the hovering lighted object, which they estimated to be about 200 feet away, fifty feet wide and twenty feet high, and watched for a about two minutes. The silent object emitted white beams like search lights that first pointed downwards, as shown here, and then swung around to point upwards as the object moved away to the north, now humming softly. [http://www.nicap.org/newlook/section_IV.htm]

parade. I can see 'soldiers' in both the Redlands and Sharon sketches.

So it's not surprising that a frightened Barney Hill, his mind's agent-detection systems on full throttle, sincerely thought he'd seen beings inside the object looking at him or marching around like "German officers". In his sketch (Fig 12), the aliens' bodies closely align with the dark vertical bands between panels, and the heads of the 'leader' and the 'figure that grinned' are close to the intersections between the dark horizontal and vertical bands.

What is surprising is that neither Allen Hynek, Stanton Friedman, nor any other UFOlogist has ever pointed out that Barney Hill's report of a standing or marching alien crew makes little sense in light of the violent manoeuvres the Hills had seen the object perform a few minutes before. Betty and Barney Hill claimed to have seen the object bounce back and forth in the sky, even apparently spinning at one point. The g-forces on any humanoid crew would have been colossal. Had flesh-and-blood creatures survived such manoeuvres, they would have been in no condition to calmly march around or grin, as Barney claimed.

If dark vertical bands separating luminous panels might have given the illusion of space aliens, then so might antennas, sensors or other surveillance equipment projecting from a probe against a lighter sky background or a background plasma glow. These are the conditions under which, in June 1959, Father William Gill and his flock at Boianai, New Guinea had reported those after-dark sightings of machine-like anomalous objects that so intrigued James McDonald.

As we've seen, in 1966, James McDonald interviewed Gill in Melbourne and, as an atmospheric physicist, was particularly interested in the glow that Gill said had traced the main object's periphery and had intensified when the object moved. That's a non-anthropomorphic observation if there ever was one and later we'll look further at its scientific implications.

Allen Hynek was as interested in the Boianai reports as James McDonald had been and he too interviewed William Gill in Australia. Hynek even visited Boianai and interviewed the local witnesses, Gill's Anglican missionary colleague Father Norman Cruttwell acting as

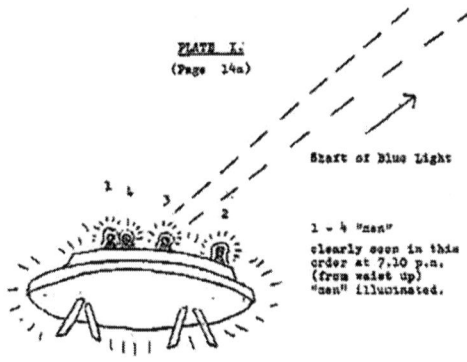

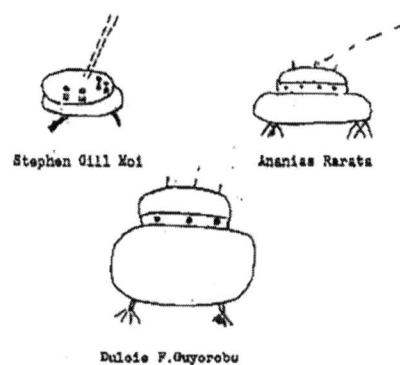

Fig 16. Plate published by Father Norman Cruttwell, showing witness sketches of the main object seen by multiple witnesses at Boianai, New Guinea, during and after dusk on 26 June 1959. At its closest the object spanned a hand's width at arm's length – about ten degrees – and was estimated to have been several hundred feet away from the witnesses. Above: Sketch by Father William Gill. Below: Sketches by Stephen Gill Moi, Ananias Rarata and Dulcie Guyorobo. [Cruttwell 1960a p 14a]

interpreter. But while McDonald had focused on the atmospheric physics of the Boianai sightings, Hynek was more interested in the alleged humanoids.

Father Cruttwell had compiled a private report on the Boianai sightings and many others that had been reported in New Guinea at this time.[8] In it Cruttwell noted that, according to Gill, the background halo showed up the outlines of protrusions that Gill had interpreted as 'men' on top of the main object (Fig 16). Father Cruttwell commented that such weird details were most unlikely to have been invented and in a separate report suggested that the anomalous object may have had a high electrical charge and the halo may have been caused by the resulting ionised air.[9] Not bad physics from a man of God.

So let's look at the eyewitness drawings in Father Cruttwell's private report.

Fig 16 reproduces a plate published by Cruttwell[10,11] comparing William Gill's sketch of the main Boianai object seen on 26 June 1959 with those made independently by three other eye witnesses, Stephen Gill Moi, Ananias Rarata and Dulcie Guyorobo.

All four sketches show projections below the anomalous object, three show protrusions above it. Gill interprets the protrusions above as heads and shoulders of 'men' outlined (though leaving a small gap) against the luminous halo. Rarata and Guyorobo make no such 'head and shoulders' interpretations of the protrusions. Gill Moi shares Gill's 'head and shoulders' interpretation of the protrusions but places these features inside a transparent 'cabin'.

Gill supported his 'head and shoulders' interpretation with the claim that, on 27 June, the second night of observations, when it was getting dark, he'd waved to the 'men' and they had apparently waved back.

Three of the sketches in Fig 16 show the central feature above or inside the object emitting a 'beam' at an angle, described in Cruttwell's plate caption as a "Shaft of Blue Light". Gill described this beam as a "thin electric blue spotlight". Gill shows it coming from the 'head and shoulders' in the middle of the group. Gill Moi shows the beam emerging from the head and shoulders inside the 'cabin'. Rarata shows the beam emerging from or near the central external protrusion.

Guyorobo and Rarata show three or four features on the side of the object below the protrusions. These appear to correspond to what Gill told Cruttwell "appeared to be panels in the side of the object, which glowed somewhat brighter than the rest, but I did not interpret them as portholes."[12]

In his report Father Cruttwell pointed out that while Father Gill and his flock were observing the anomalous objects at Boianai after dusk on 26 June, at Giwa, about fifteen miles to the north of Boianai on the opposite side of Goodenough Bay, a trader called Ernest Evennett was having an equally astonishing similar experience.

Evennett, who later made an official report on his sighting to the local District Commissioner, told Father Cruttwell that at about 1915 hours local time on 26 June 1959 an anomalous object descended and hovered about 500 feet above him. It had four or five semi-domed portholes that glowed brightly (Fig 17). After hovering for a few minutes, Evennett said, the object glowed a brilliant greenish white and "shot off like a shooting star."

Cruttwell found it "inconceivable" that Father Gill and Mr. Evennett could have independently invented such similar stories on the same night and concluded that the objects simultaneously seen at Boianai and Giwa may have been "part of the same fleet of aerial vehicles which visited Goodenough Bay that night."[13]

Let's try to make sense of all this. First, could Father Gill, the other Boianai witnesses and Ernest Evennett at Giwa have all misinterpreted Venus as an anomalous object? The astronomy software tool *Stellarium* shows that on 26 June 1959 a very bright Venus at magnitude −4.21 was about 30 degrees of arc along the ecliptic east of the sun, not far from the position of Gill's reported object. Harvard astronomer and UFO debunker Donald Menzel argued that Gill had not worn his spectacles and that he had misinterpreted Venus as an anomalous object.

But Gill said that he had worn his spectacles and, regarding Venus, told Cruttwell:

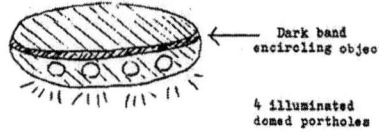

PLATE IV.
(Page 23a)

Dark band encircling object

4 illuminated domed portholes

A. U.F.O. of 27th June 1959 at GIWA, 7.15 p.m.
After E. Evennett,

(see Page 21)

The date on this drawing is wrong. It should be June 26th and not June 27th.

Fig 17. Sketch of anomalous object reported by Ernest Evennett at Giwa, New Guinea, at about 1915 local time on 26 June 1959. Evennett's sighting coincided with William Gill's at Boianai about 15 miles to the south. The note correcting the date from 27 June to 26 June was added in Gross (1999). [Cruttwell 1960a p 23a, as reproduced in Gross (1999)]

"I saw Venus, but I also saw this sparkling object which to me was peculiar because it sparkled, and because it was very, very bright, and it was above Venus and so that caused me to watch it for a while, then I saw it descend towards us."[14]

Although it's odd that Gill didn't mention Venus in his initial report, his later testimony to Cruttwell refutes Menzel's idea. In any case, the Venus idea doesn't explain the detail observed by the many other Boianai witnesses with good sight and the continuation of the 26 June sighting long after Venus had set behind the mountains to the west of Boianai.

With Menzel's Venus theory out of the way, and with no other realistic prosaic theories in sight, we can move to the hypothesis that the perceived anomalous objects on both sides of Goodenough Bay on 26 June 1959 were indeed real objects. The question then is Gill's 'human head and shoulders' interpretation of the protrusions above the main Boianai object (shown in Fig 16) reasonable or should we give due weight to the sketches of Rarata and Guyorobo and postulate that the protrusions may represent ancillary sensory or communications equipment temporarily deployed above the main body of a pilotless surveillance device?

Once we recall the notion of hyperactive agent-detection systems, it's a no-brainer. Remembering that the Boianai witnesses saw the object hundreds of feet away in gathering or complete darkness, Gill might easily have interpreted the enigmatic protrusions sketched by Rarata and Guyorobo as the heads and shoulders of 'men'.

So the way is now open for scientists to develop alien-free models that can provisionally interpret the Goodenough Bay sightings of 26 June 1959 as a surveillance operation by a group of machinelike devices of ET origin, perhaps communicating with the aid of 'blue beams' of the kind sketched by the Boianai witnesses.

As in the 1960s incidents discussed above, the main Boianai object's luminous panels may have served both to illuminate the scene and collect reflected photons. In the case of the Giwa object, the tasks of emission and collection of photons may have been handled separately. The former by the glowing semi domed portholes and the latter by the conspicuous black band that, according to Ernest Evennett, surrounded the object (Fig 17).

Why might ET probes have been attracted to isolated communities in New Guinea as dusk fell on successive evenings in June 1959? Perhaps for precisely the reason that another probe followed the Hills' car on its lonely journey on that fateful New Hampshire night in 1961. Lights. Perhaps the photons emitted by our artificial lights attract ET probes just as they attract moths.

In the 1950s, before electricity had come to this corner of New Guinea, as darkness gathered, people at the settlements in Goodenough Bay would have lit their paraffin lamps, both hurricane lamps and much brighter pressure lamps.

Attracted by the lights, probes might have moved into suitable positions and deployed their luminous panels and sensors. The main Boianai probe may even have taken advantage of Venus, taking up an observation position that exploited the bright planet both as a photon source and an aid in concealment.

When James McDonald visited Australia and New Zealand in 1966, one of the UFO witnesses that impressed him the most, apart from William Gill, was a woman called Eileen Moreland who, together with her husband, a New Zealand Air Force officer, farmed near Blenheim, a town in the north of South Island, New Zealand. Her 1959 sighting of a domed disc apparently accommodating two humanoid occupants was carefully investigated by Bryan and Phyllis Dickeson and, although Mrs. Moreland was the only witness, the quality of the technical detail and sketches she provided make it one of the most instructive of all UFO reports from that period.

On 13 July 1959 at 0530 local time, when it was still dark, Mrs. Moreland was walking across a paddock, torch in hand, to fetch some cows for milking. She noticed an unusual green glow emanating from the low covering of cloud and then was astonished to see two green lights, 'like eyes', circled by a band of orange lights, appearing through the clouds.

Desperately seeking safety, Eileen Moreland ran to join her cows sheltering beneath a clump of pine trees bordering the paddock. Then she saw the domed disc descend to a point about thirty feet above the centre of the paddock and around 120 feet away from her. As it hovered there, two rows of lights around the top and bottom of the disc started to counter rotate, eventually spinning so fast as to appear as continuous bands of light. Mrs. Moreland heard a loud humming noise.

The non-rotating dome above the disc was transparent and filled with flickering white light. Inside it Eileen Moreland saw two "scintillating" multifaceted metallic structures. She interpreted these as the heads and shoulders of two little men, wearing suits and shoulder-length helmets and facing away from her (Fig 18). After two or three minutes the bands of lights stopped whirling, the craft tilted slightly, rose vertically and, to the accompaniment of a high-pitched whine, vanished into the cloud with a movement that was "unbelievably fast". A moment later Eileen Moreland felt a warm wave of air and noticed a strange "hot pepper" smell.

The Royal New Zealand Air Force carefully investigated the incident and even arranged for Mrs. Moreland to have a session with an audiologist to throw light on the frequencies of the sounds she had heard the object emit. They also investigated possible radiation effects on the local environment. Eileen Moreland herself may have suffered from radiation effects. After the incident, brown, pigmented patches developed on her face, about which she consulted her doctor. One of these patches, above her right eyebrow, reportedly persisted for six years after the incident.[15]

The Moreland incident is particularly significant because in the 1960s and 1970s, at least eight other witnesses, or groups of witnesses –

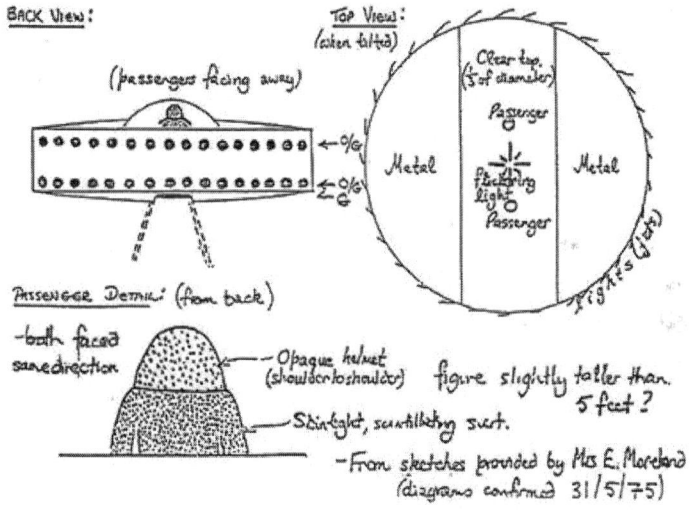

Fig 18. Sketches by Bryan Dickeson based on original sketches by Blenheim, New Zealand farmer Eileen Moreland of an anomalous disc-shaped object, about 20-25 feet in diameter, that she claimed approached her on 13 July 1959 at 0530 local time, well before dawn, when she was walking across a paddock, torch in hand, to fetch some cows for milking. Annotations by Dickeson based on discussions with Mrs. Moreland. [Dickeson F. and P. (1959)]

three in the US, two in the UK and the others in Canada, Brazil and Italy[16] – reported close encounters with similar brightly lit discs, surmounted by transparent domes and, in some cases, equipped with rotating, coloured lights. In most cases the object tilted so that the witnesses could peer into its eye-like dome and, in all cases, the witnesses reported seeing two (in one case three) structures inside. Like Eileen Moreland, most of the witnesses interpreted the structures as the heads and shoulders of little men, usually wearing metallic suits and helmets that concealed their faces. One of these witnesses, Ethel Field, who had her sighting at Parkstone, Dorset, UK, in 1977, tried to protect herself from the object's intense light with her hands, palms held outwards. Reportedly her palms later developed a skin condition of a kind that she'd never experienced before.[17]

But in an eighth case, in 1975 at Machynlleth, Wales, UK,[18] in the place of the twin structures with hundreds of scintillating facets that Eileen Moreland had seen, the young male witness reported twin jellylike structures with hundreds of moving white discs (Fig 19).

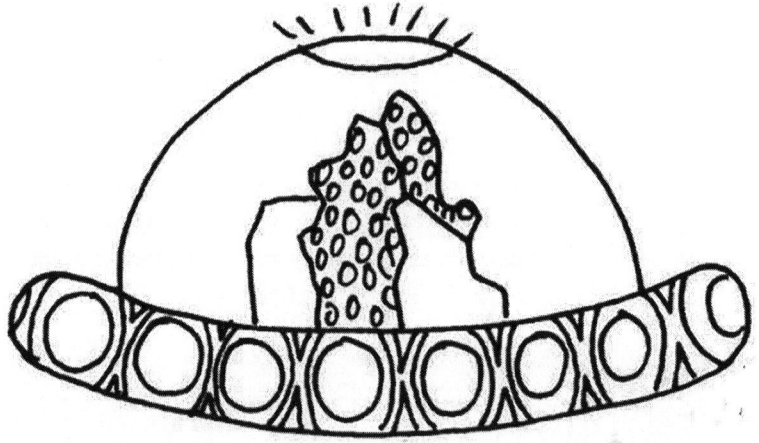

Fig 19. Sketch of anomalous object about 40 feet in diameter with transparent dome reported by a young male witness at Machynlleth, Wales, UK in 1975. It resembled the 1959 Blenheim, New Zealand object reported by Eileen Moreland (Fig 18) in several aspects. But instead of Eileen Moreland's twin multi-faced metallic structures the witness reported twin jellylike structures with hundreds of moving white discs. [Collins 1978, p 15]

Postulating that all the witnesses perceived real objects, did seven out of eight really contain pairs of little men operating 1950s-style aircraft controls? After looking at Eileen Moreland's sketches of these structures (Fig 18), anyone familiar with the work of Pascal Boyer and other cognitive scientists on the nature of our hyperactive agent-detection systems might suspect that, like Barney Hill's sexually curious space aliens and William Gill's 'men', the little men existed only in the minds of the witnesses. Moreover, in these Moreland-type incidents, the 'little man' theory faces not only the objections we've seen in the Gill and Hill incidents – the inability of flesh-and-blood humanoids to withstand excessive g-forces – but also additional objections. In Eileen Moreland's case, why would the humanoids travel many light years only to turn their backs on the good lady and her cows? At one point, she said that the closer of the two men suddenly "stood up". Yet, her own sketch contradicts this by showing that that there was no headroom for even a little man to stand up. Indeed, why design craft that gave the alien crew so little space anyway? And what about radiation exposure? If Eileen Moreland and Ethel Field suffered damage from only a few minutes exposure, how could the little crewmembers survive irradiation for long periods of space travel?

By contrast with Allen Hynek's 'little man' theory, James McDonald's notion of machinelike ET surveillance devices provides an elegant explanation for these eight reported incidents. When Eileen Moreland compared the two green lights on the bottom of the descending craft with eyes, perhaps that's what they were. Those on the bottom of the craft may have been low-resolution devices, serving both to illuminate the environment below and guide the craft to interesting targets.

The giant 'eye' on the top of the Moreland object may have been a much more sophisticated instrument. Protected from the environment by a cornea-like transparent dome, the pair of sensory devices may easily have been perceived by Eileen Moreland as the heads and shoulders of two little men. In reality however, the structures may have functioned somewhat like the retinas of our eyes or the charge couple devices of digital optical equipment. In addition to acting as sensors, the scintillating facets may have served to direct multiple beams of white 'light' – possibly extending well beyond the visible spectrum, possibly highly complex in nature – from the hidden light source towards the female human and bovine targets.

Why did the putative sensors, both on the top and bottom of the Moreland device, come in pairs? Perhaps for the same reason that we have two eyes – stereoscopic vision. Depth perception would be important both in navigation towards targets and acquisition of detailed imagery.

Of course there's a danger of over-interpreting these fallible witness reports in terms of known human technology when as James McDonald repeatedly emphasised, any ET technology would necessarily be beyond easy human grasp. But having said that, two further points are germane.

First, Eileen Moreland wasn't the only witness to report a buffet of air immediately after the craft accelerated away. One of the US witnesses, Alois Olenick, who had an encounter in his pick-up truck south of San Antonio, Texas in 1975,[19] reported that as the object departed his truck was buffeted to the accompaniment of a loud wind sound. And the two Italian witnesses, Mauro and Carla Bellingeri, who had their encounter near Casale Monferrato in 1974,[20] and who had fearlessly got out of their car to observe the hovering object, felt a blast of air when it sped away emitting a whistling sound. Such reported buffets of air are consistent with the notion that the witnesses encountered real objects that displaced air when they accelerated away.

Second, Eileen Moreland stated that when the descending disc started to hover close above the ground, two rows of lights set in the top and bottom of the disc started to counter-rotate, soon spinning rapidly in opposite directions. Mauro and Carla Bellingeri also reported that the ring of red, green and yellow lights below the transparent dome began to rotate rapidly during their close encounter. It's possible that counter-rotating 'wheels' coaxial with the disc-like parts of Moreland-type objects when hovering close to the ground may have analogies with the spinning reaction wheels that act as stabilising gyroscopes in human spacecraft. It was the failure of two of the Kepler Space Telescope's stabilising reaction wheels that led to the degradation of the space telescope's planet-hunting mission in 2013 – followed by its clever resurrection as the K2 mission.[21] If the function of the Moreland object was, like that of Kepler, the acquisition of detailed imagery, spinning wheels may have had similar stabilising functions in both devices.

Endnotes

1 Hynek 1972.
2 Bowen 1969.
3 Vallée 1969.
4 Boyer 2001.
5 Fuller 1966.
6 Hynek 1972, p.155–161.
7 Hynek 1972, p.159.
8 Cruttwell 1960a.
9 Cruttwell 1960b, p.3.
10 Cruttwell 1960a, p.14a.
11 Gross 1999, p.64.
12 Cruttwell 1960a, p.16.
13 Cruttwell 1960a, p.21.
14 Cruttwell 1960a, p.15.
15 Dickeson F. and P. 1959.
16 Hall 2001, p.456–470.
17 Hall 2001, p.463.
18 Collins 1978, p.15.
19 Hall 2001, p.461.
20 Hall 2001, p.460.
21 See Kepler and K2 Science Center Keplerscience.arc.nasa.gov.

4

Probe Theory Evolves

Allen Hynek's aliens were music to the ears of the US Air Force. James McDonald's ET probe theory, based on his meticulous study of their own Blue Book files and steadily gathering support from leading scientists like Thornton Page and Frank Drake, posed a dire threat to them. The last thing the Air Force wanted was to have well-funded independent scientists exposing their inability to explain high-quality UFO reports and probing the latest US military secrets. 'But Dr Hynek's space aliens can help us', the Air Force decision makers thought. 'Let's pass them on to our counterintelligence people.'

Hynek's aliens were music to the ears, too, of scientists wishing to detach themselves from the UFO problem. The most influential of these was Carl Sagan, editor of *Icarus* from 1968 to 1979. Having already decided to distance himself from McDonald's ET probe theory for career reasons under the Condon regime, McDonald's suicide followed by Hynek's open endorsement of space aliens would have proven a godsend. Should any scientist suggest that by banning UFOs from science Sagan was in effect endorsing the Air Force's junk science and Edward Condon's free-floating Executive Summary, all Sagan need now do was point to Allen Hynek and his aliens. Nothing more need be said. And with the contempt of Sagan and *Icarus*, Hynek's new venture, CUFOS (Center for UFO Studies) was virtually doomed from the start.

James McDonald's ET probe theory never recovered from the triple blow of Edward Condon's free-floating Executive Summary, Allen Hynek's endorsement of aliens and Carl Sagan's dismissal of the

UFO problem. From then on, scientists aware of the Fermi Paradox and wishing to test the possibility that robotic ET probes might have carried out surveillance missions in the near-Earth environment had to be discreet. As amateur UFO researchers, following Allen Hynek's lead, developed UFOlogy as a set of pseudoscientific interpretations featuring stories about space aliens revealed by hypnosis, the UFO taboo, in itself irrational, became strengthened by the perfectly rational wish of McDonald supporters like SETI's Frank Drake to distance themselves from Allen Hynek and his aliens.

Another leading SETI figure, Allen Tough, of the University of Toronto, found himself in the same quandary as Frank Drake. Tough, who died in 2012, remains well-known to scientists for his speculations, based on comparisons with projected earthly nanotechnology, that we might expect ET probes to be tiny, smart and able to replicate themselves in von Neumann fashion from materials they might find on their missions.[1]

Publicly, Tough took pains to distinguish the SETI field from the UFO field, pointing out that the latter had developed outside science, and lacking a peer-review system, contained erroneous data and interpretations. But privately Tough was very interested in James McDonald's suggestion that some UFO reports may have been triggered by ET probes. We know this from Tough's correspondence with a British aerospace engineer called Roy Dutton who had used UFO data to assemble a complex hypothesis suggesting that ET mother probes had repeatedly entered the near-Earth environment from specific directions in space and then remained in orbit while releasing and retrieving smaller surveillance devices.[2]

For aerospace engineers the position was different. The American Institute of Aeronautics and Astronautics (AIAA) had defied Condon and taken McDonald's arguments seriously. Its UFO Subcommittee carried out important work throughout the 1970s, as we'll see. And in 2001 NASA aerospace engineer Scot Stride published an important paper in the *Journal of the British Interplanetary Society*,[3] setting out his ideas on what kinds of ET probes we might expect here and how we might search for them.

Stride first pointed out that as many planetary systems in our galaxy are much older than our own solar system, and our own solar system probes had developed so much in only four decades, mature programmes for robotic space exploration were likely to have deeply probed the galaxy, including the solar system. We should therefore try to detect such vehicles.

Stride noted that our own probe designs had evolved over the years and by the turn of the twentieth century included a wide range of shapes and sizes. He pointed out that our existing exploratory probes at that date weren't sufficiently independent. The goal was – and remains – the building of self-sufficient, autonomous robotic probes that manage their own control, navigation, stability and systems maintenance.

Since Stride published his key paper, the trend to increased autonomy has continued. For example, NASA's Mars rovers, including the Curiosity Rover, can manage their own navigation and target selection. Even more autonomy was designed into the European Space Agency probe Rosetta, that with its lander Philae, performed a detailed study of Comet 67P/Churyumov-Gerasimenko in 2014 (Wikipedia: 67P/Churyumov-Gerasimenko).

Although, like Tough, Stride expected that future human-built autonomous probes would be small and smart, he understood that we shouldn't reject certain observed shapes and sizes as not being ET probes on subjective grounds. After all, if our own solar system probes have evolved so many shapes and sizes after only a few decades, we might expect ET probes, the products of much longer periods of evolution, to exhibit a very wide range of physical features. Stride argued that some might even be organic in nature.

Stride pointed out that, like some advanced US military projects, ET probes may be designed to conceal themselves from detection. Some might therefore have stealth or LO (low observable) characteristics. They might mimic terrestrial aircraft or use cloaking strategies to conceal themselves optically or from radar. Another possible LO technique might be to remain stationary over a certain region, appearing as a 'pseudostar'.

Such ET probes might be carried to the near-earth environment in large mother probes, perhaps entering from above or below the ecliptic plane to avoid collisions with space debris. Once here, the big mother probes would deploy arrays of smaller probes, each with specialised functions.

How to detect such probes? In his *JBIS* paper,[4] Scot Stride proposed setting up what he called ETPs (Experimental Tactical Platforms). These would be rugged units constructed around automated weather stations, with autonomous power from renewable sources. In addition to the collection of meteorological data, platforms would include optical cameras, spectroradiometers, microwave sensors, ion sensors, ground vibration detectors, and instruments for collecting magnetic and other geophysical data. False triggers, such as aircraft lights, lightning, birds, insects, star scintillations, intermittent sunshine or moonshine through clouds, would be added to a trigger signature database, allowing for the pinpointing of residual phenomena of interest. Such residuals might include not only possible ET probes, but also natural mobile luminous plasma phenomena.

Indeed, since 1998, when Ostfold College, Norway, installed a semi-autonomous ETP-like platform in the Hessdalen valley, Norway (followed by IRA, the Italian Institute for Radio Astronomy in 2000 and France's CEA, Commissariat à l'énergie atomique et aux énergies alternatives, in 2010), some limited work has been proceeding along the lines proposed by Stride. Accredited experts including Erling Strand and Bjørn Gitle Hauge, of Ostfold College, and astrophysicist Massimo Teodorani, formerly of National Institute of Astrophysics (INAF), in Medicina, Italy, have organised the Hessdalen work and made provisional interpretations. Although the majority of responses appear to have been stimulated by as yet poorly understood highly mobile plasmas of local origin, Teodorani has claimed that at least five per cent of the Hessdalen anomalous detections seem to have been triggered by "structured objects" – in other words, possible ET probes.[5]

So the use of automated systems for capturing data regarding possible probes has already had some success. With the development of high-frame-rate video cameras, allowing capture of high-speed plasma phenomena and the growing deployment of always-on CCTV cameras, the potential for advancing probe theory is now huge. Indeed impressive

CCTV and digital camera footage has already been captured. The problem, discussed further in Chapter 18, is one of success rather than failure. The data is too good to be publicly released.

Where might such probes be coming from? Writing in 2001, Scot Stride envisaged ET probes as emanating from advanced biological civilisations, still bound to their parent planetary systems.

But in 2003 Steven Dick, former Chief Historian for NASA, an original thinker whose nuanced assessment of the UFO problem[6] should be better known to scientists than it is, proposed a revolutionary idea. He suggested that any evolved intelligences in our Milky Way galaxy are likely to be postbiological in nature and perhaps no longer confined to the planetary systems that nurtured them.[7]

What precepts might guide the cultural evolution of such civilisations? Dick proposed his Intelligence Principle:[8]

> The maintenance, improvement and perpetuation of knowledge and intelligence is the central driving force of cultural evolution, and that to the extent that intelligence can be improved, it will be improved.

Dick later speculated that biological ET civilisations may typically make the transition to machinelike postbiological cultures through an intermediate 'cyborg' stage lasting only one thousand years or so – an instant in geological or astronomical time.[9]

But perhaps Dick underestimated the creative possibilities of designing artificial life forms and merging them with machinelike elements. Paul Davies, the well-known physicist and SETI figure, who agreed with Dick that any ET intelligence is overwhelmingly likely to be postbiological in nature, pointed out the advantages of hybrids that combine the virtues of life forms and machines. Davies saw these entities as being self-designed systems that grow, improve and adapt through their own intellectual creativity – in other words, they heed Dick's Intelligence Principle. To describe them, Davies could only come up with the clumsy but accurate moniker "auto-teleological super-systems" or ATSs.[10]

So the likely repositories of ET intelligence now look very different from the humanlike 'beings' imagined by old-style SETI researchers and scorned UFOlogists. These machinelike postbiological entities would be immortal, robust, and tolerant to extremes of environment, temperature, radiation and acceleration. Like so-called von Neumann probes they might be capable of self-replication by exploiting locally available materials. They might grow organically and repair themselves by regenerating components biologically. They might even be capable of merging with others or separating into autonomous components when necessary. Readers of hard science fiction authors like Stephen Baxter and Gregory Benford will quickly get the idea.

Crucially, these postbiologicals need not be confined to planetary systems. Driven by the Intelligence Principle to seek information of all kinds, Dick suggested, postbiologicals or their "robotic surrogates" might roam the galaxy like free spirits, perhaps communicating with each other by means of electromagnetic signals and self-replicating like von Neumann probes.[11] Dick suggested that such postbiologicals might be keen to study emerging cultures like ours, for each galactic civilisation's evolutionary pathway to the postbiological stage would be unique and instructive. They may be "closer than we think," Dick said.[12]

So we now have an overarching conceptual framework within which we can relate Scot Stride's notion of mother probes to Dick's own idea of roaming, information-hungry postbiologicals. We can then view Stride's expected ET probes, in all their weird variety of shapes, sizes, functions and concealment strategies, as sensory organs or robotic surrogates of postbiological minds based in the mother probes. The eye-like shapes of the Moreland-type objects discussed in the last chapter may be significant.

The probes we might expect here would likely possess propulsion systems tailored for exploring planets with atmospheres and hydrospheres like our own. These probes might be expected to themselves deploy smaller bots for exploring intricacies beyond the reach of larger objects. When not surveying our technology or infrastructure, these bots might conceal themselves from human landlubbers by lurking in Earth's vast hydrosphere.

And here's a related thought. Given that human designs for interstellar probes involve the use of metals that retain strength over a large temperature range – like the molybdenum alloy used in the British Interplanetary Society's Project Daedalus (see Chapter 16), we might expect postbiologicals to be interested in accessing such hi-tech metal resources, for their own use in von Neumann-type repair or self-replication activities of their bots. Emerging technological cultures like our own, that have obviously developed hi-tech metal resources, would give Dick's roaming postbiologicals valuable clues as to where such resources might be found.

Thus we have another reason why postbiological minds based in mother probes exploring our galactic neighbourhood and alert for new technological civilisations, might head for Earth and get their bots to explore it once they had detected a culture of that kind here. James McDonald's argument that anomalous events like the October 1956 Castle AFB F-86 chase, the Red Bluff, California events of August 1960, the Portage County, Ohio events of April 1966, and the Redlands, California events of February 1968, could be instances of surveillance by ET probes now looks stronger than ever.

How smart would any robotic activity have to be to qualify as evidence of McDonald's "something in the nature of surveillance"? Reflecting on Stride's ideas in the context of Dick's Intelligence Principle, we see that the lower limit is low. There's no need for ET bots to show human intelligence, the skills of felines or hawks stalking their prey would do perfectly well. All a bot need do is manoeuvre into an observing position, deploy passive sensors or radar-like 'beams', collect information, make a rapid exit and send the acquired information for processing to data interpretation units in nearby mother probes.

ET bots operating here may lack our silicon-based chips and all the smartness that comes with them for a variety of reasons. Such reasons might include the need to perform for thousands of years in high-radiation environments and the possibility that the postbiologicals' biological precursors never invented silicon chips. So, for all his insights into ET possibilities and the silliness of the UFOlogists' belief in abduction-bent space aliens, Paul Davies got it wrong in his book *The Eerie Silence* (2010) when he dismissed evidence for ET surveillance bots because of reports of them "chasing cows or aircraft or cars like bored teenagers."[13] "Not what one would expect of cosmic superminds," Davies wrote.[14] Postbiological superminds based in roaming mother probes may indeed mastermind surveillance missions in this galactic neighbourhood but there's no need for their bots operating here to be smarter than cats.

Likewise, bit rates for information transfer from surveillance bots to interpretation units in the mother probes needn't be high. Consider NASA's New Horizons spacecraft that undertook a flyby of the dwarf planet Pluto in 2015. The bit rate for transmission of data to Earth was low – one kilobyte per second per transmitter (see Wikipedia: New Horizons). But because the information was salient, the 'group mind' of computer networks and human minds on Earth has already exploited it to greatly enrich scientists' understanding of the outer solar system.

Endnotes

1 Tough 1998.
2 Dutton 2011.
3 Stride 2001.
4 ibid.
5 Teodorani 2006.
6 Dick 2001, p.137–168.
7 Dick 2003.
8 ibid.
9 Dick and Lupisella 2009, p.476.
10 Davies 2011, p.161–3.
11 Dick and Lupisella 2009, p.479.
12 ibid.
13 Davies 2011, p.21.
14 ibid.

5

Did World War II attract Probes?

Imagine postbiological minds based in roaming mother probes exploring our galactic neighbourhood, perhaps over thousands or even millions of years. Traces of their von Neumann-type mining activities might remain in the solar system's asteroids or even in the Earth's own geological record. That no such traces have yet been found doesn't mean they don't exist.

Nevertheless, the lack of such traces is consistent with the hypothesis that until ET noticed the technological explosion of the nineteenth and twentieth centuries, roaming postbiologicals had little interest in our planet. After all it's only one of billions in the Milky Way galaxy.

Nineteenth century urbanisation and steam-powered trains and ships may have first attracted the postbiologicals' attention but the radio emissions, motor vehicles, aircraft and wars of the early twentieth century could have convinced them that something important was happening here.

Then came World War II. With its vast night bomber raids and night fighter operations, air combat, mechanised land forces and naval operations of 1942-1944, culminating in the atomic bombings of Hiroshima and Nagasaki in 1945, the second global conflict presented a spectacle grand enough to grab the attention of the dimmest ET surveillance bot.

So if ET bots were already operating here under the aegis of Steven Dick's Intelligence Principle, we might expect a spate of reports from Allied aircrews reporting encounters with mystery objects. That's precisely what we have. Reports included clusters of small discs and balls of orange light that paced aircraft. Indeed, in 1944, so concerned was US General Hap Arnold that such reports might be evidence of new enemy weapon systems that he commissioned geophysicist David Griggs to investigate.

Remembered by earth scientists for his pioneering experimental studies of rock creep and its application to mountain-building theories, Griggs was then serving in the US Army Air Force as a radar expert. Risking his life on several occasions, Griggs investigated the anomalous reports for Arnold, first in Europe and then in the Pacific theatre, compiling several reports, which have remained secret.

Enter James McDonald. In the late 1960s he interviewed Griggs, by then a distinguished figure who had served as the US Air Force's Chief Scientist, and Mac left behind interview notes in his challenging handwriting. Fortunately, Professor Michael Swords, who could read McDonald's handwriting, studied McDonald's interview notes and reported that Griggs told McDonald that the objects were real, that there were many reports of them and that neither the Germans nor the Japanese knew what they were.[1]

RAF crews also reported encounters with mystery objects during World War II. British researchers David Clarke and Andy Roberts found that, although most of the reports concerned small spherical objects, some of them describe encounters of RAF crews with giant devices.

For example, they found a report in the UK National Archives of the encounter of a World War II RAF Lancaster bomber crew with a giant mystery object in 1942.[2] According to the intelligence officer's report, after dropping their bombs on Torino on the night of 28 November 1942, the entire crew of the Lancaster twice observed an object, estimated to be two hundred feet long, with four pairs of red lights spaced along it, travelling at 500 miles per hour. At 2240, with the Lancaster at 11000 feet and 10 to 15 miles south-west of Torino, the crew saw the huge object travelling to the north-west at about their height, then at 2245, having climbed to about 14000 feet, the crew spotted the object travelling to the south-west "up a valley in the Alps below the level of the peaks."

RAF top brass took this report with the utmost seriousness. Air Vice Marshal William Coryton of No.5 Group, RAF, sent the intelligence officer's report to the headquarters of Bomber Command, noting in his covering letter that "the crew refuses to be shaken in their story in the face of the usual banter and ridicule".[3]

Clarke and Roberts also drew attention to a statement by Sgt. Pilot G.N. Cockroft, flying with a squadron of Halifax bombers in the second wave of a mass 500-bomber raid targeting the German city of Essen on the night of 26/27 May 1943. Cockroft observed "a long cylindrical object, silvery gold colour, very sharply defined, hanging in the sky at an angle of approximately 45 degrees."

According to Cockcroft, the Halifax's captain, the bomb aimer, the flight engineer, the mid-upper gunner and the wireless operator all saw the giant as well as himself. The crew was amazed because it "had no right to be there." Cockcroft described its size as being like a "small cigar at arm's length" – perhaps spanning 15 degrees – and reported that he saw what looked like portholes evenly spaced along its length. After about twenty to thirty seconds, Cockcroft reported, the object started to move, retaining its angle of 45 degrees, accelerated, climbed rapidly and soon vanished from sight. Cockcroft estimated that the object reached velocities of thousands of miles per hour, its outline becoming blurred and its shape foreshortened as it accelerated away. On debriefing, the Halifax crew reported their encounter to an intelligence officer.[4]

So researchers have confirmed McDonald's suspicions, based on his interview with David Griggs, that the modern UFO era began not with private pilot Kenneth Arnold's massively publicised sighting of 'flying saucers' in 1947, but a few years earlier with the Allied bombing raids of World War II. James McDonald would have been delighted to see these documents emerging, confirming that Allied air crews reported mystery objects, some of them giants, that aroused concern at the highest Allied military levels.

This recently demonstrated link of anomalous objects with the RAF's visually spectacular night raids over Axis-held Europe in 1942 and 1943 supports McDonald's conjecture of "something in the nature of extraterrestrial devices engaged in something in the nature of surveillance." We can speculate that giant mother probes, capable of interstellar travel and hosting postbiological minds, including interpretation- and decision-making units, brought large probes here, and that the latter gave rise to reports like those of the 1942 Lancaster crew and the 1943 Halifax

crew. The large probes, in turn, may have deployed smaller devices that bomber aircrews reported as small spherical objects. Such devices, large and small, could have monitored the anomalous (to ET) airborne objects that humans call bombers and the anomalous emissions produced by burning cities like Torino and Essen.

What the putative interpretation units in the mother probes may have made of this data is anyone's guess. But if ET bots gathered data on conventional mass bombing in World War II, it's likely that they also monitored emissions linked to the atomic bombing of Hiroshima and Nagasaki in 1945 and all the events that followed. The manufacture of atomic and then thermonuclear warheads, the atmospheric testing of these devices, and the deployment of the latter in ICBMs might all be expected to interest ET postbiological minds guided by Steven Dick's Intelligence Principle.

There is evidence consistent with this hypothesis. In 1981 astronomer Walter Webb, of the Charles Hayden Planetarium in Boston, interviewed an airman, who claimed that he and two other military witnesses, including a sergeant, had seen a formation of domed discs hovering a few thousand feet above Ground Zero during the preparations for an airdrop atomic test. Webb, later identified the test as the Buster-Charlie 14 kiloton shot, held at 0700 local time on 30 October 1951.

According to the airman, who was only about three miles east of Ground Zero, the discs shone in the early morning sunlight and, after hovering for up to a minute, abruptly departed upwards at an angle and vanished in seconds. After about 15 or 20 minutes the Buster-Charlie air shot exploded.[5]

And then there were the enigmatic 'Green Fireballs'. Observed in New Mexico between 1948 and 1951, this localised phenomenon was of great concern to the US military because of its apparent link with sensitive sites like Los Alamos National Laboratory, Sandia and Kirtland Air Force Base, near Albuquerque. The bright lime-green fireballs with their flat trajectories differed so much from ordinary meteoric fireballs (bolides), that the chief investigator, meteor expert Lincoln LaPaz, of the University of New Mexico, believed them to be artificial (Wikipedia: Green Fireballs).

LaPaz, who had himself observed the phenomenon, believed humans – either Americans or their enemies – had constructed self-destroying spying devices that appeared as green fireballs. But a group of scientists at the Atomic Energy Commission's Los Alamos National Laboratory, who had also seen the green fireballs, begged to differ. In a 1952 brainstorming session with Blue Book chief Captain Edward Ruppelt, the Los Alamos group proposed that the green fireballs "could be some type of unmanned test vehicle that was being projected into our atmosphere from a 'spaceship' hovering several hundred miles above the earth".[6]

So the green fireballs of 1948-51 were the first objects seriously regarded as possible ET probes and the Los Alamos group of scientists and engineers were the first ET probe theorists. In 1952, well before Sputniks and the space age, the design of space vehicles that could survive reentry into planetary atmospheres was a major challenge. But humans have long since vanquished such problems and so, of course, would have any ET culture sending bots to explore this planet or any other with a sizeable atmosphere. The Los Alamos scientists' suggestion that the green fireballs were the signatures of ET test vehicles studying atmospheric entry problems is now of historical interest only.

What then may have been the true nature of these objects? Apart from the unrealistic suggestion by the Condon Committee's Bill Hartmann that they represented material ejected from the moon as a result of meteorite impacts there, scientists appear to have abandoned this challenging problem. UFOlogists, rushing in where scientists feared to tread, have claimed that some green fireball sightings followed the movements of fallout clouds in the US after atmospheric tests of atomic weapons.[7] So perhaps these objects were disposable devices intended to collect radioactive dust particles after the US atomic testing, analyse them and transmit the information to interpretation units in nearby mother probes. To use disposable devices to collect information about the radioactive material rather than contaminate the mother probes would have been a smart move on the part of ET mission control.

Blue Book chief Captain Edward Ruppelt was so readily able to exchange ideas regarding green fireballs with the Los Alamos group of scientists and engineers in 1952 because he thought like them. After flying with the Air Force in World War II, Ruppelt graduated as an aeronautical engineer at Iowa State College. Combined with exceptional ability and track record, this expertise establishes him, along with the Los Alamos people, as one of the founding fathers of ET probe theory.

Indeed as he wrote himself of his *Report*,[8] it was more than a book, "it is a report because it is the first time anyone, military or civilian, has brought together in one document all the facts about this fascinating subject."

Captain Ruppelt's honest efforts, unmatched at the time, to use science and technology to throw light on "this fascinating subject" made him a favourite of two of the greatest minds referred to in this book. James McDonald read and re-read Ruppelt's *Report* many times. And, in reviewing Ruppelt's *Report* in the *Journal of the British Interplanetary Society*,[9] legendary British science fiction writer Arthur C. Clarke could hardly have been more complimentary. He wrote "one is tempted to say he [Ruppelt] is the only author of a book on UFOs in a position to write about them..." "Some of the completely authenticated sightings he [Ruppelt] reports (several of which involved simultaneous visual and radar sightings) are quite inexplicable..." "Unless there is an improbable amount of synchronised and motiveless lying in progress, the fact must be squarely faced that there are some very odd things going on in our atmosphere."

Among Arthur C. Clarke's "very odd things going on in our atmosphere" seem to have been not only the enigmatic green fireballs but also disc-like surveillance bots, which, according to Walter Webb's airman, monitored atmospheric testing of atomic bombs in Nevada in 1951. So when the Los Alamos scientists and their colleagues elsewhere went on to develop thermonuclear warheads, we might expect such discs to have also monitored the atmospheric testing of those far more powerful weapons of mass destruction.

Evidently alert to such possibilities and confident that aeronautical engineer Ruppelt's Blue Book team, advised by astronomer Allen Hynek, was competent to investigate, Pentagon high-ups ordered Captain Ruppelt to swing into action. The top-secret Operation Ivy series of thermonuclear tests in the Pacific was due to take place in November 1952, so the Pentagon high-ups told Ruppelt to "get transportation to the test area to set up a reporting net, brief people on how to report, and analyze their reports on the spot."[10]

In the end this project was cancelled at the last minute "because we couldn't get space on an airplane".[11] But the huge point is that in 1952 US Air Force top brass were aware of the possibility of ET or Soviet devices spying on atmospheric tests of new thermonuclear weapons and ordered their Blue Book officers to get as much relevant information as possible. And although no UFO reports from Operation Ivy came in to the Blue Book centre at Dayton, Ohio,[12] there is evidence from recently unearthed documents and interviews with ex-military people that supports the notion that ET bots may have monitored the Operation Castle series of thermonuclear tests in the Pacific in 1954.[13]

If in the 1950s and 1960s putative ET postbiological intelligences based in interstellar-capable mother probes were focusing on the new human nuclear weapons technology, why get their bots to spy on the Boianai mission in New Guinea in 1959, to alarm two Highway Patrolmen in their vehicle at Red Bluff in California in 1960, or chase Barney and Betty Hill's car at Indian Head, New Hampshire in 1961? If such reports had been triggered by spaceships occupied by humanoids it would indeed be difficult to explain why, after many years of surveillance, the beings from space were still wasting time spying on American cars or Anglican mission stations. But if bots triggered the reports, it all makes sense. How would an intellectually challenged ET bot know any more than a cat would know that Father Gill and his flock weren't manufacturing thermonuclear warheads in their well-lit Anglican mission buildings in New Guinea?

The rule of thumb for these generalist bots might be 'collect any information that might be relevant'. Only later would ET interpretation units in nearby mother probes extract salient details – such as data pointing towards thermonuclear warheads – from the mass of information collected by the bots. And then, if they needed further details, the mission-control units in nearby mother probes might deploy specialist bots tailored to the task in hand – for example disposable devices with radiation detectors that appeared as 'green fireballs.'

After atmospheric testing of thermonuclear weapons ended in 1963, any bots gathering information relating to testing and deployment of thermonuclear warheads would have to monitor a new set of targets. There were now many to choose from. For example, by 1962 the US military had deployed some of its thermonuclear warheads in its first set of Minuteman intercontinental ballistic missiles (ICBMs). These missiles would be launched from underground silos in five areas in the continental US, called Strategic Missile Wings.

We might therefore expect the ET bots to focus attention on these silos, perhaps using penetrating beams to obtain information on the warheads within. And some reports of such monitoring would likely have reached Project Blue Book. Though Edward Ruppelt left Blue Book in 1953, the unit continued to operate under a succession of chiefs, but with Allen Hynek remaining as scientific consultant until the project's closure in 1969.

Indeed in his 1978 book *The Hynek UFO Report,* Allen Hynek drew attention to a series of anomalous events that occurred at one of these Strategic Missile Wings, the 91st, at Minot Air Force Base in North Dakota, in the early hours of 28 October 1968.[14] In 2005 French physicist Claude Poher (founder of GEPAN, the French government agency devoted to the analysis of UFO reports), helped by other experts, including British radar expert Martin Shough and the US researcher Tom Tulien, published online a new study of the 28 October 1968 Minot AFB events.[15]

Poher based his analysis on a set of radarscope photographs – not available to Hynek or McDonald – from a B-52H Stratofortress long-range bomber, already airborne, that Minot AFB Radar Approach Control (RAPCON) requested investigate the anomalous activity. The Poher-led group supported their analysis of the B-52 radarscope data by interviewing many other experts, including the two B-52 pilots, its navigator, radar navigator and the Minot ground officers who had witnessed and reported anomalous activity. The team also made use of original Blue Book forms completed by multiple Air Force witnesses soon after the events, and transcriptions of recorded conversations between the B-52 pilots and RAPCON.

In 1968 the 91st Strategic Missile Wing at Minot AFB included 150 Minuteman I solid-fuelled ICBMs with thermonuclear warheads, in underground silos spread over a large area south of the Canadian border. According to the Poher-led study, the first report of anomalous activity at Minot on 28 October 1968 was at about 0215 local time when ground security staff radioed an alert concerning a glowing object manoeuvring near Launch Facility O-6 northwest of Minot AFB, where a maintenance team was working on a Minuteman I missile. Because the thermonuclear warhead was exposed to the possible attentions of the unknown object, the team was ordered to stop work on the missile and secure the site.

Maintenance crews and security staff continued to report apparent surveillance activity by a large bright reddish-orange object that changed colour from time to time. At 0335 RAPCON requested the B-52, now over Minot AFB and heading to the Tactical Air Navigation (TACAN) initial approach fix, 34 nautical miles northwest of Minot AFB, look out to their right "for any orange glows out there". At 0352 RAPCON informed the B-52 pilots that the ground-based weather radar had located an object three miles to the right of the B-52 and, at about 0353, the B-52 navigator reported the aircraft's radar, emitting pulses at 9000 MHz, had detected what was presumably the same object three nautical miles off the right wing.

Having completed its turnaround, the B-52 circled around a point about three nautical miles to its right, and the aircraft's radar detected the object three nautical miles off its left wing. Then at 0358, within one three-second sweep of the radar beam, the object apparently reduced its distance from three to one nautical miles, alarming the radar navigator and one of the pilots. At the same time the RAPCON controller could no longer hear the B-52's radio communication at 270 MHz – but the aircraft's crew could still hear RAPCON. Two-way communication was restored by 0402.

After studying the fourteen B-52 radarscope photographs, the B-52 crew's testimony, the Blue Book forms and other evidence, Claude Poher concluded that a reflective object, surrounded by a mass of plasma (the latter perhaps responsible for the B-52's radio transmission failure) did indeed perform a series of manoeuvres in the vicinity of the B-52. In one jump, at about 0406 local time according to Poher, the object moved 1.98 nautical miles within 1.29 seconds, for which Poher calculated an acceleration of at least 449 g (Fig 20).

In his conclusion[16] Poher pointed out "we are dealing in one or more devices in which the dynamics and energy characteristics are quite simply phenomenal, and have the theoretical potential to allow for an interstellar voyage."

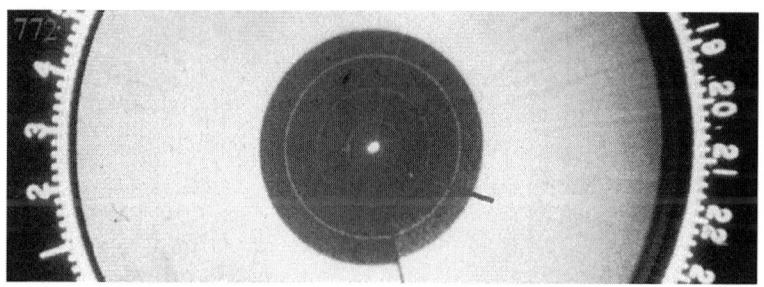

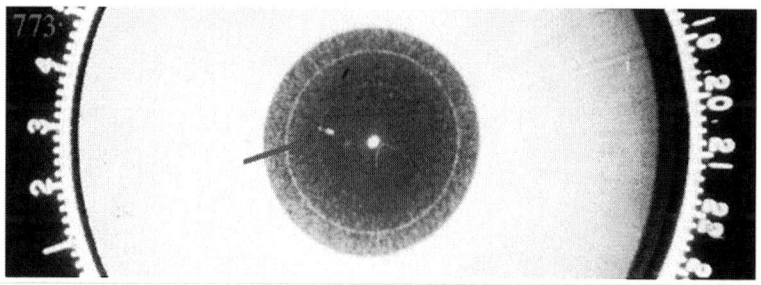

Fig 20. B-52 radarscope photos, Minot AFB, Montana, about 0406 local time, 28 October 1968. Above: part of photo 772, below: part of photo 773. According to French physicist Claude Poher, within 1.29 seconds the anomalous radar echo moved 1.98 nautical miles, for which he calculated an acceleration of more than 449 g. [Poher, 2005, p 134]

Endnotes

1 Swords 2009.
2 Clarke and Roberts 2003c.
3 Clarke and Roberts 2003b.
4 Clarke and Roberts 2003c.
5 Hastings 2008, p.60–3.
6 Ruppelt 1956, p.53.
7 Hastings 2008, p.64–81.
8 Ruppelt 1956, p.3.
9 Clarke 1956.
10 Ruppelt 1956, p.154.
11 ibid.
12 ibid.
13 Hastings 2008, p.97–104.
14 Hynek 1978, p.137. Note that Hynek gives the wrong year, 1956, for the 1968 Minot incidents.
15 Poher 2005.
16 Poher 2005, p.134.

6

Project Identification

Recall that one of the developments that prompted James McDonald to start developing his version of ET probe theory publicly was a wave of UFO sightings in Michigan in March 1966 that had had aroused the local press. Allen Hynek, then still debunking for the Air Force, had famously talked about swamp gas, but McDonald adopted a more constructive approach. He suggested to NASA's Al Eggers that a team of scientists, equipped with precision cameras and other monitoring equipment, be established. When repeated UFO sightings took place in a particular area, as had just happened in Michigan, the mobile team could be rushed in to collect scientific data under controlled conditions. Al Eggers liked the idea and had Edward Condon adopted it in the Colorado Project, the history of post-1969 science might have been quite different.

One physics professor who, after reading the Condon Report, recognised this basic flaw in Condon's approach – that his teams always arrived on the scene too late – was Harley Rutledge, Chairman of the Physics Department at Southeast Missouri State University. In 1973 an opportunity occurred for him to put McDonald's ideas into effect.[1]

In that year, there was a spate of UFO reports in the area of Piedmont, Missouri. Cars had become stalled on highways, their occupants reporting lights flying by nearby, or beaming down from above. Such witnesses often reported that, when their cars stalled, their car radios stopped functioning. Other local people reported that TV screens had become scrambled. Some of these people stepped outside and saw silent balls of light float by. On one night, even the police radio system had stopped working after Dennis Hovis, the manager of a local radio station had seen a lighted object pass directly over his radio transmitter tower.

Much of the apparent anomalous activity centred on two bodies of water near Piedmont. One was Clearwater Lake, a dam of the Black River, completed in 1948, that serves the local community as a reservoir and recreation area. The other was Brushy Creek, also part of the Mississippi watershed system, about 40 miles to the northwest of Clearwater Lake.

This spate of anomalous activity locally offered an opportunity to rectify the fundamental flaw in Condon's approach and the professor decided to investigate. After going through the same kind of soul-searching that James McDonald had done in 1966, Rutledge obtained funding from various sources, including the US University Research Council, and took the plunge. Together with his colleague James Sage, Rutledge put together a small scientific team.

Typically working at night, they set up field stations for triangulation measurements and sometimes even used light aircraft for their photography and observations. Within a few months the team had acquired a large amount of data. They obtained time exposures of 'lights', typically orange in colour, moving at hundreds of miles per hour at heights of several thousand feet. Successive movements of the lights, located by triangulation measurements, suggested activity that could be loosely characterised as surveillance. Unexplained radio frequency emissions at television frequencies were also monitored.

Knowledge of astronomy was important in their studies of moving lights in the night sky and the Southeast Missouri Astronomy Club lent its enthusiastic support. Rutledge himself became a star spotter and amassed photographic evidence consistent with Stride's suggestion that probes might sometimes conceal themselves by remaining stationary over a certain region, appearing as 'pseudostars'.[2]

As a test of their competence in this field, I checked Rutledge's claim that on 30 August 1975 his team identified and photographed a 'pseudostar' in the constellation of Cygnus. Because it didn't move, Rutledge suspected that it might be a very rare astronomical event, the flaring of a star to create a nova.[3]

The next day Rutledge found from the newspapers that this was indeed the case. The team had photographed Nova Cygni 1975, the second brightest nova of the twentieth century, discovered by Minonu Honda in Japan on 29 August.[4] The flaring of Nova Cygni 1975 resulted from the deposition of material from a red dwarf onto its high-mass white dwarf companion (Wikipedia: V1500 Cygni). Had the local Missouri skies not been overcast on that night, Rutledge's team might just have pipped Honda to the post.

So the team knew how to distinguish anomalous lights from stars. Sometimes Rutledge's team observed such anomalous lights performing 'impossible' manoeuvres such as right angle turns. And sometimes the anomalous lights appeared to react to the actions of the observing teams. In particular, when the team members pointed their cameras or other instruments at them, there was some evidence that, after a short delay, estimated to range from one fifth of a second to one second, the lights would react by turning off and on, altering their brightness, changing course, or shooting away.[5]

In the course of their observations team members also observed through binoculars and the naked eye anomalous structured 'craft' of the kind that James McDonald had considered so significant. For example, on the night of 24 May 1973, after making time exposures of moving 'lights' at Farmington Airport, Rutledge and two other observers witnessed what appeared to be a giant 'flying wing' silently pass overhead beneath an overcast sky and then disappear within seconds. Four lights, two white and two red, seemed to be molded to the trailing edge of the metallic-looking wing that subtended an angle of at least fourteen degrees of arc. With binoculars Rutledge observed that illumination from the white lights seemed to be reflecting from metallic surrounds while one of the red lights appeared to have a raised 'ribbed' structure (Fig 21).

In summary, Rutledge and Sage showed that the 1973 Piedmont UFO flap involved anomalous behaviour of two kinds of moving objects. First, lights – small objects the movement of which teams of observers studied by triangulation measurements and captured on film. Second, larger structured objects. The activities of these two kinds of anomalous objects were consistent with possible surveillance by ET microprobes and probes.

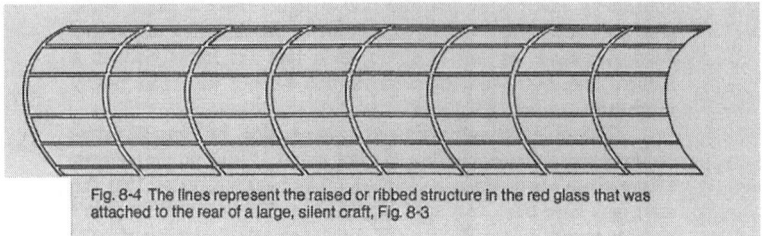

Fig. 8-4 The lines represent the raised or ribbed structure in the red glass that was attached to the rear of a large, silent craft, Fig. 8-3

Fig 21. On the night of 24 May 1973, at Farmington Airport, Missouri, Professor Harley Rutledge and two other observers witnessed what appeared to be a giant 'flying wing' silently pass overhead beneath an overcast sky and then disappear within seconds. Four lights, two white and two red, seemed to be molded to the trailing edge of the metallic-looking wing. With binoculars Rutledge observed that illumination from the white lights seemed to be reflecting from metallic surrounds while one of the red lights appeared to have this raised 'ribbed' structure.
[Rutledge 1981, p 81]

Rutledge reported some of the results of this prodigious effort in a letter in *Physics Today*.[6] In November 1973, he presented the preliminary results of his and Sage's study to a meeting of the Missouri section of the American Association of Physics Teachers in a paper titled *The Anomalistic Lights in the Sky over Southeastern Missouri*.

After the meeting, John Schuessler, an aerospace engineer with McDonnell Douglas, told Rutledge that he was amazed at the amount of data the group had collected. It was the first instrumented field study of UFO phenomena, Schuessler observed, and therefore broke new ground.

Although the local spate of anomalous activity declined in 1974, sporadic reports continued and Rutledge's team continued their fieldwork. In 1981 Rutledge published a book including an account of his team's post-1974 studies, correctly titled *Project Identification, the First Scientific Field Study of UFO Phenomena*.[7]

Endnotes

1 Rutledge 1981.
2 Rutledge 1981, plate 33.
3 Rutledge 1981, p.198.
4 ibid.
5 Rutledge 1981, p.232.
6 Rutledge 1974, p.11.
7 Rutledge 1981.

7

Searching for Gold?

Imagine that instead of closing Project Blue Book, the US government took heed of the criticism of the Colorado Project's failure to respond quickly to reports of local UFO activity. Imagine that the US Air Force therefore trained teams to undertake rapid-response field studies of anomalous events, along the lines that James McDonald had proposed to NASA's Al Eggers.

Imagine further that, in response to reports of life-threatening anomalous activity, US authorities sent a trained and suitably equipped team of Air Force investigators into the field not just for a few days but for a period of four months, with the objective of capturing imagery and movies, observing relevant details and then producing a comprehensive report.

All of this happened in 1977 and 1978. But the government that acted in this way wasn't that of the USA, but of Brazil.

The anomalous activity that prompted the Brazilian Government's response in 1977 was a much larger and more threatening affair than the Missouri flap that Professor Harley Rutledge's team had investigated four years earlier. The chief reason for the Brazilian government's intervention – the largest field study of anomalous aerial objects ever mounted by any government – was because several communities in the Amazon region reported that objects had emitted 'beams' that had allegedly hit people, causing lesions that required medical treatment at local hospitals. The locals called the phenomenon *chupa chupa* (suck-suck) believing that the beams were sucking blood from those they struck.

Night fisherman reported objects emitting blue light emerging from the water, sometimes also apparently targeting them with harmful beams. As a result, men had stopped fishing in some areas, local communities were terrified and some mayors had successfully appealed to the Air Force for help.

Physical harm resulting from beams reportedly emitted by anomalous objects had happened before. James McDonald investigated a case that had occurred in Beallsville, Ohio in 1968, when a ten-year-old boy called Gregory Wells claimed to have encountered a bright, red oval object on his way home from his grandmother's house. The boy reported that the object projected a tube that emitted a beam of light, which knocked him down and set his jacket on fire. As a result Gregory suffered from burns, which required medical attention.[1]

But in the Amazon region of Brazil hundreds of people living in the communities of Colares, Vigia, Santo Antonio do Tauá, Mosqueiro and Baía do Sol were now reporting similar 'attacks.' This created a large medical problem. Hence the local government requests, the central government intervention and the prolonged field operation by a team of a captain and six sergeants, all trained as intelligence agents. Called *Operação Prato* (Operation Plate) by its commander, Captain (later Lieutenant-Colonel) Uyrange Hollanda, the Air Force team's mission was to reassure the frightened locals and to scientifically document, with photographs, film and witness sketches the activities of the anomalous aerial objects that were apparently causing the medical problems.

Since the 1990s material from Colonel Hollanda's report has been leaked to researchers. But because the Brazilian Air Force lacked a scientific consultant – Brazil had no Allen Hynek – it was essential that those researchers included scientists qualified to interpret the voluminous and complex technical material that Hollanda and his team had compiled.

Disgracefully, this hasn't been the case. Frightened off by the UFO taboo, scientists in Brazil and elsewhere have so far largely ignored the largest government field investigation of anomalous activity ever undertaken.

And, not for the first time, where scientists feared to tread, pseudoscientists rushed in. On 20 May 2005, at the Air Force Headquarters in Brasilia, Brazilian military high-ups released selected parts of

Fig 22. General setting for the anomalous events that took place in the Amazon provinces of Brazil in 1977 and 1988. Place marker locates the community of Baía do Sol in the state of Pará, one of the localities where a unit of the Brazilian Air Force monitored anomalous activity. [Google Earth]

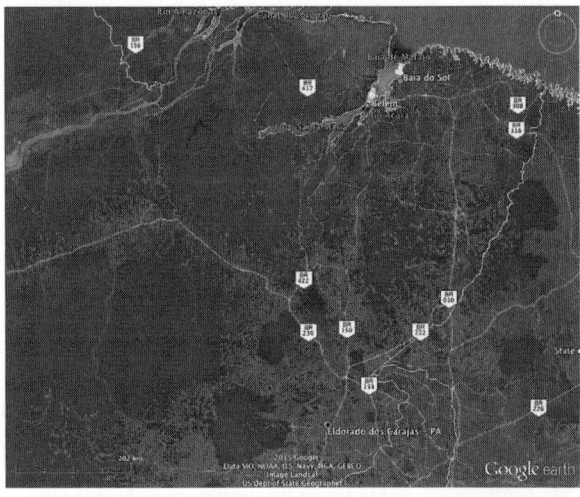

Fig 23. Baía do Sol lies on the eastern shore of the Baía de Marajo, a body of water of variable salinity. Fresh water flows into the Baía de Marajo from the Tocantins River, which, together with its tributary the Araguaia River, flows north from the gold-rich Carajás Metallogenic Province. The settlement of Eldorado dos Carajás, shown here, lies within that gold-rich region. [Google Earth]

Fig 24. Colares, the settlement where Dr Wellaide Carvalho treated patients allegedly injured by 'beams' from anomalous objects, lies about 15 kilometres northeast of Baía do Sol along the shore of Baía de Marajo. The Brazilian Air Force unit established a centre of operations in Colares in October 1977. Colares is also the name of the river-bound 'island' of which Colares town is the chief settlement. [Google Earth]

Colonel Hollanda's technical report to a group of UFOlogists. Much of the material from Colonel Hollanda's report that can be found through Internet searches has therefore suffered the same tragedy as the physical material on display at the National Atomic Testing Museum, Las Vegas. It has been contaminated by interpretations from believers in humanoid space aliens.

With agent-detection systems as active as Barney Hill's, it was likely that some of the terrified Brazilian witnesses would report aliens inside the objects they saw. For example Manoel do Espirito Santo, a 20-year-old high school student, claimed that outside his house in the town of Santo Antônio do Tauá at about 2330 local time on 12 October 1977, he'd seen a lady alien and a gentleman alien crewing a barrel-shaped object (Fig 25).

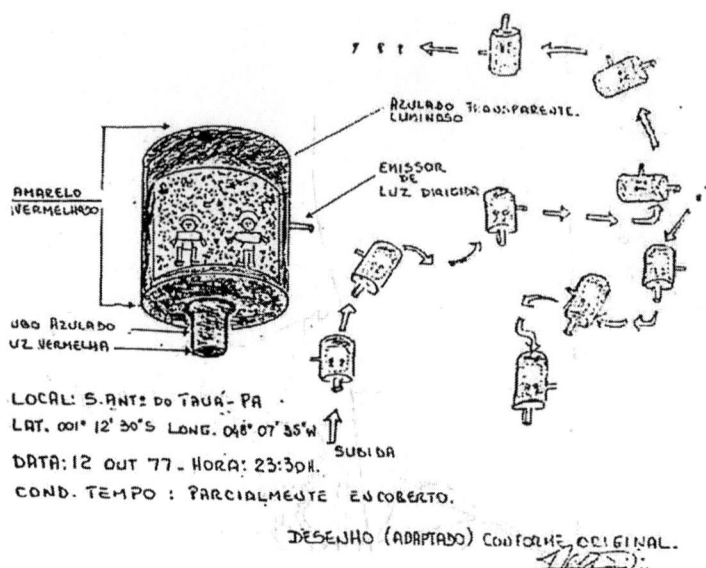

Fig 25. Hyperactive agent-detection systems at work? Drawing by the Brazilian Air Force's Sergeant Flavio Costa to illustrate the anomalous activity reported by 20-year old high school student Manoel do Espirito Santo outside his house in Santo Antônio do Tauá at about 2330 local time on 12 October 1977. Manoel claimed to have seen a lady alien and a gentleman alien inside a cylindrical object that was capable of emitting beams in two directions. He reported that after emitting a beam that hit him, the object climbed straight up in a wavy motion, abruptly varying its speed like a leaf in the wind. Courtesy: Brazilian Air Force.[http://www. mufon.com/bob_pratt/fabufo3.jpg]

He claimed the object emitted blue and red beams of light in various directions and that one of the red beams had hit him. It felt like an electric shock, leaving him feeling numb for some minutes. He reported that, after emitting this beam, the object climbed straight up in a wavy motion, abruptly varying its speed like a leaf in the wind.

Failing to grasp how our agent-detection systems can add in humanlike beings to perceptions possibly otherwise reasonably accurate, UFOlogists have used reports like this to construct pseudoscientific interpretations of the 1977-78 Brazilian activity. Thus leading Brazilian

UFOlogist Marco Petit has speculated that aliens used their beams to extract blood from their human targets. From these samples they could produce vaccines to create protection for their own bodies. So when the day arrived for contact with humankind, the space aliens would no longer be susceptible to human diseases (YouTube: Hostile UFO Encounters in Colares, 2017, 46 minutes). Such naïve, anthropomorphic interpretations have further discouraged scientists from attending to the Brazilian Air Force report on the 1977/8 anomalous activity in the Amazon region.

Until an English translation of the original text of Colonel Hollanda's report is available, together with photographs, film and other supporting material, the best option for scientists interested in the Brazilian evidence and keen to bypass UFOlogy, is to listen to the two people most qualified to tell us about the events of late 1977 and early 1988. They are Colonel Hollanda himself (Fig 26) and Dr Wellaide Carvalho (Fig 27), the 24-year-old doctor who was responsible for treating the injured people when they turned up at the local medical centre in one of the worst hit localities, Colares Island. Old interviews with the doctor and the colonel show them recounting their experiences of anomalous activity (YouTube ibid.)

Fig 26. Lt-Col Uyrange Hollanda [http://4.bp.blogspot.com]

Fig 27. Dr. Wellaide Carvalho [public domain image]

At the time of the events in late 1977 the Brazilian authorities discouraged the courageous and capable Carvalho from talking of how she coped with the crisis that struck the area. But later, after leaving Colares Island in December 1977 and serving in responsible public health positions in the state of Para, she gave several interviews, including to the French-born scientist Jacques Vallée and the American investigative journalist, Bob Pratt.[2,3]

In her interviews Wellaide Carvalho made clear the scale of the disaster that had hit the area in late 1977. Most people left the island of Colares because the fishermen were too scared to fish and only eggs and *farinha* (manioc flour) were available. Those locals who were able to leave stayed with family members in other areas and at the height of the flap only three professionals remained in the town – Dr Carvalho, the priest and the mayor.

Wellaide Carvalho stated that in 1977 she had treated about forty people for burns received at nighttime from light beams from UFOs. She said the burns did not form blisters or resemble burns caused by fire, but were similar to burns caused by cobalt-60. This artificial radioisotope, used in industry and medical therapy, emits gamma rays at 1.33 and 1.17 Mev (1 Mev is one million electron volts).

Carvalho said that the patients felt no pain in the affected areas, only itching and, after two days, the skin began to peel. She often found two small punctures, very close together, at the center of most of the burns (Figs 28, 29). In a 1993 interview, Carvalho stated that two of the victims died within twenty-four hours of being burned.

Dr Jacques Vallée also investigated and asked forensic pathologists to review the medical data. They observed that many of the reported injuries were consistent with high-power pulsed microwaves.[4]

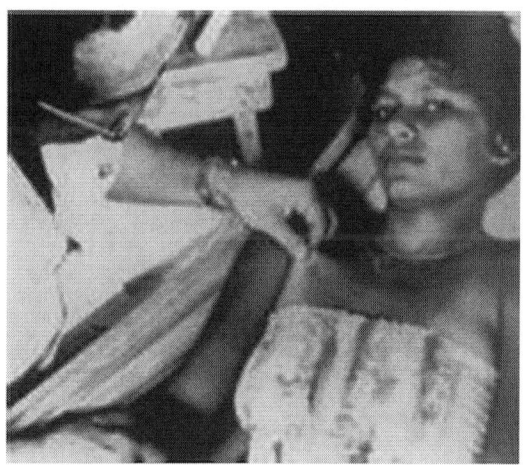

Fig 28. Doctor examines Colares woman allegedly injured by a beam from an anomalous object. [public domain image]

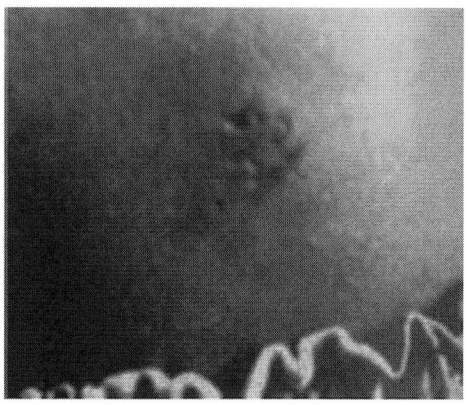

Fig 29. Close up of punctures shown in Fig 28. [public domain image]

Dr Carvalho was initially sceptical of her patients' claims that beams from anomalous objects had caused their injuries. But then, on the evenings of 16 and 22 October 1977, she herself observed anomalous aerial activity of precisely the kind that her patients had reported.

On 16 October Dr Carvalho was outside her medical centre at about 1830 local time – the town's lights would have been recently turned on – when, as she later told Vallée, she and her secretary saw "a brilliant, large cylinder with a purple light at the top and at the bottom, shining in concentric rings. It flew low over the street, dancing in majestic circles as it moved. There were no doors or windows."[5] In other interviews, she described a bright metallic object of conical-cylindrical shape (narrow end at top), initially maneuvering over the Cajueiro beach, northeast of the village, at a height of about 100 metres. There was no sound. The object moved in a wavy or irregular way, making sudden stops and turning at the same time.

Carvalho said that her secretary fainted when she saw the object. Many other people saw it, were also frightened and told the doctor to run away. But Wellaide Carvalho was made of sterner stuff. She told Pratt that she stayed and observed the dancing device for more than ten minutes.[6]

Wellaide Carvalho reported this incident and a similar one on the evening of 22 October to Colonel Hollanda's team and Sergeant Costa prepared a sketch to illustrate what the doctor had seen (Fig 31). The sketch shows a resemblance to the Project Mercury Space Capsules of the 1950s and 1960s. It well illustrates the object's dancing, irregular movements, comparable with the falling leaf motions of the barrel-like, beaming device described by the high school student Manoel do Espirito Santo in Santo Antônio do Tauá on 12 October (Fig 25).

Like Dr Carvalho, Colonel Hollanda initially doubted that strange objects really were shooting harmful beams at the locals. At first, while his sergeants had reported seeing structured objects close up, he had merely seen moving lights in the sky, of the kind that Harley Rutledge and James Sage had investigated in Missouri. Interesting scientifically, but not close enough to inflict the injuries that Wellaide Carvalho was having to deal with. Then in November 1977 Colonel Hollanda had several close-up sightings himself.

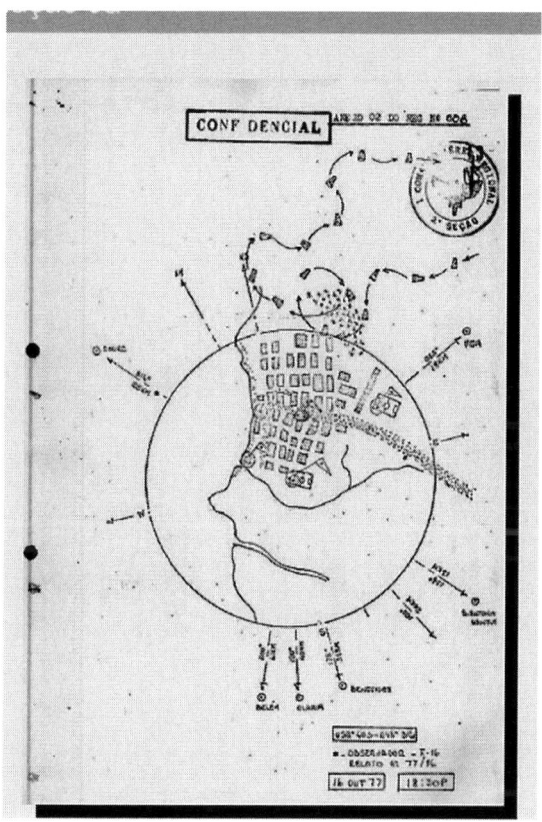

Fig 30. Drawing prepared by the Brazilian Air Force intelligence agent Sergeant Flavio Costa to illustrate, in plan view, the anomalous activity observed by Dr. Wellaide Carvalho and other witnesses in Colares at 1830 local time on the evening of 16 October 1977. While other witnesses ran away, Dr Carvalho stayed on to observe. She described witnessing the 'dancing' of a conical-cylindrical metallic object about three metres long that had a narrow end at the top. The object resembles the well-known Project Mercury space capsules of the 1950s and 1960s. Courtesy: Brazilian Air Force. [http://www.mufon.com/bob_pratt/fabufo2.jpg]

One was at Baía do Sol, 25 kilometres north of Belém (YouTube Ovnis No Brasil 1977 Operation Saucer). At about 1900 local time, just after nightfall, although they saw nothing approaching, Hollanda

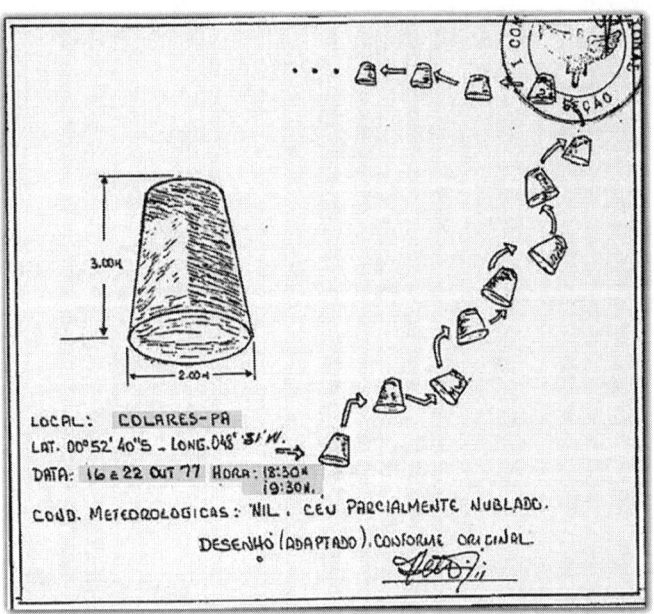

Fig 31. Drawing prepared by a Brazilian Air Force agent to illustrate, in vertical section view, the 'dancing' of the conical-cylindrical metallic object observed by Dr. Wellaide Carvalho and other witnesses above the beach near Colares town on the evening of 16 October 1977. Courtesy: Brazilian Air Force.[Brazilian Air Force]

and his men were startled to see a big disc-shaped object, estimated to be about 30 metres in diameter, hovering directly above them. Trained to carefully observe sounds, Hollanda observed, "It made a noise like an air conditioner, on which was superimposed the sound of a bicycle sprocket when you pedal backwards."

The object emitted a yellow glow that grew and dimmed every two or three seconds, the cycle repeating about five times. Hollanda and his sergeants saw small yellow and orange lights in the middle of the object. After the fifth cycle ended, the lights turned light blue, dimmed and the object "disappeared with incredible speed towards the sea."

Colonel Hollanda related to Bob Pratt that his sergeants told him one night that they had just photographed a luminous object diving into the water near a fishing boat. Hollanda interviewed the fisherman, who confirmed the frightening incident. Several weeks later Hollanda himself saw a blue light close to a fishing boat some way off shore and illuminating its sail. Hollanda saw the light circle the boat once or twice and then dive into the water.

In another sighting, at about 0200 in the early morning of 12 November 1977, in the strait separating Colares Island from the mainland, Hollanda and his men photographed an object coming down the right side of the strait. "It looped out and swung back towards us and stopped for a minute above the opposite shore. It looked like the sun had stopped in front of us about seventy metres away and six to eight metres high. It was a very, very big ball of bluish light".[7]

The team again took many photographs. Then the object ascended rapidly and its light dimmed. All Hollanda and his team could see was a green light on top and a red light below but, when the colour photo was developed, Hollanda was surprised to see a large disc-shaped object standing vertically, its left side white and light yellow, with several circular marks, and its right side dark yellow. The photo showed that the object had a 'window' at the top that emitted a beam of light towards the team's location.[8]

Hollanda didn't tell Pratt what the shutter speed for this important photo had been, but other photos captured by the team at this time, recorded on 35 mm film taken with a Yashica SLR camera, were at 1/30 of a second (Figs 32 and 33). As we'll see, studies of high-speed plasma phenomena surrounding anomalous objects are now emerging as a key line of evidence bearing on their nature and we can only hope that this crucial photograph is made available to scientists.

As Hollanda explained in various interviews before his death in 1997, his Air Force team devoted much effort to experimenting with different films and filters in order to capture images of anomalous objects they saw and described at various localities in the region. In the end, with the help of a professional photographer from the provincial capital of Belém, they succeeded and amassed at least five hundred still images and several movie films.

The still images included cylindrical objects, ones shaped like the Mercury Space Capsule observed by Dr Carvalho and disc-shaped ones

Fig 32. Photograph of anomalous activity recorded by Brazilian Air Force agents at Baía do Sol at 0325 on 11 December 1977. The photographer used a Yashica Electro 35 TLS camera to capture the image on black and white film, speed 1000 ASA. Exposure was 1/30 second. Courtesy: Brazilian Air Force. [http://www.mufon.com/bob_pratt/fafo4b.jpg]

such as those captured in the Colares strait on the early morning of 12 November 1977, as well as objects of other shapes and sizes. The latter included objects that flew very high and, on several nights, working from Baía do Sol, the agents photographed a very large object, perhaps a hundred metres long with 'windows' along it (Fig 34).[9] The agents observed up to six smaller objects emerge from the large object and return later.

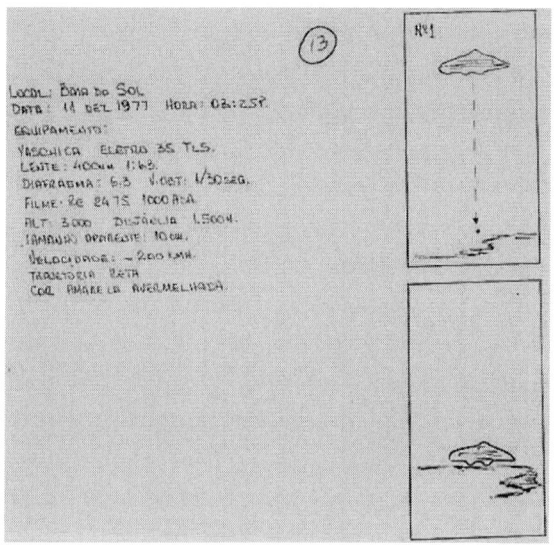

Fig 33. Eyewitness sketch of anomalous activity recorded by Brazilian Air Force agents at Baía do Sol at 0325 on 11 December 1977. The eyewitness evidently added observed details to a tracing of the photographic image shown in Fig 32. Courtesy: Brazilian Air Force. [http://www.mufon.com/bob_pratt/fafo4b.jpg]

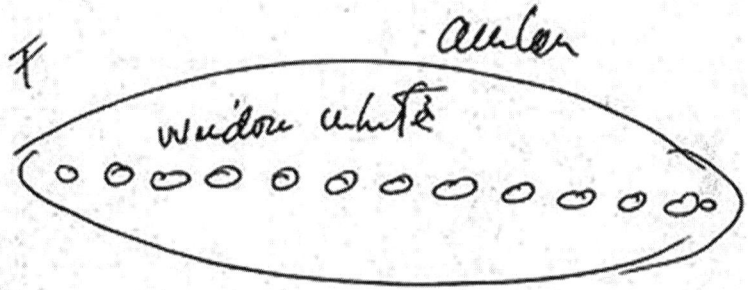

Fig 34. Lt-Col Uyrange Hollanda, commander of the 1977/8 Operação Prato *(Operation Plate) made this sketch of a huge 'mother ship' with 'white windows' along its length for the American journalist Bob Pratt in 1997. Hollanda told Pratt that his team had photographed the giant object, estimated to be a hundred metres long, on several nights near Baía do Sol. Hollanda said that the team photographed (or filmed) up to six 'little ones' coming out of the large object and later returning to it. [http://www.mufon.com/bob_pratt/hsketch22.jpg]*

Another Brazilian Air Force officer, Colonel Gabriel Brasil, confirmed the existence of 1977 Brazilian Air Force films of a large object discharging and retrieving smaller objects, and of smaller objects entering and leaving the waters of Marajo Bay. After Colonel Hollanda's death in 1997, Brasil confirmed to Bob Pratt that, together with other Air Force officers, he had viewed *Operação Prato* films showing such anomalous activities at a local Air Force base in 1977.[10]

But the Brazilian Air Force team wasn't the only group to succeed in capturing abundant photographic evidence of anomalous aerial activity in the region during 1977 and 1978. The provincial press was very active in this respect and, crucially, the press photographers continued to monitor anomalous activity after the official end of *Operação Prato* in January 1978.[11] For example, the regional *Jornal do Pará* sent a reporter, Biamir Siqueira, and a photographer, José Ribamar, to cover the story. The newspaper published a summary in its issues between 25 June and 28 June 1978.

On 24 May 1978 the pair had their first encounter. At about 0200 they were taking a nap in a car belonging to the editor of the newspaper *O Estado do Pará*, parked on the waterfront of Baía do Sol. They were suddenly awoken by an intense flash of blue light, verging on grayish. They felt a powerful impact, got out of their car and saw a craft flying overhead, perhaps about 20 meters or so high. It then turned off the light and vanished.

Though the pair didn't manage to take a photo that night, during their later night watches from Baía do Sol in mid-1978 they obtained many photographs, using high sensitivity film and a Nikon camera with a telescopic lens. The objects they saw and attempted to capture on film included 'mother ships', some of which, like the objects photographed by Hollanda's Air Force team, had a row of lighted 'windows.' On several occasions, like the Air Force team, the journalists saw 'mother ships' release smaller objects. They reported that the smaller objects departed from a sort of cockpit which opened up in the lower part of the larger object.

During their nighttime photographic missions, the *Jornal do Pará* newsmen reported a novel phenomenon, repeated on several nights.

First, Siquieira said, they would observe flashes, in which beams of light crossed the sky from north to south. These beams would be repeated seven to nine times during an interval of ten to forty-five seconds. Then the journalists would see the silent 'mother ships' appear.

Siqueira suggested that the purpose of the 'light beams' might be to prepare the routes of the 'mother ships.' Perhaps by removing beforehand all matter existing along the intended north-south trajectory of the craft, the beams could enable the 'mother ships' to move silently.

A good scientific idea. Unfortunately, the journalists' key evidence of about two hundred negatives, including coverage of this 'mother ship' activity in mid-1978, has disappeared. Siqueira and Ribamar told later interviewers that, on the orders of the newspaper office, their entire collection of negatives was sold to a North American group for an undisclosed sum.

Interesting. American UFOlogists have certainly not publicised the Brazilian journalists' material. Did a secret US science group use these Brazilian negatives together with other photographic material and movies to construct models of ET surveillance activity in the Amazon in 1977 and 1978?

That's possible. But whatever the fate of the journalists' material, with no access either to it or to the full archives of Brazilian government material, including the films viewed by Colonel Brasil, the best option now for technical people seeking to construct open scientific interpretations of the 1977/8 anomalous activity in Brazil is to continue to pay attention to Colonel Hollanda's assessments.

As a trained intelligence agent, Hollanda was familiar with aerial surveillance campaigns and, in his interviews, he observed that the anomalous activity in 1977 and 1978 appeared to have followed exactly such a pattern, moving from one area of the vast Amazon rainforest area to another in a grid-like fashion over the course of several months. His own hardworking sergeants compiled maps illustrating the local surveillance patterns they observed in the Colares area on specific nights (Fig 35). It's therefore possible that the anomalous objects systematically surveyed the whole Amazon rainforest region in a similar way over a period of many months.

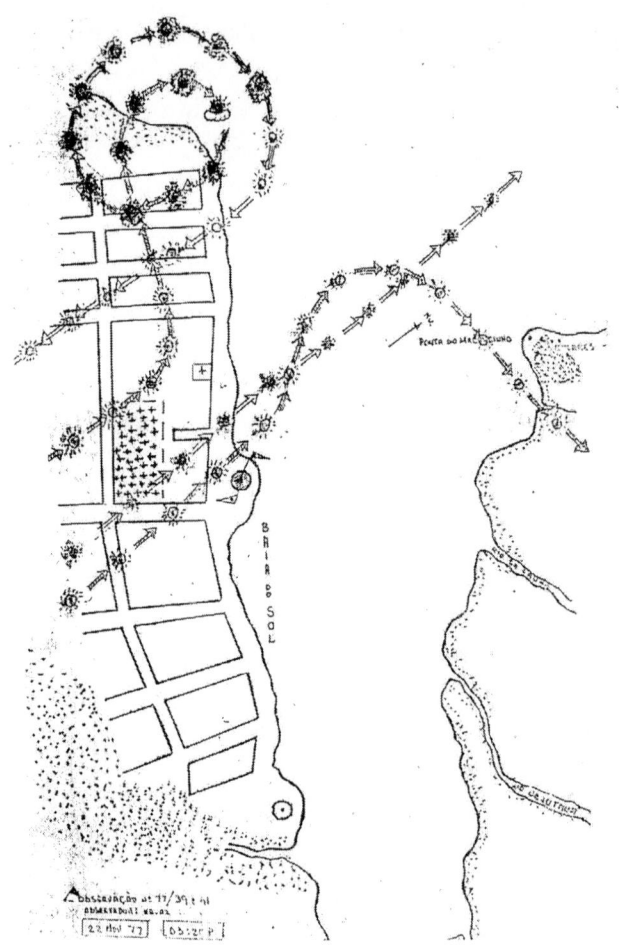

Fig 35. Brazilian Air Force intelligence agents in Baía do Sol (flag) recorded much nighttime apparent surveillance activity by anomalous objects. For example at 0320 on 22 November 1977, they observed a yellow flashing light, estimated to be about 400 metres high, that first appeared about 600 metres away from them. Then it suddenly moved to a location about two kilometres to the northwest of their position and completed two circles, as shown. Finally it disappeared to the southwest. Throughout their observation of it the object moved with irregular changes in speed. Courtesy: Brazilian Air Force. (http://documents.theblackvault.com/documents/MUFON/Pratt/prato.pdf) [http://www.fenomenum.com.br/ufo/casos/1970/imagens/página%20017.jpg]

As Hollanda explained to Cynthia Luce and Bob Pratt in 1997, "They (the anomalous objects) were moving from Maranhão to Colares, Belém, Monte Alegre, Santarém and Manaus. They were covering the Brazilian air space and the Amazon region in strips, like we do in aerial photography".[12,13]

Why might the anomalous objects have been carrying out systematic surveillance of such a vast region? Given that much of the area was uninhabited or lightly inhabited, it's unlikely that the objectives were connected with the human population. But the area possessed vast mineral wealth and, as Hollanda pointed out, a Brazilian-Japanese historian, Claudio Tsuyoshi Suenaga, had suggested that the beam-emitting objects might have been secret craft of terrestrial origin exploring the mineral deposits of the Pará region.

That's a good starting point for scientific analysis. The problem is the near-magical beam technology and propulsion systems displayed. The devices observed by Dr Carvalho and Colonel Hollanda suggest technology far beyond present human achievements, let alone what would have been available in the 1970s.

So once again our thoughts turn to possible ET bots. Not only generalist bots, as the objects Rutledge and Sage observed in Missouri may have been, but also specialist prospecting bots. To get a handle on how beam-emitting ET prospecting devices might function, we should first look at the exploration activities of our own Solar System probes.

One of the scientific functions of NASA's Curiosity Rover in its mission on Mars (Wikipedia: Curiosity (rover)) has been to zap tiny areas of target rock – that Curiosity can select autonomously – with pulsed infrared laser beams, up to seven metres in length (Fig 36). The pulsed beams, delivered through a telescope that can be autonomously focused on its target, convert minute samples of rock into plasma. As the plasma cools, the ionised atoms of the sample emit characteristic spectral lines that yield information on the chemical composition of the samples. This remote sensing technique is known as LIBS (Laser Induced Breakdown Spectroscopy).

Fig 36. NASA's Curiosity Rover zaps a Martian rock with an infrared laser beam.

The pulsed laser beam at 1067 nanometres delivers a high energy density, over 10 megawatts per square millimeter, to targets up to seven metres away, which Curiosity can select autonomously. The beam induces breakdown of target material into plasma. Ionised species in the plasma emit characteristic spectral lines that permit identification. This technique is known as LIBS (Laser-Induced Breakdown Spectroscopy).

An optical fibre transmits the laser-induced plasma light to spectrometers in Curiosity's body unit. Spectrometer data containing information on the chemical composition of the target is processed by a data processing unit in Curiosity's body unit that also serves as a command-and-control centre for all Curiosity's remote sensing LIBS operations on Mars. This unit interfaces with Curosity's central computer, which can select the rover's LIBS targets autonomously.

Curiosity radios its collected data to an orbiting satellite that later uses its large antennas to transmit the data to Earth. [NASA]

Recall that Jacques Vallée's team of forensic pathologists found that many of the injuries of Dr Carvalho's patients were consistent with the effects of high-powered pulsed microwaves. We can postulate that, like both Curiosity's infrared laser beams and pulsed microwaves, the beams that gave rise to the injuries Dr Carvalho had to deal with were energetic, penetrating and pulsed, designed to obtain information on the chemical composition of certain targets. Like Curiosity's laser beams, they may have been projected from telescope-like attachments that witnesses described as tubes (Fig 25).

So perhaps Suenaga was on the right track with his idea of surveying for minerals. But instead of humans seeking wealth or strategic advantage, the prime movers may have been Steven Dick's roaming ET postbiologicals seeking hi-tech metals for their von Neumann activities, in repair and replication.

The beams would have to be energetic enough to penetrate the rain forest canopy or shallow depths of water and that might explain reports of beams penetrating roofs. Although primarily intended to identify superficial deposits rich in hi-tech metals, the ET beaming devices might also have served to investigate mobile or stationary sources emitting energy at infrared or visible frequencies. In other words the long-suffering fishermen and householders of the Amazon region with their intriguingly warm bodies and luminous lamps and cigarettes.

What hi-tech metals might ET beaming devices have been looking for? Suenaga's suggestions included placer deposits of gold, cassiterite (a source of tin) and monazite (a source of rare earth elements). Indeed, as I well know from monitoring the global tin industry when I was with the UN, the Amazon region is rich in placer deposits of cassiterite and native gold, as well as other minerals. In particular, about five hundred kilometers south of Baía do Sol, the locality from which the journalists saw the 'mother ships' heading south, lies the Carajás Metallogenic Province. Here, weathering in tropical conditions of primary gold mineralisation in ancient suites of rocks called greenstone belts, has resulted in rich placer deposits of native gold or, rather, gold-rich alloy containing up to 98 percent gold, the balance being silver, copper and other metals.[14]

Such elongated near-surface alluvial ore bodies are up to ten million cubic metres in size, with the gold fragments typically dispersed in a gravelly or sand-clay rich matrix, and with gold content between 0.1 and 1 grams per cubic metre. Following the discovery of gold deposits in this region in the early 1970s, much small-scale mining by illegal miners called *garimpeiros* took place. By 1988, many thousands of *garimpeiros* were mining the massive Pelotas gold placer deposit near Eldorado dos Carajás (Fig 23).

Some of these old gold placer deposits are exposed at the bottoms of modern rivers and have been mined by dredges on a large or small scale. Gold-rich river bottom sediments were disaggregated with mechanical devices and brought to the surface by large-diameter hoses. Then *garimpeiros* used the environmentally catastrophic mercury amalgam process to recover gold from its matrix.

So we have to consider the mind-boggling possibility that the beaming devices that plagued Brazil's Amazon provinces in 1977 and 1978 were ET bots prospecting for gold. Perhaps initially alerted by earlier *garimpeiro* activity monitored by generalist surveillance bots, by mid-1978, small underwater-capable specialist ET devices could have been accessing river-bottom placer deposits of gold by night, transferring the disaggregated sedimentary material to large 'mother ships,' like those witnessed by Colonel Hollanda and the journalists at Baía do Sol.

It's therefore possible that these 'mother ships' were in fact mineral processing vehicles, containing facilities for processing the mined material. Because many hundreds of tons of material would have to be processed to recover significant quantities of gold or other hi-tech metals, these vehicles would need to be big. In these large vehicles the final extraction of gold or other metals could take place from large quantities of quartz-rich sedimentary matrix.

This outlandish interpretation of the anomalous 1977/78 events in Brazil has been strengthened by evidence that in April 2008 objects that could be interpreted as beaming hi-tech surveillance devices once again operated over an Amazon Basin river floored by accessible placer deposits of gold. On this occasion the events took place near the town of Pucallpa in Peru's Amazon region, where illegal gold mining dredges had recently been active on the Ucayali River. Just as in the Colares region of Brazil, beams reportedly hit local night fishermen and caused local terror. As in Brazil, local authorities and the Air Force confirmed the reality of the events and did their best to investigate.

Although the Peruvian Air Force office that studies anomalous activity of this kind lacked the capacity to mount full scientific investigations, three students at the University of Lima undertook a modest investigation of the 2008 activity as part of their degree course work. One of the students, Teresa Lucia Chamorro, is the daughter of Commander Julio Chamorro, former chief of the Air Force's UFO office, the OIFAA (the Office of Investigations of Anomalous Aerial Phenomena). The students interviewed the traumatised locals and participated in a mass witnessing of after-dark anomalous activity over the Ucayali River that was captured on two separate video cameras (YouTube search Pucallpa Chamorro).

With the 2008 events in Peru following the pattern of the 1977/8 events in Brazil, the need for a proper scientific investigation of this type of anomalous activity is more urgent than ever. And as a key to make sense of it all, rather than abduction-bent space aliens, we now have the notion of ET prospecting bots searching for gold.

Endnotes

1 McDonald 1968b, p.48.

2 Vallee 1990, Kindle locations 1924, 1929 of 4216.

3 Pratt 1996, p.178–83, p.281.

4 Vallee 1990, Book 2, Kindle location 1955.

5 Vallee 1990, Kindle location 3146.

6 Pratt 1996, p.182.

7 Pratt 1996, p.279–80.

8 Pratt 1996, p.280.

9 Pratt and Luce 1999.

10 Giese *et al.* 2001.

11 'Kandinsky' 2010.

12 Pratt and Luce 1999.

13 Before his death in 1997, Colonel Hollanda gave an interview with the Brazilian journal UFOVia, http://www.oarquivo.com.br/index.php? Using Google Translate, I translated this interview, including Hollanda's references to the work of Brazilian-Japanese historian Claudio Tsuyoshi Suenaga, discussed in the main text, from Portuguese into English. Downloaded 5 May 2013.

14 Veigia and Barros 1991.

8

The Faraday Effect

On 12 December 1977, after night had fallen in Colares and Colonel Hollanda's sergeants had started monitoring the anomalous activity in that area, four thousand miles to the northwest, a Braniff Boeing 727 bound from New York to Dallas was cruising above Memphis, Tennessee. On board among the small group of passengers was Ray Stanford (Fig 37), a man now well known to palaeontologists for his discoveries of Cretaceous dinosaur tracks in Maryland[1] but then best known as the director of the privately-funded scientific UFO venture, Project Starlight International (PSI). With Stanford was his pregnant wife, Kitty-bo, and his 8-millimetre movie camera.

Fig 37. Ray Stanford, dinosaur tracker. Stanford uses a brush with water to help define a dinosaur footprint on the NASA Goddard property in Greenbelt, Md., on Friday, August 17, 2012. Stanford discovered this fossil and believes it is the right back foot of a nodosaur, an armoured browser that lived about 115 million years ago.
[Washington Post photo by Tracy A Woodward]

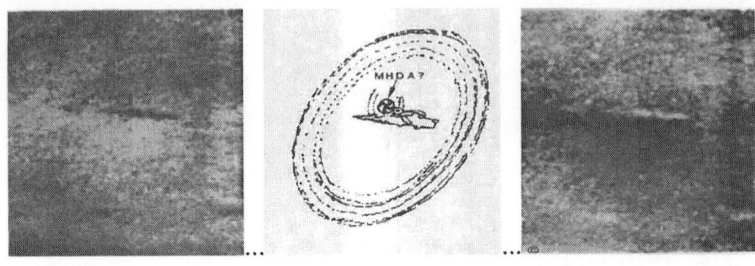

Fig 38. Left: Negative print, slightly contrast enhanced, of roughly 1/40 second exposure frame from Ray Stanford's movie taken 3.28-30 pm CST time on 12 December 1977 with Elmo 104 move camera, 24 frames per second, looking SSW through window of Boeing 727 at about 39,000 feet above Memphis, Tennessee on flight from New York to Dallas. The background light was partly horizontally polarised and the aircraft window and the camera's beam splitter appear to have functioned like analysers. Daniel Harris PhD, staff physicist with Stanford's Project Starlight International (PSI) group, provisionally interpreted the large light and dark ellipses in this frame as a result of the Faraday effect, the rotation of plane polarised light by a powerful magnetic field. Right: Positive print of this movie frame. Centre: Ray Stanford's interpretation of this movie frame, clarifying the large but hard-to-see light and dark ellipses and outlining the perceived shape of the giant tube-like object. Stanford has pointed out that the ellipses could be projections on the film plane of circles centering on the axis of the tube-like object.

The letters MHDA ?, pointing to a small elliptical object, allude to the possibility that the swastika-like pattern represents MHD (magnetohydrodynamic) flow around an object resembling the theoretical disc-like MHD aerodynes proposed by French physicist Jean-Claude Petit. Stanford suggested that the small light and dark ellipses to either side of the disc-like object may result from Faraday rotation caused by this small object's own magnetic field. [PSI]

Cruising at about 39,000 feet above Memphis, the ground hidden by a nearly continuous layer of cloud at 11,000 feet, at about 1528 Central Standard Time, Ray and Kitty-bo Stanford observed a very long anomalous object above the southern horizon. The tube-like object subtended about 90 minutes of arc – about three times the angular size of the sun or moon – and was tilted at about 13 degrees to the horizon, its left end uppermost (Fig 38).[2]

Stanford later recalled[3] that it was incredible in appearance. It looked as if an artist had painted his canvas a deep sky blue and had then made a thin slit in the canvas, allowing a brilliant light to shine through. Moreover, Stanford recalls, the brilliant tube seemed to periodically project narrow beams from both ends.

The Stanfords could also see a number of smaller objects going to and fro from the giant tube. One of these devices closely approached the Boeing 727, as if on an investigative mission. Ray and Kitty-bo Stanford remarked that it resembled the then well-known Mercury space capsules, with the narrow end uppermost. Recall that on 16 October 1977 Dr Wellaide Carvalho had observed a similar object near her clinic at Colares also apparently engaged in surveillance (Fig 30).

Ray Stanford managed to get his movie camera out and started filming the giant tube. He filmed through the aircraft window, shooting at 24 frames per second, zooming in and out and capturing the images on Ektachrome G colour film. While Ray was filming, Kitty-bo and the Captain of the Braniff airliner, who later visited Stanford's home and watched Stanford's processed film, also observed the object through separate windows. According to Stanford, after watching the film, the Captain acknowledged that he had departed from the normal flight path, J42, to give the object a wide berth and confirmed Stanford's description of the amazing brightness of the giant tube.

After two minutes Ray Stanford ran out of film but he visually observed that the giant tube shot two blue flame-like jets from its lower surface, rotated about its midpoint and then began to ascend vertically. Stanford missed the rest of the action because he then tried to get the two airhostesses to witness the goings on. That was a mistake. They were a tough pair. Stanford recalls that they thought he was trying to distract them while he hijacked the airliner. Taking up military postures they ordered Stanford to return to his seat.

While all this was happening, Kitty-bo Stanford continued to observe the object from her window seat. About five minutes after the start of observations, she called out "It's gone". The giant tube had disappeared.

In his two minutes of filming, Stanford had struck gold. Later Stanford's PSI group spent a fortune studying the 2800 movie frames, the funds paying for the purchase of special equipment to analyse the frames and make prints from them, and to cover salaries and consultation fees of the physicists who interpreted the prints.

Even before Stanford's team had embarked on a frame-by-frame analysis of the footage, leading experts studied the film and agreed that it presented a challenge to science. First, astronomers Allen Hynek and Elaine Hendry of CUFOS (Center for UFO Studies) concluded, from analysis of the way the bounce of the tube matched the bounce of the horizon, that it was genuine footage of a vast, distant object.

Then a more highly regarded technical body took an interest in Stanford's film. In 1978 the AIAA (American Institute of Aeronautics and Astronautics) organised a special meeting to analyse and discuss the footage. A large group of scientists and aerospace engineers, including Peter Sturrock, a physicist at Stanford University, projected the PSI material in a planetarium on the Caltech campus in Los Angeles and confirmed Allen Hynek's and Elaine Hendry's assessment of the vast size of the apparition.

But did Stanford really film a giant tube, perhaps several miles long, hovering in the stratosphere above Memphis and emitting beams of some kind from both ends? Or did he in fact capture a satellite reentry event on film? The 'beams' from each end of the tube could perhaps be misinterpretations of the single plasma trail created by a satellite reentry.

According to Stanford, this was the prosaic explanation for the footage initially favoured by many of those at the AIAA meeting. But if this was the correct explanation, it should have been possible to later verify it by consulting appropriate catalogues. Such a satellite reentry identification was never made.

Presumably the reentry of a secret military satellite remained a theoretical possibility for some time after the AIAA meeting. But after PSI physicist Daniel Harris had undertaken detailed preliminary frame-by-frame studies of the movie with the newly arrived equipment, the evidence of plasma ball growth and collapse at both ends of the giant tube ruled out the satellite reentry possibility altogether.

Moreover, Dr Harris's studies of plasma ball growth and collapse allowed the use of a subtle method to refine the assessments of the size of the giant object. As each plasma ball collapsed, emitting a plasma beam as it did so, it left behind a sphere that appeared dark because of its relatively high refractive index.

From the rate of expansion of shock waves that followed the collapse of each plasma ball, knowing the speed of sound at various levels in the atmosphere, Harris calculated that the large tubular object, estimated to be about twenty miles above the Earth's surface and about 150 miles to the southeast of the aircraft during filming, was about 14000 feet (2.7 miles) long.

Utterly outrageous. Even if an ET mother probe did visit the Earth on 12 December 1977, somehow maintain its integrity despite huge gravitational stresses and conceal itself above continuous cloud cover while releasing and retrieving smaller devices, why would it have to be so colossal?

We've already seen one possible answer. As well as bringing surveillance devices to this planet, for the gathering of general information, under the aegis of Steven Dick's Intelligence Principle, the mother probes may have needed to accommodate large vehicles linked with the mining of low-grade gold deposits exposed on the bottoms of rivers draining Brazil's Carajás Metallogenic Province. If the 'mother ships' witnessed nightly in mid-1978 by the journalists at Baía do Sol were mineral processing vehicles emerging from underwater cover and heading south to receive shipments of gold-containing material, then the giant tube filmed by Ray Stanford may have been one of the final destinations for these large vehicles. The extraction of gold and possibly other hi-tech metals from low-grade quartz-rich material might take place slowly as the giant mother probes cruised from one resource-rich planet to another.

There's more technical evidence for the mother probe interpretation of the events filmed over Memphis. Studying the prints of the individual movie frames, Stanford claims to have identified at least four classes of 'probe' interacting with the giant tube in a manner that might have come from a Star Wars movie. One variety was the 'Mercury space capsule' type already mentioned. A second class consisted of big black triangular objects with sunken-in backs, which appeared to have domes on top. These may have corresponded with similar devices observed and sketched by police in Lumberton, North Carolina in May 1975.[4] Stanford's prints clarified the movements of these objects, apparently showing them docking into the vast tube with one vertex pointing down.

A third class were wing-shaped objects which Stanford called 'Star Wars objects' because of their astonishing manoeuvrability. They apparently achieved this, in part at least, by laterally shooting off narrow columns of plasma. The prints showed a fourth class of object, round with a small dome on top, docking into the upper surface of the giant tube.

Hahaha, scientists will say.

But wait. One thing shifts the whole scenario from entertaining science fiction to possible science fact.

The prints, which, at 24 frames per second, captured snapshots of the action lasting about 1/50 of a second, showed that, as the 'Mercury space capsule' manoeuvred around the Boeing 727, it was accompanied by glowing curves of plasma reminiscent of the pattern that iron filings assume on a piece of paper when a bar magnet is placed underneath. According to Stanford, the prints showed similar glowing curves of plasma spiraling around the domes of the large triangular objects when they approached the giant tube.

These curved paths are the telltale signs of charged particles moving at high speed in the presence of powerful magnetic and electric fields. Experts who have studied the prints from Stanford's movie frames have concluded that the swiftly manoeuvring objects may have been using propulsion systems based on magnetohydrodynamics (MHD).

Some physicists, such as Jean-Pierre Petit, formerly of CNRS, France, and Auguste Meessen, formerly of the Catholic University of Louvain, Belgium, both working in the Francophone domain where

Edward Condon's free-floating Executive Summary was less influential than in the English-speaking world, have for many years suggested that any ET probes operating in the Earth's atmosphere and hydrosphere might use MHD-type propulsion systems. Probes might use unknown compact energy sources to generate pulses of X-rays or other means to ionise surrounding air molecules and intense alternating magnetic and electric fields to 'push' against the resulting charged plasma particles, using Lorentz forces. By pushing a large mass of charged particles in one direction, by Newton's Third Law, probes could accelerate in the opposite direction.

When operating in the Earth's atmosphere, by controlling charged particle movements in their surrounding plasma coronas, ET probes could also minimise drag and shock wave effects, permitting silent travel. With large enough energy sources and nimble control of the high-speed charged particles in their surrounding plasma coronas, probes could display silent movement, astonishing acceleration and apparent right angle turns – all the alien-killing features of a supertechnology that so alarmed the US military and fascinated James McDonald.

Another clue to the possibility that the anomalous objects may have used powerful magnetic fields in propulsion or shock wave control lies in the Faraday effect. In 1845 Michael Faraday carried out experiments showing that both an electromagnet and a permanent magnet could rotate a ray of horizontally polarised light passing through a special glass (silicated borate of lead), when "the [magnetic field] lines are parallel to the ray or in proportion as they are parallel to it: if they are perpendicular to the ray, they have no action upon it."[5]

Faraday's demonstration that magnetic fields could rotate plane-polarised light paved the way for the notion that light was an electromagnetic wave and the classic mathematical formulations of James Clerk Maxwell. It also led to a means of detecting magnetic fields. Astronomers use the Faraday effect to measure magnetic fields in the interstellar medium and geophysicists use it to study polarised radio waves passing through the ionised plasmas of the Earth's ionosphere.

So the Faraday effect offers an elegant potential test for MHD-type theories of probe propulsion. When James Harder, an engineering professor at the University of California (Berkeley) made his statement to the Congress committee in 1968,[6] although he focused on the implications of the 1960 Red Bluff event, he also drew attention to some remarkable observations made by Wells Allen Webb, an applied chemist, near Yuma, Arizona at about 1000 local time on 5 May 1953.

Wearing polarised sunglasses, Webb noticed a small white cloudlike oblong object moving eastwards in the northern part of a cloudless sky. The object spanned about 15 minutes of arc. When it reached a point to Webb's northeast, it altered to a circular shape, spanning about 5 minutes of arc.

The circular object continued to decrease in size, as if moving away from him. At the same time, Webb noticed a series of dark rings appearing around the object, the outermost having a diameter of about 30 minutes of arc. To see if the rings remained visible without the polarised sunglasses, which preferentially blocked horizontally polarised light, Webb repeatedly removed and restored his sunglasses. The rings disappeared each time he removed the sunglasses. As Webb carried out these tests, the object got smaller and eventually disappeared.

Webb understood the scientific importance of his observations, but it was Harder who first interpreted them as a possible example of the Faraday effect. Harder was thinking of a static magnetic field and in this era before the Francophone physicists' MHD theories of probe propulsion were available, he could make no further interpretations. But the later MHD theories suggest the possibility that the object's powerful magnetic field was pulsing at a frequency too high for Webb to notice the flickering and that the rings were generated because the background plane-polarised light passed through the object's plasma corona rather than through ordinary air.

That's a matter for physicists to pursue. What's important is that, as physicist Daniel Harris continued to study Stanford's 12 December 1977 movie frames, he noticed that, in some frames, sets of bright and dark ellipses appeared. Some of these ellipses were apparent projections of circles centered on the axis of the giant tube itself and others of circles centered on the axes of smaller disc-like objects interpreted as probes. Noting that the background light had been partially horizontally polarised, as in the case of Webb's observations, Harris tentatively suggested that the circles might have been created by Faraday rotation of plane-polarised light that had passed through strong magnetic fields.

This is an interpretation of staggering potential importance. Several factors add up to give the PSI studies of the 12 December 1977 Memphis event far more scientific weight than James Harder's anecdotal evidence presented to the Congress committee in 1968. First, the effect was captured on photographic prints. Second, the scientific importance of this material has been validated by the study of the film by physicist Daniel Harris and then by the AIAA's UFO subcommittee at the Caltech campus.

Third, in early 1979, when Harris had been working on the movie frames for many months, the PSI team were able to take advantage of a fortuitous development that resulted from the January 1979 145th annual meeting of the American Association for the Advancement of Science at Houston, Texas, not far from Stanford's PSI project in Austin, Texas. Attending the Houston AAAS meeting was an expert – he asked Stanford not to reveal his name – who was at the time the world's leading authority on pulsed plasma propulsion technology. Aware of the AIAA interest in Stanford's movie frames, the expert contacted Stanford and asked if he could visit PSI and see the latest results of Daniel Harris's analysis of the 12 December 1977 Memphis event.

According to Stanford, the AAAS expert, concerned to detect any hoaxing, did not reveal his world expert status to Stanford. The expert may have reasoned, suggests Stanford, that if any hoaxing was involved, Stanford would not wish to expose the PSI's scientific studies to an accredited world authority and would call off the expert's visit.

In the end, again according to Stanford, the expert was highly impressed with the PSI studies of the 12 December 1977 Memphis event and confirmed that Daniel Harris's interpretations involving generation of powerful magnetic and electric fields were soundly based. The expert even offered his own interpretation of one of the high-speed events captured in the prints. After the giant tube had emitted a plasma beam to the left, a small dish-shaped object approached this beam. According to Stanford, in the expert's interpretation, the small object's own magnetic field broke the magnetic confinement of the giant tube's plasma beam, causing an explosion of plasma out of the beam that pushed an expanding shock wave in front of it.

So by confirming that powerful magnetic fields were involved in the 12 December 1977 Memphis event, the AAAS expert contributed further credibility to the mother probe interpretation.

More recently, one of the above-mentioned Francophone physicists, Auguste Meessen, added even more credibility to the mother probe interpretation of the 12 December 1977 Memphis event in a series of well-received presentations at a conference held in Moscow in 2012 and subsequently published in PIERS (Progress in Electromagnetic Research Symposium).[7,8,9] The US-based Electromagnetics Academy, which organises these symposia, is devoted to developments in electromagnetic theory and their applications.

Because the ellipses in Fig 38, although certainly present, aren't detailed enough for intensive scientific analysis, Professor Meessen chose to reproduce a spectacular set of bright and dark ellipses captured by Stanford on another, occasion, 4 December 1980, above Tizayuca, Mexico, on a flight from Mexico City to San Antonio, Texas (Fig 39).

In this case, also involving a giant tube and smaller objects, the circles, projected on the film plane as ellipses, centered not on the axis of a tube-like object, but on a smaller disc-shaped object, at the moment when, according to Stanford, this small object accelerated away from the top of the large object. Professor Meessen's interpretation was that, in order to accelerate, the small disc-like object produced a very intense magnetic field, together with an intense ionisation pulse.[10] In his paper, Meessen further claimed that his version of MHD theory could account for the spacing of the rings in Fig 39.

So after all those decades, published in the proceedings of a reputable global technical body, the members of which include luminaries of the US National Academy of Sciences, and reproduced here in Fig 39, was the smoking gun that many had been waiting for. How delighted James McDonald would have been.

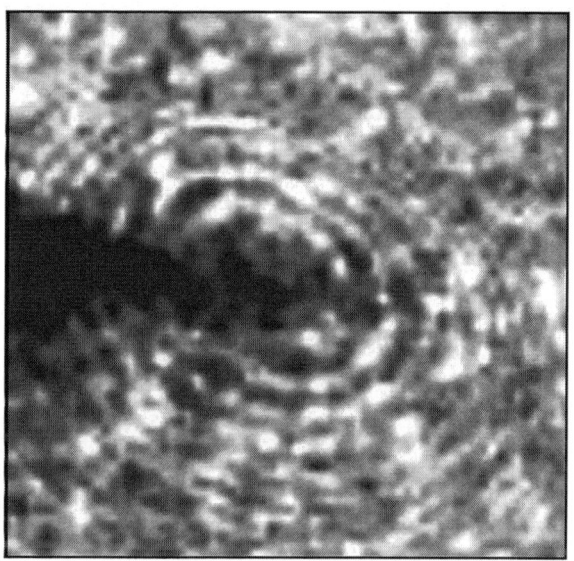

Figure 5: Ray Stanford's set of Faraday rings.

Fig 39. Part of movie frame, exposure around 1/100 of a second, captured by Ray Stanford through window of Braniff Flight 56, Mexico City to San Antonio, Texas, on 4 December 1980, using a Super 8 Canon with a 70 mm focal length lens at 54 frames per second. As in Stanford's 12 December 1977 movie frames, the aircraft window and the camera's beam splitter appear to have functioned like analysers, allowing capture of phenomena due to Faraday rotation of background partially plane polarised light by a powerful magnetic field. The bright and dark ellipses are not present on the preceding and subsequent movie frames.

Stanford claimed that this frame records the moment when a small disc 'took off' from the top of the large object shown in the left of the frame. The disc was not present in the next frame. Stanford interpreted the ellipses as projections of circles caused by the Faraday effect, centring within this disc.

Belgian physicist Auguste Meessen studied this movie frame (Meessen 2012b). Professor Meessen also interpreted the ellipses as due to the Faraday effect and suggested that in this frame in order to accelerate away from the large object on the left the small object, using MHD-type propulsion, simultaneously produced a very intense magnetic field and a short ionisation pulse. [PSI, Auguste Meessen]

McDonald grasped the potential importance of Wells Allen Webb's 1953 observations of concentric rings around an anomalous object when viewed through Polaroids and he interviewed Webb on 5 June 1966. McDonald noted the interview in one of his journals, but gave no details of his conclusions, merely writing "See small notebook".[11] In this yet-to-be-found notebook, McDonald evidently recorded details that he did not want to be accidentally discovered and revealed.

Had James McDonald lived on, he would have appreciated the smoking gun nature of Fig 39 and likely used the image as a battering ram to storm the fortifications erected by the grandees of US science around Edward Condon's free-floating Executive Summary. The metaphor 'smoking gun' can be a tired cliché. But when applied to the rings in the iconic Fig 39 it is remarkably apt. According to probe theory, the circles, seen as ellipses in this 1/100 second frame, centre precisely on a point on the top surface of the putative mother probe as the probe accelerates away, just like a bullet leaving the barrel of a gun. Like telltale smoke from a gun, the circles testify to the strength of the magnetic pulse that, according to MHD theory, accelerated the probe by accelerating charged atmospheric particles in the opposite direction.

If the set of relatively small circles in Fig 39 attests to the MHD mechanism by which this probe shot away from its mother probe in the Tizayuca event of 4 December 1980, then the set of much larger circles in Fig 38, centring on the axis of the giant tube, suggests that the Memphis giant of 12 December 1977 also used an MHD-type mechanism to combat the acceleration of gravity and maintain its position in the stratosphere above Memphis. Because the circle's axis of symmetry (imagine the circles as wheels on this axis) appear to point obliquely towards the ground rather than along the axis of the giant tube, if the skies above Memphis had been clear that afternoon, someone on the ground looking in the right direction and wearing polarising sunglasses might have seen near-circular rings around the object, just as Wells Allen Webb claimed to have done in 1953.

Such MHD concepts aren't likely to be the whole story. As any ET propulsion technologies will have evolved for a much longer period than our own aerospace technologies, they may incorporate physical principles not yet understood by human scientists. Intriguingly, according to Stanford, PSI's studies of the Tizayuca event contain hints of such exotic physics.

But now, when most scientists still dismiss the very concept of ET probes, is not the right time to time to highlight exotic possibilities such as 'antigravity' with its aura of pseudoscience. Many scientifically literate visitors to the Las Vegas 'Authentic Alien Artifact' exhibit were likely put off by the pseudoscientific statement that "the core of the material is composed of a substance with anti-gravitational properties." Instead of talking about antigravity, now is the time to focus known peer-reviewed science on the question of ET probe propulsion, as James McDonald tried to do in the late 1960s, as the physicists working with Ray Stanford's PSI group attempted to do over the decades and as Auguste Meessen finally succeeded in doing in his presentations at the PIERS meeting in Moscow in 2012.

Endnotes

1 Stanford *et al.* 2004.

2 Images downloaded from http://www.nicap.org/madar/psi-sympap80-part8.htm on Monday 9 December 2013.

3 Stanford interview on US radio show *Night Search* December 28 2011, downloaded from www.blogtalkradio.com/memphisufo/page/6 on 12 January 2014.

4 Marler 2013, p.92–94.

5 Faraday 1846, p.4, paragraph 2160.

6 Harder 1968.

7 Meessen 2012a.

8 Meessen 2012b.

9 Meessen 2012c.

10 Meessen 2012b, p.258.

11 Druffel 2003, p.239.

9

Like Baxter's Angelia

If ET mother probes of interstellar origin really did enter the Earth's atmosphere and release and retrieve probes of various kinds above Memphis, Tennessee on 12 December 1977 and above Tizayuca, Mexico on 4 December 1980, these events ought to have been picked up by radar. Why weren't they?

Perhaps they were. But a moment's reflection shows that if US or Mexican military or civilian radar did paint solid targets of this size or their plasma trails in the stratosphere, the utmost secrecy would have descended on the information, particularly in view of the Cold War standoff at the time. This would have happened whether detections were prompted by the reentry of secret military satellites or by the entry of ET mother probes. For obvious reasons any data relating to radar detection techniques for plasma trails in the upper atmosphere, which might represent incoming missiles, were and remain classified.

If civilian or military radar systems in other countries have detected such giant tubes in Earth's atmosphere, similar secrecy would apply. But in rare cases details of such radar detection may have leaked out. That's what may have happened near Barcelona, Spain, in the early morning of 30 November 1985.[1]

In the late evening of 29 November witnesses reported a strong bluish white light, elongated when viewed through binoculars, in the clear starry sky of Tarrasa, about 30 kilometers northwest of Barcelona. Police informed the Air Traffic Control Centre at Barcelona Airport, who used ASR-7 radar to locate a fixed echo north of Tarrasa (height of echo unknown) implying a target over 200 meters long.

Air Traffic Control radar at Barcelona Airport continued to monitor the anomalous activity above Tarrasa through the night. At 0420 local time on 30 November a very long moving target suddenly appeared on the radar and the controllers switched on MTI mode (moving target indication, exploiting the Doppler effect). Some nine kilometers (five miles) long but of 'imperceptible' breadth, the target was oriented east-west, but moved south, at right angles to its length, at about 50 knots (about 90 kilometres per hour). About 50 seconds after its appearance, the giant target ejected from its east end a smaller target, equivalent to that of a fighter aircraft, about 20 metres in size. The small target travelled south at about 900 kilometres per hour for some 15 seconds and then vanished from the screen. The very long target soon vanished too, about 90 seconds after it first appeared.

Concerned about the possible danger that these unknown objects posed to air traffic leaving Barcelona, Air Traffic Control rerouted a postal service aircraft bound for Madrid at 0431 to a path taking it over the sea to the southeast of Barcelona rather than its usual route to the north over Tarrasa. When following this alternative route, the pilots reported that they could see a white glow over Tarrasa that flashed every two or three seconds, then zigzagged and finally vanished.[2]

Spanish military radar reportedly also detected the objects and, unlike the Air Traffic Control radar, was able to assess their height. A subsequent military report was classified as the events clearly involved "the national defence and the security of the realm".[3]

TV journalists interviewed both the local police and Air Traffic Controllers at Barcelona Airport. One of the Air Traffic Controller interviews has been preserved and is accessible on YouTube (Search UFO Sabadell Tarrasa 1985). Such testimony therefore bypasses both UFOlogy and military secrecy, and provides radar evidence supporting the notion that large tube-like mother probes have entered the earth's atmosphere and released smaller devices.

There have been other reported radar detections of giant tube-like or cigar-shaped objects in the atmosphere that may have been ET mother probes. The 20 October 1990 issue of the Moscow newspaper *Robochaya Tribuna* carried a statement by an interceptor pilot who had been ordered to chase an anomalous object after a blip had suddenly appeared on radar screens at 1100 local time on 8 October 1990.[4] At 1122 he received the coordinates of the object and the order to investigate. The military radar had determined the object's height as 4.5 kilometres. Although the weather was clear and visibility excellent, the pilot stated that he saw nothing at first. Then, turning his head, he saw two giant "cigar-shaped objects" to the rear and to the right. One he estimated to be about two kilometers long, the other about 400 metres long.

Although the objects were too far away for the interceptor pilot to see details, he noted that the smaller giant appeared silver in reflected sunlight, and the larger one lustreless. Both were moving sideways, similar to reports of the Tarrasa radar-painted giant. Then, as the Russian pilot attempted to close in on the giants, they both suddenly disappeared from his vision. But the ground radar continued to paint both the twin giant targets and his own aircraft, the radar post telling the pilot that his interceptor was about 15 kilometres from the targets at this point.

It's interesting to compare this reported 1990 Russian event with the reported 1985 Spanish event. In both cases giant high-aspect-ratio targets low in the troposphere that could be interpreted as possible mother probes were detected by military radar. In the Spanish case, Air Traffic Control radar also detected the object. In the Russian case, an interceptor was vectored to the target's location within two minutes, and the pilot visually reported the two high-aspect-ratio objects to be moving *sideways,* as the Spanish Air Traffic Control MTI radar had found in the case of the 1985 Tarrasa object.

In both cases the anomalous objects had reportedly displayed an ability to switch on and off cloaking abilities. But whereas in Spain the cloaking had been at radar wavelengths and its temporary suspension had been apparently linked with the ejection of a smaller device, in Russia the cloaking had been at optical wavelengths and both anomalous objects apparently switched it on when the approaching interceptor reached a range of fifteen kilometers, according to the military ground radar. It was as if the objects interpreted the interceptor's approach as potentially aggressive and reacted appropriately.

Other anomalous objects in the lower atmosphere that may have been giant tube-like mother probes were the two large objects of very high aspect ratio reported by Captain Ray Bowyer, at around 1406 UTC on 23 April 2007, when he was piloting an Aurigny Airline Trislander airliner from Southampton, UK, to the island of Alderney in the English Channel. Viewing through binoculars, Bowyer noted that the very bright yellow anomalous objects ahead of him were like flattened disks, sharply defined and pointed at both ends. Another pilot, Captain Patrick Patterson, flying a Blue Islands Jetstream aircraft from the Isle of Man to Jersey, also reported seeing one of these objects.

According to Bowyer, both objects had dark bands towards the right side (Fig 40) and, in the nearest object, Bowyer noticed a pulsating boundary layer between the dark band and its yellow surroundings. He described the boundary as "some sort of interface with sparkling blues, greens and other hues, strobing up and down about once every second or so".[5]

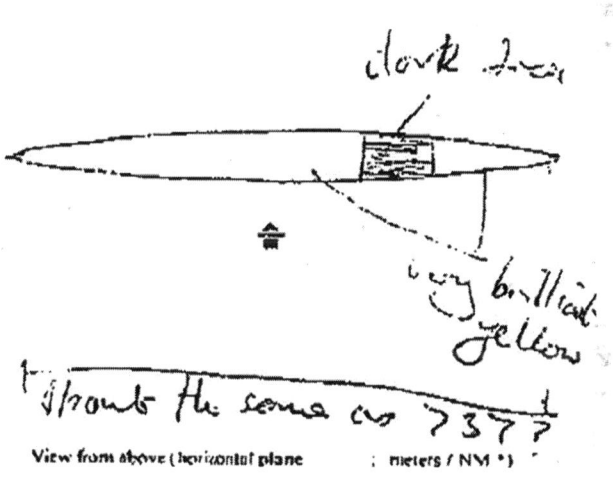

Fig 40. Sketch of one of two anomalous objects seen by Captain Ray Bowyer, pilot of an Aurigny Airline Trislander flight from Southampton, UK, to the channel island of Alderney at around 1406 UTC on 23 April 2007. Viewing through binoculars, Bowyer noted that both objects had dark bands towards the right side and in the nearest object, shown here, he noticed a pulsating boundary layer between the dark band and its yellow surroundings. He described the boundary as 'some sort of interface with sparkling blues, greens and other hues, strobing up and down about once every second or so.' [Kean 2010 p 76, Captain Ray Bowyer]

Bowyer's description of a dark band towards the right end of the objects recalls Ray Stanford's account of the 12 December 1977 giant tube above Memphis, so a confirmed radar detection of Bowyer's anomalous objects would be particularly interesting. Nearby French Air Defence radar reported no detection at the time, but Captain Bowyer believed that two slow-moving traces captured by Jersey Air Traffic Control (ATC) radar, which, like Barcelona's radar, did not record height, might have represented the large objects he saw. But in a joint paper with David Clarke and two other authors, Martin Shough, the British radar expert who contributed to the SOHP team's 2011 study of the 1968 B52 radarscope photographs (Chapter 5), suggested that "An ATC radar echo reported below the approximate visually-estimated position of one UAP may have been associated with an identifiable moving surface vessel".[6]

Because ATC radar does not record height, the authors of the joint paper were wrong to write that the radar echo was 'below' the visually estimated position of the northernmost anomalous object. But Captain Bowyer had more substantive criticism of the surface vessel theory. Having viewed the decluttered Jersey ATC radar trace of the events, which showed both of the aircraft and the two unidentified echoes that may have corresponded with the anomalous objects, Bowyer pointed out that both unidentified radar echoes began and ended at precisely the same time over the sea. Difficult to explain if the echoes were returned from surface vessels, but compatible with the notion that the echoes came from two anomalous hi-tech vehicles in the atmosphere coordinating their movements. Moreover, according to Bowyer, the northernmost echo disappeared at or above the Casquets Lighthouse, the site of many notorious wrecks.[7] Yet no shipwreck was reported there on 23 April 2007.

So the inherent limitations of ATC radar prevented an unambiguous conclusion that the giant high-aspect-ratio objects reported by pilots in the English Channel on 23 April 2007 were detected on radar. Nevertheless, this multiple pilot sighting of a pair of giant objects in the lower atmosphere adds weight to the similar 1977 Memphis, 1980 Tizayuca, 1985 Tarrasa and 1990 Russia candidate mother probe sightings.

If military secrecy has bedevilled attempts to discuss detections of possible mother probe operations within the Earth's atmosphere, such secrecy will also have applied to any detections by the US or other militaries of mother probes entering or leaving the atmosphere from space. In this connection, there's been internet discussion of alleged leaked information from a US 'top secret' document reporting the detection in 1981 of a group of objects entering the near-earth environment on a trajectory suggesting an origin outside the solar system. Presumably that means that space radar showed the objects making a large angle with the ecliptic plane, a strategy Scot Stride suggested mother probes might adopt.[8]

The 1981 objects reportedly entered low earth orbit. The report allegedly stated that three of the objects broke off from the group in orbit and headed for the Moscow region of the Soviet Union, where they remained for about an hour. These three objects were reportedly tracked by an AWACS system to the limit of the latter's capabilities.[9]

If that was counterintelligence it was far more sophisticated than the silly stories about space aliens that US counterintelligence agents have promoted over the years. But intelligent US counterintelligence is possible. The reference of the 1981 report to the Moscow region might point to cleverly contrived counterintelligence designed to be picked up by Soviet agents and confuse Soviet decision makers. On the other hand the leaked report might be true.

In the Soviet Union, as in the US, military secrecy would likely have blocked any reports of detection by radar of candidate mother probes operating in near-earth space. However, in the early 1990s, after the end of the old Soviet state but before Russia had set up as a military rival to the US, there was a period during which senior Russian experts felt free to talk to journalists about such matters. One of the most authoritative of these figures was academician Rimili Fedorovich Avramenko.

During this period Avramenko, a leading expert on the radar-tracking of ICBMs reentering the earth's atmosphere from space and the design of plasma beam weapons systems intended to throw them off their flight trajectories, gave a number of interviews.[10] He told US journalist George Knapp that in 1959, when only a few artificial satellites were orbiting earth, new Soviet radar systems detected, in addition to meteor trails, "tens" of objects "whose technical characteristics we can't match, even now" entering and leaving the Earth's atmosphere. He added that the early warning systems of both the US and Russia no longer detected these targets because the computer systems were programmed to weed out anomalous objects, focusing only on objects of known origin, such as ICBMs.[11] This echoed a similar point that Robert Baker had made in his address to the US Congress Committee on Science and Astronautics in 1968.[12]

To check Knapp's account of Avramenko's work, I used *Google Translate* to see if the academician had spoken in a similar vein to Russian journalists. He had. In one 1991 talk,[13] Avramenko stated that in the 1959-60 time frame, as well as detecting the new satellites, such as the US Echo 1, an inflatable 30 metre sphere launched on 12 August 1960, orbiting at about 1500 kilometres height, and the plasma trails of meteors entering the atmosphere, the new Soviet space radars detected tens of anomalous objects.

One of these, Avramenko stated, was tracked for about a minute at a height of 300 kilometres, had a size of 300 metres and a velocity of 20 kilometres per second, which was much higher than expected from an object in a near-circular earth orbit at that height. Avramenko pointed out that the only natural object that could reach such a speed at 300 kilometres height would be an earth-grazing asteroid in elliptical orbit around the sun.

But, even if that prosaic explanation was workable, it could only account for one exceptional instance, not tens of objects with anomalous characteristics. Avramenko and his colleagues therefore prepared a report on the anomalous radar detections of the 1959-60 period. Needless to say, it was never openly published.

The detection of putative ET mother probes entering or leaving the Earth's atmosphere since 1960 is clearly a complex subject that military secrecy has made largely off-limits to probe theorists. In any case a lack of reported detections in this period means little. Since they 'felt' the first human space radars around 1959, incoming mother probes may have adopted stealth technologies to prevent US and Soviet military space radars or optical trackers from detecting them, even if they were attempting to do so. For example the MTI radar detection of the Tarrasa giant in 1985 may have been a lucky chance. Perhaps it disappeared from Barcelona Traffic Control MTI radar because it switched on a suitable stealth mode. Perhaps it continued to operate its radar screening as it left the Earth's atmosphere.

The combination of anomalous accelerations and the use of radar and optical cloaking technologies would mean that in the post-1960 period incoming or outgoing mother probes may have easily evaded human detection.

So back to 1959-60. Or rather 1958-60 because on 8 September 1958 one of the most well-qualified group of people ever to report anomalous activity made a key report to the US Air Force. Representing more than 25 Air Force officers, airmen, missile engineers and the tower operator at Strategic Air Command headquarters, Offutt Air Force Base, Omaha, Nebraska, Major Paul Duich, reported a display that could be interpreted as the release of probes by a giant tube-like mother probe (Fig 44).[14]

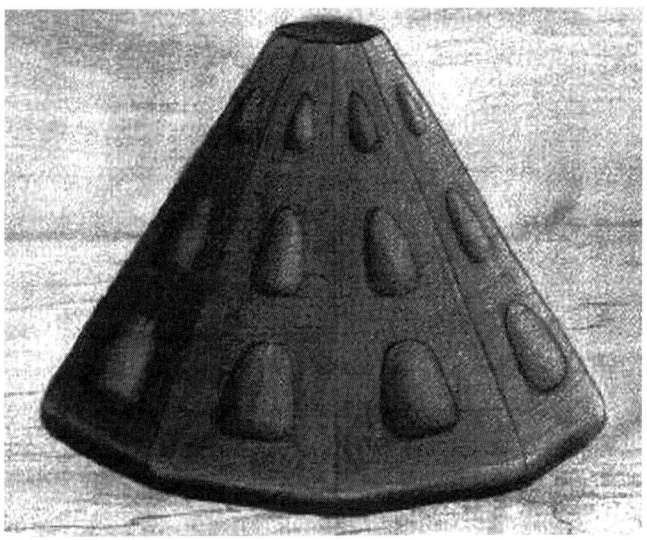

Fig 41. Drawing by artist Sergio Porres of the Engineering College at the Catholic University of Pelotas, Brazil. It depicts a giant conical object about 100 metres in diameter that local private pilot Haroldo Westendorff and three air traffic controllers in the tower at Pelotas airport claim they saw at about 1030 local time on 5 November 1996. [http://www.rense.com/istoe3.jpg, Sergio Porres]

131

In 1959, recall, the year during which according to Rimili Avramenko Soviet space radars detected 'tens' of anomalous objects entering and leaving Earth's atmosphere, there were some classic reports of anomalous activity at ground level. Recall the reported activity at Boianai, New Guinea, on 26 and 27 June 1959 (Chapter 2) and at Blenheim, New Zealand, on 13 July 1959 (Chapter 3).

And on 13 August 1960 the important Red Bluff, California incident took place (Chapter 2). All we need to complete the picture is a film of a candidate mother probe in this 1959-60 period.

We have two – separate films of the same candidate tube-like mother probe on 28 July 1959. The two cameramen were a young Ray Stanford and his friend, Don Jammer. Seven other witnesses also saw the anomalous objects.

The story started on the afternoon of 28 July 1959 when a friend of Stanford, then living in Corpus Christi, Texas, phoned him to say she had seen a tiny bright dot in the sky. Already a well-equipped UFO spotter, Stanford started filming the object using his 16 mm movie camera with a 75 mm high-quality telephoto lens. Other UFO spotters turned up, including Don Jammer, wielding an 8-mm movie camera.

As they watched and filmed, the object moved slowly westwards. Suddenly Stanford realised that the tiny dot was Venus. When it's bright enough, Venus is sometimes visible in the daytime sky and has generated countless UFO reports.

So this UFO quickly became an IFO (Identified Flying Object). But then the observant Stanford noticed something else. Some distance away from Venus was a white tube-like object that Stanford described as looking like a piece of thin white translucent bone china with sharp parallel edges and a bright blue-white light inside it. While Stanford tried to swing his tripod-mounted movie camera around to film the tube-like object, a whitish cloud began to envelope it.

Nevertheless, both Stanford and Don Jammer succeeded in filming the tube-like object. From its angular size, Stanford estimated a length of about 400 feet at a height of 20 miles.

Although one other witness saw little bright objects flying away from the tube, these smaller objects weren't clearly confirmed on Stanford's 16 mm movie film until many years later when Stanford's group acquired equipment to obtain prints from movie film. Then, Stanford claims, he could see that the smaller objects were triangular in shape and concluded that this was a possible mother probe event.

Project Blue Book initially listed this 28 July 1959 Corpus Christi sighting as an unknown[15] and James McDonald copied information for his own files. Stanford's 28 July 1959 Corpus Christi 16 mm movie frames were later studied by various groups, including Allen Hynek and one of his assistants. Parts of Don Jammer's 8 mm movie were widely publicised, shown on one of Arthur C Clarke's popular UK ITV series and today there is a digitalised version on YouTube of what appears to be a part of Jammer's film, incorrectly attributed to Stanford and complete with the usual garbled information that is the hallmark of a YouTube UFO clip (YouTube UFO – Corpus Christie (sic), Texas, July 25 (sic), 1959).

But this clip is worth watching. Although a telescope would have shown Venus with a crescent phase on this date (thank you, Stephen Wolfram), the video shows it as a bright fuzzy dot. The camera swings through a partly clouded sky towards a long white object that looks like a section of a contrail. But it's not a contrail and its very high aspect ratio places it with the other mother probe candidates discussed in this chapter.

That very high aspect ratio is worth thinking about. People who have read Stephen Baxter's brilliant novel *Proxima* will recall that to reach the fictional exoplanet Proxima c (alternative name Per Ardua, not to be confused with the real planet Proxima b),[16] Angelia, an advanced Artificial Intelligence, reconfigured herself as a long thin needle, only a few microns thick, pointing towards the exoplanet. By assuming a needle shape, Angelia minimised the hazards of high-velocity collision with the gas, dust grains, radiation and other material that constitute the interstellar medium.

The 1959 Corpus Christi object and the other giant tube-like objects discussed in this chapter aren't quite needles, but they all have very high aspect ratios, 15:1 or higher. Like Baxter's Angelia, they appear superbly adapted for travel through the interstellar medium.

What other adaptations for or legacies of interstellar travel might we look for in mother probe candidates? Look at Fig 41. This is a drawing by technical artist Sergio Porres of the Engineering College at the Catholic University of Pelotas, Brazil. It depicts a giant object that three air traffic controllers in the tower at Pelotas airport claim they saw about eight kilometres southeast of the airport at about 1030 local time on 5 November 1996. Local businessman Haroldo Westendorff, a private pilot who investigated the object in response to a request from the tower, made the detailed observations that Porres used in this drawing, subsequently published by the respected Brazilian general news magazine ISTOÉ.[17]

At first glance this massive cone, about 100 metres in diameter and brown in colour, could hardly differ more from the giant tubes we've just discussed. But imagine what the nose cone of a tube several kilometers long that's been travelling through the interstellar medium might look like. Its 100-metre diameter would fit a 15:1 aspect ratio object 1500 metres long and its brown colour (like some asteroids) might well result from the prolonged high-velocity travel of an iron-rich or organic-coated object through the interstellar medium.

Before discussing how its prominent external bulges, too, might represent adaptations to travel through the interstellar medium or planetary atmospheres, let's continue the narrative of the 5 November 1996 events.

Piloting a single engine Piper Apache, Westendorff had taken off from the small radar-lacking Pelotas airport for a joyride at about 1018 local time. On his return, flying at about 5000 feet over a coastal body of water southeast of Pelotas, he saw an unusual object ahead of him. At about 1030 he radioed the Pelotas control tower to ask if the people there could see it too.

They responded that they could and asked Westendorff to investigate. That he did. He later reported that the giant faceted cone was about 100 metres in diameter at its base, rotating slowly and moving southeast towards the ocean at about sixty knots.

Heedless of the danger, Westendorff made a close inspection, flying round the slowly moving brown giant three times. After his third lap, the rounded apex of the cone seemed to disappear and he saw a disc, about ten metres in diameter, its long axis vertical, rise from a now open hole at the top of the cone. When it had cleared the top of the giant cone, the disc tipped over to an angle of about 45 degrees and accelerated away, quickly reaching a velocity that pilot Westendorff estimated as Mach 10 (about 12,000 kilometres per hour at an altitude of 5000 feet).

Intending to view the giant cone from above, Westendorff began a steep climb. While doing this, he noticed that the cone was rotating faster. Next, he saw the still-open top of the cone emit multiple beams of red light vertically upwards (Fig 42).[18] Finally, the giant cone itself shot upwards in the wake of the beams, and disappeared into a layer of nimbostratus cloud.

The intrepid pilot was scared. Only a few hundred metres away from the giant cone when it accelerated upwards, the pilot anticipated that the ensuing turbulence would destabilise his small Piper Apache and he began emergency procedures. But Westendorff felt no turbulence and lived to tell his tale.

When he landed at Pelotas airport, Westendorff was greeted by a crowd of media folk, alerted by other private pilots who had overheard his radio exchanges with the control tower. However, instead of blurting out his story, the pilot told the journalists that he'd say nothing until he'd conferred with the officials in the tower. The chief traffic controller in the tower, Airton Mendes da Silva, thereupon phoned his boss, an Air Force colonel in Porto Alegre, who told da Silva to decide for himself whether or not the tower controllers should confirm Westendorff's story with statements of what they themselves had seen.

Da Silva reported to the media that looking towards runway 15/33 in the eastern sector he had seen a grey triangle with rounded edges on the horizon. One of his assistants, Gilberto Martins dos Santos, added that to the naked eye the object had appeared the size of a power pole.

But what really shook the three observing officials in the tower was the object's later rapid vertical ascent and disappearance into the cloud layer. Da Silva commented that such a performance was beyond the capability of known aircraft. Jorge Renato Dutra, the third official in the Pelotas tower, commented that he'd "never seen a flying monster of that size."

Fig 42. Intending to view the giant cone (Fig 41) from above, Westendorff, piloting a single-engine Piper Apache, began a steep climb. While doing this, he noticed that the cone was rotating faster. Next he saw the still-open top of the cone emit multiple beams of red light vertically upwards as shown here. Finally according to Westendorff, the giant cone itself shot upwards in the wake of the beams, and disappeared into a layer of nimbostratus cloud.
[http://www.rense.com/istoe4.jpg, Sergio Porres]

Fig 43. External and submerged air inlets on a jet engine cowling. Compare the external air inlet with the conspicuous external bulges Westendorff reported having seen on the giant Pelotas cone (Fig 41). [Wikipedia: NACA duct]

With professional testimony like this supporting Westendorff's account, the Pelotas incident quickly became a national media sensation in Brazil. As a result the Brazilian Air Force decided to mount a modest investigation.

Because the Westendorff case was thus taken up by the Brazilian national media, including by the respected news magazine ISTOÉ, I was able to avoid UFOlogy sources and confirm using Google Translate that the events, as reported in this chapter, match those reported in the Brazilian media at the time.[19]

So the Pelotas event of 5 November 1996 passes a preliminary reality test. The only prosaic explanation would be a prearranged hoax, including prearranged cooperation with the traffic controllers' boss, the Air Force colonel in Porto Alegre. It's beyond reason that all these professional and military people would jeopardise their careers in this way. And all that the standard sceptical scientist wheeled onto Brazilian

TV could do was repeat the irrational mantra that so irritated Allen Hynek – 'It couldn't have happened therefore it didn't happen'. Not much awareness of the Fermi Paradox there.

And, indeed, if there is no Fermi Paradox and the McDonald Conjecture is correct, deliveries by mother probes of surveillance devices to the Earth's atmosphere, as may have happened above Memphis, Tennessee in 1977, Tizayuca, Mexico in 1980, Tarrasa, Spain in 1985 and now at Pelotas, Brazil in 1996, are precisely what scientists should expect.

So how could probe theory apply to this case? The Pelotas object could, just conceivably, have been a large military balloon or blimp until, according to Westendorff, it did three things and failed to do one thing.

First, it ejected a ten-metre disc that, after clearing the cone's top and tipping over to an angle of about 45 degrees, shot away with an anomalously high acceleration. Second, the cone emitted multiple red beams vertically upward and, third, in the event also witnessed by the Air Traffic Controllers in the Pelotas tower, the object itself shot upwards in the wake of the beams, again with an anomalously high acceleration. Fourth, as it shot upward, the giant cone failed to create sufficient turbulence at Westendorff's location, a few hundred metres away, to threaten the stability of his small Piper Apache.

Recall that in mid-1978 Brazilian newsman Biamir Siqueira speculated that the 'beams of light' that José Ribamar and himself had seen crossing the sky from north to south at Baía do Sol before the 'motherships' appeared were preparing the way for the large vehicles to travel silently through the atmosphere (Chapter 7). Perhaps the Pelotas object's red beams served a similar purpose, helping to reduce subsequent turbulence and energy loss when the giant cone ascended. That could be a key feature for a mother probe – or perhaps in this case the detachable nose cone of a giant tubelike mother probe – designed to operate in planetary atmospheres.

But what then of the Pelotas cone's most conspicuous features, the triangular shaped external bulges that, after detailed discussions with Westendorff, Porres depicted in his drawing (Fig 41)? A quick Internet search showed intriguing similarities between these bulges and supersonic external air intakes for jet engines (Fig 43).

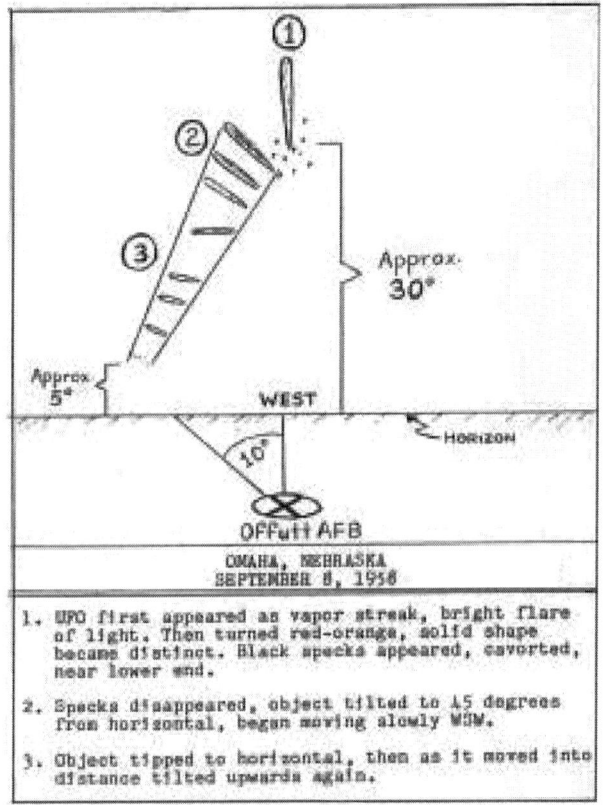

Fig 44. From about 1840 to 1900 local time on 8 September 1958 a group of more than 25 Air Force officers, airmen and missile engineers and the tower operator at Strategic Air Command headquarters, Offutt Air Force Base, Omaha, Nebraska witnessed and attempted to photograph anomalous activity. One of the witnesses, Major Paul Duich, prepared this self-explanatory sketch and summary of what he saw. Major Duich collected names of fellow witnesses and reported the sighting to ATIC (Air Technical Intelligence Center). But despite promising to contact him for interview within 48 hours, ATIC never did so.

Five years later, after retirement, Major Duich sent this sketch and summary to NICAP (National Investigation Committee on Aerial Phenomena). One interpretation would be that a giant pencil-like mother probe, spanning about 10 degrees of arc, positioned itself vertically in the atmosphere west of Omaha and then released a set of smaller vehicles from its lower end. [Hall 1997, p 25-27]

So did downward jet-like expulsion of air taken in through these vents contribute to the cone's astonishing upward acceleration in the atmosphere? And did the bulges continue to function in a similar jet-like way in the interstellar medium, perhaps in the manner of the Bussard ramjets beloved by science fiction fans?

Those are questions that only a team of scientists and aerospace engineers can answer.

Endnotes

1 Crivellen 1986.

2 Crivellen 1986, p.4.

3 Crivellen 1986, p.5.

4 FBI 1991.

5 Kean 2010, p.76.

6 Baure *et al.* 2008, p.298.

7 Kean 2010, p.79.

8 Stride 2001.

9 See posts of 26 January 2014 on UFO Casebook: Deep Space Tracking & UFOS http://ufocasebook.conforums.com/index.cgi?board=general&action=display&num=1390750047 Downloaded 18 February 2015.

10 Gallagher 1993.

11 Gross 1999, p.19.

12 Baker 1968.

13 Avramenko 1991, 2012.

14 Hall 1997, p.25–27.

15 Sparks 2016, Case No.1365.

16 Anglada-Escudé *et al.* 2016.

17 Image downloaded from http://www.rense.com/istoe3a.jpg on 20 April 2011.

18 Image downloaded from http://www.rense.com/istoe4.jpg on 20 April 2011.

19 Downloaded on 26 March 2011 from: http://translate.google.co.uk/translate?hl=en&sl=pt&u=http://srv-net.diariopopular.com.br/05_10_02/cv041001.BWestendorff%26start%3D10%26hl%3Den%26sa%3DN%26prmd%3Divns.

10

Kirtland

In the last chapter we looked at claims by Russian academician Rimili Avramenko that in 1959 Soviet space radars detected 'tens' of anomalous objects entering and leaving the Earth's atmosphere. And we saw that US Air Force testimony and filmed evidence exists for anomalous events in the atmosphere in 1958 and 1959 that are consistent with the 'ET mother probe' interpretation of that Soviet radar data. Given that World War II, followed by human development of atomic and thermonuclear weapons, may have prompted putative postbiological ET minds to intensify their surveillance operations here in the 1940s and 1950s, what additional events might have triggered a surge of surveillance activity in 1959?

No prizes for spotting one possibility.

In 1957 humans became a space-faring species. On 4 October the Soviets put the first artificial satellite, the radio-transmitting Sputnik 1, into low earth orbit and on 3 November they launched the second, Sputnik 2, containing the shortly-to-die space bitch Laika. Space-faring creatures equipped with nuclear weapons would present a challenge that no ET minds could ignore and we can speculate that the apparent ET surveillance spike of 1958-9 actually started soon after the 4 October and 3 November Sputnik launches of 1957.

There's evidence to support this idea. On Sunday 6 October 1957, two days after the Sputnik 1 launch, in Tucson, Arizona, at about 1615 local time, together with other observers, amateur astronomer Earl Sydow, an engineer by profession, observed anomalous activity through his small (70 mm objective) telescope.[1] He later sent his telescope

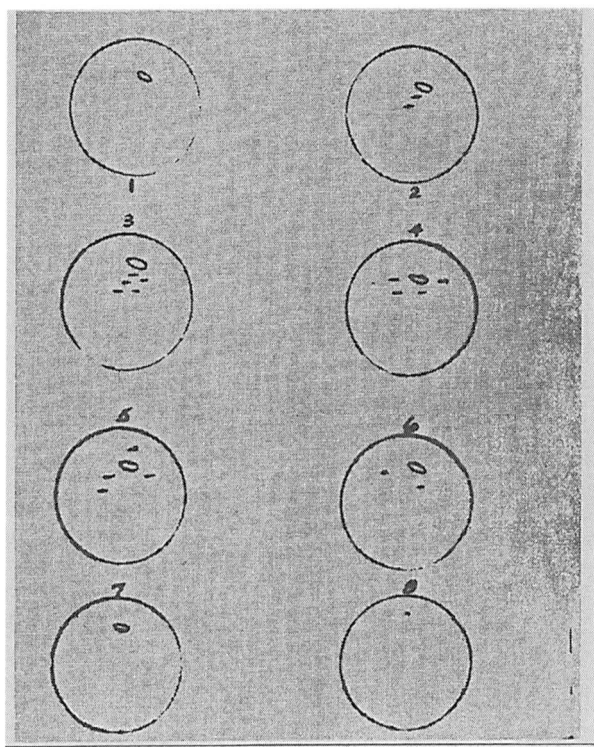

Fig 45. At about 1615 local time in Tucson Arizona, on 6 October 1957, two days after the Sputnik 1 launch, amateur astronomer Earl Sydow observed this anomalous activity through his small (70 mm objective) telescope. He later sent this drawing and report to James McDonald at the Institute of Atmospheric Physics in Tucson.

In a clear blue sky, Sydow first saw a single elongated object, that he estimated had the magnitude of about -3 (comparable to Venus) spanning about 3 minutes of arc. He estimated the object's elevation at 60 degrees and its azimuth as 135 degrees. Then the large object seemed to emit smaller objects, 6-10 in number, 15 to 30 seconds of arc in diameter, which sometimes appeared as short traces of light and sometimes appeared semi-wedge shaped.

Over a period of about 15 minutes the objects moved to the northwest, the smaller ones leaving the field of view until only the large one remained. It got smaller and smaller, finally disappearing as if into the distance at an elevation of about 85 degrees. [Gross 2003b 1957 Oct-Nov- 2- SN p 5] drawings (Fig 45) and report to James McDonald at the Institute of Atmospheric Physics in Tucson. Mac was already known locally as that rarest of creatures, a scientist interested in UFO reports.

In a clear blue sky, Sydow first saw a single elongated object, that he estimated had the magnitude of about -3 (comparable to Venus) spanning about 3 minutes of arc. He estimated the object's elevation at 60 degrees and its azimuth as 135 degrees. Then the large object seemed to emit smaller objects, 6-10 in number, 15 to 30 seconds of arc in diameter, that sometimes appeared as short traces of light and sometimes appeared semi-wedge shaped (Fig 45).

Over a period of about 15 minutes the objects moved to the northwest, the smaller ones leaving the field of view until only the large one remained. It got smaller and smaller, finally disappearing as if into the distance at an elevation of about 85 degrees – heading almost vertically upwards into space.

A nice set of observations from an amateur astronomer consistent with Scot Stride's notion of mother probes delivering surveillance devices to our planet and the timing invites interpretation as an event possibly linked with the Sputnik 1 launch of 4 October. Although no observations have surfaced reporting possible mother probe activity after the launch of Sputnik 2 on 3 November, what does correlate with that event is a huge surge of reports of anomalous activity in the US Southwest. Often called 'whatniks' by the local press in honour of Sputnik 2, the typically egg-shaped objects were associated with vehicle stoppages and surrounded by what can now be interpreted as plasma coronas. The latter showed classic air plasma colours, for example orange and blue-green, that appeared to change in correlation with the objects' movements.[2]

Among the dozens of professional witnesses who reported sightings of egg-shaped anomalous objects in the US Southwest during the period 3-5 November 1957, were two tower operators at Kirtland Air Force Base, R.M Kaser and E.G. Brink. They had made reports to Blue Book's Captain Patrick Shere on 6 November 1957.[3] James McDonald interviewed the pair in 1969 when checking important Condon cases and found that their statements confirmed their earlier testimony to Captain Shere.[4]

At about 2245 hours on 4 November 1957 the tower operators had observed with binoculars an elongated egg-shaped device with a white light on its base but no wings descend to the runway area at Kirtland, hover near the ground for some tens of seconds, and then climb into the overcast sky at a speed the operators considered beyond the capacity of the latest jet aircraft. The Blue Book files confirmed that radar then tracked the object to the south, where it circled for some minutes before returning to follow an Air Force plane outbound from Kirtland.

Good evidence for an unknown device engaged in surveillance, one might conclude, especially in view of the many reports in November 1957 of similar egg-shaped devices seen in New Mexico and Texas.[5] But Edward Condon had other ideas. Brushing aside the lack of wings, the anomalous lighting and climb rate, the radar evidence for surveillance, and failing to interview the tower operators, the Condon Report concluded that the operators probably saw an aircraft.

No comment. Let's quickly move on to December 1979. By this time, the US Air Force had excavated tunnels in the small hills within the Kirtland AFB area, detached from the southerly trending Manzano mountain range that lies east of Albuquerque. The tunnels housed facilities for the underground storage of thermonuclear weapons.

This was the Manzano Weapons Storage Area. To acquire data related to the stored weapons, surveillance discs would need to hover close to the bunker entrances and direct their beams laterally into the bunkers.

And that is what may have happened. About two miles to the northwest of the storage bunkers, in the southern outskirts of Albuquerque, was the house of a physicist called Paul Bennewitz. Bennewitz was then President of Thunder Scientific, a hi-tech company specialising in the design and manufacture of humidity-measuring instruments, which it supplied to the Air Force.

Bennewitz had been interested in local UFO reports for years and by December 1979 he had turned the observation deck of his Albuquerque house into an observatory for studying anomalous activity. His equipment included binoculars, a Hasselblad still camera, an 8 mm movie camera that operated at 24 frames per second, an 8 mm movie film editor and a binocular microscope that allowed him to study the individual movie frames taken on ASA 25 Kodachrome colour film. He was therefore equipped to study images capturing the too-fast-for-the-eye plasma activity surrounding anomalous objects of the kind that PSI physicist Daniel Harris was also studying at this time.

According to Bennewitz's notes, as reported by his friend Chris Lambright,[6] shortly before midnight on one moonless night, probably between 16 and 20 December 1979, while viewing from his observation deck, Bennewitz noticed strange pulses of light appearing towards the base of the Manzano Weapons Storage Area. A few minutes later he observed four simultaneous pulses of light there, each lasting ten to twenty seconds before fading away. Bennewitz called his wife and together they watched as the four objects, one larger than the other three, repeated the sequence of synchronised brightening and fading. This sequence repeated itself many times during the night.

Then after several hours Bennewitz saw a quick flash and seconds later the objects shot up vertically to a height he later estimated as 300 to 400 feet. After hovering for a moment, the objects then shot off near-horizontally to the south, disappearing from view behind the small range of hills.

Bennewitz observed this same broad pattern of activity on several later nights in December 1979. He spent many hours filming the activity with his 8 mm movie camera equipped with a telephoto lens and capturing still images with his Hasselblad. He later projected the individual Kodachrome movie frames on the screen of his film editor, made prints of them and studied them at leisure.

What might these objects have been doing? Bennewitz's observations are consistent with the possibility that the objects, either hovering or landed, positioned themselves close to the entrances of the excavated nuclear weapons storage bunkers and probed their contents with penetrating 'beams'. Given the apparently slow nature of ET data acquisition, we can understand why the whole mission may have taken many hours spread over several nights.

And the objects did, apparently, deploy beams of some kind. Bennewitz filmed the objects emitting what he called "blue standing beams" or "force field spikes"[7] and speculated on their nature. For example, he speculated that increasing magnetic field strength could cause these beams to slowly extend.[8] Any beams directed into the storage bunkers would not of course have been visible from Bennewitz's position.

But what Bennewitz's colour prints did capture were snapshots of the successive stages in the appearance of the luminous plasmas surrounding the objects as the latter descended, hovered, ascended and then shot away laterally. Bennewitz gave some of the colour prints from his film image editor to Chris Lambright, who processed them digitally, enhancing some of the frames, and published the images in his eBook, *X Descending*.[9]

I've reproduced some of these images in Colour Plates 1-6. Bennewitz's notes, some of which Chris Lambright reproduced in his eBook, make clear that the same sequence of events was repeated on several nights and I've arranged the pictures in that sequence. I've also made minor changes to show more clearly what the original images looked like on the screen of Bennewitz's movie editor.

Look first at Colour Plates 1 and 2. This frame (images in Colour Plate 1 enlarged and juxtaposed in Colour Plate 2) captures two objects, hovering close to the ground or actually landed, just before ascent after completing a nightly mission. Bennewitz estimated the larger object to be around 36 feet in diameter and the smaller one around 18 feet.

The blue-green colour of the plasma patches around the larger object evidently represents spectral lines around 500 nanometres wavelength, perhaps emitted by ionised nitrogen molecules. The discrete nature of the blue-green ionisation patches suggests multiple local sources of ionising radiation, perhaps 'emitters' located on the rim of the hidden disc. Within the blue-green patches are arcs that may represent the trajectories of clumps of ions that have moved under the influence of strong magnetic and electric fields during the exposure time. Using the rule of thumb that exposure time (shutter speed) is half the frame rate, that would be roughly 1/50 second.

Above the blue-green patches are faint orange patches that may represent emission lines around 600 nanometres, emitted by other ionised species of nitrogen or other ionised air molecules. The sources of ionising radiation that gave rise to these orange emission lines aren't obvious.

Now look at the smaller object on the right. Instead of being blue-green the lower plasma patches appear white and the patches of orange emission are more intense. One interpretation could be that the smaller object's output of ionising radiation was greater than that of its larger companion – or more effective because of its smaller size – and the resulting plasma emissions around 500 and 600 nanometres have therefore increased. In the case of the blue-green lines around 500 nanometres the emission intensity may have saturated the Kodachrome emulsion's color response ability, leading to the misleading white colour.

This may also be the explanation for the white patches in Bennewitz's movie frame of the large object reproduced in Colour Plate 3. This remarkable frame apparently records a moment when the large disc's output of ionising radiation is greater than in Colour Plate 2, so the blue-green patches around the emitters appear white. Multiple curved orange arcs seen here may represent the trajectories of clumps of charged particles, emitting spectral lines around 600 nanometres, moving in the presence of strong magnetic and electric fields during the 1/50 second exposure time.

What happened next? Colour Plate 4, again with an exposure of 1/50 second, shows the large object and two of its smaller companions 'flaring' in the instant before all three simultaneously accelerated and shot upwards. Evidently, the discs' output of ionising radiation had suddenly increased and their plasma coronas now appeared as much expanded ellipses of intense white light. An enlargement of the largest disc (Colour Plate 5) resembles photographs of the solar corona and suggests streams of plasma moving radially outwards.

Bennewitz observed that, after shooting upwards to an estimated height of around 300 to 400 feet, the discs decelerated and hovered for an instant before accelerating away laterally. In Colour Plate 6, Bennewitz's movie frame appears to have captured a moment when one of the smaller discs, surrounded by its plasma corona, is hovering at this height. A blue-coloured spike rises from the point on the ground from which the object has just ascended. This spike may represent emission lines from ionised nitrogen and could be interpreted as a corona discharge from the ground.

Such a discharge would be consistent with MHD-type propulsion. The powerful electric and magnetic fields associated with the disc's propulsion system may have left a huge but unstable electric charge temporarily stored in the ground.

Bennewitz's notes show that he carefully observed salient features of the discs' behaviour as captured in the prints of the movie frames he made. Thus, he noted that the simultaneous 'flaring' captured in Colour Plate 4 happened both when the objects were 'landing' and during 'power up' for ascent. In other words the flaring accompanied their acceleration and deceleration.

Moreover Bennewitz observed the synchronised behaviour of the objects, coordinated to within the 1/50 second exposure time of the frames. He understood that the objects used electromagnetic fields in some way and suggested that an understanding of this might lead to an understanding of the 'synchronizing signal' that enabled the discs to precisely coordinate their flaring and acceleration.

Indeed, the objects' electromagnetic effects appeared so intense that he believed he could likely detect them on his roof top laboratory two miles away. Bennewitz therefore started to construct sensitive detection equipment that would allow him to investigate these electromagnetic aspects.

He also observed that the intense bursts of energy from the objects during 'flaring' ought to generate sound waves, similar to the atmospheric shock waves caused by lightning. He therefore expected flaring to be followed by a rumble of thunder-like noise after the ten seconds or so needed for sound waves to travel the two miles to his rooftop. Instead, there was silence.

So Paul Bennewitz observed several remarkable effects linked with the anomalous objects apparently operating within the Kirtland Air Force base in December 1979 and tried to interpret them scientifically. But although trained as a physicist and a very hands-on technical man,

Bennewitz lacked the expertise of the world-class plasma physicists and aerospace engineers who at that very time were helping Project Starlight International to interpret the prints made from Ray Stanford's movie frames of the 12 December 1977 Memphis event.

And although not himself a UFOlogist, Bennewitz stubbornly clung to the UFO buffs' absurd notion of humanoid alien pilots. This was despite his own demonstration that the objects coordinated their behaviour to within 1/50 second, and displayed alien-killing accelerations and outputs of radiation.

Moreover, working in 1979 and 1980, Bennewitz naturally lacked access to the later interpretative work we've looked at in this book. Particularly relevant is the groundbreaking analysis that Auguste Meessen presented at the Electromagnetics Academy's 2012 Moscow conference, involving the concept of anomalous objects using very brief synchronised ionisation pulses and magnetic pulses to accelerate in the Earth's atmosphere.[10,11,12] Therefore, the time is ripe for expert teams outside UFOlogy to make fresh interpretations of Bennewitz's 1979 data using the material that Chris Lambright has published in his eBook and which I have copied here in Colour Plates 1-6.

What the rest of us can immediately take from these extraordinary images is an appreciation of the significance of a meeting held at Kirtland Air Force Base on 10 November 1980. The images published by Chris Lambright and reproduced here give only a hint of the quantity and quality of the data that Bennewitz, motivated by a patriotic concern for national security, presented at that meeting.[13]

In his quest to alert the Air Force authorities to the potential security threat at Kirtland revealed by his data, Bennewitz had a formidable ally – New Mexico senator Dr Harrison Schmitt. A former NASA astrogeologist who in 1972 had collected rock samples from the moon, Schmitt took Bennewitz's data very seriously and was pressing for a full Air Force scientific investigation into the events that Bennewitz's data showed had taken place.

In preparation for the 10 November meeting, on 26 October 1980 Jerry Miller, the Chief Scientific Advisor for the Air Force Test and Evaluation Center at Kirtland, who had been a former Blue Book officer and Richard Doty, a counterintelligence officer, visited Bennewitz at his home and studied his film, photographs and other data. The official Air Force report on this visit[14] emphasised that Miller was "one of the most knowledgeable and impartial investigators of Aerial Objects in the southwest." It then stated, "After analyzing the data collected by Dr BENNEWITZ (sic), Mr MILLER related the evidence clearly showed that some type of unidentified aerial objects were caught on film; however no conclusions could be made whether these objects pose a threat to Manzano/Coyote Canyon areas."

The next step was that crucial official meeting of Air Force authorities with Paul Bennewitz in a conference room at Kirtland on 10 November 1980. A Freedom of Information Act document, with the same file number as quoted in Note 14 above, revealed that Brigadier General William Brooksher and Dr William Lehmann, the civilian Director of the Air Force Weapons Research Laboratory, together with other significant Air Force personnel, were present. The document[15] states that Bennewitz "presented film and photographs of alleged unidentified Aerial Objects photographed over KAFB, NM during the last 15 months." Dr Lehmann "advised Dr. BENNEWITZ (sic) to request a USAF grant for research" and assured him "he would assist him in filling out the proper documents."

So we have official US documents stating that Jerry Miller, former Blue Book officer, believed that Bennewitz's film and other imagery depicted real unknown objects manoeuvring within Kirtland Air Force Base and that William Lehmann, the US Air Force Weapons Research Laboratory chief, stated that Bennewitz's material merited further scientific study. Senator Harrison Schmitt, a man of unique experience as scientist, lunar astronaut and politician, strongly supported these assessments.

Wow. There could hardly be a more conclusive endorsement of James McDonald's arguments than that. Decades of effort by the US military to manage 'the UFO problem' had collapsed. An independent scientific investigation would no doubt reveal the full scale of anomalous activity in US airspace and the inability of the military to do anything about it. What were the shadowy military decision makers to do?

Their solution, as Chris Lambright has documented,[16] was something that many people might at first refuse to believe. A counter-intelligence operation was mounted against Bennewitz, exploiting his irrational belief in humanoid alien pilots by forging documents that led him to believe crazy ideas – for example that the humanoids had local underground bases – that, if released, would destroy his scientific and professional credibility. Nobody would believe anything he said again, and his 1979 Manzano film would be discredited and forgotten.

Why not just seize Bennewitz's films and other data on the grounds that he'd been spying for the Soviets? With William Lehmann, the civilian Air Force Weapons Research Laboratory chief, impressed by Bennewitz's data and Senator Schmitt on the warpath, that may not have been practicable. At any event the US policy of supplying disinformation to discredit Bennewitz and make scientists think he was crazy was successfully implemented. Bennewitz ended up in hospital.

While the discrediting of Bennewitz appears to have been the chief policy of the shadowy US counterintelligence bosses, as backup they seemingly used another well-known trick. Sow confusion. If you have Black Project craft to conceal, spread stories about UFOs and aliens. And if you're faced, as in this case, with objects displaying supertechnology that baffled even the Air Force Weapons Research Laboratory chief, acknowledge privately that there was a counterintelligence operation to discredit Bennewitz and his films. But give out that, in reality, he'd merely filmed the testing of Black Project vehicles – projects so secret that even William Lehmann knew nothing about them. Uncle Sam was in control after all.

Technically savvy readers who've looked through Colour Plates 1-6 will reject this idea instantly. Even with this very limited selection of the material that Bennewitz presented to William Lehmann and his staff at Kirtland AFB in 1980, we don't need to be world experts to see that these frames capture a technology beyond current human capabilities, one that Uncle Sam would dearly love to have.

Endnotes

1 Gross 2003b 1957, Oct-Nov- 2- SN, p.5.

2 Gross 1997, p.3.

3 Sparks 2016, case 1232.

4 McDonald 1969b, p.3.

5 Rullan 2006.

6 Lambright 2011.

7 ibid.

8 Lambright 2011, Kindle location 2090 of 4754.

9 Lambright 2011.

10 Meessen 2012a.

11 Meessen 2012b.

12 Meessen 2012c.

13 Lambright 2011, p.188–9, Attachment D Report of meeting at Kirtland AFB in November of 1980, File No. 8017D93-O/29.

14 Lambright 2011, p.186–7 Attachment C AFOSI Report of Doty and Miller's visit with Paul Bennewitz File No. 8017D93-O/29.

15 Lambright 2011, p.188–9 Attachment D Report of meeting at Kirtland AFB in November of 1980 File No. 8017D93-O/29.

16 Lambright 2011.

11

Bentwaters and Whiteman

On 14 July 2015 the UK quality newspaper *The Independent* surprised its readers with a piece about UFOs, then the preserve of down-market newspapers like *The Sun*. *The Independent*'s headline read:

> **Former Air Force Colonel claims he has new evidence that aliens visited Rendlesham Forest in Suffolk in 1980**

The substance of the piece concerned statements from radar operators at the RAF Bentwaters base in Suffolk about their painting of objects with anomalous velocities and accelerations on the night of 27/28 December 1980. On that night Colonel Charles Halt (then a Lieutenant-Colonel and Deputy Commander of the base) was leading a USAF team investigating reported anomalous activity in and above Rendlesham Forest.

In 2015, Colonel Halt told the BBC:

"I have confirmation that (Bentwaters radar operators)…saw the object go across their 60 mile (96km) scope in two or three seconds, thousands of miles an hour, he came back across their scope again, stopped near the water tower, they watched it and observed it go into the forest where we were,

"At Wattisham [an adjacent radar station], they picked up what they called a 'bogie' and lost it near Rendlesham Forest.

Endnotes

1 Gross 2003b 1957, Oct-Nov- 2- SN, p.5.

2 Gross 1997, p.3.

3 Sparks 2016, case 1232.

4 McDonald 1969b, p.3.

5 Rullan 2006.

6 Lambright 2011.

7 ibid.

8 Lambright 2011, Kindle location 2090 of 4754.

9 Lambright 2011.

10 Meessen 2012a.

11 Meessen 2012b.

12 Meessen 2012c.

13 Lambright 2011, p.188–9, Attachment D Report of meeting at Kirtland AFB in November of 1980, File No. 8017D93-O/29.

14 Lambright 2011, p.186–7 Attachment C AFOSI Report of Doty and Miller's visit with Paul Bennewitz File No. 8017D93-O/29.

15 Lambright 2011, p.188–9 Attachment D Report of meeting at Kirtland AFB in November of 1980 File No. 8017D93-O/29.

16 Lambright 2011.

11

Bentwaters and Whiteman

On 14 July 2015 the UK quality newspaper *The Independent* surprised its readers with a piece about UFOs, then the preserve of down-market newspapers like *The Sun*. *The Independent's* headline read:

> **Former Air Force Colonel claims he has new evidence that aliens visited Rendlesham Forest in Suffolk in 1980**

The substance of the piece concerned statements from radar operators at the RAF Bentwaters base in Suffolk about their painting of objects with anomalous velocities and accelerations on the night of 27/28 December 1980. On that night Colonel Charles Halt (then a Lieutenant-Colonel and Deputy Commander of the base) was leading a USAF team investigating reported anomalous activity in and above Rendlesham Forest.

In 2015, Colonel Halt told the BBC:

"I have confirmation that (Bentwaters radar operators)...saw the object go across their 60 mile (96km) scope in two or three seconds, thousands of miles an hour, he came back across their scope again, stopped near the water tower, they watched it and observed it go into the forest where we were,

"At Wattisham [an adjacent radar station], they picked up what they called a 'bogie' and lost it near Rendlesham Forest.

"Whatever was there was clearly under intelligent control."

(BBC Local News, Suffolk, 13 July 2015)

In 1997 Colonel Halt had clarified what his search team saw on the night of 27/28 December 1980, and recorded on tape at the time, with a statement to the journalist A.J.S. Rayl.[1]

"[After leaving the woods, our search team] crossed the farmer's field past his house and across the road, stumbled through a small stream, and went out into a large plowed field. Somebody noticed several objects in the sky to the north – three objects clearly visible with multiple-colored lights on them. The objects appeared elliptical and then they turned full round, which I thought was quite interesting. All three doing that. They were stationary for awhile and then they started to move at high speed in sharp angular patterns as though they were doing a grid search. About that same time somebody noticed a similar object [in the southern sky]. It was round – did not change shape – and at one point it appeared to come toward us at a very high speed. It stopped overhead and sent down a small pencil-like beam, sort of like a laser beam. It was an interesting beam in that it stayed – it was the same size all the way down the beam. It illuminated the ground about ten feet from us and we just stood there in awe wondering whether it was a signal, or warning, or what it was. We really didn't know. It clicked-off as though someone threw a switch, and the object receded, back up into the sky.

Then it moved back toward Bentwaters, and continued to send down beams of light, at one point near the weapons storage facility. We knew that because we could hear the chatter on the [two-way] radio."

Three elliptical objects with multiple-coloured lights that later turned full round, perhaps synchronously. The objects sent pencil-like or laser-like beams towards weapons storage facilities believed to contain tactical nuclear weapons. We are evidently in the same territory as that illuminated by Chris Lambright's publication of images from Paul Bennewitz's movie frames capturing anomalous activity in the Manzano Weapons Storage area at Kirtland AFB in December 1979. At Bentwaters, however, we now have the additional evidence that on the night of 27/28 December 1980 one anomalous object was painted by military radar and displayed anomalous velocities and alien-killing accelerations.

So where did *The Independent's* aliens come from?

At Kirtland the anomalous objects' synchronous behaviour ruled out humanoid alien pilots and at Bentwaters the huge accelerations recorded by the radar operators would have killed any such beings. But the UFOlogists' belief in humanoid 'occupants' seems to defy rational argument and as we saw in the Kirtland case US counterintelligence agents exploited this silly idea in an effort to discredit Paul Bennewitz and his data.

So perhaps *The Independent* inserted aliens into Colonel Halt's story with a similar intention. I'm not suggesting that *Independent* journalists work secretly for counterintelligence – there's a thought – but they might have sound reasons for making the good Colonel appear a kook. By turning Halt's statement about 'intelligent control' into one about 'aliens' (ignoring the likelihood of AI and the radar evidence for alien-killing accelerations) they moved the story from legitimate science into the pseudoscientific field of UFOlogy. This evidently allowed them to publish the piece in a tongue-in-cheek manner while preserving their reputation as an intelligent newspaper with their alien-sceptical readers.

That's enough about aliens. Returning to science, it's now clear that the anomalous activity at Kirtland AFB in December 1979 and at RAF Bentwaters in December 1980 show common features and ought to be studied together. There's now sufficient technical evidence to warrant attention by a team of accredited experts including aerospace engineers and plasma physicists.

And as a working hypothesis, instead of humanoid aliens piloting flying saucers, we now have the notion of ET bots of various kinds using passive and active sensors to obtain salient information. In the Kirtland and Bentwaters cases, as in the 28 October 1968 Minot AFB case

(Chapter 5), the sought information may have concerned the nature and disposition of thermonuclear warheads.

Consistent with the idea of robotic surveillance is Colonel Halt's statement that the anomalous objects "started to move at high speed in sharp angular patterns as though they were doing a grid search."

A grid search is just what we might expect from not-too-bright ET bots. Recall Colonel Uyrange Hollanda's statement that, over a period of months, anomalous objects had been moving methodically from one area of the vast Amazon rainforest area to another in a grid-like fashion (Chapter 7).

So "Initiate grid search routine for…" might be a command to which surveillance and prospecting bots respond. Such commands might be stored in the bots' software and implemented in response to sensory data received either by the bot itself or by a nearby bot acting as a local command-and-control unit.

Depending on the task in hand, such routines could be implemented on various scales, ranging from the deployment of passive sensors over regions spanning hundreds of kilometres, such as the Amazon basin, to the use of 'pencil beams' to investigate nuclear weapons silos on the centimetre scale. To confirm that small-scale operations of the latter kind have taken place, we would need an account by a military eyewitness of a putative bot using a thin beam to carry out a grid search over a stored thermonuclear warhead. Here, instead of the stable isotope gold-197, of interest to prospecting bots, the targets might be fissile isotopes such as plutonium-239 and uranium-235 that are believed to play key roles in thermonuclear warheads. To identify such warheads, the devices would need to compile detailed maps showing the distribution of such fissile isotopes.

We have such an account.[2] In 2010 Dale Hogan, who in 1984 had been an Airman serving at Whiteman Air Force Base, Missouri, claimed that one night in September-October 1984, he and a fellow Airman, both on security duties, witnessed an anomalous object hover in succession over three round-roofed nuclear weapons storage igloos at Whiteman and in each case implement grid search routines with a pencil-wide reddish-blue beam (Fig 46).

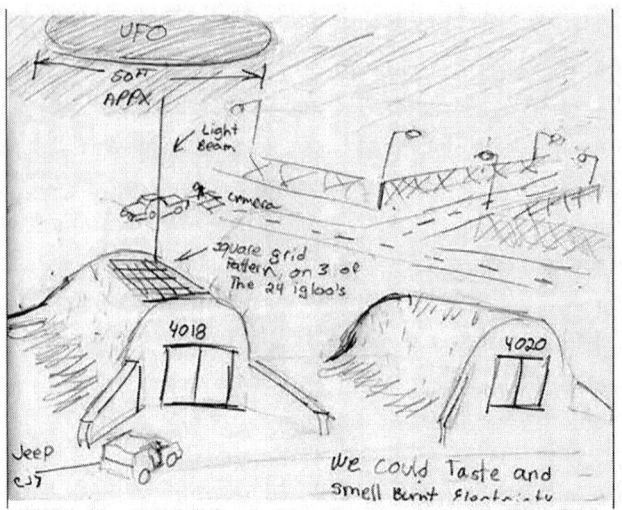

Fifty-foot-diameter black disc hovering over nuclear weapons storage igloo 4018 and 4020 emitting pencil-wide reddish-blue beam straight down on to 4018 and making a precise grid pattern with the light on top of the igloo. Illustration © 2010 by Dale Hogan.

Fig 46. Former US Airman Dale Hogan's 2010 sketch of an anomalous event he claimed was witnessed by a colleague (Airman George) and himself about 0200 local time one night in September-October 1984 at Whiteman Air Force Base, Missouri. He claimed that the two airmen had witnessed an anomalous object (UFO) hover in succession over two round-roofed nuclear weapons storage igloos at Whiteman and in each case implement grid search routines using a pencil-wide reddish-blue beam. Courtesy: Dale Hogan. [Howe (2010)]

Around 0200 local time on that clear, cloudless night, Hogan and his fellow Airman (simply referred to by his surname George) found that the engine of their security jeep kept cutting out and their radios were affected by static. The Bravo Flight Shift Commander told them to park their vehicle so they pulled up in front of one of the igloos.

Hogan then felt sluggish and both he and Airman George found their hair was standing up. Hogan noticed that when he touched the jeep, sparks came from his fingers. Then he saw a bluish-red pencil beam going up from one igloo. He traced it upwards and saw that it came from a hovering black disc about 50 feet in diameter. A sketch made by Hogan (Fig 46) suggests that the disc was hovering about fifty feet above the top of the igloo.

Hogan tried to radio for assistance, but without success because the radio kept breaking up. Meanwhile he'd climbed on top of the igloo to get a closer look at the pencil beam. It now started to trace a three-inch-square grid pattern on the top of the igloo. Curiosity outweighing common sense, Hogan put his hand in the bluish-red beam whereupon its color changed to "like a purple", it stopped doing the grid and his hand "felt like pins and needles".

On removing his hand the beam resumed its former bluish-red color and "started to do the grid pattern again" (Fig 47). According to Hogan the disc then used its beam to complete grid search routines on two other storage igloos despite harassment by Air Force Harrier jump jets (that Hogan had seen arrive on the base earlier that day). After two or three hours, the black disc turned "silverfish white" and then shot straight up. Having reached a point where "it was almost nothing" within three seconds, the disc then shot off at a 90-degree angle and disappeared.

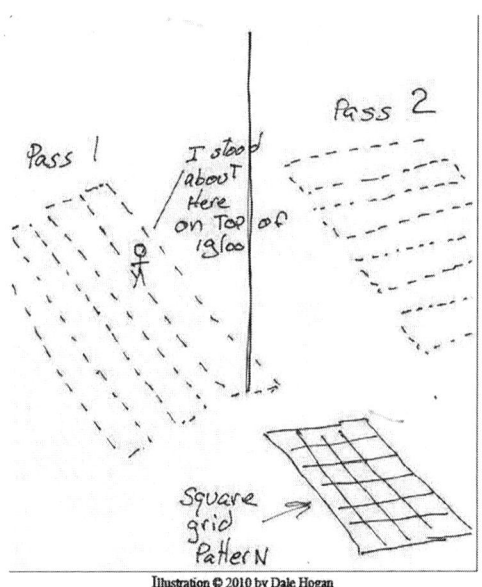

Fig 47. Former US Airman Dale Hogan's 2010 sketch of a three inch square grid pattern he claims to have seen traced by a bluish-red pencil beam emitted from a hovering black 50-foot disc on the tops of two nuclear weapons storage igloos at Whiteman Air Force, Missouri in 1984. Courtesy: Dale Hogan [Howe (2010)]

Hogan's 2010 account to veteran journalist Linda Howe contains other claims regarding an alleged stressful debriefing experience with three other eyewitnesses that are typical of statements by ex-military US personnel who claim to have witnessed anomalous activity. Uniquely though, Hogan claimed that a two-man film crew with a special camera, under instruction by an Air Force Major or Lieutenant-Colonel, filmed the disc's grid search activity. Hogan told Howe that he couldn't tell which rank the officer held "because all I could see was the clover leaf". In the US Air Force, the insignia for both ranks includes an oak leaf, which, to me, is a telling detail that supports Hogan's story. Only the subtlest of hoaxers would replace 'oak leaf' with 'clover leaf' to mimic an Airman's understandable confusion of the two.

What to make of Hogan's story? Like Paul Bennewitz, Howe, an intelligent and courageous investigative journalist specialising in anomalous reports, especially those of puzzling bloodless animal excisions, was considered important enough to be targeted by US counterintelligence and fed forged documents and silly stories about aliens. Though never driven crazy like Bennewitz, she swallowed and regurgitated some of the forged documents and alien stories and therefore lost some credibility.

So Dale Hogan's account of events at Whiteman AFB in 1984, as told to Howe in 2010 and summarised above, is not in the same category of solid evidence for probe theory as Colonel Halt's testimony to the BBC on the radar support for his team's observations at Bentwaters on the night of 27/28 December 1980.

The reason for including Hogan's story here is that his account of the alleged 1984 Whiteman AFB events includes descriptions of electromagnetic and ionisation phenomena similar to those that Bennewitz filmed at Manzano Weapons Storage area in 1979 and presented at that key meeting with General William Brooksher, Dr William Lehmann and other high-ups at Kirtland on 10 November 1980 (Chapter 10). For example, Hogan reported that, after completing its surveillance tasks, the Whiteman disc turned white, shot up to a certain height and then shot off laterally, just as the Manzano discs had reportedly done in 1979.

This turning white before acceleration links Hogan's account with probe theory, and invites interpretations by teams of accredited experts, including plasma physicists, comfortable with concepts such as MHD propulsion, Lorentz forces and shock wave control. This is the world of the technical experts who assembled at the Electromagnetics Academy's Moscow conference in 2012 (Chapter 8), not that of UFOlogists and UFO debunkers.

But until 2012, when Chris Lambright published some of Paul Bennewitz's 1979 Manzano images, people like Hogan would have had no means of knowing such technical details. Therefore the resemblance between Hogan's technical details and Bennewitz's suggests that, at the very least, we should consider the possibility that Hogan's story is true. Indeed, for global security reasons we have to do so.

And if Hogan's story is true, it immediately becomes one of the most important witness accounts of possible ET surveillance to be considered by probe theorists. For while other references to 'grid search' are imprecise, Hogan's sketches (Figs 46 and 47) are detailed.

Starting in one corner, the moving pencil beam slowly but economically built up the three-inch-square pattern in two passes, just as we might expect a bot to do. Although Hogan doesn't explicitly say so, it seems that the bot and its pencil beam moved together, allowing the bot's normal positioning reference frame to also serve as the reference frame for the grid.

Foolhardy Hogan may have been to put his hand in the path of the beam, but future scientists may thank him. The device's response – to stop the beam's movements and change the beam's colour was in line with that expected from a simple AI-controlled system. And, after Hogan had removed his hand from the path of the beam, the device returned the beam to its former colour and "started to do the grid pattern again" – just how we might expect a simple ET bot to respond to such interference.

What may the bot have actually been looking for? In Chapter 10 I noted that "Space-faring creatures equipped with nuclear weapons would present a challenge that no ET minds could ignore..."

This assumes the putative ET postbiological minds – perhaps with physical substrates located in nearby mother probes – that interpret data from bots like the one Hogan described, have arrived at concepts like 'criticality', 'fissile isotopes', 'fission bomb', 'nuclear fusion', 'fusion bomb' and 'thermonuclear warhead'. That seems reasonable, considering that putative ET minds, like our own, would have evolved in a cosmos wherein stars shine because of the nuclear fusion of hydrogen and helium and heavy fissile isotopes are created by exploding supernovae or merging neutron stars. If ET has developed technology that can build and propel high-acceleration interstellar-capable vehicles, then it's reasonable to assume that the ET minds in the mother probes can handle concepts such as those listed above. Representations of such concepts may even be stored in the software of specialist surveillance bots like the Whiteman device.

Therefore we can speculate that the Whiteman bot's three-inch-square grids showed plans of the distribution of the manmade fissile isotope plutonium-239 (half life around 24,000 years) in each of the igloos it surveyed. A particular distribution of plutonium-239 may have triggered a representation of the concept 'thermonuclear warhead' in the bot's software. By employing multiple specialist bots, and surveying many sites, in the Soviet Union and Eastern Europe as well as in the US and its NATO allies, ET minds in the mother probes may have built up a comprehensive picture of the quantity and distribution of human nuclear weapons in the 1980s.

Endnotes

1 Hastings 2008, p.394.
2 Howe 2010.

12

Beam Forward

We've looked at evidence that putative ET prospecting and surveillance devices have deployed a variety of thin laser-like beams that, like the infrared laser beams of NASA's Curiosity Rover on Mars, are apparently capable of focusing energy on small nearby targets. As we've seen, such thin beams may have served to identify different elements, or isotopes of those elements.

But we've also looked at reports that anomalous objects may have used thicker luminous beams, apparently involving the production of plasmas from Earth's atmospheric gases. For example California Highway Patrolman Charles Carson reported to James McDonald that one of the anomalous objects involved in the Red Bluff event of 13 August 1960 emitted a beam that "seemed to extend out into the air, and then to end in some curious manner" (Chapter 2). And the 'blue standing beams' filmed by Paul Bennewitz at Kirtland AFB in 1979 (Chapter 10) may also have been of this nature.

Like the thin laser-like beams, such thicker beams could serve a variety of purposes. Their 'solidity' and mass would give them a range of applications – manoeuvring, propulsion and shock wave mitigation – beyond those of the thin laser-like beams. As an example of shock wave control, consider the multiple beams of 'red light' that, according to pilot Haroldo Westendorff, a massive conical anomalous object directed upwards before it shot up into the cloud layer above Pelotas, Brazil on 5 November 1996 (Chapter 9). Had those beams not drastically reduced subsequent local turbulence, Westendorff may not have lived to tell his tale.

And although not so easy to direct and manipulate as thin beams, magnetic and electric fields could perhaps control them. Paul Bennewitz speculated that increasing magnetic field strength could cause the 'standing beams' he'd seen and filmed to slowly extend (Chapter 10). Physicist Auguste Meessen, looking at similar anomalous reports, has formulated his own theory of how increasing magnetic field strength could cause such solid beams to extend.[1]

"Let's see a photograph of a putative ET vehicle emitting one of these solid beams," scientists will say. Look at Colour Plate 7. PhD student Ellen Crystall captured this 1/60 second exposure on Kodacolor negative film after 2200 local time on 18 July 1980 at Pine Bush, Orange County, New York State. On that occasion, *Omni* science journalist Harry Lebelson and other people, including Crystall, witnessed and tried to photograph close-range activity of what Crystall claimed to be large triangular vehicles.[2] The witnesses were surprised to find that the developed film either failed to capture the images, as happened with Lebelson, or, as in the case of this exposure taken by Crystall, the image on the emulsion did not capture precisely what the eyewitnesses claimed to have seen.

In the case of this image, Crystall claimed to have seen a device shaped like a triangular platform about sixty feet wide, with a square front divided into four vent-like or window-like units by a yellow illuminated panel in the shape of a 'plus sign' (Fig 48). But the photographic image (Colour Plate 7) only faintly registered these visually observed details. Instead a spectacular orange truncated beam, apparently emitted from the bottom left of the four vents, dominates the photograph.

Such discrepancies between what witnesses claim to have seen and what they have captured on film or digital media illustrate once again the need for research in this area to be undertaken by teams of accredited technical experts, not UFOlogists. While the amateur researchers of UFOlogy naively expect photos to match what was allegedly seen, experts take a different view.

To her credit Crystall tried to find a scientific explanation for the puzzling discrepancy discussed above. She noted that while the human eye could not detect ultraviolet radiation (radiation with wavelengths

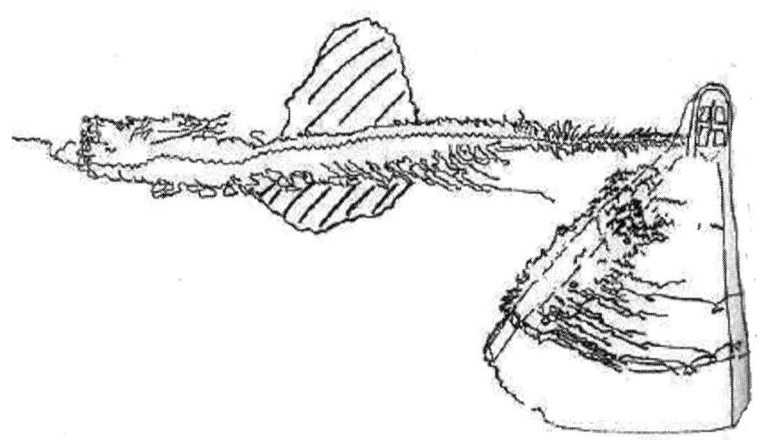

Fig 48. Sketch by Ellen Crystall of the large metallic triangular object that she claimed to have seen while taking the photograph reproduced in Colour Plate 7. Crystall has added details of the invisible beam and other invisible emissions apparently captured in that photograph. [Crystall 1991, Fig 21]

shorter than about 400 nanometres) the Kodacolor emulsion she used could. Therefore, she argued, the beam and other emissions in Colour Plate 7 could have been captured on film because they represented ultraviolet wavelengths invisible to the eye.[3]

To make her theory credible, Crystall would have had to show that the glass lens of her Russian Zenith 35 mm SLR camera was transparent to ultraviolet radiation in this wavelength range. But in fact there was no need for Crystall to bother, because her suggestion that the beam represented ultraviolet emissions failed to account for its orange colour, representing wavelengths around 600 nanometres, as recorded by the Kodacolor negative film.

A better explanation than Crystall's was needed to account for the failure of the witnesses to see the orange beam recorded by the 1/60 second exposure of the Kodacolor emulsion. As a science journalist Harry Lebelson had good contacts with the US scientific community and he worked hard to procure expert interpretations for this image and others captured by Crystall at Pine Bush on 18 July 1980.

In an interview with Robert Jastrow, founding director of NASA's Goddard Institute for Space Studies, parts of which were published in *Omni* (September 1981), Jastrow stated:

"I am unable to interpret these images as atmospherical electricity. Perhaps they represent something totally unknown to us at this time."[4]

Encouraged by Jastrow's comments, and by the opinion of experts at Stevens Institute of Technology at Hoboken, New Jersey,[5] Lebelson continued his quest for expert interpretations of Crystall's images, including the key one reproduced in Colour Plate 7. In the end he managed to interest Paul van Dyke, a scientist at Sandia Laboratories at Livermore in California whose research activities there had included an assessment of the effects off lightning strikes on rockets launches. After studying Crystall's image at Sandia, Van Dyke wrote to Lebelson in 1983 that the image was "very interesting and looked quite different from any of the thousands of photographs of static discharges taken at Sandia Laboratories." Moreover, he wrote, "it has a unique pattern that clearly implies periodicity." With a shutter speed of 1/60 second, van Dyke wrote, he could "ballpark the period somewhere around 130 microseconds. That's too fast for any large mechanical object I know of."[6]

Both Robert Jastrow and Paul van Dyke were intrigued by the image in Colour Plate 7 and recognised that it wasn't a hoax and presented a big challenge to science. But in the post-Condon climate of the early 1980s neither of these accredited experts felt they could publicly take the analysis further and compare the photograph with what Lebelson, Crystall and the other eyewitnesses claimed to have seen. In the end, Crystall published her erroneous interpretation in a book bursting with thoughts about space aliens[7] while the experts' views went unheeded. Naturally the scientific community ignored the whole affair.

But today, with probe theory much strengthened by events since the Atomic Testing Museum's 2012 display of some of the Height 611 remains in Las Vegas, the time is right for the technical experts now entering the field to refocus attention on Crystall's photographic image in Colour Plate 7.

First, the fast nature of the phenomenon, as discussed by van Dyke, points to an obvious explanation for the eyewitnesses' failure to see the orange beam captured by the Kodacolor emulsion. It wasn't because human eyes can't see at ultraviolet frequencies; it was because they can't, particularly at night, record events shorter than about 1/20 second.

Let's postulate, then, that the highly structured orange beam represented emissions around 600 nanometres from ionised species in the air excited by a very brief leftward-directed pulse of ionising radiation, perhaps X-rays, from one of the object's vents. If the ionising pulse was shorter than the exposure time of 1/60 second, then the stimulated emission at 600 nanometres may also have lasted for a very brief period, too short to be registered by the human eye. But Crystall's 1/60 second exposure evidently captured it.

The next step is to interpret the structure of the beam. Although a period of 1/60 second is too short for human eyes to cope with, for plasma phenomena it's like a time exposure. The complex orange trails of Colour Plate 7 therefore appear to represent the surprisingly long travel paths completed by small, high-speed packets of plasma during this short period.

In some cases the trails fade away before they end, suggesting that the excited ions' emission at around 600 nanometres decayed before Crystall's camera shutter closed. But what's exciting is that, in some cases, the trails are looped and the shapes of the loops correspond to the expected trajectories of charged particles moving in the presence of magnetic and electric fields (see Wikipedia: Lorentz force). The repetition of the loops indicates periodicity, as Sandia's Paul van Dyke noted, indicating a powerful, pulsed magnetic field.

And although the travel directions of the plasma packets in Colour Plate 7 vary from place to place, perhaps responding to variance in local magnetic and electric field vectors, the overall direction of mass movement of ions, both in the left-directed ionisation beam and the other emissions from the vehicle's left side, is towards the bottom right. According to Newton's Third Law, the acceleration of mass towards the bottom right would give rise to an opposing accelerating force directed towards the upper left. Or, if the downward component of the thrust served only to counteract gravity, then the pull would be horizontally to the left.

An intriguing feature of Colour Plate 7 and Fig 48 is the way the rectilinear horizontal beam emerges from the bottom left of four rectangular 'vents' at the front of the putative vehicle as if the vents were precisely designed to project such beams. If this is so, we could speculate that the four vents could project ionisation beams forwards, sideways and up or down. Adroit control of such brief directed ionisation pulses from the front of the vehicle, together with similar control of ionisation pulses from the sides and coordination of all these ionisation pulses with brief magnetic pulses, could allow the device to manoeuvre with great dexterity. This brings to mind Ray Stanford's claim (Chapter 8) that studies of the prints of the 12 December 1977 Memphis event showed that one class of smaller devices associated with the giant tube were a group of wing-shaped 'Star Wars' objects that appeared to manoeuvre by laterally shooting off narrow columns of plasma. Could Crystall have captured a close-up snapshot of a device of that kind emitting just such a plasma column?

Whether or not that was the case, a team of aerospace engineers and plasma physicists might now be able to use the data in Colour Plate 7 to develop models of how probes could use ionisation beams and magnetic pulses to generate directed thrust when operating in planetary atmospheres like that of the Earth. Of the possible directions, forward movement would be the most important. After all, forward movement into space already mapped by forward directed sensors is crucial for surveillance devices, whether human drones or putative ET bots.

To help move forward in an ionisable planetary atmosphere, the putative vehicle in Colour Plate 7 might direct one or more ionisation beams forward instead of to the side. Mass movement of ions to the rear in such a directed energy beam, perhaps also partial vacuum in the space between the packets of ionised material, would help to propel the vehicle forward and reduce drag and shock wave effects.

Such ideas have immense commercial and military potential. As far as shock wave mitigation at supersonic speeds is concerned, Paul Hill, a leading aerospace engineer at NASA's Langley Research Center, who received NASA's Exceptional Service Medal in 1969, pointed out in his posthumously published book[8] the possibility that anomalous objects could mitigate shock wave effects by beaming forward speed-of-light signals to 'tell' the air in front to move aside.

Another even more celebrated aerospace engineer, Professor Leik Myrabo, who now operates Lightcraft Technologies, has also long been aware of such possibilities. Recall that, partly as a result of James McDonald's campaigning, the American Institute of Aeronautics and Astronautics (AIAA) set up a UFO Subcommittee. Academics mindful of their careers looked away, but aerospace engineers were intrigued. The solid evidence – for example McDonald's study of the 4 November 1957 Kirtland Air Force Base incident – suggested to them that they might learn a thing or two by studying reports of what McDonald was already calling possible ET probes. We've already seen (Chapter 8) one example of the AIAA Subcommittee in action in that 1978 AIAA meeting at which experts analysed Ray Stanford's groundbreaking 12 December 1977 Memphis footage.

And, also in 1978, John Warren, then at Los Alamos National Laboratory, where ET probe theory was first hatched in 1952 (Chapter 5), published an article in the MUFON Journal entitled *The Scientific Method of Investigating UFOs*. Having come across Warren's article, Myrabo, then a young aerospace engineer, sent Warren a draft copy of his own paper, *Solar Powered Global Aerospace Transportation*,[9] which he later presented at the AIAA 13th International Electric Propulsion Conference, held at San Diego that same year.[10]

Myrabo's draft paper included several sketches of disc-like vehicles and included a discussion of how beamed energy might be used to mitigate shock wave effects. It was therefore natural for Myrabo to consult Warren, a scientific UFO expert, in preparing his own AIAA paper on advanced aerospace transportation.[11]

Leik Myrabo maintained an interest in what aerospace engineers might learn from UFO reports. About nine years later, when he was at Rensselaer Polytechnic Institute, Troy, New York, Professor Myrabo heard of impressive footage and prints resulting from the filming of an anomalous event that appeared to involve the forward beaming of energy from a disc. Naturally, he was intrigued. In March 1987, when attending a symposium at the Goddard Space Flight Center in Maryland, Myrabo, accompanied by one of his PhD students at Rensselaer, spent a lot of time at the home of the man who had filmed the events, studying and discussing the slides made from the footage.[12]

Who was the person who had acquired this scientifically important footage? It was none other than Ray Stanford, who had recently moved from Texas to Maryland. Had he not later won international scientific acclaim for his skills at spotting dinosaur tracks and remains,[13] we might doubt that this one individual could consistently film anomalous activity.

Part of Stanford's secret is that he always had his movie camera ready. On the afternoon of 5 October 1985, Stanford, with his two daughters and three other witnesses, was walking on a pier at Corpus Christi, on the Gulf Coast of Texas. Stanford had agreed to pay his children ten dollars if they ever spotted a bona fide anomalous object, and now they cashed in. They both pointed to the sky and said "Daddy, what's that?"

Stanford whipped out his movie camera equipped with a ten-power telephoto lens and started filming a group of seven or eight anomalous objects travelling from the north-northeast towards Corpus Christi. All but one of the objects appeared to be identical domed discs and they were travelling on edge, the domes to the rear and the flat sides facing the direction of travel (see Fig 49).[14]

Having captured the first part of the event on film, Stanford later tried to obtain radar confirmation of the incident. With his tape recorder on, he phoned the FAA headquarters in Dallas, explained that he was with Project Starlight International and told them what had happened. He claims to have received the following response: "Do you just want the regular radar paints or do you want the plasma penetration images?"

Stanford had to reveal that he wasn't with the US government, but claimed to have been so shaken by the implications of the response that he could not remember, when later interviewed on radio, how the rest of the conversation went. But Stanford claimed to have recorded it all on tape.

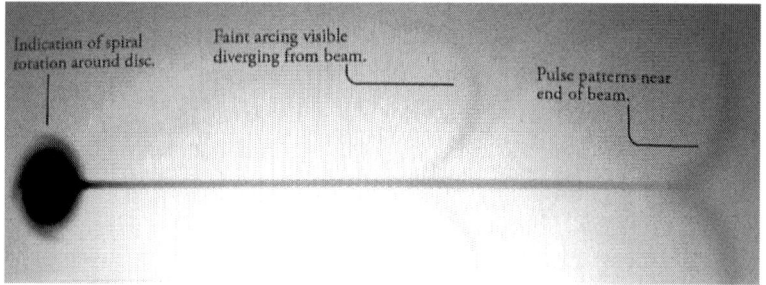

Fig 49. Researcher Chris Lambright's impression from memory of a slide made from a movie frame of an anomalous object captured by Ray Stanford above Corpus Christi, Texas on 5 October 1985. Lambright viewed the projected slide in Stanford's house in 1986 and published this impression in his eBook X Descending *in 2011.*

According to Lambright, the Corpus Christi object appeared to project beams forward in a series of pulse regimes. These beams apparently played a key role in the object's propulsion and quiet travel through the atmosphere. [Lambright (2011) p 38]

The FAA has never been known for its UFO enthusiasm so Stanford's story that the Dallas FAA had obtained technical radar information regarding the 5 October 1985 anomalous activity above Corpus Christi and was ready to pass the details on to him is extraordinary. What gives his account some credibility is independent evidence that the FAA Traffic Control radar at Tucson also monitored activity of multiple groups of anomalous objects during this 36-hour period – perhaps including the very same group of objects that Stanford filmed.

The Tucson-based *APRO Bulletin*, run by Coral and Jim Lorenzen, a quality UFO journal of the time, carried a report that, in the early hours of 7 October 1985, the traffic control radar at Tucson International Airport detected the passage of fifteen formations of objects without transponders, travelling in groups of four to seven, moving at about 300 miles per hour from the southwest to the northeast over Tucson. The Tucson air traffic controller alerted the local Tucson police helicopter, whose pilot confirmed lighted objects over Tucson between scattered cloud at 3000 feet and heavy cloud at 7000 feet.[15,16]

So Stanford's claim that an FAA radar expert in Dallas offered him "plasma penetration images" in connection with the anomalous objects painted above Corpus Christi on 5 October 1985 is not incredible. If true, it might support the idea that at that time PSI International operated under contract as a data interpretation unit for the US Air Force. Perhaps the technical expert Stanford spoke to at the FAA knew of this arrangement and assumed that one of the shadowy high-ups had already approved release of this data to Project Starlight International.

Now let's return to the story, first unearthed by Chris Lambright[17] of how some aspects of the TAV (Trans-Atmospheric Vehicle) designs of Leik Myrabo's corporation Lightcraft International go back to the legacy of James McDonald's campaigning and the work of the AIAA's UFO subcommittee that made it respectable for aerospace engineers to study UFO reports. The next stage in that story continued to involve the AIAA. In 1994, together with Yu P Raizer, Leik Myrabo published a seminal AIAA paper entitled *Laser Advanced Induced Air Spike for Trans-Atmospheric Vehicles (TAV)*. In it the authors proposed to reduce drag and heating by focusing a powerful pulsed laser or microwave beam ahead of the TAV flight path to create a "thermal spot."[18]

This is the Directed-Energy Air Spike (DEAS) effect (Fig 50). In Myrabo's conceptual models,[19] hypersonic airflow is diverted around a parabolic shock wave created by such a thermal spot towards MHD engines on the periphery of a disc-like craft.

Tests of models of such devices (Fig 51), some looking precisely like the disc-shaped anomalous objects reported so many times by eye witnesses, have continued, for example, in the Hypersonic Shock Tunnel at the Laboratory of Aerothermodynamics and Hypersonics at the Instituto de Estudos Avançados in São José dos Campos, Brazil.[20] Such shock tunnel experiments involve cameras operating at 100,000 frames per second capturing laser-induced air breakdown and plasma phenomena on microsecond timescales in front of models exposed to airflows in the order of Mach 7 at gas pressures between 4 and 12 millibars. Looking at these microsecond timescale photographs, it's evident how inadequate the twenty-four per second and fifty-four per second frame rates of Stanford and Bennewitz were at capturing the high-speed plasma phenomena linked with anomalous objects.

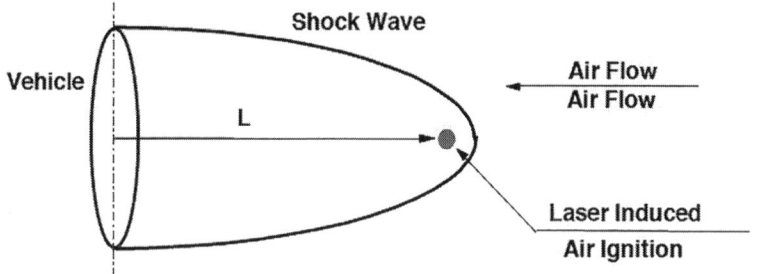

Figure 2. Schematic of the DEAS concept.

Fig 50. Principle of the Directed Energy Air Spike (DEAS) concept. A pulsed forward directed laser beam creates a thermal spot ahead of a disc-shaped vehicle, where air ignition takes place. Hypersonic airflow is diverted away from the vehicle's path by the thermal spot and feeds hypersonic MHD (magnetohydrodynamic) engines on the periphery of the disc-shaped vehicle. [Minucci et al, 2005, p 52]

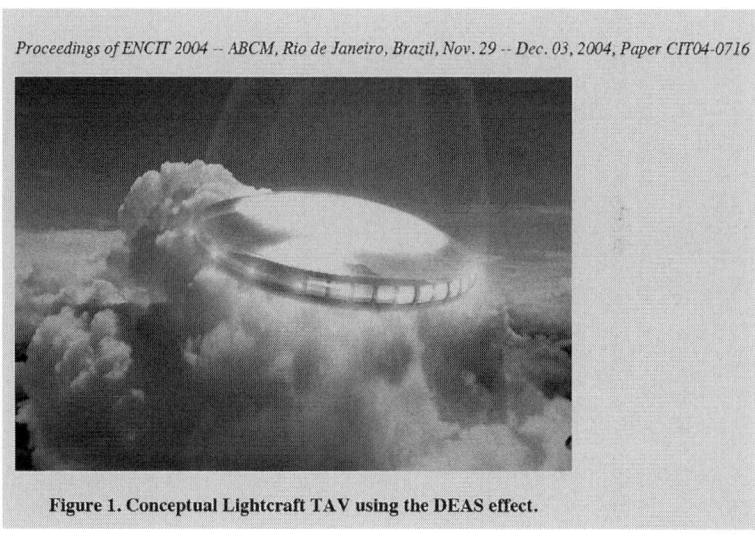

Fig 51. Conceptual model of a Trans-Atmospheric Vehicle using the DEAS concept (see Fig 50) to achieve hypersonic velocities in the atmosphere. [Minucci et al, 2005, p 52]

Equally this ongoing experimental work shows the enormous potential of what might be achieved by capturing digital movies of plasma coronas around anomalous objects at very high frame rates. Perhaps there could even be progress towards understanding the nature of the compact energy sources that apparently allow these objects to create ionisation pulses and magnetic pulses of such intensity.

Endnotes

1 Meessen 2000.

2 Lebelson 1981, p.33–8.

3 Crystall 1991, p.168.

4 Lebelson 1981.

5 ibid.

6 Lebelson 1980s, The Hidden Harry Lebelson Files, downloaded from: www.pinebushufo.com/lebelsonfiles.htm, 26 August 2011.

7 Crystall 1991.

8 Hill 1995, p.182.

9 Myrabo 1978.

10 Lambright 2011, p.51.

11 Myrabo 1978.

12 Lambright 2011, p.50, Kindle location 1030 of 4754.

13 Stanford *et al.* 2004.

14 Lambright 2011, p.38.

15 Lorenzen 1987a.

16 Lorenzen 1987b.

17 Lambright 2011.

18 Myrabo and Raizer 1994.

19 Minucci *et al.* 2005, p.52.

20 ibid.

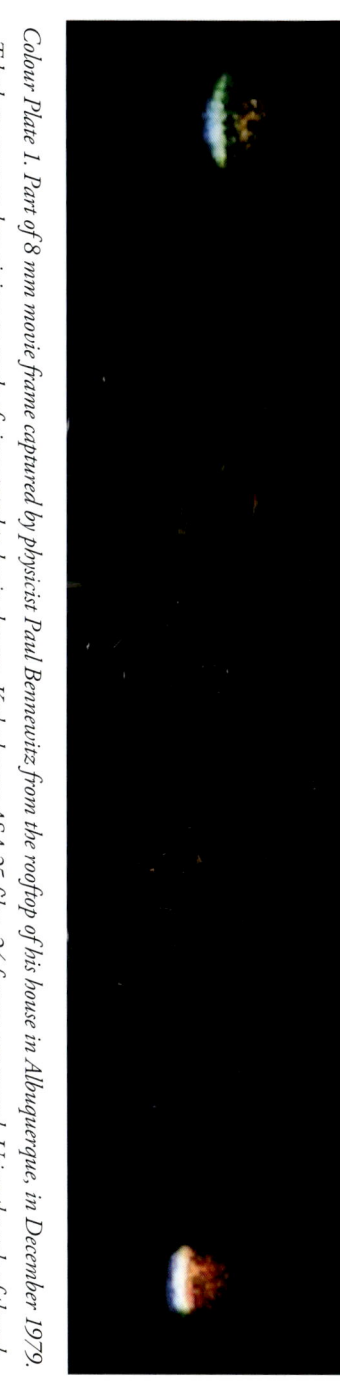

Colour Plate 1. Part of 8 mm movie frame captured by physicist Paul Bennewitz from the rooftop of his house in Albuquerque, in December 1979. Telephoto or zoom lens giving an angle of view stated to be six degrees. Kodachrome ASA 25 film, 24 frames per second. Using the rule of thumb that exposure time (shutter speed) is half the frame rate, the exposure time for each frame would be about 1/50 second.

Paul Bennewitz studied the frames with his 8 mm film editor, produced prints from them, some of which he sent to his friend Chris Lambright. Lambright converted the prints to high-resolution digital scans, enhanced them with computer software and then published them in his ebook (Lambright 2011, location 4744).

This frame shows two anomalous objects surrounded by their plasma coronas hovering close to the ground within the security fence of the Manzano Weapons Storage Area about two miles to the southeast of Bennewitz's house.

From intensive studies of the images he collected over many nights of observations in December 1979, Bennewitz concluded that the hidden objects causing the visible plasma phenomena shown here were discs or ellipsoids ranging from about 36 feet in diameter (object on left) to 18 feet in diameter (object on right). [Lambright 2011 location 4744]

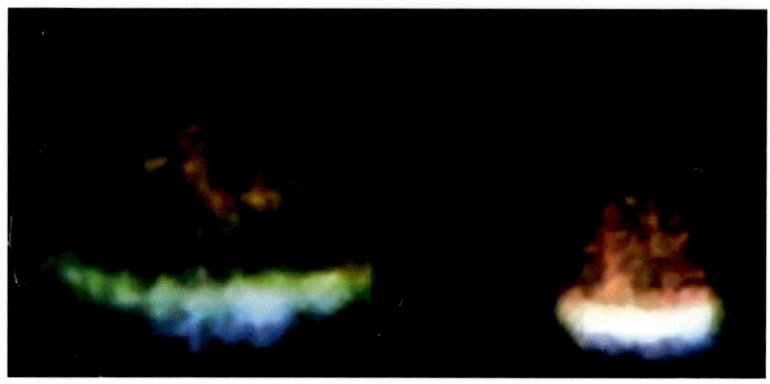

Colour Plate 2. Objects shown in Colour Plate 1, enlarged and juxtaposed. Original images captured by Paul Bennewitz on Kodachrome ASA 25 film, exposure time about 1/50 second. The blue-green colour of the patches around the object on the left probably represents spectral lines around 500 nanometres emitted by ionised nitrogen molecules. The discrete nature of the ionisation patches suggests close sources of ionising radiation, perhaps 'emitters' located on the rim of the hidden object.

In these blue-green plasma patches there are indications of curved arcs that may represent trajectories of charged particles that in the 1/50-second-exposure time have followed curved paths under the influence of strong magnetic and electric fields.

The white colour of the clumps of plasma on the right may represent emission from multiple lines of many different ionized species, as in a lighting flash. Alternatively the white colour may be a photographic effect resulting from saturation of the emulsion's colour response functionality. In either case, the white colour is consistent with a higher output of ionising radiation from the 'emitters' on this disc compared to those on the larger disc to its left.

The orange colour of the clumps of plasma above both objects may represent emission lines around 600 nanometres emitted by other ionised species of nitrogen or other air molecules. The larger volume of orange plasma above the disc on the right is again consistent with a higher output of ionising radiation from this disc at this moment compared with the one on the left. [Lambright 2011 location 4744]

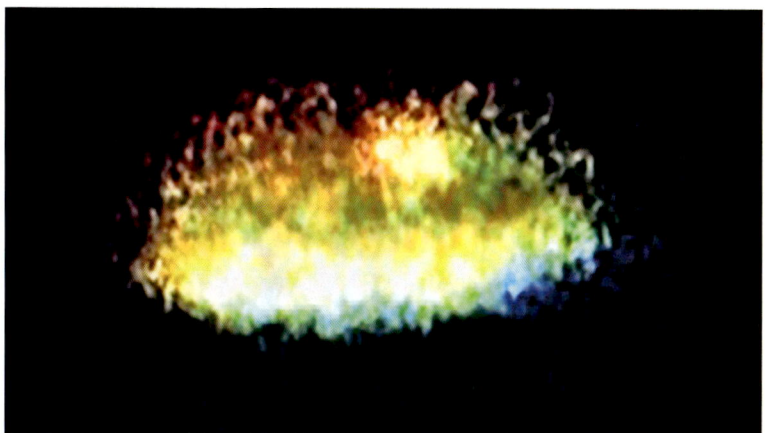

Colour Plate 3. Enlargement of the larger object of Colour Plate 2 and its plasma corona as captured in a later frame. Output of ionising radiation has apparently increased, causing the clumps of plasma near the 'emitters' and above the disc to enlarge. Multiple curved orange arcs may represent the trajectories of clumps of charged particles, emitting spectral lines around 600 nanometres, moving in the presence of strong magnetic and electric fields during the 1/50 second exposure time. [Lambright 2011 location 4744]

Colour Plate 4. Part of 1150 second movie frame showing three of the anomalous objects simultaneously 'flaring'. Output of ionising radiation has evidently increased further and the objects are now surrounded by much-expanded ellipses of intense white light.

[Lambright 2011 location 4744]

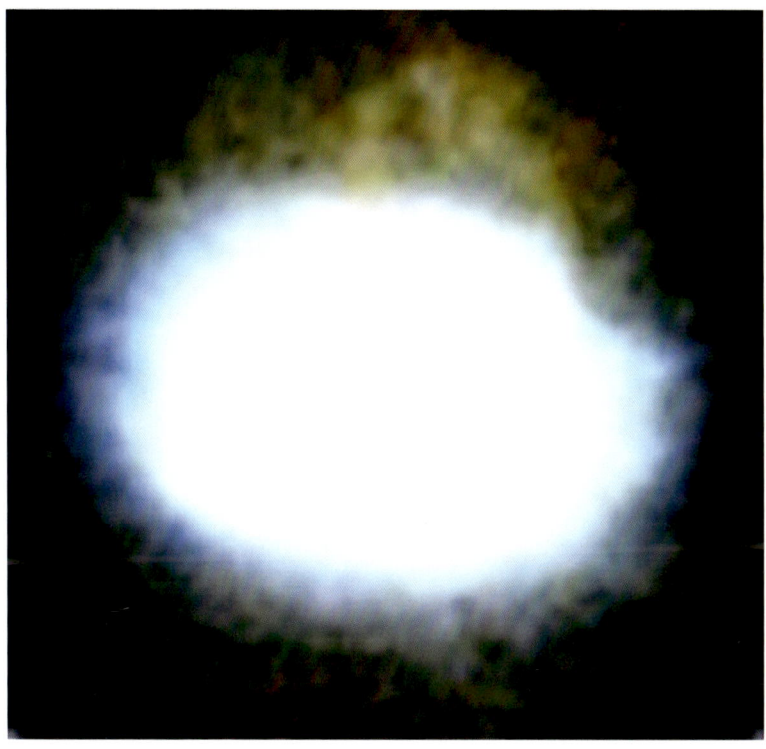

Colour Plate 5. Enlargement of largest anomalous object. Note the resemblance to photographs of the solar corona, suggesting streams of plasma moving radially outwards. [Lambright 2011 location 4744]

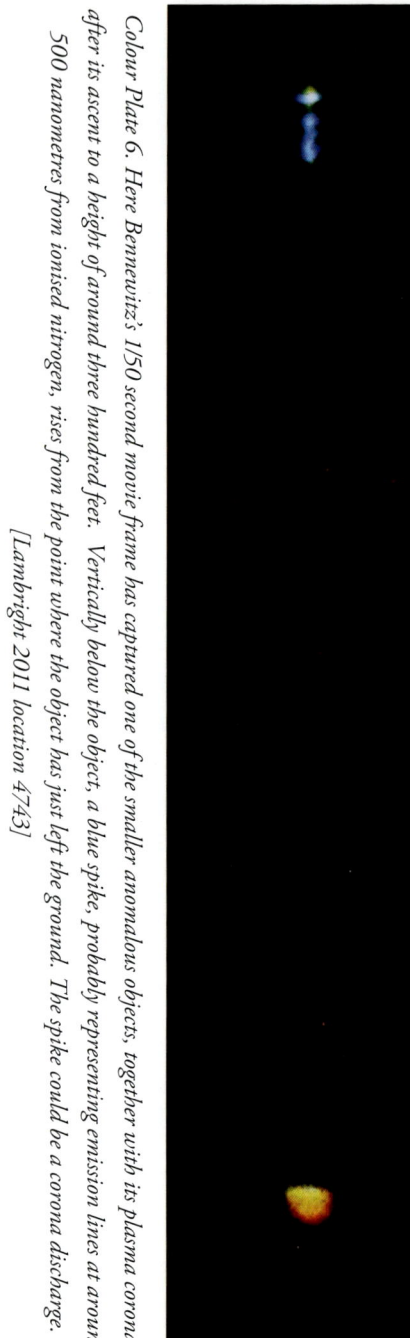

Colour Plate 6. Here Bennewitz's 1/50 second movie frame has captured one of the smaller anomalous objects, together with its plasma corona, after its ascent to a height of around three hundred feet. Vertically below the object, a blue spike, probably representing emission lines at around 500 nanometres from ionised nitrogen, rises from the point where the object has just left the ground. The spike could be a corona discharge.
[Lambright 2011 location 4743]

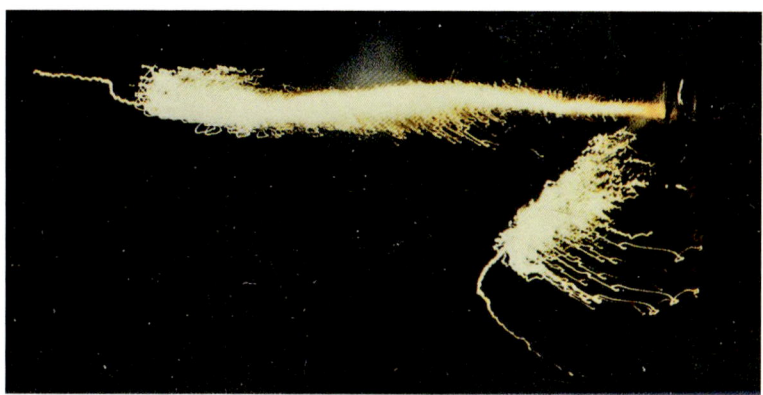

Colour Plate 7. PhD student Ellen Crystall captured this 1/60 second exposure on Kodacolor negative film after 2200 local time on 18 July 1980 at Pine Bush, Orange County, New York State. While taking the photograph, Crystall claimed to have seen a device shaped like a triangular platform about sixty feet wide, with a square front divided into four vent-like or window-like units by a yellow illuminated panel in the shape of a 'plus sign' (Fig 48). But this photographic image registered these visually observed details faintly. Instead a spectacular orange truncated beam apparently emitted from the bottom left of the four vents dominates the photograph. [Crystall 1991, cover photograph]

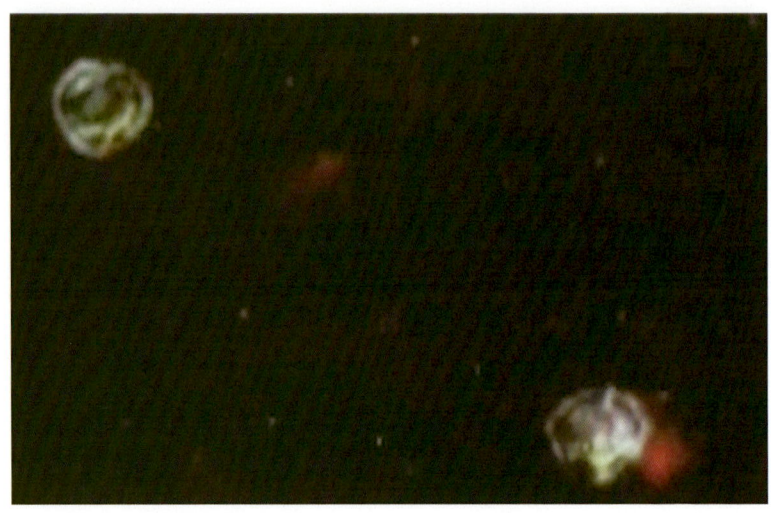

Colour Plate 8. Waltraud Kaliba and Jürgen Trieb, two professional sports photographers, claim to have captured this image, apparently showing anomalous objects emitting red plasma beams, from the north-facing balcony of their house in Knittelfeld, Austria at 2311 local time on 24 August 2003. Nikon D1X DSLR camera, exposure time 3 seconds.

The two objects appear to have grown organically. Each seems to comprise an inner polyhedron linked by four 'struts' to an incomplete outer polyhedron. The struts of the first object appear to parallel those of the second, as if the objects are coordinating their activities.

The red areas to the lower right of each object could be interpreted as the effects of beams of ionising radiation from the devices, the excited species in the air emitting at around 650 nanometers. The cratered appearance of the objects could have resulted from micrometeorite impact or could be a consequence of their organic growth.

[YouTube 'UFO Hotspot Knittelfeld–Gerhard Gröschel'. Image downloaded 20 July 2014]

13

The French Connection

The scientific study of the remains of the Height 611 high-temperature event of 29 January 1986, some of which were displayed at the National Atomic Testing Museum, Las Vegas in 2012 (Chapter 1), and which will be discussed in detail in the next three chapters, is easily the most important set of evidence for ET probe theory. But there are two other cases in which teams of experts working for the French government studied traces and environmental effects on soil and vegetation left behind after witnesses had reported the arrival and departure of anomalous objects. There is also a third case, in France's old ally, Scotland, in which police officers and a police forensic laboratory in Edinburgh studied ground traces, torn clothing and other evidence for assault against a forester that was so strong that a legal case remains in place more than four decades after the anomalous events took place.

First, the two French cases. At Trans-en-Provence in the south of France on 8 January 1981 at about 1700 hours local time Monsieur Renato Nicolai, a householder engaged in building work outside his hillside property, heard a faint whistling noise and observed a grey disc about two metres in diameter (he called the device *l'engin*) descend from the sky and rest on a hillside platform below him about 80 metres away. After remaining there some seconds, according to Nicolai, the device, whistling again, lifted off, ascended vertically to a point above the trees and then left at high speed towards the northeast.[1,2]

In the northern city of Nancy, on 21 October 1982 at about 1233 hours local time, Monsieur Henri, an experimental biologist, working in his small terrace and garden, looked up and noticed a small object high in the clear sky. It grew bigger every moment and descended towards him on a curved trajectory. Within a few seconds the object (he too called it *l'engin*) was revealed as a metallic disc about 1.5 metres in diameter, hovering silently about one metre above the lawn of his tiny walled garden (Fig 52).[3] Shocked, he stepped backwards, fetched a camera from the house, and tried and failed (because of a camera fault) to photograph the device. Then Monsieur Henri observed it from various angles while it hovered above the lawn for the surprisingly long period of twenty minutes. Finally the disc shot upwards vertically, reflecting the sun, until it was too small to be seen. The biologist noticed that, as the object rose the somewhat curled blades of grass beneath it straightened to a vertical position.

In both cases the reported *engins*, too small to accommodate humanoid occupants, could have been generalist ET surveillance bots.

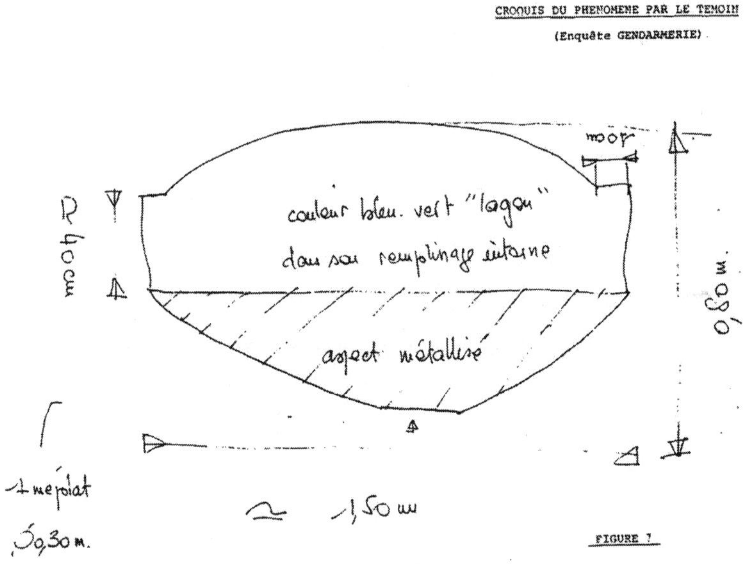

Fig 52. Nancy, France. Drawing by Monsieur Henri, biologist, of engin, *about 1.5 metres in diameter, that he reported viewing close-up on 21 October 1982. Local gendarmerie investigated on 22 October and Monsieur Henri deposited this drawing as part of their investigation. [Centre Nationale d'Etudes Spatiales 1983a, p 23]*

On both occasions the movements of the isolated witnesses engaged in outdoor activity could have attracted the attention of the cruising bots' optical sensors, just as movements of small potential prey animals attract attention from the visual systems of cats or other predators.

At Trans-en-Provence traces remained in the limestone-based soil on the platform that corresponded to the witness's description of the device having landed there and subsequently taken off (Fig 54). Analysis of samples collected by local gendarmes was undertaken at the SNEAP (Société Nationale Elf Aquitaine Production) laboratory in Boussens, the Paul Sabatier University in Toulouse and other laboratories. The results of these studies were consistent with expected effects of mechanical pressure and frictional forces on the terrace soil.[4,5]

J.-J. Velasco

Fig. 12. Location of the trace.

Fig 53. Trans-en-Provence, France. Trace in limestone-based soil corresponding to the position where on 8 January 1981 Monsieur Renato Nicolai, working outside his property, reportedly observed a disc of about two metres diameter land and remain for some seconds. Photograph by Draguignan Gendarmerie, 9 January January 1981. [Velasco, 1990, p 40]

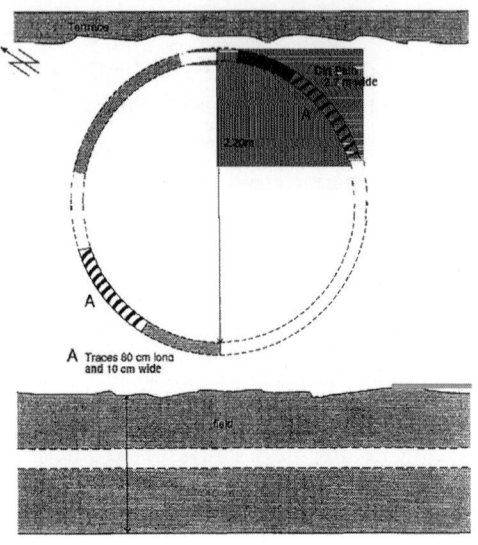

Fig. 11. **Drawing of the trace by the Gendarmerie.**

Fig 54. Trans-en-Provence, France. Drawing by Draguignan Gendarmerie on 9 January 1981 of traces photographed in Fig 53. [Velasco, 1990, p 39]

Michel Bounias, of INRA (Institut National de la Recherche Agronomique), Avignon, conducted a sophisticated biochemical study of apparent effects of the 8 January 1981 Trans-en-Provence event on the subsequent growth of a wild strain of alfalfa plants, collected within the landing trace. He concluded that his results "were consistent, for instance, with an electromagnetic source of stress." Bounias observed that one possible source of such stress might have been an MHD-type propulsion system of the kind proposed by CNRS physicist Jean-Pierre Petit.[6,7]

While no permanent ground traces remained at Nancy, apart from the anomalous object's observed straightening effect on the grass blades when it ascended, the object apparently had other more lasting effects on the plants in Monsieur Henri's little garden. Flowers and leaves from an amaranth plant and several others were afterwards found to be desiccated. This was noted by the local gendarmerie who investigated on the following day, 22 October 1982, shown in their published photographs and confirmed by a small study carried out by Monsieur Henri in the biological laboratory where he worked.

To throw light on the grass straightening, GEPAN consulted the atmospheric physicist S. Chauzy of the Paul Sabatier University in Toulouse.[8] Chauzy concluded that the minimum intensity of an electric field capable of causing the grass straightening was 30 kilovolts per metre, but much higher field strength may have been needed. Such an electric field could have played a part in the desiccation of the amaranth, GEPAN noted. But whatever the role played by a possible brief electric field, emissions of some kind from the hovering and then accelerating object could obviously have caused the desiccation of the amaranth and other nearby plants.

Why might the object have remained in the little Nancy garden for as long as twenty minutes? Sensibly, the GEPAN investigators refrained from speculating. But having already suggested that the cruising device may have been a generalist surveillance bot attracted to the garden by the movements of Monsieur Henri himself – perhaps conspicuously reflecting light from the near-midday sun – it's reasonable to point out here that the biologist's continued activity after the object's arrival may have been the reason why it stayed so long.

Monsieur Henri reported to GEPAN that on the object's arrival in his garden, he initially stepped back some metres on his terrace. Then, scientific curiosity overcoming fear, he reported having moved to eight successive positions, approaching the object, fetching his camera, trying and failing to take a photograph, observing it from various angles and so on. So, while the biologist's eyes and other sense organs were collecting data on the device as he moved around, we can speculate that the device's sensors were gathering data on him.

Monsieur Henri's close study of the object yielded observations compatible with this idea. For example, he noted that the sideband around the device and the dome above it (Fig 52) were very difficult to describe. He stated to the GEPAN team that this upper part was not homogeneous and that being close to it was like being in the presence of *"un volume translucide"* (a translucent volume). He compared it to a blue-green lagoon and also to Plexiglass.

The upper part of the Nancy object including its dome therefore had a transparency or translucence recalling the transparent domes of the eye-like Moreland-type objects discussed in Chapter 3. Contrasting with the blue-grey metallic appearance of its lower part, which reminded Monsieur Henri of the metal beryllium, the biologist's description of the upper part is compatible with the presence of optical sensors of some kind.

Another aspect of the Nancy object that struck Monsieur Henri was its perfect finish. Despite having sharp angles in places, for example the top of the sideband (Fig 52), there were no signs of welding, machining or factory work of any kind. It was *"un bel objet, joli"*, a beautiful object. Worthy, therefore, of ET.

The Trans-en-Provence and Nancy reports show that other events in addition to the 1986 Height 611 high-temperature event can be interpreted as near-ground activity of possible ET probes giving rise to environmental effects that have been studied by accredited science

Fig 55. Scottish Forester Robert Taylor, 1979 [Keatman and Collins 1980 p 25]

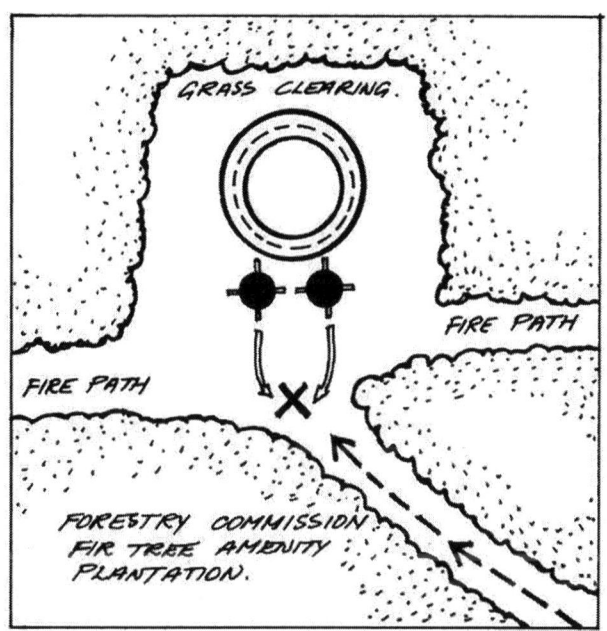

Fig 56. On a routine inspection on 9 November 1979, having left his truck nearby, forester Robert Taylor walked (dashed arrows) along a fire path towards a grass clearing (X) in Dechmont Woods, Livingston, west of Edinburgh, Scotland. There, as he later reported to his boss, the police and investigators, Taylor was surprised to encounter a dark grey spherical object, about seven metres in diameter (Fig 57). [Keatman and Collins 1979 p 5]

teams in reputable laboratories. The fact that both studied events happened in France doesn't mean that ET probes are Francophile but rather that in the relevant period France was the only nation that openly deployed properly funded science teams on such studies. It's therefore probable that many events of this kind have happened worldwide over the last few decades.

Indeed, in one of these, a 9 November 1979 event that became one of the most celebrated UFO cases of all time, a Scots forester, Robert Taylor (Fig 55), reported being assaulted in the course of his duties by two mine-like devices that emanated from a larger spherical landed object (Fig 57).

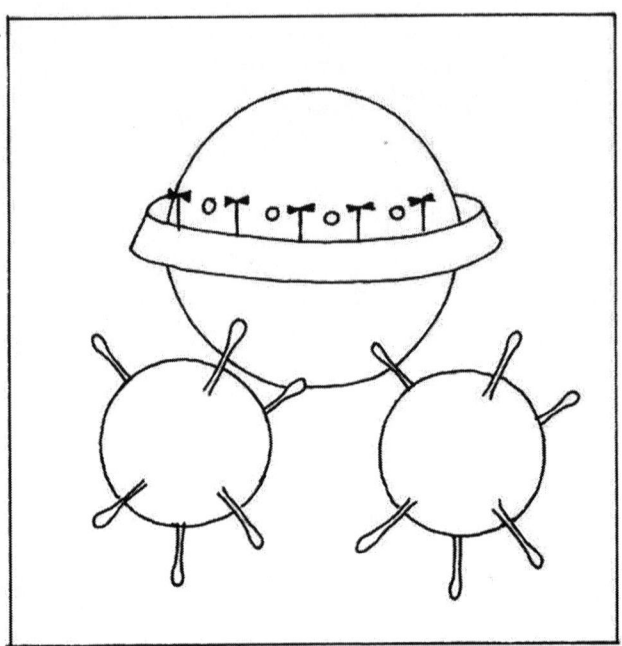

Fig 57. The dark grey spherical object reported by Robert Taylor in Dechmont Woods on 9 November 1979 and the two mine-like devices that it later emitted. Around the larger object's equator was a downward-slanting flange surmounted by a set of rods and blades. Just above the equator was a series of darker markings that may have been optical sensors. [Keatman and Collins 1979 p 5]

On a routine inspection, having left his truck nearby, Taylor walked along a fire path towards a grass clearing in Dechmont Woods, Livingston, west of Edinburgh. There, as he later reported to his boss, Malcolm Drummond, the police and investigators, he was surprised to encounter a dark grey spherical object, about seven metres in diameter. Around the equator of the sphere was a downward-slanting flange surmounted by a set of rods and blades as indicated in Fig 57. Just above the equator were a series of darker markings that may have been optical sensors.

Taylor reported that parts of the spherical object then began to fade allowing background to show through. Then the forester was startled to see two smaller mine-like devices, each about 76 cm in diameter and projecting six 45 cm spikes at right angles to each other (shown correctly in Fig 56 and incorrectly in Fig 57) hurl towards him from the object. The mine-like devices appeared to roll with one spike at a time in contact with the ground. Each ground contact was accompanied by a thud, suggesting heavy weight.

The mine-like spheres approached Taylor and began to tug his trousers. He was overpowered by a heavy odour and became unconscious for a short time.

Taylor next recalls lying face down in the mud. He tried to talk to his dog, Lara, an Irish setter, but couldn't speak. Neither could he walk, so he crawled back to his truck and tried to radio his boss, Drummond, and, although he made contact he still couldn't speak.

Robert Taylor tried to drive back to his house, but lost control of the vehicle and had to walk. When he reached his house, still in a state of shock, his wife telephoned Drummond and the local doctor. Both rushed to Taylor's house. The doctor found that he was suffering from a headache and minor injuries only.

While Taylor received medical attention, Drummond alerted the local police. Within the course of the day a police team documented and photographed abundant trace evidence in the form of depressions in the grass apparently left by the objects.

In the absence of a government-funded scientific investigation, a private UK UFO research group moved into action.[9,10] They obtained full cooperation from Taylor, Drummond, local police superintendent David Scott and his officers, and Lester Knibb of the police forensic laboratories at Edinburgh (whose team studied Taylor's torn trousers). Starting their own site investigations on 15 November, the investigators cleared new snow that had helped preserve the indentations, made sketches and took photographs of the indentations (Figs 58, 59, 60).

The two kinds of depression left in the grass – twin rows each of about eight rectangular depressions and horseshoe indentations – corresponded to Taylor's account and the results of the police investigations.

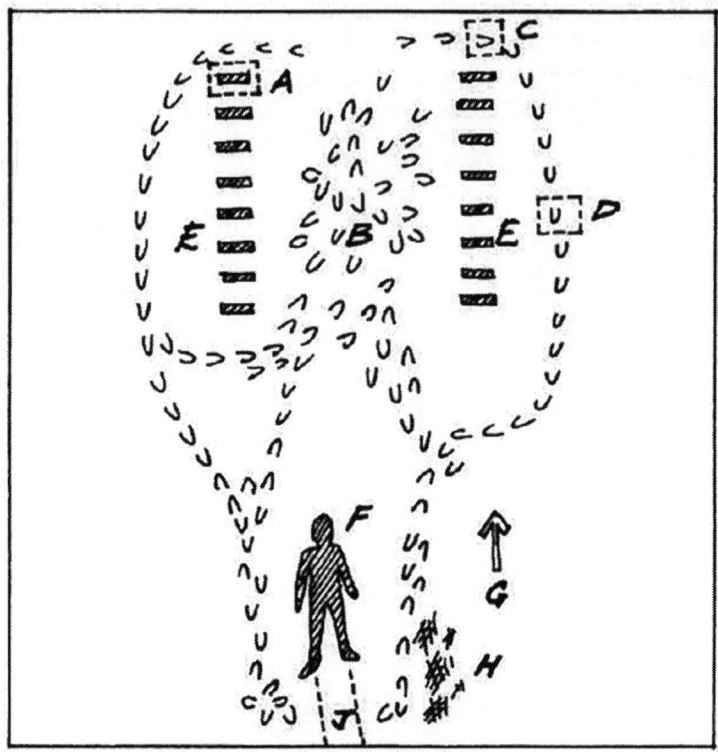

Figure 5: The traces left behind.
Key: A. Depression sample from here.
B. Indentations facing in every direction.
C. Indentation sample taken here.
D. Turf sample taken here.
E. Lines of rectangular depressions.
F. Bob Taylor regained consciousness here.
G. Direction Bob viewed the object.
H. Unidentifiable gashes and scuff marks.
J. "Drag" marks stated to have been seen here.

Fig 58. Self-explanatory diagram by private investigators based on their measurements on 15 November 1979 following their removal of snow that had preserved these traces at the Dechmont Woods site of Robert Taylor's 9 November encounter. [Keatman and Collins 1979 p 6]

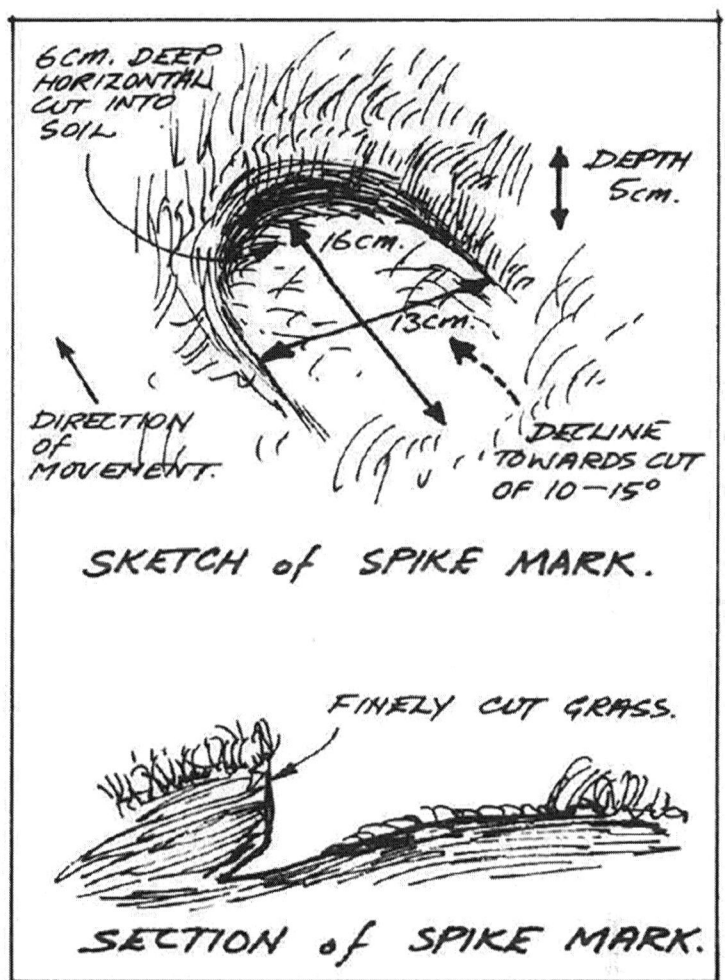

Fig 59. Investigators' detailed sketch of one of the horseshoe imprints at the Dechmont Woods site shown in Fig 58 and apparently left by the 'spikes' of the two mine-like devices shown in Fig 57. [Keatman and Collins 1980 p 26]

One of the large track marks.

Fig 60. Photograph by private investigators of one of the lines of rectangular depressions at the Dechmont Woods site labeled 'E' in Fig 58. [Keatman and Collins 1980 p 26]

The rectangular depressions could represent the indentations left by the landing gear of the heavy large spherical device and the horseshoe marks those by the 'spikes' of the two mine-like devices.

The pattern of indentations apparently left by the landing gear of the large spherical device suggests that it was designed to resist destabilising forces when resting on a space object with a weathered or soil covered surface and significant gravity. Such a design compares with the zigzag grooves in the tires of NASA's Mars Curiosity Rover (Fig 36). The sectional view of one horseshoe mark (Fig 59) suggests a complex design that could have enabled the mine-like devices to use their weight to exert tractional force when resting on such an object.

But what may have been the purpose of the assault on Robert Taylor at Livingston? If the two French events discussed above can be interpreted as the operations of small generalist surveillance discs, attracted by the activities of the two witnesses, perhaps the 1979 Scottish event can be understood as the actions of a specialist ET device, that had hidden in the forest clearing in a project to study local biological activity. Indeed according to Taylor, his dog Lara had been pursuing similar enquiries in that patch of forest just before Taylor's own encounter.

Once again NASA's Curiosity Rover may give us a clue. Recall that Curiosity looks at Martian rocks and (in autonomous mode), if they pass certain criteria, zaps them with laser beams to see what they are made of. It then radios the information to NASA Mars orbiters that transmit the data to Earth for human interpretation.

We can speculate that the Livingston device first looked at potential biological local targets with its optical sensors. If the targets met certain criteria, the device may have commanded its mobile bots to retrieve them, sedate them and place them on its flange for testing. The device may later have sent the resulting data to a nearby mother probe for interpretation.

The surgical nature of the equipment, including rods and blades, displayed around the equator of the large device (Fig 57) suggests that living biological targets would not survive the testing procedure. Fortunately for Taylor, although sedated and dragged some inches, he was not pulled all the way to the large device, perhaps because he weighed much more than the device's normal biological targets.

Endnotes

1 Velasco 1990, p.39–40.
2 CNES 1983a, p.23.
3 CNES 1983b, p.170.
4 CNES 1983a, p.1–66.
5 Velasco 1990.
6 Bounias 1990, p.17.
7 Petit and Lebrun 1986.
8 CNES 1983b.
9 Keatman and Collins 1979, p.5.
10 Keatman and Collins 1980, p.26.

14

The Dalnegorsk Events

To prove beyond doubt that ET surveillance devices have carried out missions in the Earth's atmosphere, we need a scientific study of the remains of an ET probe. James McDonald understood this well. For he said, "Despite stories to the contrary" – perhaps he'd heard rumours about the alleged Roswell crash – "there seem to be no crashed UFOs." This "can be whimsically explained away," McDonald told scientists at an Astronautics Symposium organised by the Canadian Aeronautics and Space Institute in Montreal on 12 March 1968, "by asserting that 'they' seem to have attained 'zero defects'".[1]

The period during which there was no hard scientific evidence for the remains of an ET probe ended in the summer of 1988. Scientists at Tomsk Polytechnical University (TPU) then began to study remarkable fragments from the Height 611 event of 29 January 1986 collected by Dalnegorsk school biology teacher Valery Dvuzhilni (Chapter 1). So challenging were these remains that the TPU scientists abandoned their current projects and turned their full attention to the exciting new material. As the 2012 display of some of the Height 611 remains at the National Atomic Testing Museum in Las Vegas stated, many academic centres and research institutes subsequently studied the material.

Scientists immediately ask why, after so much attention by many teams of technical experts, there are no papers on the research in the peer-reviewed science literature. The short answer given in Chapter 1 was "the scientists' UFO taboo". But rather than the global taboo, that was largely shaped by military decision makers in the USA, what likely prevented open publication of the Height 611 studies was the particular version of the taboo that operated in the Soviet Union and then Russia in the late 1980s and early 1990s with the connivance of the KGB and its successors.

It could have worked out differently.

For the Soviet Union soon disappeared and in the mid-1990s a window of opportunity for the scientific development of ET probe theory opened up in the USA. Laurance Rockefeller, a man with high-level political contacts and billions of dollars, got together with Peter Sturrock, then Director of the Center for Space Science and Astrophysics at Stanford University, with the aim of reawakening scientific interest in 'the UFO problem'. Like James McDonald, Sturrock had carefully read the Condon Report and, like McDonald, had concluded that the body of the Report – as opposed to the Executive Summary – suggested that something was going on that ought to be investigated by scientists.

Both Sturrock and Rockefeller agreed that physical evidence for UFOs was the kind most likely to convince sceptical scientists that a major scientific challenge truly existed. The pair therefore organised a meeting focusing on such evidence, which was eventually held in 1997, starting in New York and continuing, after a break, in San Francisco.[2]

By this time Russian and Ukrainian scientists had completed substantial studies of the Height 611 remains. So at the very time when solid scientific evidence for a possible ET probe was first available, the director of a prestigious American space science institute was organising a meeting focusing on physical evidence of anomalous activity. Here by serendipity was a huge opportunity to advance science. Theoretically it should have been possible to bring to the US five or six of the Russian and Ukrainian academics, with translators, and their papers could have been presented at the Sturrock meeting.

The effect could have been shattering. Imagine six professors, each with some standing in his or her field, each from a different academic institute, delivering technical papers on their teams' analyses of one aspect of the Dalnegorsk high-temperature event of 29 January 1986. Some papers would have focused on the nature of the remains themselves and others on the event's geological and geophysical context and its environmental effects. Each paper would have left open the possibility that the event represented the disintegration of an ET probe.

They would have stolen the show. The nine Sturrock panelists would have been suitably impressed, the UFO taboo might have subsequently disintegrated and ET probe theory might now be the hottest area in science.

But it didn't work out that way.

Rockefeller money was indeed used to bring Russians with some knowledge of the Dalnegorsk material to the USA. But instead of bringing those six accredited experts, it brought the talkative former school teacher Valery Dvuzhilni, one scientist and one politician.[3]

With Dvuzhilni's lack of a relevant scientific track record and his links with pseudoscience, it's no surprise that Peter Sturrock decided not to refer to the Height 611 evidence at his 1997 meeting. That may have been precisely the outcome that Russian intelligence agents had worked for.

Having said that, it's important to stress that Valery Dvuzhilni is a sincere researcher who has done his best to do good science and if he hadn't investigated the site of the 1986 high-temperature event and hadn't brought the Height 611 material to the attention of the TPU researchers in 1988, there may have been no academic studies of the Height 611 material at all.

So how did it all start? Here's one account of the original event.[4] On 29 January 1986, at about 1955 local time, many people in Dalnegorsk witnessed a remarkable event. Some were students. One of them, Eugene Serebrov, then a fifth-grade school student who later became a candidate in physical and mathematical sciences, recalled, "The ball was flying parallel to the ground, rising and falling several times."

Another, Sergei Olkhovoy, reported, "I saw a ball of red. There was no sound, no sparks or smoke trail. It flew in a straight line, without any twists. I ran to Sasha Sinitsky's house. When he came to the door, we saw how the ball fell and hit the top of the mountain. There was a flash. Then there was long burning."

Sergei's mother also came out to see what was happening. According to Valery Dvuzhilni's report on the incident, she reported that something was burning on the hill for over an hour.

Another witness was V.M. Korytko, editor of the regional newspaper, *Labour Word*. He was in the hills at the time.

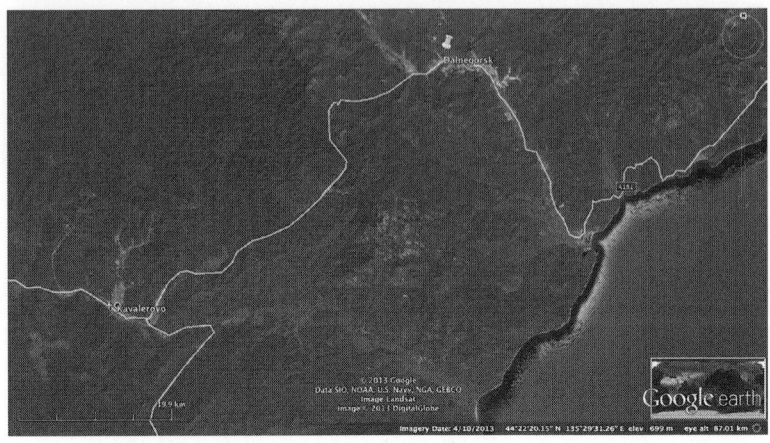

Fig 61. The Dalnegorsk settlements in the Rudnaya river valley, Russia. The A181 road from the regional centre of Kavalerovo enters the Rudnaya valley near Dalnegorsk and follows it southeastwards to the port of Rudnaya Pristan. Place marker indicates the approximate location of the 29 January 1986 high-temperature event near Height 611.

Fig 62. View of the Dalnegorsk settlements from the south. To the right of centre are the opencast workings of the 24-hour boron mining operation. Place marker indicates approximate location of the high-temperature event of 29 January 1986 near Height 611.

"I saw something fall on a rock. There was a dull thud, not booming, but fairly strong. It lasted a split second. There was a flash – large white-red flames. It seemed there was something badly on fire. All this I watched for about five minutes. It burned for one to two minutes and then stopped."

Julia Krichnina saw the ball fly, but did not see it fall. "I saw the flying yellow ball. The shape and colour did not change. There were no sparks or sounds. Behind the ball was a yellow-white ray, similar to a flashlight beam. Close to the ball the ray was darker, of uniform thickness."

Mechanic Vladimir Kondakov was at the bus station. "The ball was flying low and it seemed that it would hit part of the Dalpolimetall factory chimney. It was round with no protrusions or indentations. It seemed to be made of metal and the colour looked a little like red-hot stainless steel. I thought that it was a military missile. I did not hear any noise. I saw it fall. At this point it burned the earth."

As author Michael Gerstein pointed out,[5] the witnesses' descriptions varied. Estimates of duration of burning on the hill varied from one minute to one hour. There was even a report that it burned "deep into the night". Some witnesses described the object 'bouncing' on the hill, up to six times. Some reported the object burned in one locality on the hill, others claimed two.

On 2 February, Sergei Olkhovoy's father, Gennady, his sister, Catherine Yassin, and several students organised an expedition to the place where the ball was seen to fall, the peak known from its height in metres as Height 611. They found a charred stump, a shallow notch in a tree and broken fragments of branches, but no major parts of the object.

They did however find fused droplets of a substance that had a metallic sheen, blackened stones and pieces of the stump. They took this treasure to the local lore club, run by Valery Dvuzhilni, a biology teacher at a local school.

The boys tested the metal drops with a couple of different acids, but there was no reaction. So they sought the advice of the geologist V. V. Berliozov, one of the oldest scientific professionals in Dalnegorsk.

Berliozov had participated in the 1947 expedition to locate the site where a massive iron meteorite had fallen in the Sikhote-Alin Mountains in eastern Siberia.

Berliozov said that he could make no judgment on what the boys had found. "It requires the attention of authoritative experts," Berliozov said.[6]

But the authoritative experts did not appear immediately. And Valery Dvuzhilni had already started investigations of his own. He climbed to the site with the school children and some colleagues. The slope was covered with about sixty centimeters of snow, apart from the small area of ledge, about three by three metres in size, where the children had found the remains. On the ledge, Dvuzhilni and his friends found scattered fragments of the local rock, together with some silver droplets of solidified metal, later identified as lead-based. He found some of the rock fragments had apparently been magnetised enough to deflect a compass needle. Some of the rock fragments were cracked and some had been turned coal-black.

At the site Dvuzhilni noticed a sharp smell "of something chemical" that, with his scientific knowledge he later interpreted as a smell caused by the dry sublimation of wood products. The smell appeared to have its origin in the charred stump, which, from its roots, he identified as the remains of a Korean Pine. Dvuzhilni was astonished to discover streaks of black glassy material on the remains of the stump facing the southwest, as if it was dripping with black oil. It appeared that the wood on that side of the pine had melted rather than burned. Dvuzhilni observed that the wood on the other side had no signs of heat damage.

A small distance away from the charred stump of Korean Pine, Dvuzhilni noticed that a rhododendron bush had been badly affected by the event. The bark had cracked and large fragments of its branches were hanging down. Later examination of a branch cross-section showed that one side of the rhododendron branch had been blackened, evidently by radiation from the event (Fig 63).

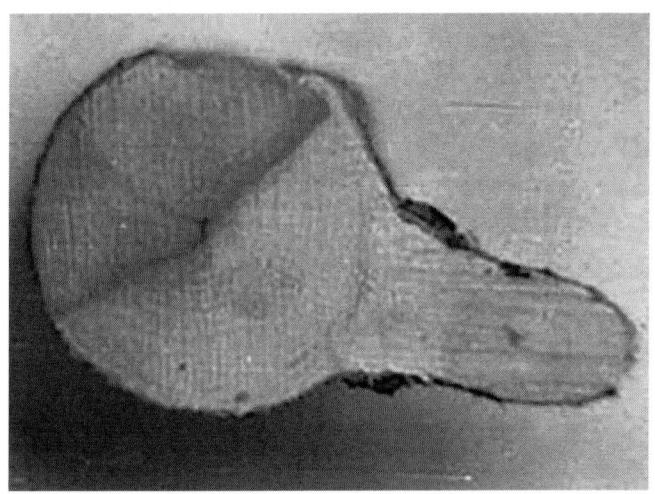

Fig 63. Dark band in rhododendron branch near Height 611 attests dead tissue resulting from unknown radiation during high-temperature event of 29 January 1986.[http://www.74rif.ru/nlo.files/177866.jpg.] [Google Translate of interview with Valery Dvuzhilni by Natalya Ostrovskaya of "Komsomolskaya Pravda' in 2006, http://www.74rif.ru/nlo-dv.html]

Altogether Dvuzhilni and his friends found at the Height 611 site about thirty grammes of solidified metallic drops of dark colour. Most were small – from 0.5 to 2.0 mm in diameter – but others were larger – 3 to 5 mm.

Dvuzhilni approached the laboratories of the two mining operations, Bor and Dalpolimetall, based in the town. Bor was concerned with opencast mining of the large borosilicate deposit exposed near the town (Fig 62) and Dalpolimetall was involved with the recovery of lead and zinc by underground mining of metal sulphides from nearby skarn deposits.

Analysis by the two laboratories showed that the smaller drops, one to two millimetres in diameter, recovered from the Height 611 site were lead-based and contained up to seventeen elements, including zirconium, lanthanum and yttrium. The analysts found up to two per cent of praseodymium in one of the drops.

Each analysed drop seemed to have a different composition, as if it had been produced during the event. It was rather as if a television had exploded, producing droplets of different composition.

The larger balls were iron-based, and included chromium, nickel and aluminium. Typically very hard, they could only be cut with diamond tools.

No further analytical work on the Dalnegorsk material seems to have been done for some time. But residents of the town witnessed further anomalous events.

First, at about 2030 on 6 February 1986, eight days after the first event, two yellow balls were seen to fly over the town from northeast to south. They reportedly completed four laps around Height 611 and then disappeared at high speed.

Then, the following year, between 2200 and 2330 hours on Saturday 28 November 1987, according to Valery Dvuzhilni and his co-investigator, N.L. Nikolaev, the people of Dalnegorsk and other settlements in the area – such as Kavalerova and Rudnayaa Pristan – witnessed one of the largest and most spectacular anomalous events in history. A very large number of people reported seeing these objects, some of which were huge (Figs 66, 67, 68). Dvuzhilni and Nikolaev interviewed more than one hundred of these witnesses and together compiled a report.[7]

Reported meteorological data show that it was a clear night in the area, with a light wind of around seven metres per second from the northwest. I checked from *Stellarium* that the moon that night was then near first quarter and would have been low in the east, probably providing enough light both for the putative anomalous objects to 'see' what they were doing and for the witnesses to see what the objects were doing. The Dalnegorsk town lighting would have also illuminated the scene.

Here are a few highlights of the 28 November 1987 events as quoted from the report by Dvuzhilni and Nikolaev.

At 2230 that Saturday evening, a Department Chief at the Bor mining operation, who had once been a pilot, saw a very large anomalous object. "I noticed a bright glow in the window" this official said, "and then drifting slowly, about 300 metres above the ground, was a large cigar-shaped object with yellow portholes in the middle, behind which

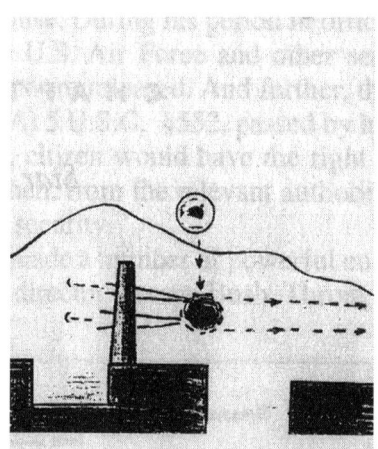

Fig 64. Artist's impression of manouevres allegedly carried out by a bright ball witnessed at Dalnegorsk on the night of 28 November 1987. The ball descends vertically, shines two beams onto a factory chimney and then moves off laterally. [Hesemann 1998, p 301]

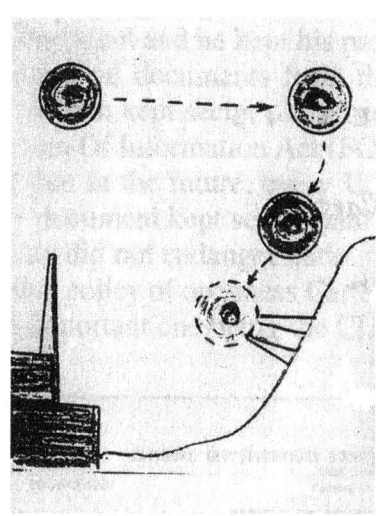

Fig 65. Artist's impression of event reported by Police Sergeant N Kotov in Dalnegorsk at about 2240 on 28 November 1987. Sergeant Kotov reported that a bright ball, its centre brighter than the outer shell, descended over the mountains near Height 611, moving in a stepwise fashion. He then saw the ball shine two beams onto the mountain. [Hesemann 1998, p 301]

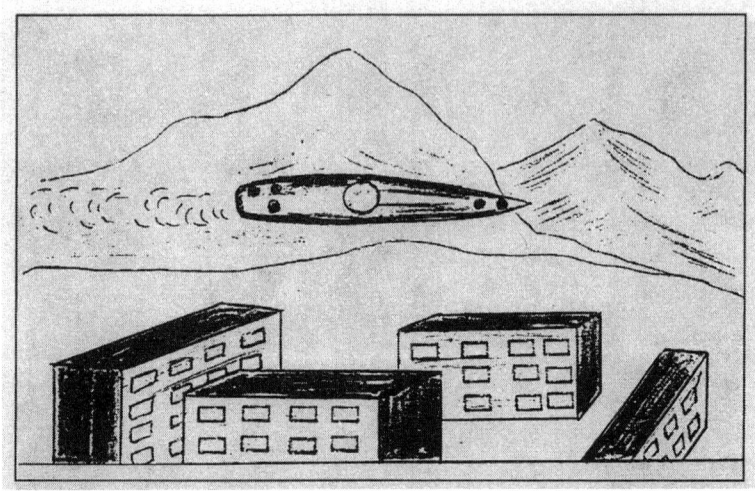

Fig 66. Artist's impression of a large object reported by witnesses in Dalnegorsk between 2200 and 2330 local time on 28 November 1987. The artist shows a streamlined vehicle with docking ports on its starboard side for six smaller devices, one much larger than the others.

The vehicle could be interpreted as a probe carrier designed for high-speed operation in planetary atmospheres, hydrospheres, other viscous fluids or even the interstellar medium. The small ports might be docks for small surveillance or prospecting bots. The larger port might accommodate a surveillance disc. [Hesemann 1998, p 300]

was a bright vapour trail." The official continued, "I felt like a Stone Age man witnessing a locomotive. As a former pilot, I'm familiar with aerodynamic theory. But this object flew silently, without wings or engine."

At about the same time, kindergarten teacher T.J. Markina saw a bright ball flying at the height of an eight- or nine-storey building. "The ball was surrounded by a less bright shell," Markina said. "In front of the ball was a silently moving object of metallic colour with four square windows through which shone a yellow light."

According to Markina, the ball stopped over School No. 27. It emitted a blue-violet ray, about fifty centimetres in diameter, which shone towards the ground and lasted for about two seconds. But the

Fig 67. Artist's impression of a 'huge black cylindrical object' that operatives on a night shift at the Dalnegorsk opencast boron workings claimed to have seen at around 2300 local time on 28 November 1987. The frightened witnesses claimed that after approaching the opencast workings, its front part 'shining like burnt metal', the object flew silently eastwards along the valley towards the port of Rudnaya Pristan. [Hesemann 1998, p 300]

Fig 68. Artist's impression of a scene reported by witnesses on ships in the port of Rudnaya Pristan, between 2200 and 2330 local time on 28 November 1987. A large teardrop-shaped vehicle directs a 'searchlight beam' down towards the settlement, while six smaller devices cluster around it. [Hesemann 1998, p 300]

objects it illuminated gave no shadows. The ball then moved towards the TV tower on the mountain near the Height 611 'crash' site. "It emitted a beam of reddish light, illuminating the middle of the mountain, as if looking for something. Then it disappeared."

At about 2240 Police Sergeant N. Kotov described what might have been the same object. He was in a fifth floor Dalnegorsk apartment belonging to a friend's son. The son first noticed a bright ball slowly descending over the mountain. It moved in a stepwise fashion. Its centre was brighter than the outer shell. It circled the hill and stopped. Then, like a searchlight, it shone two beams of light onto the hill.

These beams weren't all harmless, apparently. Reportedly, one beam struck a man standing at the bus stop in Dalnegorsk. He was badly affected, with local swelling.

At 2300 D.I. Bystryantsev was operating an excavator at the Dalnegorsk opencast borosilicate mine, Top of the Day. He said "The time was about 11 pm. I saw a huge black cylindrical object flying directly towards the quarry (Fig 67). Its front part shone like burnt metal. It flew towards Rudnaya Pristan [the port of Dalnegorsk], its height declining slightly. I quit my job and jumped from the excavator. We were terrified. What if this object fell on us? But it passed over our heads at a height of about 700 metres. Technology Chief Anokhin estimated its light output at 3.4 lux. It was about 25 metres long – as high as a 130-apartment building. We heard no noise."

The crews of two ships at the port of Rudnaya Pristan did indeed report objects of this kind around this time. Crews reported one object at a height of about 500 metres, which apparently deployed a 'searchlight' that lit up the whole settlement at once (Fig 68).

People in Dalnegorsk reported widespread electromagnetic effects at the time when the anomalous objects were seen. There was interference with TV and radio reception, telephone communication was disrupted, as were computers and ventilation equipment in underground mines. There were even reports that some objects were tracked on radar, and Soviet fighters mobilised.

Could there be a prosaic explanation for these spectacular 28 November 1987 Dalnegorsk events? Nobody has correlated the timing of the display with that of a space spectacular, such as the Cosmos 2355 disintegration that, thanks to the work of Ted Molczan, Jim Oberg and his colleagues, we now know to have been the stimulus for the reported 11 December 1996 'Giant Yukon UFO'.[8] In any case, such a stimulus could not account for the relatively close-up eyewitness reports of objects moving in the Dalnegorsk valley against a background of mountains (Fig 66), the reported electromagnetic effects or the objects' emission of strange 'beams' without shadows.

The Far Eastern Branch of the KGB came up with a prosaic explanation of a kind – weather conditions. Like Hector Quintanilla's "refraction of Capella", this obviously wasn't a genuine attempt to explain hundreds of eyewitness reports, but an attempt to divert serious technical attention from those reports. Soviet military authorities could no more afford to acknowledge loss of control of their airspace than their US opposite numbers.

So scientists should consider the possibility that the artists' impressions in Figs 66-68 represent honest attempts to illustrate the anomalous events described by hundreds of witnesses on 28 November 1987 and linked with widespread electromagnetic effects. And inasmuch as the 'search beams' reportedly directed towards the Height 611 site on that date (Fig 65) link the 1987 events both with the high-temperature event of 29 January 1986 and the 'search beams' reportedly directed at Height 611 on 6 February 1986, we can put all three Dalnegorsk events together in one mental box, linked by one provisional narrative.

The key concepts underlying that narrative may already have popped up in some readers' minds. Like Brazil's Amazon provinces with their accessible placer deposits of gold and tin, the equally remote and unpopulated Russian Far East is rich in hi-tech metal deposits that might interest ET. So the remains from the 29 January 1986 Dalnegorsk high-temperature event, rich in lead and other hi-tech metals like REEs (Rare Earth Elements), could be those of a prospecting bot. And the small beaming objects of 28 November 1987 (Figs 64 and 65) could have been similar prospecting bots. These small near-spherical beam-emitting objects differed in appearance from the small cylindrical objects observed emitting beams in Brazil but, like those of the Brazilian objects, their beams may have been intended to identify metals of interest.

And perhaps not only identify metals but actually collect samples from ore bodies or tailings dumps. Obviously laser-like beams, like those of NASA's Curiosity Rover, couldn't do that. But thicker, plasma-like beams, in principle, could. Convert some of the target material into plasma, transport it 'upbeam' and then convert it into small spheres. In Chapter 12 we discussed a spectacular photograph, captured by Ellen Crystall at Pine Bush, New York, on 18 July 1980 (Colour Plate 7), which appears to show small plasma packets travelling long distances 'upbeam' within 1/60 second. Given an understanding of physical principles not yet known to humans and aeons of technical evolution, ET prospecting bots could perhaps have used exotic plasma-type beams to collect surface samples from earthlike planets with appropriate atmospheres.

Recall witness Julia Krichnina's description of the original Height 611 object emitting a beam on 29 January 1986. "Behind the ball was a yellow-white ray, similar to a flashlight beam. Close to the ball the ray was darker, of uniform thickness." Her description compares in some respects with Crystall's Pine Bush beam. Recall also witness T.J. Markina's report of another possible Dalnegorsk example of this kind of beam on 28 November 1987. She reported that a bright ball surrounded by a less bright shell emitted a blue-violet ray, about fifty centimetres in diameter, and that the ground objects, which the beam illuminated, gave no shadows. According to Markina, the ball then moved towards the Height 611 site and directed a beam of reddish light towards the mountain.

Blue-violet or 'electric blue' from ionised nitrogen is a classic air plasma colour, generated by ionising radiation or ground discharge (Colour Plate 6). Therefore, it is possible that, like the original Height 611 29 January 1986 object seen by Julia Krichnina, the 1987 object seen by T.J. Markina was a prospecting bot which used such beams to collect samples of interest.

So although the small near-spherical Dalnegorsk objects differed in appearance from the small cylindrical objects reported in Brazil (Chapter 7), they might all have been prospecting bots, typically deployed in the first phase of a von Neumann-type operation. And the style of movement of the Dalnegorsk objects suggests common features of propulsion and navigation with their Brazilian counterparts. For example, the step-wise movements of spherical objects observed at Dalnegorsk in 1987 (Figs 64, 65) recall the 'dancing' of the conical-cylindrical object observed by Dr Carvalho at Colares in 1977 (Fig 30).

In the 'von Neumann interpretation' of the 1977/78 Brazilian events offered in Chapter 7, I tentatively suggested that the large objects with rounded ends and 'white windows' photographed by Colonel Hollanda's Brazilian Air Force team (Fig 34) might have been mineral processing vehicles intended to transport newly mined planetary gold placer material to giant tubelike mother probes for processing. At Dalnegorsk on 28 November 1987, the large cylindrical object with rounded ends and what may have been panels along its length witnessed by night shift workers at the opencast borosilicate workings (Fig 67) could have been a similar transport and processing vehicle.

So we can provisionally interpret the large group of anomalous objects witnessed at Dalneorgsk on 28 November 1987 as a possible set of 'von Neumann vehicles' comparable in some ways with the objects studied by Colonel Hollanda's Brazilian Air Force team in 1977-8. But if the Brazilian vehicles were searching for gold placers, what were the Dalnegorsk vehicles looking for?

"The remains of the device that disintegrated in the 29 January 1986 Height 611 high-temperature event is the obvious answer. Apparently not only Valery Dvuzhilni, but also some of the academic scientists that he mobilised took this idea seriously.

But why should ET want to retrieve remains of such a small device?

"To understand what went wrong" is one possibility.

"To prevent humans from studying the remains and learning ET's technical secrets" is another more cogent reason and one that several Russian scientists seem to have taken seriously. If such a search-and-recovery operation was indeed attempted, it could have been partially successful. Some remains may have been removed from the Height 611 area with the aid of exotic beams or other means.

Now the notion of preventing your galactic rivals from understanding and copying your propulsion technology is one that science fiction writers have almost worked to death. But that doesn't mean that scientists should exclude it when considering possible interpretations of the Dalnegorsk events.

In fact if you take seriously the notion that ET interpretation units – perhaps components of postbiological minds physically based in roaming giant tube-like mother probes – have processed data retrieved by surveillance and prospecting bots, the possibility of such a search-and-recovery operation in Dalnegorsk in 1987 immediately gains plausibility.

Let's imagine the kind of picture of advancing human technology that the decision-making parts of these postbiological minds, informed by the interpretation units, may have gained by the mid-1980s. During the four decades since Air Vice Marshal William Coryton of No.5 Group, RAF, expressed his concern about a giant anomalous object lurking close to his bombing operations at Torino in 1942 (Chapter 5), ET interpretation units would likely have processed data collected by surveillance bots to paint a portrait of exploding human technology. We have no idea how much 'understanding' of the driving factors behind human technological advance – such as silicon chips – the interpretation units might have acquired. Given the apparent efforts of a beaming surveillance device to identify a thermonuclear warhead in the 1984 Whiteman AFB incident (Chapter 11), it would be logical for ET to have also captured samples of critical human technology, have their bots study them at leisure and thereby acquire some in-depth understanding.

But whether or not that has happened, the overall picture pondered by the ET decision-making units in the mid-1980s would have been one of rapidly advancing and potentially threatening human technology. Indeed, the potentially threatening nature of human technology, including thermonuclear weapons and their delivery systems, may be one of the chief reasons why ET surveillance operations have been maintained here since World War II.

How could human technology, even space-going missiles with thermonuclear warheads, possibly threaten ET? If UFOlogists like the late Stanton Friedman were right, and reports such as the 1961 Indian

Head, New Hampshire account, were sparked by spaceships piloted by little humanoids from the Zeta Reticuli system forty light years away, it's indeed difficult to see how we could possibly threaten such distant ET strongholds. But if Steven Dick is right and roaming postbiological ET minds operating under the aegis of his Intelligence Principle are "closer than we think" (Chapter 2), the position is different.

Let's posit that such postbiological minds based in giant tubes operate in a region within, say, a thousand light years of Earth. Within this volume, the tubes may have wandered freely for thousands or even millions of years, moving from one resource or object of interest to another like desert nomads moving from waterhole to waterhole.

Now, so the postbiological decision-making units might conclude after considering the interpretation units' analysis of the post-World War II surveillance bot data, the lightning-like explosion of technology on Sol c, particularly the appearance of space-going missiles with thermonuclear warheads, could threaten this long-established way of life. For all the postbiologicals would know, the ICBMs at Minot, and the thermonuclear warheads at Kirtland and Whiteman, may have been constructed with their own bases, the giant tubes, in mind as potential targets.

For the moment, the tubes' rapid-exit abilities and the Sol c biologicals' need to propel their thermonuclear warheads with slow chemical rockets meant the local postbiologicals were reasonably safe. But what if humans were to study remains of failed ET devices such as the Height 611 bot and learn to propel thermonuclear warheads with propulsion systems that could achieve accelerations of at least 449 g, as at Minot AFB in 1968 (Chapter 5)? Soon, the postbiological decision-makers might fear, the whole postbiological system of freely roaming giant tubes might be at risk. With the humans' warlike record, the atomic bombs of Hiroshima and Nagasaki, the thousands of thermonuclear warheads by the 1980s, ever advancing chip-based missile guidance and AI capabilities and, now, human science teams learning ET propulsion secrets from the remains of the Height 611 bot, the outlook for ET in this part of the galaxy could be grim.

So the local postbiologicals may have decided to act:

"We've received a self-destruct signal from prospecting bot SL 537 on Sol c. Eight Sol c rotations later, messages from bots SL 243 and SL 244 confirmed self-destruction of SL 537 but with some remains still in the area.

"This is our first loss on Sol c. We'll collect relevant information from the area including, if possible, remains of SL 537 to understand what went wrong and prevent the Sol c biologicals from studying the remains.

"So Mind 324, now at communications sweet spot Sol a [550 AU from Sol] will travel to Sol c and organise a search-and-retrieval mission."

Readers may laugh at my attempt to fictionalise the interpretation, but the three successive Dalnegorsk events in 1986 and 1987 do suggest a science fiction style scenario of this kind. The eight-day time gap between the high-temperature disintegration of an object near Height 611 on 29 January 1986 and the reported Height 611 reconnaissance by two apparently similar objects on 6 February 1986 invites interpretation as the time taken for two Earth-based prospecting bots to travel to Height 611 after receiving a speed-of-light distress signal from the failed bot. The 22-month time gap between the high-temperature event of 29 January 1986 and the putative 'search and recovery' operation of 28 November 1987 invites interpretation as the time taken for a giant mother probe, containing the physical substrate of a postbiological mind and a set of 'von Neumann vehicles', to travel to Earth after receiving the same or a similar signal.

If we guesstimate the mother probe's speed at a modest 0.01c (3,000 kilometres per second), it would have been about 1200 AU from the Earth when it set out for our planet. That's within one of the outer Solar System's radio communications 'sweet spots' (beyond 550 AU from the sun) that, according to Italian SETI expert Claudio Maccone, may be present as a result of gravitational lensing by the Sun.[9]

Endnotes

1 McDonald 1968a.

2 Sturrock 1999.

3 Google Translate from: http://anomalia.kulichki.ru/text6/176.htm Downloaded 25 November 2012.

4 Google Translate from: http://real-ufo.ru/articles_about_ufos/447-krushenie-nlo-v-dalnegorske.html Downloaded 12 Feb 2012.

5 Google Translate from: http://www.smoliy.ru/lib/000/003/00000302/gershtain_nlo_i_tayni_prishelzev3.htm Downloaded 9 Feb 2012.

6 Google Translate from: http://real-ufo.ru/articles_about_ufos/447-krushenie-nlo-v-dalnegorske.html Downloaded 12 Feb 2012.

7 Google Translate from http://lib.rus.ec/b/3225/read of Librusek document authored by V.N. Salnikov, V.P. Skavinsky, M.V. Korovkin, V.V. Dvuzhilni, and S.V. Lebedeva entitled *Geological and geophysical characteristics of the place of landing of the anomalous object near Dalnegorsk*. Downloaded 17 April 2012.

8 See 29 April 2012 Above Top Secret Forum (www.abovetopsecret.com) thread Yukon UFO 'Mothership' Incident: December 11th, 1996, including discussion between Jim Oberg and myself, posting as 'Lowneck'.

9 Maccone 2011.

15

Scientists Start Work

The anomalous events of 1986 and 1987 aroused much local interest and controversy among the people of Dalnegorsk and neighbouring settlements in the Soviet Far East. However the KGB and other agents of Soviet power were anxious to quell popular interest in the events and, had nothing further happened, there would likely have been no more scientific studies of the Height 611 material.

But Valery Dvuzhilni would not let matters rest. And his wish to pursue further scientific investigations was shared by the town's senior scientist, geologist V.V. Berliozov, and the laboratory chemists on the staff of the two organisations, Bor and Dalpolimetall, that had made the first analyses of the strange material left behind after the high-temperature event of 29 January 1986.

An opportunity presented itself in April 1988. At Tomsk Polytechnical University (TPU), an inter-disciplinary conference was then held on the theme *Non-periodic fast phenomena in the environment*. This enigmatic wording was evidently designed to permit the presentation of papers on anomalies of various kinds and the Height 611 remains were certainly anomalous. So Dvuzhilni sent a package containing samples of collected material from the Height 611 event to TPU.

The TPU scientists were so intrigued by the material, which was clearly not the remains of a meteorite, that they put their other projects on hold and started research on Dvuzhilni's material immediately. Clearly the Soviet authorities would not have permitted such a study had the material been the remains of a Soviet military device.

Given the focus of the Tomsk conference on the environment surrounding anomalous events, it was important to undertake a survey of the Height 611 environment as soon as possible. So from 18 May to 25 June, 1988, a team led by Vladimir Salnikov of the "Natural and man-made electromagnetic systems" laboratory, Tomsk Branch of the Institute of Geology and Geophysics of the Academy of Sciences of the USSR, conducted a field study of the Height 611 remains in their geological and geophysical context.[1]

Salnikov was a specialist in 'plasmoids', a highly theoretical concept of discrete plasma bodies accompanied by local electromagnetic fields in the atmosphere and lithosphere. Locally generated mobile plasmas such as those studied at Hessdalen, Norway by the Ostfold College group (Chapter 4) do indeed exist and present an intriguing challenge to science. But clearly such plasmoids could not produce metallic droplets of the kind analysed by the chemists at the Bor and Dalpolimetall laboratories at Dalnegorsk in 1986.

Nevertheless, from the start Salnikov tried to interpret the remains of the Height 611 high-temperature event within his own version of this 'plasmoid' paradigm. While his motivation for this move may have owed more to politics than science, at least it allowed scientists to carry out research on the Height 611 remains without confronting the Soviet version of the UFO taboo.

Whether a plasmoid or solid, to appreciate the significance of the Height 611 object's trajectory and to understand the effects of its high-temperature disintegration on the local rocks near Height 611 required an assessment of the local geology and a geophysical survey of the site. In their subsequent 1990 report,[2] Salnikov and his colleagues set out the geological context of the event, as then understood.

Since 1990 there has been a revolution in understanding the complex geology of the Dalnegorsk region, interpretations being couched in terms of increasingly sophisticated plate tectonic theories. Interpretations have now become so refined that only a tiny number of specialists have a command of the subject. Not being one of those, all I offer here is a very simplified account.

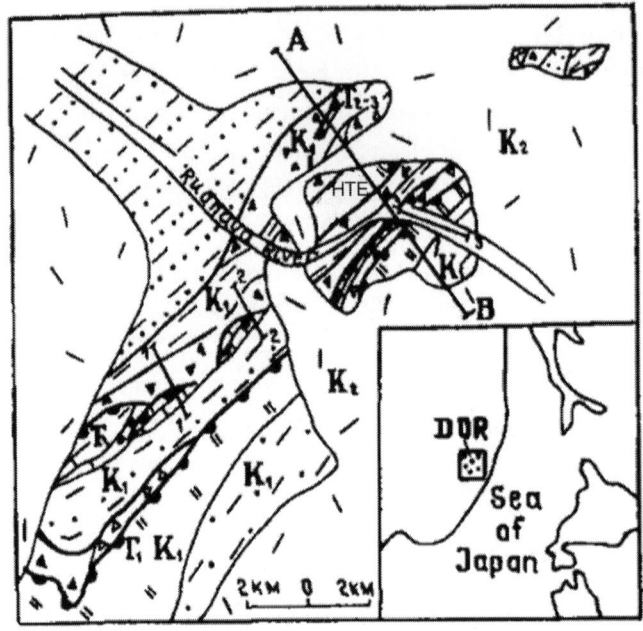

Fig 69. Sketch map of the Dalnegorsk Ore Region (DOR) illustrating the approximate location of the high-temperature event (HTE) near Height 611 on 29 January 1986 in relation to the Rudnaya river valley and various geological units. The line AB indicates the cross section shown in Fig 70. Inset shows location of the Dalnegorsk Ore Region (DOR)

K2 Late Cretaceous volcanic cover.

K1 Nazhdanka Formation (Lower Cretaceous)

T2-3 Fragmented Tetiukhe nappe (Middle-Upper Triassic)

T1-K1 Gorbusha thrust sheet packet (Lower Triassic–Lower Cretaceous)

[Original based on Parnjakov, Valerii P, Tectono-Sedimentary Complexes of the Dalnegorsk Ore Region, In : Late Paleozoic and Early Mesozoic Circum-Pacific Events: Biostratigraphy, Tectonic and Ore Deposits of Primoryie Far East Russia)

Volume 272 of International Geological Correlation Programme: IGCP project, Editor Aymon Baud, page 183-189, Université de Lausanne, 1997]

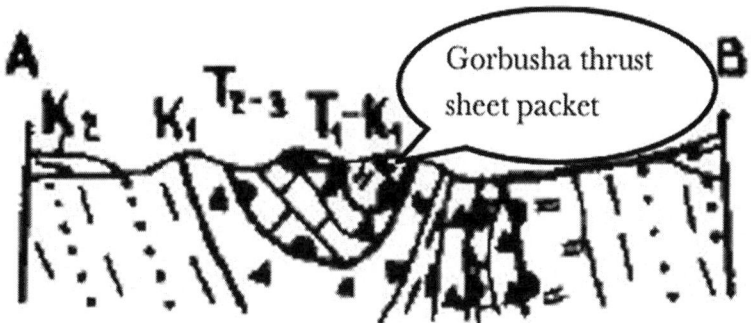

Fig 70. Schematic vertical northwest-to-southeast cross section (AB in Fig 69) through the Gorbusha thrust sheet packet and other units. The initially sub-horizontal thrust sheets have been tightly folded. The rock units are labeled as in Fig 69.

[Original based on Parnjakov, Valerii P, Tectono-Sedimentary Complexes of the Dalnegorsk Ore Region, In : Late Paleozoic and Early Mesozoic Circum-Pacific Events: Biostratigraphy, Tectonic and Ore Deposits of Primoryie (far East Russia) Volume 272 of International Geological Correlation Programme: IGCP project, Editor Aymon Baud, page 183-189, Université de Lausanne, 1997]

    Today the northward-dipping Pacific plate dives beneath the ocean floor to the south of Japan, generating earthquakes and tsunamis. Over the last three hundred million years, the Pacific plate's forbears dived beneath the North Asian continent, squeezing various rock assemblages including the steeply dipping siliceous rocks and limestone fragments of the Gorbusha thrust sheet packet (Fig 70) against older, more rigid rocks to the northwest.

    Then, after a period of erosion, there was a time of intense volcanic activity when magma rose through cracks to feed the volcanoes of the Sikhote-Alin belt. Fluids containing boron deposited the large borosilicate ore body near Dalnegorsk that at the time of the 1986 and 1987 events was being worked by opencast mining.

    Later boron-rich fluids containing lead, zinc and other metals, including small amounts of gold, silver and rare earth elements, deposited the polymetallic sulphide ore bodies worked in underground mines by

Dalpolimetall. Concentrates from these mines were transported by rail car to Rudnaya Havens for smelting, together with recycled material such as used lead batteries from the Soviet Navy.

Following the volcanism and genesis of ore bodies, a period of erosion created 'windows' exposing older rocks in the volcanic cover. As the ancestor of the Rudnaya river made its way southeastwards towards the sea, its course became perturbed locally by the northeast strike of the steeply dipping hard siliceous sedimentary rocks exposed in one of the 'windows'. Thus was created the rather unusual topography of a steep-sided S-shaped valley.

Therefore, as the 1986 object followed the short northeast-trending middle section of the S-shaped Rudnaya valley before its disintegration near Height 611, in an area where siliceous rocks of the Gorbusha thrust sheet packet are exposed, it would inevitably have been traveling in a direction closely aligned to the strike of the rock units below, including faults and folded thrusts as shown in Fig 70.[3] These were the same fractures that had guided the boron-rich mineralising fluids that may have given rise to the metallic deposits of lead and zinc together with minor amounts of gold, silver and rare earth elements.

All this opened the way for Vladimir Salnikov to theorise that the 'plasmoid' had somehow been guided by the fracture trends, had picked up metallic elements from the polluted atmosphere on its northeast directed trajectory, and had deposited these elements in the form of metallic droplets.

In this way, Vladimir Salnikov could present his 'plasmoid' explanation for the Height 611 event in a manner that appeared consistent with the local geological setting. But what about the geophysics of the Height 611 site? Another member of the Tomsk team, Victor Skavinsky, of the Institute of Geology and Geophysics, Siberian Branch of the USSR Academy of Sciences, conducted a series of geophysical surveys at the site.

These included magnetic surveys made with a proton magnetometer and measurements with a magnetic susceptibility meter. Skavinsky found magnetic anomalies at the Height 611 site in the location where droplets from the event had been found.[4]

Fig 71. The site near Height 611 where Valery Dvuzhilni and others collected material after the high-temperature event of 29 January 1986. Photograph was taken in summer showing the exposed steeply dipping siliceous rocks of the Gorbusha thrust sheet packet, the thin patches of soil and the local vegetation. The six areas outlined in white allegedly correspond to the magnetic anomalies measured in 1988 by Victor Skavinsky, of the Institute of Geology and Geophysics, Siberian Branch of the USSR Academy of Sciences.

[Widely reproduced image of uncertain origin. This particular image was downloaded from Internos's Above Top Secret (www.abovetopsecret.com) thread 'The Height 611 UFO Crash' on 31 March 2011]

Full interpretation of the magnetic anomalies near Height 611 can't be made until experts have openly published scientific papers in the normal way. What seems certain is that strongly magnetised material was found at the site, including some of the 'iron droplets', fragments of the siliceous rocks and ancient flint arrowheads. Many of these fragments were darkened, possibly by absorption of iron atoms in the vapour phase from the anomalous object as it disintegrated at very high temperatures. During the cooling that followed, ferrimagnetic and antiferromagnetic minerals, such as magnetite and pyrrhotite, formed in some of the local rocks. Such minerals evidently became magnetised as they further cooled below their Curie temperatures – in the range 300 to 600 degrees centigrade – in the presence of a very strong static magnetic field.

Because Salnikov's postulated 'plasmoids' would be accompanied by complex electromagnetic fields, all the evidence that the high-temperature disintegration of the anomalous object near Height 611 had been accompanied by an intense magnetic field could be shoehorned into the framework of plasmoid theory. With the unmentionable acronym 'UFO' replaced by the acceptable term 'plasmoid', scientific research on the Height 611 remains could continue.

And so it did. Indeed, the initial study by the Tomsk scientists sparked an explosion of scientific research at various institutes. In terms of the cost and duration of the work, the number of expert teams involved and the scientific importance of their findings, the Soviet era studies of the Height 611 remains dwarfed the efforts of Edward Condon's University of Colorado Project. That all this important work has sunk without trace is the greatest scandal in the history of science.

We've already seen one reason for this disappearance – the developments that allowed pseudoscience to enter the National Atomic Testing Museum's 'Authentic Alien Artifact' exhibit at Las Vegas in 2012. For while experts were working quietly and invisibly in their laboratories, the pseudoscientists of UFOlogy were feasting on garbled versions of the scientific studies that journalists had picked up. If the UFO taboo had already made it difficult for scientists to publish their findings in scientific journals, the promotion by some commercially minded UFOlogists of the Height 611 high-temperature event, as 'Russia's Roswell Incident' was the last straw.

Somewhere in the middle of all this was former schoolteacher Valery Dvuzhilni. As curator of the now scientifically valuable remains and with his own training as a biologist, Dvuzhilni was in a position to cooperate and exchange information with the scientific experts that he himself had mobilised. But equally, having given up teaching and set up shop as a self-employed UFOlogist (and herbalist), he came under pressure to give 'the UFO community' and, later, the local UFO tourism industry what they wanted – and that was talk about space aliens. For example, in a 2007 magazine interview,[5] Dvuzhilni interpreted the identification by scientists using a microprobe of high levels of phosphorus in the Height 611 remains as the bones of a space alien crewmember. To fit into the small Height 611 object, the alien would have had to be very small but then, as UFOlogists know, space aliens are very small.

In this dire situation, any honest attempt to extract good science from the morass of pseudoscience and garbled material can help, and in the Internet age with online translation facilities and images escaped from laboratories into the public domain, even someone with modest relevant expertise can do useful work. What follows is my own attempt to identify some of the salient findings resulting from this explosion in scientific studies of the Height 611 material.

One important clue concerning the environmental effects of the high-temperature event was the evidence that it was accompanied by an intense static magnetic field that left its legacy in the local siliceous rocks as ferrimagnetic and antiferromagnetic minerals such as magnetite and pyrrhotite, possibly newly formed as a result of diffusion of iron from the disintegrating object, cooled below their Curie temperatures. Following Victor Skavinsky's magnetic surveys, two scientists from IZMIRAN (Institute of Terrestrial Magnetism, Ionosphere and Radiowave Propagation of the Russian Academy of Sciences), V. Gernikom and E. Gorshkov, investigated samples of siliceous rocks from the Gorbusha thrust sheet packet at Height 611 that had been 'magnetised' as a result of the Dalnegorsk event.[6]

IZMIRAN is a highly regarded organisation. Its experts collaborate with scientists from NASA, the European Space Agency and other national space agencies on multidisciplinary research in areas focusing on the electrodynamic properties of plasmas in the near-Earth, solar and interplanetary environments. The fact that two of its experts devoted time to analysing the magnetic properties of these Height 611 rock samples gives weight to the reported findings that the samples recorded 'structural changes' – presumably the growth of new iron-rich minerals during the high-temperature event – and recorded a magnetic field nearly two orders of magnitude greater than the Earth's field of around 50 microteslas. Given that the samples are likely to have been at least ten metres or more away from the disintegrating object, the intensity of the magnetic field closer to the disintegrating object would have been many orders of magnitude greater than that.

If the disintegrating Height 611 object generated a powerful magnetic field, what about its electric field? To shed light on this question, experts from yet another highly regarded research institute, the E. O. Paton Electric Welding Institute, Kiev, Ukraine, became involved.[7] Engineers there would have talked with the experts who had already studied the Height 611 material and their familiarity with the physical processes involved in high-temperature plasma electric arc welding would have contributed a valuable new perspective.

The experts from the far-away Paton Institute studied how the high-energy event affected silica-rich material at Height 611, perhaps somewhat in the way that lightning strikes can create structures known as fulgurites in silica-rich soils or sands. Dvuzhilni quoted a statement from the Paton Institute concluding that the power of the object in its disintegration phase may have reached 10 to 100 million volts with a current of 100,000 amps. The power, therefore, would have been of the order of 10,000 megawatts – which, as Dvuzhilni pointed out, is twice the power output of the Krasnoyarsk hydroelectric power station. An amazing output of power and, given the high reputation of the Paton Institute, one that shows how a renewed high-quality study of the Dalnegorsk event will be of value to all scientists and engineers seeking new sources of energy.

The total energy released during the Height 611 high-temperature event of 29 January 1986 and the extent of its environmental effects would have depended on the time during which highest power output was maintained. Though intense, the environmental impact was limited in extent. For instance, the only part of the stump of the Korean Pine that melted was the part facing the southwest. So the high power output may have lasted for a very short time.

Since rather than melting, carbon sublimes at temperatures of about 4000 degrees centigrade at atmospheric pressure, the highest sublimation temperature of any element, the melting rather than sublimation of carbon in the stump is one of the many puzzles stemming from the Height 611 high-temperature event.

Slightly to the east of the stump of Korean Pine at the Height 611 site, the rhododendron bush also suffered damage, as discussed in Chapter 14. Other reported local biological effects included charred nests of ground wasps in the soil. Once again the only way forward to advance an understanding of the biological effects of the Height 611 event will be the publication of expert studies. In this specialty Valery Dvuzhilni is a genuine expert with a fund of crucial local knowledge resulting from decades of dedicated study. So let's hope that younger Russian-speaking biologists, interested in publishing a high-quality paper on the biological effects of the Dalnegorsk high-temperature event will consult Dvuzhilni in the near future.

Even more important than biological and geological materials that recorded magnetic fields, electric fields and radiation effects of the Height 611 high-temperature event, are the actual remains of the disintegrated object. In some respects, these remains resembled those created by an explosive volcanic eruption. Thus the solidified metal droplets bear some analogy to glassy solidified droplets of molten magma ejected from volcanoes. There's no doubt that parts of a very complex object melted some metres above the ground near Height 611, some mixing of melts occurred and cooling drops of the molten material rained to the ground.

After repeated searches by Dvuzhilni and his friends, the TPU team, and other investigators, many more metal droplets were found and were studied in several laboratories. The researchers also found strange translucent yellow beads and fragments of a black glassy material they called mesh (сеточка). These 'organic style' materials are so weird and their study so challenging that they deserve separate treatment in the next chapter.

Lead-containing drops ranged from 0.5 millimetres to 3.6 millimetres in size (Fig 72). Some were found sprayed on rock and fragments, others were later discovered in the soil. Intriguingly, four of the lead-based drops were not drop-shaped at all, but rather said to be 'hexagonal' in shape with sharp edges.

Clearly, although much of the lead-containing material had relatively low melting points, not all of it melted and some original structures in the anomalous object were likely preserved.

Fig 72. Metallic balls collected from the site of the 29 January 1986 high-temperature event near Height 611. Iron-containing balls, 3-6 millimetres in diameter, include a group found sintered together (top left). Lead-containing balls (bottom right) were typically smaller in size. [http://vadim-andreev.narod.ru/ufo/art1603.jpg]

Falling into this category of possible original structures were spherical objects with openings leading from the surface to the inside. Some of the TPU researchers noted their resemblance to similar openings in metal particles emitted during the application of metal coatings by high-temperature industrial plasma spraying processes.

Modern techniques such as microprobe analysis allowed the study of the variation in composition within individual drops. Studies showed that, although some of the drops were pure lead, others contained varying quantities of other metals.

Some lead-containing drops reportedly resembled Wood's alloy, a low-melting point (70 degrees centigrade) fusible alloy containing bismuth, tin and cadmium as well as lead. The low melting point would have resulted from the 'eutectic' composition of the alloy, which is used in applications such as fire sprinkler systems. Eutectic or near-eutectic compositions of this kind are precisely what scientists would expect to result from the partial melting of a highly complex object containing the appropriate metals.

Other lead-containing drops included phases rich in refractory metals, such as molybdenum and tungsten. Yet others contained the alkali metals sodium and potassium, totalling up to three per cent in some cases. A substantial number of lead-containing drops were rich in lanthanum, praseodymium and other rare earth elements.

Where did the lead come from? According to Salnikov's theory, the 'plasmoid' picked up lead particles from the polluted local air, lead that mostly had its origin in the local Dalnegorsk lead sulphide deposits that were mined by Dalpolimetall and smelted at Rudnaya Havens. Because the isotopic composition of each lead deposit is distinctive, this hypothesis could be tested by conducting lead isotope analysis on samples of the lead-containing droplets. The TPU report recommended that this be done.

Accordingly, Yuri Pushkarev, later a well-known figure in the Russian isotope geochemistry and geochronology fields, then working with IZMIRAN, undertook a study of the lead isotopic composition in selected lead-containing drops collected near Height 611. The results were surprising. Instead of matching the isotopic composition of the locally smelted lead, the isotopic composition matched that of lead from the massive Kholodninskoye lead-zinc sulphide deposit more than 2000 kilometres to the northwest of Dalnegorsk in the northern Lake Baikal region.[8]

A rapid exit for Vladimir Salnikov's plasmoid theory, then. And an end too, for the other token prosaic theories that the TPU scientists had proposed, for example that the Height 611 material represented remains of the NASA space shuttle Challenger that had disintegrated over the Atlantic Ocean on 28 January 1986.

But what about the TPU's fourth possible explanation for the event – the disintegration of an ET probe? At first sight the isotopic match with the Kholodninskoye lead cast doubt on that too. Why would an ET probe come all the way to our planet merely to collect samples of lead from the Lake Baikal region? Yuri Pushkarev reportedly commented that obviously the extraterrestrials were "secretly developing domestic deposits and using the lead in the construction of their vehicles."

Of course Pushkarev was joking. However, joking or not, neither Pushkarev nor any other scientist has constructed a coherent prosaic explanation for the presence of Kholodninskoye lead in the Height 611 object. After doing some research, I found out why.

The vast Kholodninskoye lead-zinc sulphide deposit has never been developed on a commercial scale. During the Soviet period intense prospecting and exploration had revealed the deposit's potential and small quantities of lead and zinc were obtained from galena (lead sulphide) and sphalerite (zinc sulphide). In 1985 the Soviet authorities approved future development.

But the prospecting had already caused environmental problems. Groundwater contaminated by tailing plumes from the exploration activity seeped into the Kholodnaya River that flows into the pristine ecologists' paradise of Lake Baikal.

So anyone claiming that the Height 611 object was a human artifact would first have to explain why, instead of using lead commercially available in the Soviet Union or elsewhere, the fabricators chose to use material that had only been obtained in small quantities from exploration activities in a remote area. It's easy to see why sceptics haven't even tried to build a prosaic theory that takes Yuri Pushkarev's lead isotope evidence into account.

But if the Dalnegorsk object was an ET prospecting bot that had deployed plasma beams to retrieve lead metal samples from Kholodninskoye tailings dumps, that would solve the lead isotope puzzle. As the lead in such dumps would have been in the form of galena rather than lead metal, the plasma beam would have had to possess 'direct smelting' capabilities.

Direct smelting has been proposed in several patents and, with their capacity to convert the lead into ionic form and then transport the ions 'upbeam' (as apparently happened in the case of the plasma packets discussed in Chapter 12, see Colour Plate 7), there's no reason why, after aeons of technical evolution, ET plasma-type beams couldn't do the job. Recall that the TPU researchers noted the resemblance of some lead-containing balls, ones that had holes leading to the inside, to metal particles emitted during high-temperature industrial plasma spraying processes. If these balls predated the high-temperature event at Height 611, they could perhaps have been generated from Kholodninskoye galena through the Height 611 object's deployment of direct smelting plasma beams.

In support of this idea is the fact that exploration activity at the Lake Baikal Kholodninskoye deposit had reached a climax during the years before the 1986 high-temperature event. Surveillance bots could have monitored this early activity, allowing ET mission control to instruct prospecting bots such as the Height 611 object, to direct their smelting beams towards the dumps. Valery Dvuzhilni gave further support to this idea by claiming that two weeks before the high-temperature event of 29 January 1986, eyewitnesses in the Lake Baikal region saw a 'ball' flying toward the southeast – the direction of Dalnegorsk.

If the Height 611 object obtained some or all of its lead by directing smelting beams at ore minerals contained in tailings dumps, could it have obtained some of the other metals found in the lead-containing drops, rare earth elements, for example, in a similar way? As well as prospecting for lead, zinc and other metals, Soviet exploration teams had identified valuable deposits of monazite, a mineral containing rare earths, in the subpolar Urals and there were other sources of rare earths in Siberia that may have been accessible to smelting beams at the time. Deposits of minerals containing molybdenum and tungsten, too, may have been accessible. So the idea that the Height 611 object was a prospecting bot with direct smelting capabilities that collected rare earths and other valuable metals as well as lead isn't as crazy as it seems.

As scientists continued their research on the Height 611 remains in the wake of the TPU report, they focused also on the iron-containing balls, some of which the Dalnegorsk mining laboratory technicians had found to be so hard that they could only be cut with diamond tools. Like the lead-containing balls but typically larger, 3-6 millimetres in size, most of the iron-rich balls were drop-shaped. Many iron-rich drops had glassy outer margins, testifying to their rapid cooling from melt as they fell to the ground. Five of them, reported to weigh a total of 850 milligrammes, were found to be sintered together (Fig 72).

The fact that iron-rich parts of the object as well as lead-rich ones had melted showed that temperatures in the disintegration phase had locally approached the melting temperature of iron (1538 degrees centigrade). Microprobe analysis of the iron-containing balls showed not only that each drop had a different composition but also that there were multiple phases within each drop. For example, one part of one drop consisted mainly of alpha iron but also contained three percent of silica, 2.4 percent of tungsten and 0.5 per cent of cobalt.[9] Presumably the silica, tungsten and cobalt were in separate phases from the alpha iron, which can only accommodate very small amounts of other elements.

In another investigation of the iron balls, X-ray diffraction studies were quoted as showing an increase in the lattice parameters of alpha iron in an iron ball after one year. This report was likely the source of the misleading statement in the National Atomic Testing Museum's display that "the distance between atoms is different from ordinary iron."

It may be that the crystal structure of alpha iron in this iron ball altered over the course of a year, presumably the period 1988-9. The alpha iron may have changed from a face-centred cubic structure to a less compact body-centred cubic structure. Quenched alloys – those rapidly cooled from high temperature – have been known to 'age' in this way over the years. But to properly interpret this possible effect in the Height 611 iron balls, expert technical papers will need to be published in the normal way.

Parts of other drops collected at Height 611 were rich in rare earth elements. One local microprobe analysis of part of a drop was quoted as fifty seven percent cerium, eighteen per cent neodymium, and sixteen percent praseodymium, with small amounts only of iron and nickel.

Was this rare-earth-rich part of a drop acquired as a result of prospecting or was it part of the Dalnegorsk object's original structure? In his 2007 interview with *Golden Horn,* Dvuzhilni suggested that some fragments of the original structure survived the Height 611 high-temperature event. He drew attention to another tiny fragment, also rich in rare earth elements. Less than one millimetre in size and with three edges visible when studied with a microscope, it was not part of a drop and Dvuzhilni interpreted it as part of the original structure.

The microprobe analysis of this tiny fragment showed fifty-five percent cerium and twenty-six per cent tungsten, the balance consisting of neodymium and lanthanum. Such a combination of the refractory metal tungsten with a typical rare earth composition indicates a command of nanotechnology and is one of the many Height 611 findings that challenge current science.

This particular tiny fragment lacked an iron base. But in the iron-containing drops generally, the typical association of rare earths, in particular neodymium and praseodymium, with iron brings to mind thoughts of advanced magnetic materials.

Why were some of the iron-containing drops so hard? In parts of the drops researchers identified cementite (iron carbide, Fe_3C) a hard normal component of steels, often in the strength-conferring intergrowth with alpha iron known as pearlite, and other exotic hard and refractory ceramic phases.[9]

For example, within certain drops researchers identified the exotic refractory ceramic phases tantalum carbide and hafnium carbide. These two are not only very hard but have some of the highest melting points of any known solids (3900 and 3880 degrees centigrade, only exceeded by that of tantalum hafnium carbide, about 4215 degrees centigrade). Other exotic refractory ceramic phases reportedly identified in parts of the iron-containing drops include scandium nitride and manganese oxides.[10] Such exotic ceramics have hi-tech applications, such as jet engine components, where performance at high temperatures is crucial.

The combination of such temperature-resistant materials with those that are advanced magnetically is precisely what we might expect to find in the remains of an ET prospecting bot that used MHD-type propulsion and then disintegrated at high temperatures.

Endnotes

1 Google Translate of V.N. Salnikov, V.P. Skavinskiy, M.V. Korovkin, V.V. Dvuzilny, S.V. Lebedeva *Geological and geophysical characteristics of the place of landing of the anomalous object near Dalnegorsk*, Tomsk, 1990. Summary downloaded from: http://ufo.tomsk.ru/oldtgrufors/ptes/o-dgpt.htm on 17 April 2012.

2 ibid.

3 Parnjakov 1997.

4 Google Translate of piece written by E. Mizyurkina, member of Salnikov's TPU field team that visited Height 611, Dalnegorsk from 18 May to 25 June, 1988. Mizyurkina observed geophysicist Skavinsky's professional fieldwork using a proton magnetometer – looked like a long-barreled gun on his back – to locate the magnetic anomalies that he interpreted as the places of contact of the Height 611 object on 29 January 1986. Downloaded from http://miger.ru/1988_1.html on 9 February 2012.

5 Google Translate of piece written by Tatyana Kurochkina, Golden Horn No. 18 2007. Downloaded from http://www.pressmon.com/cgi-bin/press_view.cgi?id=2050666. March 19 2012.

6 Google Translate from: http://www.kosmodmitrov.narod.ru/5.html. Downloaded 9 February 2012.

7 Google Translate of: *Non-recurrent ultrafast phenomena in the environment*, Abstracts of the Second All-Union Interdisciplinary Scientific and Technical School Workshop 19-30 April 1990, Tomsk Part I, Tomsk, 1991. Research methods of beam diagnostics surface material objects collected at a height of 611 in Dalnegorsk. Posted story on Wed, 07/22/2015 - 17:09 material analysis Dalnegorsk study UFO thesis Tomsk, O.D. Smiyan, L.M. Kapitanchuk, P. O. Antonov. Downloaded from http://aeninform.org 25 February 2017.

8 Google Translate of piece by Alexander Milanovsky, an acquaintance of Yuri Pushkarev. http://www.meteorite.narod.ru/proba/stati/stati75.htm. After Pushkarev had made his 'joke', Milanovksy observed that the foolish believers in UFOs had taken it seriously. But, argued Milanovsky, the isotopic match between the Height 611 lead-containing drops and the Kholodninskoye lead, in fact, showed that these drops had an earthly origin. Downloaded from: http://www.meteorite.narod.ru/proba/stati/stati75.htm. 13 February 20102 at 13.02 hours.

9 Rempel 2011.
10 ibid.

16

Artificial Life

The black glassy material that the TPU researchers called mesh (сеточка) is the most challenging of all the materials collected from the Height 611 site. This carbon-based material, in all its weird variety (Figs 73-81), sparked the curiosity of the TPU researchers and remained the focus for expert attention in the period of intensive research that followed the TPU field study in 1988.

Fig 73. Two fragments of the black glassy carbon-rich material found at Height 611 and described by researchers as 'mesh' (сеточка). Mesh fragments consist of networks of multiply connected hollow tubes. Within the networks are large open spaces, which appear to connect with each other. For a guide to scale of tubes see Fig 74. [Widely reproduced image of uncertain origin. This particular image was downloaded from Internos's ATS (www.abovetopsecret.com) thread 'The Height 611 UFO Crash' on 3 April 2011]

Fig 74. Ballpoint pen and typescript show the scale of the fragments of mesh and other remains collected from the Height 611 site by Valery Dvuzhilni and his associates. [YouTube 35 'UFO Height 611'. Image downloaded from www.youtube.com on 4 November 2011]

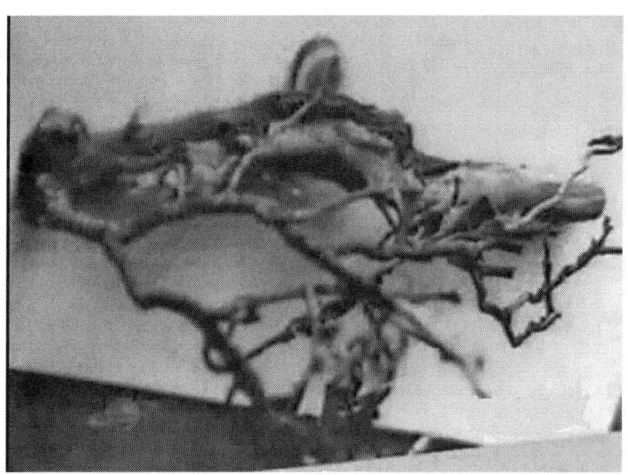

Fig 75. In this fragment of mesh the branching network of black tubes calls to mind biological growth in an unrestricted environment. Unlike the examples of mesh shown in Fig 73 and Fig 74, the tubes are filled with a whitish material. The branched structure of this 'filled mesh' brings to mind images of the human cortex. Courtesy: 'Sightings', Valery Dvuzhilni. [YouTube 15 'UFO Height 611'. Image downloaded from www.youtube.com on 2 November 2011]

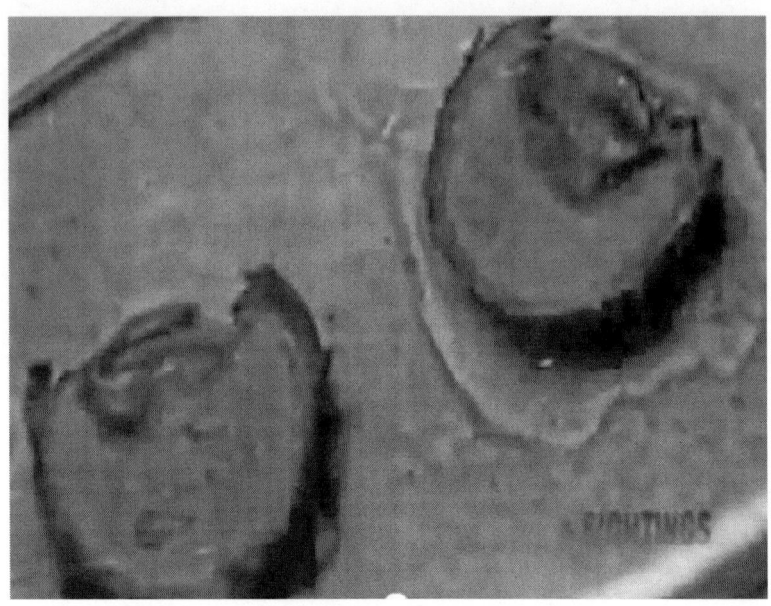

Fig 76. Here researchers have sawn through a thick tube of 'filled mesh' to reveal the internal material, rather as one might slice through the trunk of a branched tree. The complex internal structure can be understood by comparison with Fig 75. 'Branches' are already present within the 'trunk' and some of the branches contain thinner branches, in the form of projecting black tubes.

White areas within the slice on the left may be sections of quartz fibres while the gray material may be a fine-grained intergrowth of quartz threads and black 'mesh' material. Courtesy: 'Sightings'. [YouTube14 'UFO Height 611'. Image downloaded from www.youtube.com on 8 November 2011]

Vladimir Salnikov's plasmoid interpretation created confusion for those studying the mesh just as it did for the researchers studying the metallic droplets. If the metals had been picked up locally from the polluted atmosphere and deposited by the plasmoid in the form of droplets, where did the carbon-based mesh come from? Salnikov's answer was the local vegetation, particularly the stump of Korean Pine. Although Salnikov's frankly absurd plasmoid interpretation was soon ruled out by Yuri Pushkarev's lead isotope work, as far as the origins

Fig 77. Close up view of a specimen of mesh. Some of the black tubes are hollow – for example the tube that extends towards the camera in the upper right. Others are filled with fibres of a white material identified by researchers as alpha quartz. Quartz fibres splay out from the central tube, much as conducting wires might splay out from the protective jacket of an electricity cable. Small areas of the black 'protective jacket' have disintegrated, perhaps during the Height 611 high-temperature event.[YouTube 16 'UFO Height 611'. Image downloaded from www.youtube.com on 2 November 2011.]

of the mesh goes, it's had a lasting influence on the thinking of Valery Dvuzhilni. Dalnegorsk's famous UFOlogist continued to sometimes claim that, during the high-temperature event, vaporised metals from the Height 611 object were somehow absorbed by carbon from the stump of Korean Pine, magically creating the mesh.

Atomic absorption and neutron activation analytical techniques certainly showed that, apart from carbon, the black glassy mesh material contained silicon and many metals, including silver, gold, zinc, cobalt, copper, iron, manganese, calcium, sodium, potassium and rare earth elements.[1]

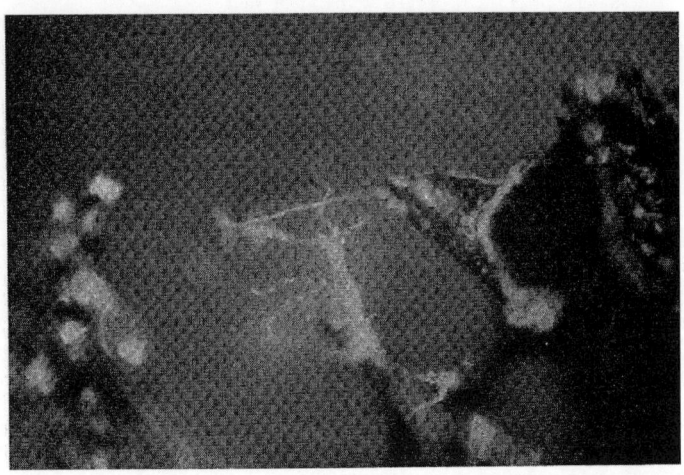

Fig 78. The mesh sample shown in Fig 77 after laboratory heat treatment. Further disintegration of the carbon-rich 'protective jackets' has taken place. The quartz fibres, reportedly about 17 microns in diameter, are arranged in bundles of twisted strands. Within such bundles, researchers have reportedly identified fine filaments of gold. [Hesemann (1998) page 296]

Fig 79. Another sample of mesh after laboratory heat treatment. During processing individual quartz fibres have apparently separated from their bundles and adhered to the carbon–rich black 'protective jacket' material. The pale crystals may have grown in the laboratory during cooling.[Hesemann (1998) page 297]

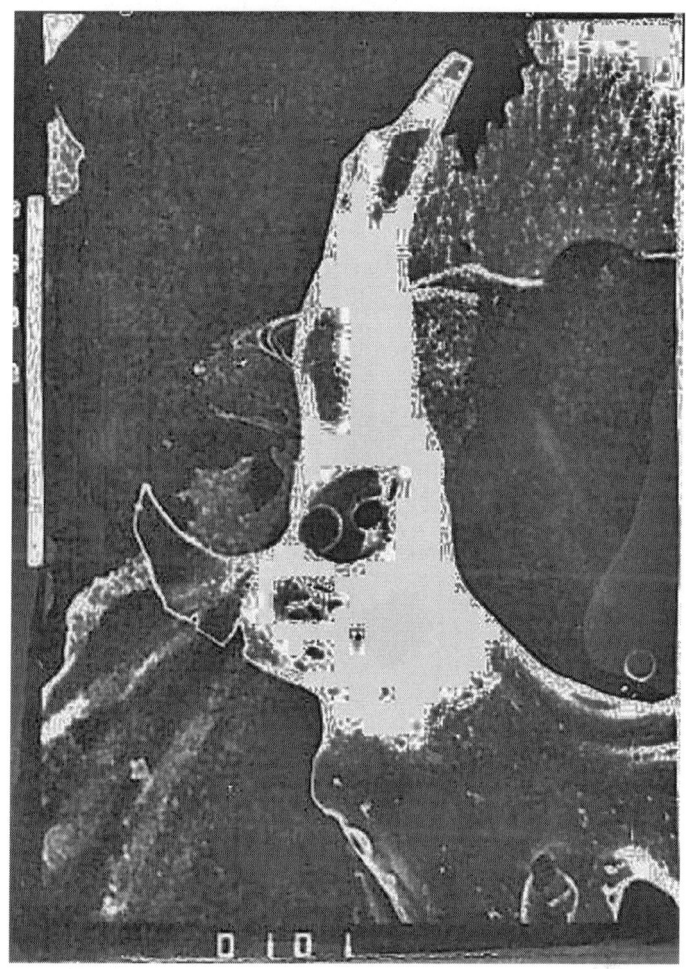

Fig 80. Scanning electron microscope image of another specimen of carbon-rich mesh. The image suggests 'organic-like' growth of the mesh on a microscopic scale.

[Image was downloaded from Internos's Above Top Secret (www.abovetopsecret.com) thread 'The Height 611 UFO Crash' on 7 August 2011]

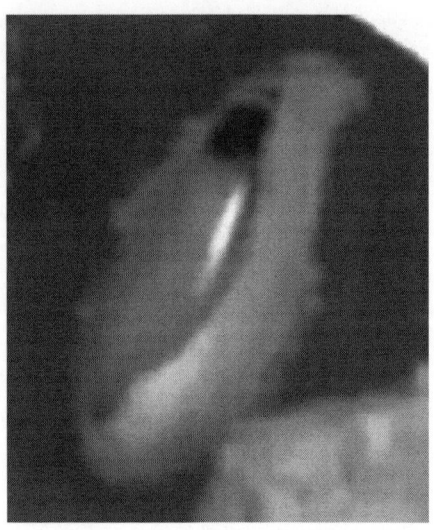

Fig 81. Enigmatic budlike structure consisting of amber bead of glassy material within pale, opaque sheath. [YouTube 18 'UFO Height 611'. Image downloaded from www.youtube.com 2 November 2011]

But it isn't clear how much of this quoted content of silicon and other elements was actually in solid solution in the black glassy material and how much in separate phases. For example, some silicon was evidently not in the black glass, but outside it in the form of separate threads consisting of silica polymorphs (Fig 79).

A. A. Makeev, a senior researcher at TPU, investigated these silica polymorphs by means of X-ray diffraction and identified alpha quartz, beta tridymite, alpha cristobalite and beta cristobalite polymorphs. At atmospheric pressure, cristobalite is the silica polymorph stable between 1470 degrees centigrade and the melting temperature of 1705 degrees, but it can persist metastably below 1470 degrees. Makeev concluded that, after the high- temperature event, the mesh material might have cooled rapidly from a temperature above 1470 degrees, allowing random preservation of the high-temperature polymorphs of silica. Such rapid cooling, rather in the manner that small droplets of magma ejected from volcanoes cool to form glassy lapilli, would be consistent with the glassy coatings of some of the metal droplets.[2]

Two chemists at the Institute of Chemistry, Russian Academy of Sciences, in Vladivostok, Alexey Kulikov and Vladimir Vysotki (В. Высоцкий), made a particular study of the mesh in their laboratories.[3,4] Kulikov was completely baffled. "It is impossible to find out what it is. It reminds one of glass carbon. The conditions under which it can be produced are unknown. Perhaps it was produced by extremely high temperatures." Glass carbon, sometimes called glassy carbon or vitreous carbon, is a hard, low-density form of carbon that is resistant to high temperatures and chemical corrosion.

The black glassy carbon-rich mesh material displayed remarkable properties. Although in air it burned at 900 degrees centigrade, when heated in a vacuum it reportedly withstood temperatures of up to 3000 degrees. This suggests that fragments of mesh survived the Height 611 high-temperature event because of the lack of oxygen in their local environment. The carbon-rich material's electrical conductivity, too, reportedly behaved in an unusual way. For example, at low temperatures, the material did not conduct an electric current, but became a conductor when heated in a vacuum.

Vysotki studied some of the mesh material with a scanning electron microscope and other analytical equipment. In some samples, he found the mesh network was filled with threads of alpha quartz only 17 microns in diameter. Sometimes the quartz threads were plaited together like a rope (Fig 77, 78) and in one of these 'ropes' Vysotki identified by X-ray diffraction a fine thread of gold, or gold-rich alloy. Later, other gold threads were identified in similar situations. Reportedly, Vysotki also identified threads of alloys of silver and other metals.

Could these be microcables, Vysotki wondered, the quartz threads acting as insulators and the gold and other metals as electrical conductors? In Vysotki's view, all of this was clearly the product of "a highly developed technology". And not terrestrial technology either, "for no earthly production technique is capable of producing such fine material."

Given the high temperatures experienced by the mesh in the disintegration event, as recorded by the cristobalite identified by Makeev, any organic compounds originally present in the black glassy material may have been altered. But aromatic and aliphatic organic compounds were reportedly identified in the black glassy material. Makeev confirmed this, making the remarkable statement: "particularly interesting is the large proportion of organic material. It could mean that we are dealing here with some kind of artificial life."

Makeev's paradigm-challenging assessment 'artificial life' is supported by the extraordinary range in morphologies of the mesh, many suggesting biological growth. This was evidently a feature that captured the imagination of the TPU researchers.

The combination in the mesh of Vysotki's "highly developed technology" with Makeev's "artificial life" returns our thoughts to the speculations of Steven Dick and Paul Davies regarding the possible physical substrates of ET intelligence. Davies emphasized the creative possibilities of designing artificial life forms and merging them with machinelike elements. As already mentioned in Chapter 4, he speculated that these hybrids could comprise self-designing systems that could grow, improve and adapt, which he called ATS's, auto-teleological super-systems.[5]

A phrase that hardly trips off the tongue and, after using Google to gauge its scientific reception, I found barely any discussion by Davies's scientific peers, but at the top of the search results was a link to a 2011 thread I had started on the ATS (Above Top Secret) forum entitled "Have Coal-eating Cyborgs visited Earth?" My thread pointed out that Davies's idea might trump the notion of space aliens in interpreting certain reports of anomalous activity.

Clearly Paul Davies's concept of auto-teleological super-systems is an idea that has yet to come of age. Could the Height 611 mesh be an example of such a super-system, the material delivered quietly to our home planet while Carl Sagan and Paul Davies stared vainly into space in their quest for ET? Davies rightly rejected Allen Hynek's humanoid aliens as anthropomorphic in origin, but if he looks through Figs 73-81, he could hardly reject the possibility that his own utterly non-anthropomorphic speculations about the possible physical substrates of ET intelligence now have solid support.

So a published high-quality study of the Height 611 mesh has the potential to overthrow the current scientific paradigm and bring Nobel prizes to theorists like Paul Davies and Steven Dick, as well as to the Russian chemists who first raised the possibility that the material they were studying in their laboratories was some kind of artificial life. Had Rockefeller money brought Kulikov, Vysotki and Makeev to the USA in 1997 to present their papers at the Sturrock meeting (Chapter 14) this might already have happened.

After a hiatus of many years, thanks to Allan Palmer of the National Atomic Testing Museum, Las Vegas, the prospect of Nobel prizes for scientists brave enough to renew studies of the Dalnegorsk mesh has been resurrected. Since the samples that Valery Dvuzhilni gave to George Knapp were displayed at the National Atomic Testing Museum in 2012, the material has been pleading for renewed scientific attention, using the latest analytical techniques.

Until that happens, what we can do is look at the many microphotographs and other images of the various varieties of mesh that have escaped from laboratories and appeared in the public domain on the Internet.

First, it's apparent that the epithet 'mesh' describes only one variety of this black glassy material. It evidently comes in a huge variety of shapes, structures and sizes. After exposure to the atmosphere for some years, the black glassy material often takes on a rusty appearance, as if iron and other metals in the surface layer of the mesh have formed particles of oxide.

In some of the mesh examples the black glass forms are filled with other material. As we've seen, in the cable-like structures that Vysotki discussed (see Fig 77 and 78) tubes of black glassy material contain braided threads of alpha quartz or other silica polymorphs that sometimes are associated with even thinner threads of gold, or gold-rich alloy. In other examples, the filling consists of composite material, which may include intricate mixtures of silica polymorphs, gold and other metal alloy threads and black glassy material. The samples displayed in the National Atomic Testing Museum in 2012 may be of this kind (Figs 1-3).

Two examples of filled mesh, shown in Fig 75 and Fig 76, are crucially important, because they show that the black glassy material has grown in an organic manner. Indeed, at first sight, the fragment of mesh shown in Fig 75 looks just like a piece cut off an earthly plant, with the bark having in some places peeled away from the interior.

But look more closely. Although the branches grow and subdivide much like something in your garden, instead of avoiding each other as they grow, different branches sometimes join up. In some cases, the junctions resemble the synapses of vertebrate nervous systems. Comparison would be with the high-speed electrical synapses, discovered in the 1950s, rather than with the better known and slower-acting chemical synapses.

Fig 76 shows two adjacent slices of filled mesh. One interpretation of these images is that during organic growth the carbon-rich fibres have gradually separated from the rest of the silica-rich material and formed tubes. It's possible that a comprehensive study of the mesh could trace organic growth from a stage involving mixed silica polymorphs and carbon-rich fibres (Fig 76), through to varieties such as the cavity-prone networks of carbon-rich tubes (Fig 74) and the varieties of filled mesh resembling hi-tech microcables studied by Vladimir Vysotki (Figs 77 and 78).

Experts may already have carried out such a study. At an early stage in the research, the TPU researchers noted the resemblance of some of the mesh structures to the human brain cortex. They speculated that if the Height 611 object was a robotic ET probe, the convoluted mesh might have acted as its command-and-control centre.

But those early speculations date from a period before the explosion in research drew in scientists and engineers from many other institutes. Later investigations of the mesh included the study of scanning electron microscope (SEM) images. One of these images has leaked out (Fig 80) and shows that the organic-style growth of nested tube-like structures in the carbon-rich mesh has taken place on the micrometer scale as well as the millimeter scale of Fig 74.

Such images present a huge challenge to science. With access to many other similar images and their technical context, experts may have made provisional overall technical interpretations during the 1990s and may have sent confidential executive summaries of their findings to selected decision makers.

But even these putative 1990s interpretations may now be outdated as a result of the recent revolution in understanding of the molecular structures and properties of two classes of carbon allotropes, the carbon nanotubes and the fullerenes. Both are based on one-carbon-atom-thick hexagonally linked sheets. In the nanotubes, the sheets of hexagons are rolled into tubes, the thinnest having a diameter around one nanometer, while in the fullerenes the sheets are curved into spheres or domes, so called after the geodesic domes of architect Buckminster Fuller.

Many of the nanotube-based materials show extraordinary electrical, mechanical and optical properties. Such bizarre properties may, therefore, explain some of the bafflement of Height 611 researchers like Alexey Kulikov and Vladimir Vysotki at the strange way the carbon-rich mesh's electrical conductivity and other properties behaved in laboratory tests. Conceivably also, reports that X-ray studies showed inexplicable appearance and disappearance of certain metals when samples of mesh were heated in a vacuum could now be explained by models involving the structural rearrangement of nanotubes on heating.

Models involving carbon nanotubes may also contribute to understanding organic growth in the mesh, perhaps helping to understand how such growth has apparently taken place on the microscopic scale. Such modeling may therefore bear directly on fundamental questions concerning the possible substrates of ET intelligence and the possible role of silica polymorphs and gold.

For example, if synapse-like structures involving micron-scale gold wires could be modified by partial melting after passage of pulses of electric current, this could provide a basis for plasticity leading to possibilities for information storage and memory. Even at the scale of Fig 74, this could contribute to simple but rapid command-and-control systems. And if analogous plasticity occurs on the micrometre scale of Fig 80, then perhaps possibilities for an advanced form of ET AI arises. Theorists familiar with emerging technologies such as carbon nanotube field effect transistors (CNFET) (see Wikipedia) might contribute relevant ideas.

Here perhaps, robust and near immortal, may lie clues to the substrates of ET intelligence as envisaged by Steven Dick and Paul Davies. The Height 611 mesh may therefore present one of the greatest scientific challenges that we earthlings have ever faced.

Endnotes

1 Rempel 2011.

2 Google Translate of document downloaded from http://flotcom on 28 April 2012.

3 Google Translate of book review of Michael Gerstein's *Secrets of UFOs and Aliens*. Downloaded from http://ufosecret.ru/page 98.html on 25 November 2012.

4 Hesemann 1998, p.294–7.

5 Davies 2011, p.161–3.

17

Molybdenum and Gold

What's the best material to use for making the hull of an interstellar probe? The British Interplanetary Society (BIS) considered this question in the 1970s. A team of its engineers faced the task of designing a conceptual mother probe that, within fifty years, would reach Barnard's Star, an old Class M red dwarf about six light years away. Aptly named *Project Daedalus*, the BIS's mother probe was to be the second stage of a two-stage fusion-rocket system, weighing a total of fifty thousand tonnes. Before reaching the Barnard's Star system, the mother probe would deploy an array of exploratory probes, rather as NASA's Scot Stride imagined possible ET mother probes might do when surveying our own planet.[1]

To serve in an interstellar probe, the chosen material would need to retain its strength through the largest possible temperature range. Bearing this in mind, the BIS boffins chose to make the craft's engine bells and supporting structure from the metal molybdenum, or rather the molybdenum-based alloy known as TZM Molybdenum. In addition to molybdenum, this alloy contains 0.5 per cent titanium, 0.8 per cent zirconium and 0.1 per cent carbon.

Despite its relative rarity, molybdenum qualified for this interstellar role because it has one of the highest melting points of any metal – 2896 degrees centigrade – a very low coefficient of thermal expansion and good corrosion resistance. Its tensile strength can be made adequate even at very low temperatures by adding other elements, as in the TZM alloy, or in the case of molybdenum wires, decreasing the diameter. Molybdenum's tendency to oxidise in the earth's atmosphere would not be a problem in the interstellar medium.

The BIS's *Daedalus* concept proved influential. When Robert Freitas designed a conceptual REPRO star probe, self-replicating along the lines originally envisaged by John von Neumann, he based his ideas on *Project Daedalus*, with its molybdenum hull. Desperate for molybdenum, which the *Daedalus* design specified in quantities second only to the abundant element aluminium, Freitas even considered – but in the end rejected on energy grounds – that his self-replicators might obtain it by fusion breeding from the more abundant element zirconium.[2]

Given the logic that before imagining what ET probes might be like, we should first examine designs for our own interstellar probes, scientists investigating the Height 611 remains ought to be alert for fragments of a molybdenum hull. To find such pieces would be like discovering the Holy Grail.

So what to make of the claims in 2006, by Valery Dvuzhilni and Vadim Chernobrov, of the Kosmopoisk (Космопо́иск) Organisation, that they had located fragments of the outer case of the Height 611 object and that chemists had found that it was made of pure molybdenum. Unlike normal molybdenum, Dvuzhilni claimed, the Height 611 molybdenum was "magnetised".

Caution is in order. Dvuzhilni is a sincere researcher and he has genuine expertise in two fields – the biological effects of the 1986 Height 611 high-temperature event and the field investigation of local reports of anomalous activity. But beyond those areas, his thinking has been contaminated by the flawed interpretations of the UFOlogists. That's why, outside those two specialties, I've given no particular credence to Dvuzhilni's own claims as an independent researcher.

Much the same could be said of former aerospace engineer Vadim Chernobrov and his Kosmopoisk Organisation, in which Dvuzhilni served as the local coordinator. Indeed, Chernobrov's reputation for constructing time machines means that Dvuzhilni's links with Kosmopoisk do nothing for the Dalnegorsk UFOlogist's scientific credibility.

On the other hand, if we view the 2012 YouTube clip (Search: YouTube НЛО в Приморском крае-Высота 611 (Дальнегорск)) in which Dvuzhilni shows a group of Height 611 tourists a scientific report including a set of photographs alleged to be of the object's molybdenum case, it's clear that scientists can't dismiss this claim. The weird, quasi-biological style of the alleged fragments of molybdenum brings to mind the same biological style of the mesh material discussed in the last chapter.

The fact that the alleged fragment of molybdenum did not oxidise in the high temperature event is consistent, too, with the claim that the carbon-rich material of the stump of Korean Pine facing the southwest didn't burn, but apparently melted and flowed.

Valery Dvuzhilni has claimed that the molybdenum's lack of oxidation means that the Height 611 object was "flying in a vacuum". But we all know that nature abhors a vacuum, so perhaps here we see the limitations of a school biology teacher when faced with a problem in plasma physics. Professional plasma physicists, like Jean-Pierre Petit and Auguste Meessen, are needed here. While awaiting interpretations from such experts, my own amateur guess would be that if the object was using MHD-type propulsion, the highly ionised air of its plasma corona might have prevented oxidation of molybdenum just as if a vacuum had surrounded the object.

The point is that given the theoretical studies of conceptual interstellar probe designs by the BIS boffins and by Robert Freitas, given the extensive Soviet-period scientific studies of the Height 611 remains, including Yuri Pushkarev's lead isotope work (Chapter 15), Dvuzhilni's claim that part of the object's case has been located and chemists have found it to be made of molybdenum is important and scientists should take it seriously. Clearly we now need an independent scientific study of the vaunted molybdenum case, including a study of its isotopic composition.

Molybdenum has several stable isotopes, including three, molybdenum-92, molybdenum-96 and molybdenum-100, that were each produced in only one kind of nucleosynthetic process inside stars. Geochemists studying the early history of the earth, meteorites and other solar system bodies are, therefore, very interested in molybdenum isotopes. If the 2006 studies of the Height 611 object's alleged molybdenum case are presented to geochemists in the context of the earlier Soviet scientific work, rather than that of UFOlogy, scientific curiosity might well prompt further research into Dvuzhilni's molybdenum claims. That's perhaps something for Yuri and Julia Milner, the paymasters of the 2015 Project Breakthrough Initiatives, a set of projects focused on the search for extraterrestrial intelligence (see Wikipedia), to think about.

Such an isotopic study of the molybdenum fragments claimed to be part of the Height 611 object's outer case could therefore shed important light on the object's origins. And fortunately for scientists wary of linking themselves with Valery Dvuzhilni or Vadim Chernobrov, there is the highly regarded name of Yuri Pushkarev to conjure with, as well as those of the other accredited scientists at respected research institutes who have already studied the Dalnegorsk material. To follow Pushkarev's lead isotope work with their own molybdenum isotope studies would be a perfectly respectable way for a team of scientists to respond to the Height 611 challenge. Indeed, given Pushkarev's demonstration of an isotopic link between the Dalnegorsk lead and Kholodninskoye lead and given the claim discussed in the next chapter that ET bots may have mined terrestrial molybdenite deposits at Spring Creek Mine, Idaho in 1965, such a molybdenum isotope study could bear on the possibility that the molybdenum in the Height 611 object's case, like the lead in its lead drops, came from planet Earth.

If eyewitness reports of the events at Dalnegorsk on 28 November 1987 are correct (Figs 64 and 65), then the original Height 611 object, with its possible molybdenum shell, was likely one of many similar small beam-deploying prospecting bots active in the Dalnegorsk area during the late 1980s. Could there be any photographs or videos of similar devices in action elsewhere?

There is one intriguing set of images. At 2311 local time on 24 August 2003, Waltraud Kaliba and Jürgen Trieb, two professional sports photographers based at Knittelfeld in Austria, captured some remarkable digital images (Colour Plate 8). Kaliba and Trieb shared a house in Knittelfeld close to the west bank of the River Mur which here flows north. On that Sunday night, after a hard day's work at a local motor racing event, Waltraud Kaliba went to the north-facing balcony overlooking the river for a smoke. There she saw a line of what looked like red luminous balls appear over a nearby hill and move towards their house. Kaliba called Trieb and the pair now saw that the balls had various geometrical shapes. The objects remained stationary long enough for the couple to take several photographs with a Nikon D1X DSLR camera, exposure time three seconds.

German technician and researcher Gerhard Gröschel, who has since collaborated with the Austrian couple to convert their Knittelfeld house into a centre for the automatic recording of anomalous activity, has studied these digital photographs (see YouTube: UFO Hotspot Knittelfeld–Gerhard Gröschel). If they are indeed bona fide images of anomalous objects, they are some of the most convincing ever captured. Appearing as if organically grown, the objects come from a different world from our own surveillance devices. As weird indeed as the Height 611 object and its alleged molybdenum case.

These images, one of which is reproduced in Colour Plate 8, show that the red colour initially noticed by Kaliba came not from the objects themselves but from areas to the lower right of each object. One interpretation would be that the red colour represents spectral lines around 650 nanometers, emitted from species excited by beams of ionising radiation from the objects. Because of the long exposure time of three seconds, any detailed image structure would have been lost.

If these 2003 Knittelfeld images captured beaming prospecting bots comparable with the Height 611 object of 1986, what metals might the devices have been looking for as they cruised over the mountains and then hovered above the River Mur in that Styrian country town? Searching for gold again? You must be joking, surely. Yet when I researched that idea, it emerged as a real possibility.

Around 1400 AD miners operated many small gold workings in the vein deposits exposed on the eastern flank of the local Tremmelberg mountain. This hilly area to the northeast of Knittelfeld is where Waltraud Kaliba first spotted the anomalous objects. Tremmelberg gold mining ceased in the seventeenth century when, as a result of the religious upheavals that shook much of Europe, the local Catholic landowner evicted his Protestant miners. Later some mining for copper and gold took place to the east of the Tremmelberg mountain but all mines had closed by the end of the nineteenth century.

Some of this local gold, from erosion of vein gold and old mine tailings would have likely been carried as gold dust by streams into the River Mur, so it's possible that the anomalous objects seen by Kaliba and Trieb on 23 August 2003 were prospecting devices following a placer gold trail in the local river in the same way that the 1977/8 Brazilian objects may have tracked placer gold in the Amazon Basin rivers (Chapter 7).

In the Amazon provinces of Brazil, the 1977 reports of possible placer gold prospecting activity were followed in 1978 by reports of activity by possible large transport vehicles for gold-quartz material. Perhaps a similar sequence of events occurred in Austria, with prospecting bot activity in 2003 followed in later years by sightings of large objects that may likewise have been transport vehicles for gold-quartz material. In this context it's interesting that on 13 August 2008 at 11.55.56 local time (note the Germanic precision) on a cloudy day one of Gerhard Gröschel's automated movie cameras, installed in the Kaliba-Trieb Knittelfeld house and directed towards the northwest, recorded the abrupt appearance of a horizontal row of four luminous rectangles (Fig 82) (Search YouTube: UFO Hotspot Knittelfeld–Gerhard Gröschel).

This image was recorded on two successive movie frames suggesting the 'flash' lasted for about 0.2 seconds. If the panels were attached to an object partly hidden by cloud beyond the trees, it would have been very large.

Could this remarkable 2008 image have captured a large transport vehicle with four bright luminous rectangular panels returning to a gold prospect initially identified by molybdenum-hulled prospecting bots on 23 August 2003?

Endnotes

1 Bond *et al.* 1978.
2 Freitas 1980.

Fig 82. Image captured at 13 August 2008 at 11.55.56 local time by one of German researcher Gerhard Gröschel's automated movie cameras installed in the Kaliba-Trieb house in Knittelfeld, Austria. Directed towards the northwest, the camera recorded the abrupt appearance and disappearance of a horizontal row of four luminous rectangles. The image was recorded on two successive movie frames suggesting the 'flash' lasted for about 0.2 seconds. The rectangles may represent luminous panels attached to a large object beyond the trees partly hidden by cloud. [YouTube 'UFO Hotspot Knittelfeld–Gerhard Gröschel'. Image downloaded from www.youtube.com 23 November 2014]

18

Von Neumann Machines

The high-melting-point metal molybdenum completes a list of hi-tech materials identified in the Height 611 remains. As we saw in Chapter 15, other metals identified in the remains include lead, gold, tungsten, rare earth elements such as cerium, neodymium, praseodymium, lanthanum, and ceramics like tantalum carbide, hafnium carbide, scandium nitride and manganese oxides.

It's quite a haul – and that's only what I've been able to glean from a cursory study of the material leaked from the Russian and Ukrainian laboratories. Given the large number of scientists and engineers that have studied the remains from the 1986 Height 611 high-temperature event, we can only guess at the wealth of materials that may have been identified and discussed in unpublished or secret reports.

But staying with the list above, once we deploy the von Neumann concept of self-replicating and self-repairing machines using local materials, we have a challenging set of predictions of what ET prospecting and mining bots may have been up to here while SETI people gazed vainly into space.

Some of the predictions have already passed preliminary tests. Yuri Pushkarev's lead isotope studies linking the Height 611 object's lead with the lead of the Kholodninskoye lead-zinc sulphide deposit, under exploration in 1986 (Chapter 15), is the key result that puts the von Neumann idea on the scientific agenda.

And, with regard to gold, in Chapter 7 we looked at the notion that 1977 reports of placer gold prospecting activity by ET bots in Brazil's Amazon provinces were followed in 1978 by reports of activity by what may have been large transport vehicles for gold-quartz material. In that chapter we also considered the possibility that further ET prospecting activity took place near the town of Pucallpa in the Amazon Basin of Peru in 2008. In Chapter 17 we considered the further possibility that this 2008 global surge in ET prospecting for gold extended to historically worked placer gold deposits in Austria.

So much for placer gold, one of Earth's key planetary resources discussed in this book. But before considering the remaining materials on the above list one by one, if ET prospecting bots have been active here, we might expect some eyewitness descriptions of specialist bots engaged in general geochemical prospecting – the quick preliminary search for multiple elements. Human geochemists exploit the Earth's water cycle to do this. They collect and analyse for trace elements in water samples from soils, streams, lakes or runoff. Expert interpretation of such data can lead to the discovery of new ore bodies. Operations of this kind lend themselves to automation and we might, therefore, expect to find eyewitness accounts of such robotic ET operations.

Here's one. It's the afternoon of 9 April 1970 and the setting is a country road near the village of Langenschemmern, in southern Germany. Walking home along the road, Max Krauss, a retired electrician, notices a strange semi-transparent spherical object about forty centimetres in diameter making its way along the other side of the road, close to a drainage channel full of rainwater draining from a sloping field. The object has a dark spherical nucleus, from which eight tapering radial spokes extend to its outer edge (Fig 83). Despite a strong cross wind, the object floats along just above the road, all the while rotating on a vertical axis.

The astonished electrician observes the object move slowly along the road for about one hundred and fifty metres. He is even more astonished to see the object stop, move over the little stream of water and insert something resembling a hosepipe into the water.

But this is no ordinary hosepipe. It bends into a U-shape, writhes sideways and, in the bend appears a gleam like that of red-hot iron. Then the hosepipe writhes around like a worm, with its far end reaching into the water. After remaining there for a short time, the worm withdraws

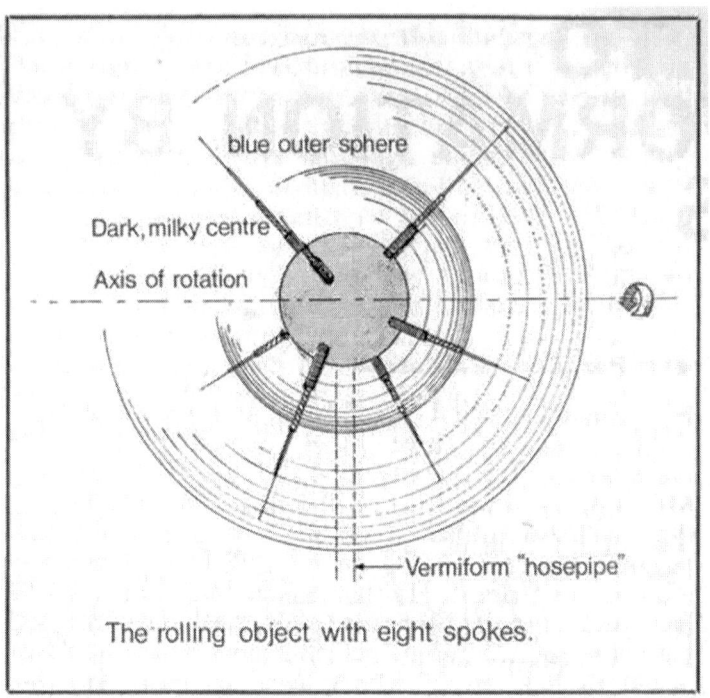

Fig 83. An ET geochemical prospecting bot? On 9 April 1970, walking home along a country road near Langenschemmern in southern Germany, electrician Max Krauss claimed to have seen a semitransparent spherical object about 40 centimetres in diameter making its way just above the road. Note that Krauss stated that the object's axis of rotation was vertical, not horizontal as shown in this figure.
[Malthaner 1972]

and the central part of the sphere becomes milky, "just like water does before it boils". At the same time, the electrician observes that the outer shell of the ball now shows a bluish tinge "like the ionised air to be seen around electrical high-tension generators."

Resuming its previous rotating, gliding movement, the object crosses the road and passes a pace or so into the field on the other side. Then it shoots up into the sky and disappears so quickly that the electrician can't follow its movement with his eyes.

Not much anthropomorphism there. And because the witness, Max Krauss, and the investigator, Hubert Malthaner, a teacher in a technical school, were both engineers trained in the thorough German technical tradition, the full account[1] contains enough technical detail to be convincing as a possible description of a small ET prospecting bot in action. Krauss estimated the object's dark nucleus, which must have housed its 'brain', to be only about ten centimetres in diameter, so the device was small and smart enough to have pleased Allen Tough. Krauss's observation that the outer shell of the ball showed a bluish tinge like ionised air may have been on the right track – perhaps that's exactly what it was. The bluish colour may have resulted from quanta emitted by de-excitation of nitrogen molecules ionised by electrical discharge from the object.

Of course the putative prospecting bot's 'interest' in the field drainage runoff might have been linked with purposes other than geochemical prospecting. It might have been monitoring human use of fertilisers or pesticide residues. But given the evidence for ET prospecting bots already presented in this book, it's reasonable to speculate that the Langenschemmern device analysed the water for trace elements of interest, recorded the information and then rapidly conveyed or transmitted the data to an ET data interpretation unit. Thousands of such small, semi-transparent geochemical prospecting bots could have operated unnoticed worldwide allowing one ET group to build up a sophisticated knowledge base concerning this planet's hi-tech metal resources.

In remote regions of this planet, much larger ET devices could have freely engaged in geochemical prospecting, their activities only coming to light on rare occasions when people such as exploration geologists caught them red-handed. That's what apparently happened about seventy miles north of Hazelton, British Columbia at about 1000 local time on a sunny morning in July 1965. Exploration geologist John Hambling and a fellow geologist had just been dropped by helicopter on a mountain ridge in this area and had set up their equipment when, on a ridge below them to the west, catching the morning sun, they saw a domed disc, estimated to be about fifty feet in diameter and with three rectangular markings or windows on its face, move into position about fifty feet above a small glacial lake. Then, to the accompaniment of a humming noise, the device lowered an appendage into the lake. The appendage came out "smoothly and steadily as if under mechanical control", Hambling reported, the disc at the same time rotating so that its three 'windows' were facing the geologists, as if observing them. After about eight minutes, the device carefully withdrew the appendage and departed, climbing slowly at first, and then shooting off, disappearing from sight within twenty seconds.[2]

What hi-tech metals might the Hazelton device have been interested in? Mining activity had already started locally and exploration targets included copper, molybdenum, tungsten, silver, lead and zinc.[3]

Analysing runoff or glacial lake water for trace elements is fine for a human geochemist or an ET prospecting bot, as long as water is circulating or ice has been melting. But how to cope in a desert? A human geochemist might still collect dry soil samples and send them for laboratory analysis. And, as already suggested, ET bots may, like NASA's Curiosity Rover on Mars, be able to quickly deploy energetic beams that can acquire information on the elemental and isotopic composition of their targets.

That's one interpretation of what two mining engineers reported having witnessed in the New Mexico desert in 1977.[4] At about 2345 local time, one night in July of that year, the pair was surveying a prospect on a mesa in the area of Los Cerrillos, 25 miles southwest of Santa Fe. The area's metal deposits, including silver and gold, attracted prospectors in the nineteenth century and several mines operated in the area from the late nineteenth to early twentieth century. Just the place where a new, well-planned mine might succeed and, after preliminary exploration, it was logical for the engineers' mining company to carry out a detailed feasibility survey for a new mining project.

This was their first night in the area and the engineers had parked their two vehicles facing each other so that they could put their drawings on the cars' top hoods and plan the next day's activities. The desert soil below was dry with only a few tufts of grass.

While they were studying the drawings by flashlight, out of the corner of his eye one of the engineers saw a light moving over a nearby ridge, flying in a zigzag pattern. "It would move very quickly and then stop in the sky," the engineer (referred to as J.S.), who was also a pilot, reported. After that, the object repeated the manoeuvre, but this time its direction made a right angle with its previous path. According to J.S., the object repeated these movements about twenty times, all the while getting closer, each movement in the sky apparently at right angles to the direction of the previous movement.

After approaching them in this odd way, perhaps related to gyroscopic stabilisation of the device, the object started hovering about six feet above the ground about sixty feet away. It was well lit by its own lights reflecting from the ground and the engineers could see that it was a disc-like object, about fifty feet in diameter and nine feet high with a raised hat-like structure in the middle. The upper surface appeared black, in contrast to its silvery lower surface (Fig 84).[5]

It hovered silently – apart from an occasional faint "mechanical clicking" – and displayed two bands of pulsating lights, one, red, yellow and green, on the outer margin of disc and the other, green and blue and less bright higher up on the central hat-like structure. All the lights pulsed at different frequencies, flashing on and off more than once per second. The engineer had the impression that the upper lights were pulsating in a clockwise direction while the lower ones were pulsating in an anticlockwise direction.

Next, while still hovering about six feet above the ground, the object extended three thin landing legs, each about ten feet long and with a small rectangular pad at the end. When the pads were about six inches

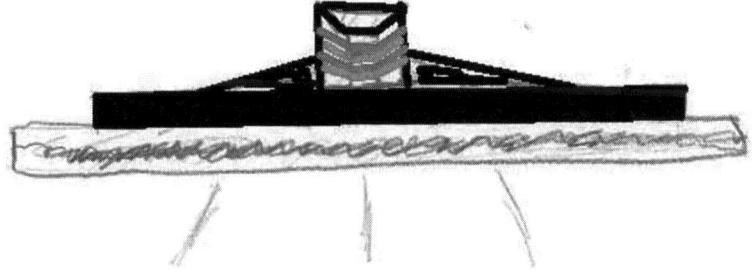

Fig 84. Profile sketch by mining engineer J.S. of a disc-like anomalous object about fifty feet in diameter, that he claimed at about 2345 local time one night in July 1977 extended three very thin legs and then landed close to a location in Los Cerrillos, New Mexico, where he and his colleague were surveying for a new mining project. [Howe 2013a]

above the flat desert surface, the object descended the final six inches slowly until its three pads rested on the surface of the mesa.

Then a hatch at the bottom of the disc opened and the machine started investigating the soil surface with a bright, white rectangular 'light' deployed at the end of an articulated arm. For several minutes the rectangular head moved around, remaining about three to six inches above the surface. The radiation from the rectangular head gave out so much heat that some of the dry grass started to smoke.

Now the articulated arm directed a beam of this intense white light directly at the two engineers who, unwisely, had left their vehicles and were now standing only about forty feet away. The articulated arm "moved fluidly like a snake", "the head whipped up and stared at us like it was alive", blinded them and forced them to cover their eyes (Fig 85).[6]

Deciding to make a rapid exit, the pair ran back to their vehicles. The bot evidently decided it was time to leave, too. It retracted the articulated arm and closed its hatch so that it emitted no light. While this was happening, the engineers tried to start their vehicles. Although J.S.'s vehicle started, his buddy's did not, so he climbed into J.S.'s vehicle and prepared to leave.

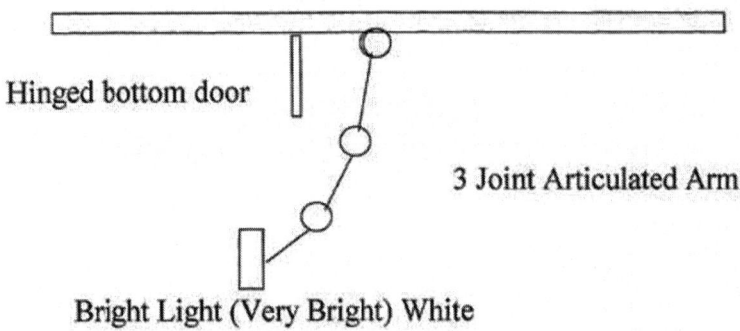

Fig 85. According to mining engineer J.S. a hatch on the bottom of the landed device shown in Fig 84 opened and the machine started investigating the desert soil with a bright, white rectangular 'light' deployed at the end of an articulated arm. [Howe 2013b]

While trying to start their vehicles, the engineers had time to observe what the bot was doing. Its lights came on as before, as if it was going through a start sequence, but its landing pads remained embedded in the ground. Then the ground started reverberating with a rum-rum-rump sound. At first, J.S. reported, the vibrations were at a sub-audible frequency, but then the frequency increased into the audible range, creating a deep rumbling sound. Fine dust started to rise from the ground, apparently caused by low-frequency vibrations passing through the landing pads into the dry soil.

The sound frequency increased steadily, first giving rise to a high-pitched turbine noise and, then, apparently, reaching ultrasonic frequencies so that the engineers could no longer hear anything. As the frequency increased, dust no longer rose from the soil and instead started to settle.

Then came lift off. The putative bot retracted its three legs simultaneously and remained hovering about six feet above the ground, as if it was rock solid. This complete rigidity of the large, silent, heavy object astonished the two engineers. Then, J.S. reported, the hovering device slowly slid forward about six inches, just as a parked car would when the driver takes his feet off the parking brake. The bot steadily gathered speed, first moving at about five or six miles per hour, then as it moved faster, it tilted to an angle of forty to fifty degrees. Maintaining the plane of its disc in line with this angle of attack, the bot accelerated, disappearing from sight within twenty to thirty seconds.

Starting at about 2345 local time, J.S. estimated, the whole episode had lasted about thirty or forty minutes. Feeling that he had to "come to peace" with the extraordinary event, to make sure that they hadn't both been hallucinating, the engineer returned to the landing site the following morning. All the traces were still there. Three rectangular imprints in the hard-packed sandy soil, about five inches by six inches in size and about two-and-a-half inches deep, represented the traces of the landing pads. The burned grass remained and the 'light' had apparently bleached some of the soil white. The prints from the wheels of the two trucks and the footprints of the two men were there too, frighteningly close to the landing traces.

The technical detail in this account suggests that the 'engineering module' in J.S.'s brain was still active, despite the dramatic and frightening nature of the events. And, on reflection, J.S. continued to think in engineering terms. For example, he worried that the machine's legs were too thin to support such a large device, the weight of which could be gauged from the two-and-a-half-inch-deep imprints its landing pads left behind in the packed sandy soil.

That of course is one argument in favour of the reality of the events. A hoaxer would hardly invent a story about an anomalous object with landing legs that were obviously too thin. But if an ET prospecting bot really did land at Los Cerrillos, its supertechnology, involving advanced superstrong materials, and perhaps including cyborg-like components, such as the lifelike articulated arm, the thinness of its landing legs might well surprise a human engineer.

The other technical details all suggest supertechnology, evidently different from the disc-like MHD-type devices that Paul Bennewitz and Ray Stanford claimed to have filmed (Chapter 10) but perhaps having something in common with the Moreland-type objects discussed in Chapter 3. Like the Moreland-type objects, key features of the Los Cerrillos device appear to have been counter-rotating gyroscopic wheels responsible for the device's rocklike stability. It clearly had the spacecraft designer's prized 'rigidity in space'.

If ET materials supertechnology meant that the machine's legs could be super strong and therefore surprisingly thin, then possibly its super-strong gyroscopic flywheels – perhaps involving carbon nanotube technology – could rotate with surprising speed. Perhaps they reached speeds orders of magnitude greater than the rates of sixty thousand or so revolutions per minute currently achieved by human-made carbon fibre energy storage flywheels with magnetic bearings. To achieve such superfast flywheel speeds, the Los Cerrillos device would need a compact source of immense energy, and that of course could have powered its quick acceleration to supersonic speeds and disappearance from sight. Whether this unknown energy source powered an MHD-type propulsion system or something more exotic, the bot would certainly have needed some MHD-like mechanism to control surrounding air or plasma in order to travel quietly at supersonic speeds.

But what was the bot actually doing as its head directed a beam of scorching white 'light' at the hard sandy desert soil? To guess that it was engaged in some kind of soil surveying is a no-brainer, as the engineer J.S. quickly pointed out. But he added no more details – remember that he and his colleague were carrying out nighttime surveying for his mining company, possibly with an element of secrecy.

A good guess is that the head of the bot's articulated arm, like the Mars Curiosity Rover's ChemCam (Fig 36), emitted energetic beams of radiation that allowed it to collect information on the concentrations of target materials in the ground. In the case of the Los Cerrillos device, these may have been metals like gold, silver, copper and molybdenum in the desert soil.[7] The bot may therefore have been a prospecting device that had parallels with the beam-emitting devices that apparently caused such mayhem in the Amazon region of Brazil and were the subject of Colonel Hollanda's investigation for the Brazilian Air Force.

Remember also that the Los Cerrillos machine apparently carried out its prospecting mission on this New Mexico mesa in July 1977, just when what may have been intense systematic surveillance in the rainforest regions of Brazil was beginning. Could this be evidence of a planetary wide ET survey for gold and other hi-tech metals, carried out at night by prospecting bots brought into the near-earth environment by vast tubular mother probes like the one apparently filmed by Ray Stanford above Memphis, Tennessee on 12 December 1977 (Chapter 8)?

If so, the Los Cerrillos machine was as well adapted to the flat, hard-surfaced desert mesas of New Mexico as Colonel Hollanda's hovering devices with their penetrating beams were to the Amazon rainforests. In comparison with the problems that the European Space Agency's Philae lander experienced when it tried to land on the boulder-strewn comet 67P in 2014, the Los Cerrillos machine's landing appeared as easy as pie. And then it had a degree of what, in his key 2001 *British Interplanetary Society* paper, NASA engineer Scot Stride called LO (Low Observable) characteristics.[8] Hidden beneath its fifty-foot-wide black upper surface, the prospecting activities of its articulated arm would not have been easily seen. Only when the device discovered that two weird aliens were in fact observing it, did it decide to leave.

After prospecting for placer gold, the next step in the suggested von Neumann sequence is the deployment of mining bots and conveyance by transport vehicles of the gold-rich placer material to the giant tubes for processing. If this happened in Brazil's Carajás Metallogenic Province in 1978, it may also have happened in other remote regions of this planet where gold placers occur. So we should be alert for eyewitness reports that could be interpreted as descriptions of mining bots excavating gold placer material and transferring it to transport vehicles.

Here's one. It's 1996 in the Indian River valley area near Dawson in Canada's Yukon Territory. Silica-rich gold placers occur here as they do in the Amazon provinces of Brazil and Peru and have been worked since the days of the 1890s Klondike gold rush.[9] But here at a latitude of 64 degrees north, with permafrost only melting superficially in the short Arctic summer (this melting has recently intensified as a result of global warming), the challenges facing prospectors and miners, whether Klondikers or ET bots, could hardly be more different from those of the Amazon jungle.

Although gold placer mining in the Dawson area has mushroomed in recent years, as Google Earth reveals, already in 1996 a view from air or space would have shown many traces of active placer mining in the valley of the Indian River and its tributary creeks. So, if such data from roving bots was available to them, ET interpretation units – perhaps, as already suggested, components of postbiological minds based in the giant tubelike mother probes – could have concluded that here, as in the Amazon region, the Sol c biologicals were mining placer gold. Here too, the interpretation units may have concluded, was an opportunity to deploy the mining bots, perhaps in the nature of quick pilot plant operations.

Pure science fiction, surely. Yet we have to consider such outlandish possibilities when we try to make sense of an eyewitness account of events in 1996, as investigated in detail by engineer Martin Jasek.[10]

One night, or rather in the twilight that passes for night at this latitude at this time of year, towards the end of July 1996, the twin sisters Sue Malcolm and Sarah Baker, restaurateurs, were returning from Whitehorse to their home near Dawson City (Fig 86).

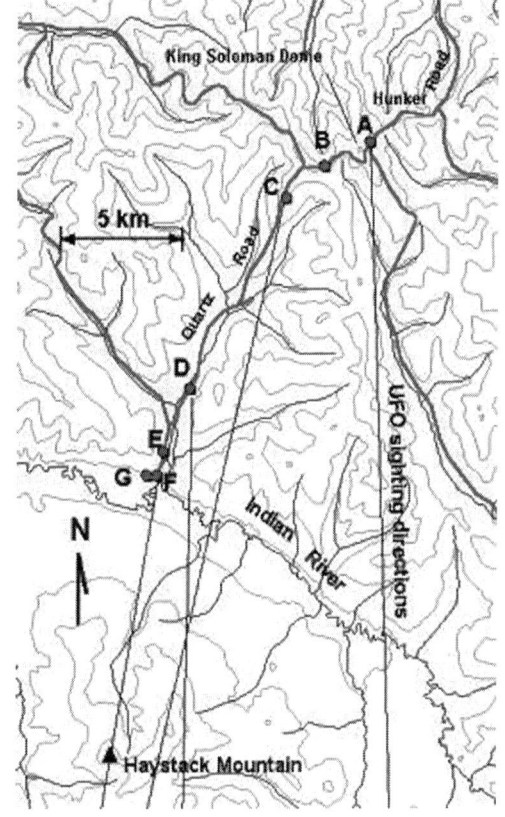

Fig 86. ABCDEFG marks the route followed after midnight one 'night' in July 1996 by twin sisters Sue Malcolm and Sarah Baker, returning from Whitehorse to their home near Dawson City in the Indian River area of Yukon Territory.

Travelling along the Hunker Road, as they reached a local high point (A) about twenty kilometers northeast of Dawson City, they were startled to see, above the mountains to the south, what they interpreted as a cigar-shaped object, tilted at a slight angle, with a row of rectangular 'windows' in the middle, (Fig 87). At point C, now driving along Quartz Road, they saw the object again, low over the mountains directly ahead of them. It was tilted with its eastern end uppermost. The twins saw twelve or thirteen bright hazy lights 'buzzing' around and going in and out of the eastern upper end of the object.

After travelling about ten kilometers further south along Quartz Road the twins saw the object a third time, at point D. The smaller objects had now 'tucked themselves away' but to Sue and Sarah the cigar-shaped object now appeared close and to be hovering directly above a gold claim the twins jointly owned in the Indian River valley. [Jasek 2003]

Travelling along the Hunker Road, as they reached a local high point about twenty kilometres northeast of Dawson City, they were startled to see above the mountains to the south, what they interpreted as a cigar-shaped object, tilted at a slight angle, with a row of rectangular 'windows' in the middle. Sue Malcolm later told Jasek that she recalled then looking at her watch and noticing that it had stopped at 0150 local time.

Instead of stopping to watch the object, they decided to get to the safety of their home and the reassurances of Sue's grown-up son, as soon as possible. About five kilometres further on, by which time they were driving southwards to Dawson City along Quartz Road, they saw the object again, low over the mountains directly ahead of them. It was tilted with its eastern end uppermost. The twins now saw twelve or thirteen bright hazy lights 'buzzing' around and going in and out of the eastern upper end of the object (Fig 87).

As they drove south along Quartz Road into a valley, the twins lost sight of the big object because of hills to the east. But after travelling about ten kilometres further south along Quartz Road, the twins saw the object a third time. The smaller objects had now "tucked themselves away", but to Sue and Sarah, the cigar-shaped object now appeared close and to be hovering directly above a gold claim the twins jointly owned in the Indian River valley.

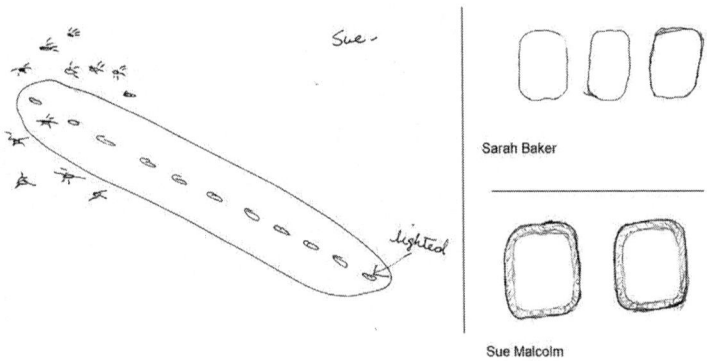

Fig 87. Sketches by twin sisters Sue Malcolm and Sarah Baker of the giant cigar-shaped object they claimed to have seen to the south from point A of Fig 86. [Jasek 2003]

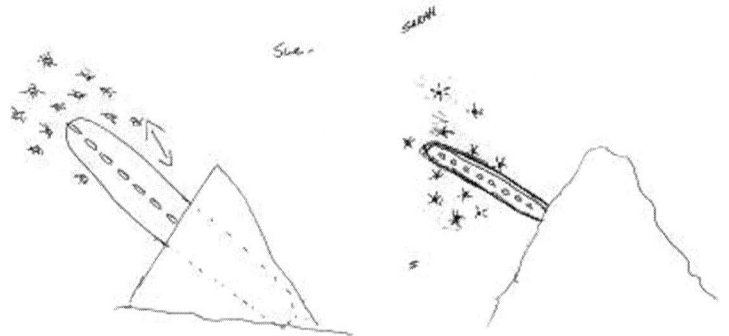

Fig 88. Sketches by twin sisters Sue Malcolm and Sarah Baker of the a giant cigar-shaped object they claimed to have seen to the south from points E and F of Fig 86. At E they recall seeing the cigar's lower western end move slowly behind the prominent local feature known as Haystack Mountain. Left, Sue's sketch, right, Sarah's. At point F, just before arriving home, they recall having seen the eastern end of the cigar finally pass behind the mountain. [Jasek 2003]

About three kilometres further south, now only about two kilometres from their home, the twins saw the cigar-shaped object once more. It had tilted further and the twins were astonished to see that its lower, western end was now concealed behind the prominent feature known as Haystack Mountain, about twelve kilometres to the southwest (Fig 88). They saw the cigar descend slowly behind Haystack Mountain, maintaining the same high angle of tilt as it did so. Just before they reached their home, they saw the upper, eastern end of the cigar finally disappear behind the western flank of the mountain. They couldn't understand how the whole thing could fit behind Haystack Mountain unless "it went into the dirt".

After the twins, overwrought by their experience, reached home, they watched Haystack Mountain for about twenty minutes while unloading their car. They did not see the cigar reappear during that time.

Upon hearing this remarkable story, engineer Martin Jasek undertook a thorough investigation.[10] He studied the local topography and found that there was a steep-sided valley to the south of Haystack Mountain. By sinking its lower western end into this valley, the cigar, which Jasek estimated might have been around six hundred metres long, could have concealed itself completely from the twins and other observers in Dawson. After waiting until any observers lost interest, it could have made an unobserved ascent.

What to make of this story? The only prosaic explanation would be a hoax by the twins, perhaps with an eye to promoting themselves and their restaurant on Prince Edward Island. But that looks unlikely. Abduction by space aliens is the name of the game when it comes to UFO stories with popular appeal. Seeing distant lights in the sky isn't likely to bring people into your restaurant. And Jasek's careful demonstration that, unknown to the twins, there was a valley to the south of Haystack Mountain that could have accommodated the lower western end of the huge object, adds weight to their narrative.

But what transforms the twins' tale from just another UFO story to a possible real event is that the notion of von Neumann machines processing gold-silica placer deposits provides an interpretative framework within which their seemingly crazy story makes sense. On this hypothesis the cigar was a mineral-processing vehicle, like those that may have operated in Brazil in 1978, been seen in the Dalnegorsk 'search fleet' in 1987 and possibly captured by an automated camera in Knittelfeld, Austria in 2008 (Fig 82). The bright, hazy objects the twins saw buzzing around and going in and out of the upper end of the object could have been MHD-propelled mining bots surrounded by their plasma coronas.

Having quickly excavated a substantial amount of gold-silica material from one or more of the many gold placer deposits in the Indian River area, the mining bots would have transported the material to the raised eastern end of the giant vehicle, allowing gravity to complete the task. It would have been this stage of the operation that the twins witnessed as they viewed the smaller objects going in and out of it as they drove down Quartz Road.

The mining bots, if that's what they were, would have been too small for the twins to make out in any detail from a distance of around ten kilometres (Fig 87). But the giant sizes of the cigar itself and of the illuminated patches that ran along it evidently led them to conclude that these patches had rectangular shapes. It was natural for the twins to interpret these patches as giant windows – perhaps they imagined giant aliens peering out through them. But if the big cigar was indeed a mineral-processing vehicle, its controlling AI systems perhaps seeking to avoid telltale radiofrequency emissions, the luminous rectangles could have been communications panels. The panels could have been sending high frequency optical signals to the mining bots.

Mining operations could have been brief, possibly lasting only a few minutes, this particular venture only coming to light by chance. Had this incident happened in France, police and science teams might have investigated and found evidence of the removal of material in line with the twins' report. But this was North America, where no official science teams had openly investigated UFO reports since the US Air Force sacked Allen Hynek in 1969.

After lead and gold, the next set of hi-tech materials that the Height 611 remains suggest may be on the ET shopping list are neodymium, praseodymium and other rare earth elements. As with gold, as a result of the Earth's gravity operating in conjunction with processes such as river and wave action, abundant placer deposits rich in these materials occur on this planet. But whereas the heavy metal gold is chemically stable and gold placers, therefore, contain gold itself (strictly gold-rich alloy), the rare earth elements are highly reactive. They are found, however, in the stable heavy minerals monazite and xenotime and these are the minerals that wave action has concentrated in old beach deposits.

One of the most important of such deposits stretches along Australia's east coast in New South Wales from the Sydney area northwards to Tweed Heads. Here, the other heavy minerals rutile, ilmenite and zircon, sources of hi-tech metals titanium and zirconium, are also found. Taken together, these add up to an economically attractive proposition and, for many years, this stretch of coast was one of the planet's leading sources of rare earths.

But there was a fly in the ointment. Thorium, making up about three per cent of monazite, consists of a mixture of radioactive isotopes and, therefore, its working presents radiation hazards. Concerns about this led to the closure in the 1980s of the Kincumber monazite processing plant near Gosford, about 50 kilometres northeast of Sydney. To minimise transport costs of monazite-rich concentrates, the Kincumber plant was located close to minerals sands quarries in the complex bar-built estuary deposits of the Brisbane Water area.

Hypothetical humanoid aliens, too, might have reservations about working with monazite. But robust ET bots could withstand high levels of ionising radiation. Given the presence of rare-earth-rich compositions in the Height 611 remains, we should check to see if there are any reports from the monazite-bearing deposits of the eastern Australian coast that might be interpreted as activities of ET prospecting or mining bots.

So if you want to catch an ET prospecting bot in action, head for Sydney's Bondi Beach? On second thoughts, bear in mind that ET bots may not like crowds, and go to a quieter beach near Sydney, perhaps in winter at dusk. That's just what Sydney resident Denis Crowe, a technical artist who had been employed by several British aircraft companies, did one winter's evening in 1965.

Crowe's account of what happened next is important for several reasons. His professional experience as a technical artist employed by British aircraft companies could hardly be more relevant to the claims and technical drawing he made (Fig 89). The large-circulation Sydney paper, *Daily Telegraph,* attracted much interest when it published Crowe's drawing, together with his careful description of his experience.[11] Many readers wrote to the paper to report having seen objects like the one sketched by Crowe, but having remained silent through fear of ridicule.

As a result of all this publicity, the Royal Australian Air Force was forced to make a statement. Crowe might have seen a tornado, they said. Neither Crowe nor the readers of the *Daily Telegraph* who had viewed his sketch were particularly struck by the brilliance of this suggestion.

But what did Denis Crowe actually claim to have seen?

About 1700 on July 19, 1965, a day of high winds and stormy showers (hence the tornado idea), Crowe was walking along Vaucluse Beach, Sydney, during a period of calm between the showers, when he noticed a glow coming from the sands and decided to investigate. He reached a point about fifty or sixty feet from the glow and discovered that it surrounded a disc about twenty feet in diameter and nine feet high, just above the sand. The upper conical surface of the disc was silvery grey on top and a darker grey lower down, with a hollow on the top that could have been a transparent dome. Around the rim of the disc was a greenish-blue glow.

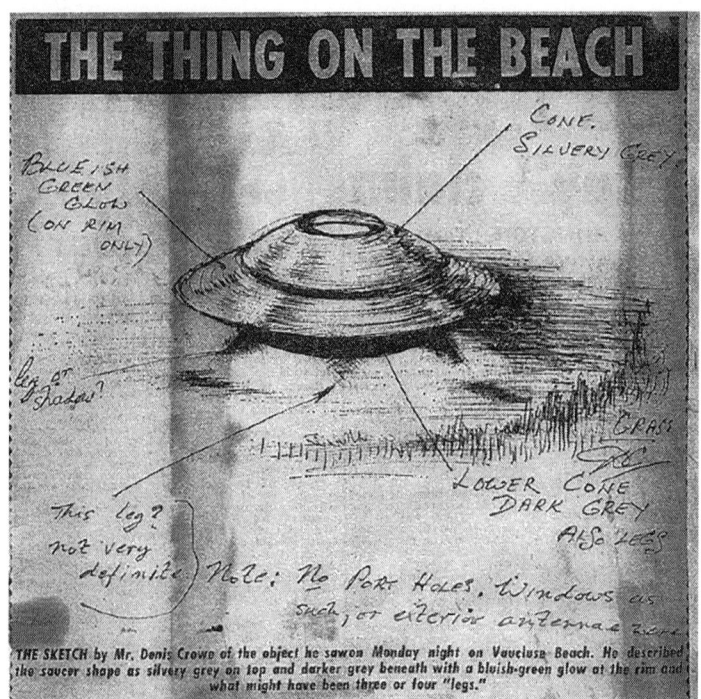

Fig 89. *The Thing on the Beach.* About 1730 local time in the evening of 19 July, 1965, technical artist Denis Crowe noticed a glow coming from the sands at Vaucluse Beach, Sydney, New South Wales, and decided to investigate. He found that the source of the glow was a disc about twenty feet in diameter and made this sketch, afterwards published in the Sydney Daily Telegraph.

Like many other sandy beaches along the eastern Australian coast, Vaucluse Beach contains the heavy mineral monazite, rich in rare earth elements (REEs). The disc may have been prospecting for these elements. *[Sydney Daily Telegraph 21 July 1965]*

The area below the disc was not clearly visible, so Crowe couldn't see whether or not the object was resting on legs. The only other witnesses were some dogs that started barking loudly at the object. With so much unwanted attention from these strange Sol c biologicals, the putative bot evidently decided to leave and Crowe saw a yellow orange glow appear beneath it as it made a short "take off run" of fifty or sixty feet. Then it "it took off with a noise like air forcibly released from a balloon" and "quite unlike any made by jet engines." Crowe claimed to have watched the object in flight for ten seconds before it disappeared in a cloud over Manly to the north. After returning home and eating his dinner he made the sketch shown in Fig 89.

Crowe told the reporter that he had wondered if he should keep silent but felt "a moral obligation to speak of what I had seen." Reportedly, a geologist afterwards inspected the site and concluded that something had definitely landed there and the nearby vegetation was dying.

In 1965 the RAAF's tornado idea may have been the only scientific interpretation available of Denis Crowe's report and technical sketch. But the recently published work discussed in this book, particularly Paul Bennewitz's 1979 Manzano images (Chapter 10) and their interpretations in terms of MHD theory, suggests more plausible alternatives.

It's now clear that Denis Crowe's key observations concerned the blue-green glow around the object's rim as it remained stationary over the sand and the yellow-orange glow he observed beneath the object just before it took off. The stationary Vaucluse Beach disc's blue-green rim glow compares with the blue-green rim glow of the stationary Manzano discs (Colour Plate 2). And the orange glow beneath the Vaucluse Beach disc before it accelerated away compares with the orange glow above the Manzano discs before they accelerated away (Colour Plate 3).

It's reasonable to speculate that the blue-green 'rim glows' represented spectral lines around 500 nanometres emitted by ionised molecules in the air and that these plasmas were created by emitters of ionising radiation located around the rims of the Vaucluse and Manzano discs. Likewise, orange glows, representing emission lines around 600 nanometres, may have been created by ionising radiation from unknown emitters on the discs.

Further, considering that at both Vaucluse Beach and Manzano an orange glow preceded acceleration, we can once again deploy Auguste Meessen's suggestion, presented at the 2012 Moscow meeting of the Electromagnetics Academy, that some anomalous objects may use synchronised ionisation pulses and magnetic pulses to accelerate.[12] That idea, together with Paul Bennewitz' s Manzano data, could now enable a team of aerospace engineers and plasma physicists to develop new interpretations of Denis Crowe's 1965 Vaucluse Beach data.

And when that team considers what the bot might have been doing on Vaucluse Beach, the studies of the Height 611 remains, coupled with the von Neumann idea, now suggest that it might have been prospecting for rare earth elements. Whether the bot used high-energy 'prospecting' beams, as the Los Cerrillos device may have done, or 'direct smelting' beams to collect actual samples of rare earths, we can speculate that the device may have been gathering data as part of a longer-term ET mission. Just as NASA's Mars rovers have gathered data as part of a decades-long human quest to better understand Martian geology, so the Vaucluse bot may have been collecting data as part of a decades-long ET assessment of the rare earth potential of the Earth's minerals sands deposits.

If so, as in the case of the human gold placer operations around Dawson in the Yukon, the human minerals sands quarrying operations in the Brisbane Water estuary deposits west of the old Kincumber monazite processing plant may have attracted the attention of ET rare earth prospecting bots. So, while remaining alert for anomalous events along the whole eastern Australian coast, it would be sensible to concentrate on this area south of Gosford.

Over the years the Gosford area has indeed been a focus for reports of anomalous activity. For example in early December 1995 several witnesses reported anomalous lights manoeuvring in the local skies. Then, in the hours after midnight in early morning of 31 December 1995, many people reported being woken up by a loud humming noise and were alarmed when they found that the noise appeared to be coming from a hovering object, about 20 to 30 metres across, that was sending four or five cylinders or columns of 'light' down into the shallow water. This was accompanied by frothing as displaced water splashed back onto the estuary surface. Some witnesses reported having seen the object away from the water, or in flight, and in these cases, with the beams 'turned off', they could see a red glow or flashing red and orange lights beneath the object.[13]

The frightened witnesses overwhelmed the duty officer at the local Gosford police station with their telephone calls. The localities where the residents observed the hovering object included Point Frederick, St Hubert's

Island, Woy Woy, Ettalong and Umina (Fig 90). Having concluded that the panicking callers weren't hoaxers, the experienced desk sergeant sent patrol cars to investigate at least thirty-five times. But the officers reported that each time their headlights got close, the object would turn off its lights and shoot up out of sight.

In view of the number of frightened witnesses, the quality of their statements and the scale of the police activity, scientists had a clear obligation to help the police by making provisional scientific interpretations of what had happened. But this was Anglophone New South Wales, not rational France. So once again the UFO taboo reared its

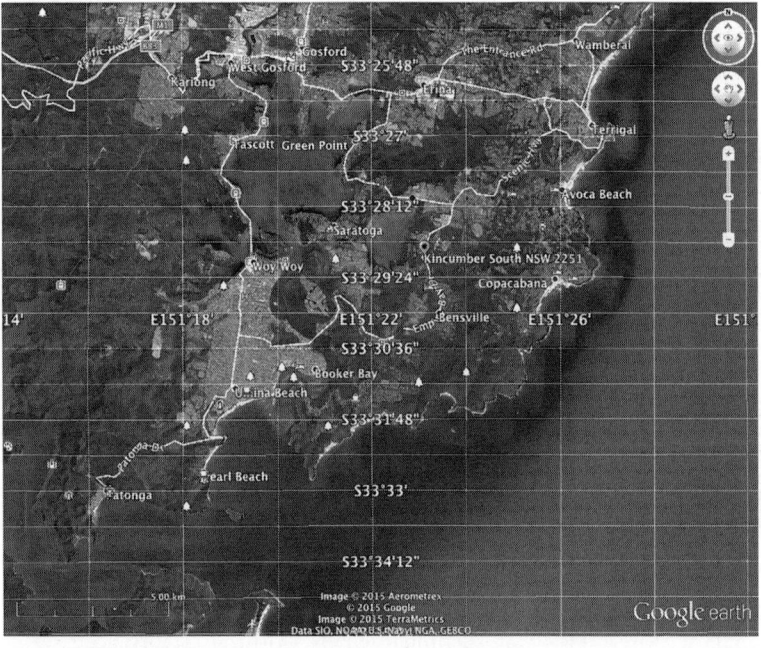

Fig 90. Gosford–Kincumber area, New South Wales. In the early hours of 31 December 1995, many residents in properties close to the Brisbane Water estuary south of Gosford reported a hovering object, about 20 to 30 metres across, that was sending four or five cylinders or columns of 'light' down into the shallow water. Beneath the shallow waters here the sands contain the REE-rich mineral monazite. Like the 1965 Vaucluse Beach disc, the 1995 Gosford device may therefore have been an ET bot prospecting for REEs.

ugly head and Aussie scientists buried their heads in their minerals sands. Fortunately, with full police cooperation, the local media and amateur UFO investigators did a fair job in interviewing witnesses and preparing provisional accounts of the anomalous events.[14] In 2012, posting as 'Lowneck', I started a discussion thread on this topic on the Above Top Secret forum (Search: www.abovetopsecret.com Gosford NSW multiple witness UFO sightings Dec 30/31 1995).

All this opens the way for the suggestion that the anomalous activity in the Gosford/Brisbane Water area in December 1995 represented a later stage in a decades-long ET assessment of the rare earth potential of eastern Australia's minerals sands. Having used bots like the Vaucluse Beach device as early as 1965 to obtain preliminary information on possible exploration targets, in early December 1995, ET decision-making units may have used further prospecting bots to conduct surveys in the region north of Sydney, giving rise to the reports of anomalous lights at that time.

Then in the early morning of 31 December 1995 a larger ET device may have deployed its multiple broad beams to obtain specific data concerning the size and rare earth potential of stratiform monazite-rich ore bodies beneath the shallow waters of the Brisbane Water estuary.

Like the Curiosity Rover's laser beam system, the beams may have been capable of identifying particular elements and quantifying their abundance. They may even have had some 'direct smelting' capabilities. If so, the compositions of the metallic particles obtained from monazite, like the products obtained from monazite concentrates at the local Kincumber plant before its closure, would have resembled 'mischmetall' in composition.

Mischmetall is an alloy containing about fifty percent cerium, with smaller amounts of lanthanum, neodymium and praseodymium. As well as being used as a source of individual rare earths, mischmetall from monazite is exploited directly in human technology. For example, one application is in flint ignition devices, with other compounds such as iron oxide and magnesium oxides being added to achieve the required hardness.

Recall (Chapter 15) that the Height 611 researchers identified similar compositions both in the lead balls and in fragments that may have been remnants of the object's original structure. Therefore, we can speculate that, like human technology, ET supertechnology has evolved to exploit monazite-derived mischmetall directly as well as having uses for individual rare earth elements, such as neodymium and praseodymium. It's even possible that mischmetall had a role in the self-destroying capabilities of the Height 611 device.

Like gold and silica, monazite is a stable mineral likely to be common in placer deposits on our galaxy's earth-like exoplanets and exomoons. Over the millennia, transported from one planetary system to another in its mother probe, the 1995 Brisbane Water device may have operated in many such environments.

If it functions as an advanced prospecting device, then the putative Brisbane Water vehicle's role in monazite processing may parallel the suggested role of ET prospecting devices in gold-silica processing. Successful prospecting would be followed by pilot plant mining operations. After extraction by mining bots, monazite concentrates would be transported to large mother probes, like the giant Stanford tubes, for further processing and the mischmetall or individual rare earth elements would be used in production, von Neumann style, of new bots or repair of damaged ones.

Alternatively, the large size of the Brisbane Water vehicle suggests the possibility that its broad 'smelting' beams may themselves have been capable of extracting useful quantities of mischmetal from the underwater ore bodies it hovered over. The device may even have been able to isolate individual rare earth metals such as neodymium and praseodymium.

Apart from rare earths, the Brisbane Water device may also be capable of extracting useful amounts of other hi-tech metals, such as gold and tin from placers on the earthlike planets or moons it visits on its rounds. After docking with its mother probe, automated systems may use these materials directly to make bot components for use in von Neumann activity.

Such scenarios may seem far-fetched, but they are perfectly plausible scientifically. Until the scientific ostriches of Oz propose viable prosaic explanations for the events of 31 December 1995, such way-out notions should remain on the table.

The next metal on the suggested ET shopping list, molybdenum, presents challenges different from those posed by gold and rare earths. If the outer hulls of some devices are made of molybdenum, then, to replace failed bots, ET's von Neumann operations will require supplies of this metal. Yet, in contrast to gold and rare earths, but like those of lead, molybdenum ore minerals, such as molybdenite (molybdenum sulphide), are not stable in the natural placer deposits of this planet with its oxygen-rich atmosphere.

Perhaps stable molybdenum-rich placers occur on some planets. Or perhaps ET bots mine vein deposits of molybdenum on some planets free of interfering biologicals. Perhaps ET bots even obtain molybdenum through that science fiction staple, the mining of extrasolar asteroids.

But here on Sol c the only superficial molybdenum sources for ET von Neumann operations would be old tailings dumps in mining areas where humans have recently exploited vein deposits of molybdenum. If the Height 611 object obtained samples of lead from galena (lead sulphide) left behind in tailings dumps at the Kholodninskoye vein deposits in 1986, then other prospecting bots could have pinpointed locations of tailing dumps containing residual molybdenite. And, in cases where such prospecting had been successful, we might expect ET bots to have progressed to the pilot mining stage. So we should look for evidence of anomalous activity near old molybdenum tailings dumps.

There is one such report. It came from two hunters, who, one early morning in the fall of 1965, were camping in the Selway wilderness in Idaho, on a ridge overlooking an old tailings dump of the Spring Creek Mine, about half a mile away.

After some Internet research, I found that this mine once had one production adit exploiting a quartz vein associated with pyrite, molybdenite and galena.[15] The mine was assessed as having 500,000 tons of ore with two per cent molybdenite. After processing of concentrates, the tailings would still have contained worthwhile amounts of molybdenum. Google Earth shows a mound, apparently the remains of the old tailings dump, close to the location of the old Spring Creek mine.

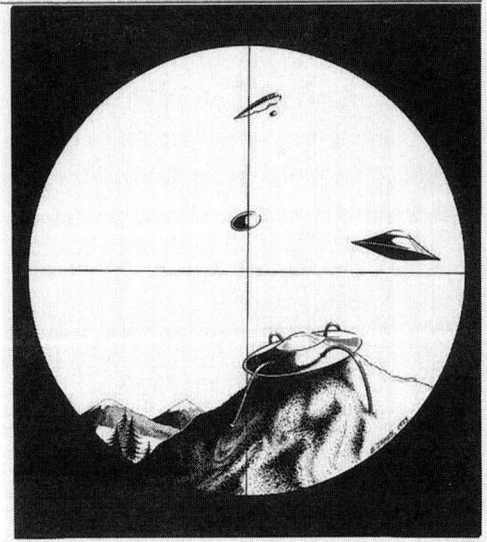

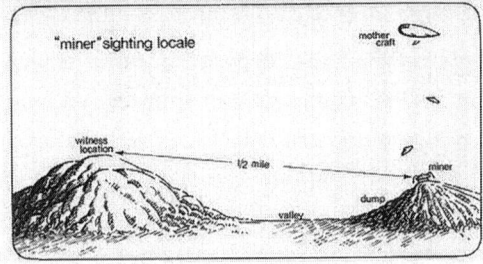

Fig 91. ET mining bots working an old molybdenum mine tailings dump in Idaho?

Hunter Buzz Montague reported that in the fall of 1965 at about 0600 local time one morning a fellow hunter and himself witnessed four discs sitting on a mine tailings dump, apparently sucking up material through hose-like pipes.

According to Montague, after some time, the discs made their way upwards towards a larger elongated object that the hunters now noticed for the first time.. When the four discs reached the larger object, they fitted snugly into four depressions in its underside and remained there for a short time. Then the four discs descended to the mine dump, repeated their mining routine and returned to the larger object. The discs repeated this routine twice more. Finally, according to Montague, after the discs had fitted into the depressions in its hull, the large object ascended slowly to the northwest and disappeared in the distance.

Aerial Phenomena Research Organization (APRO) artist Brian James subsequently contacted Montague and after discussion with him prepared this sketch to illustrate what Montague claimed to have seen. Although James's sketch makes good sense as an imaginative depiction of putative mining bots in action, it fails to capture the 'group behaviour' reported by Montague. [Lorenzen 1973]

Back to the hunters' report. One of the hunters, Buzz Montague, reported the anomalous events in a 1967 letter to Coral Lorenzen, the Secretary-Treasurer of APRO, the long-defunct high-quality UFO research organisation already mentioned.[16] Mrs Lorenzen didn't publish an account for some years, because she needed time to organise a field investigation in Idaho to check that Montague's extraordinary claims were plausible.

In the end Allen Benz, APRO's librarian, was able to investigate the Spring Creek mining area in Idaho and interview Montague. APRO's staff artist, Brian James, also contacted Montague and worked with him to produce the illustration of the incident shown here (Fig 91).

Benz and Montague agreed on the following account, to which I've added an observation of my own. On the day of the sighting, Montague and his fellow hunter woke at about six in the morning and both noticed a shiny spot on the tailings dump. If my Google Earth identification of the location of the tailings dump and of the hunters' campsite on the ridge are broadly correct, then the hunters would have been about half a mile to the east of the dump, well-placed to see any metallic objects there reflecting light from the rising sun.

Using the ten-power telescopic sights fixed to his rifle, Montague observed four shiny disc-like objects, with transparent domes on top, hovering over the tailings dump. Extending from the upper part of each disc were four hose-like pipes, the lower ends of which were embedded in the dump and 'moving around' within it.

According to Montague, after some time, the discs made their way upwards towards a larger elongated object that the hunters now noticed for the first time (Fig 91). Hovering at an estimated one thousand feet above the ground, the object had four depressions on its underside. When the four discs reached the larger object, they fitted snugly into the depressions and remained there for a short time.

Then the four discs descended to the mine dump, repeated their mining routine and returned to the larger object. The discs repeated this routine twice more, so that within the forty-five minute or more observation period, each disc had apparently transported four loads of material from the mine dump to the larger object. Finally, according to

Montague, after the discs had fitted into the depressions in its hull, the large object ascended slowly to the northwest and disappeared in the distance.

Once again we have a story that challenges the current scientific paradigm. And once again the evidence for von Neumann activity reported in this book transforms the tale from an account of something impossible to an event that may well have happened. For Montague's story now makes sense within a scenario in which ET bots have mined residual molybdenite in tailings dumps for use in the production of molybdenum hulls for prospecting devices such as the Height 611 object.

But do Brian James's illustrations (Fig 91) make sense as imaginative depictions of real ET bots in action? With their shallow transparent domes, James's discs are remarkably similar to the Sydney *Daily Telegraph's* depiction of Denis Crowe's disc sitting on Vaucluse Beach, also in 1965 (Fig 89). These see-through domes could open the way to charges of anthropomorphism but only if we imagine pairs of little men sitting inside and manually piloting the objects. Once we replace the 'little man' idea with the twin sensor concept discussed in connection with the Moreland-type devices of Chapter 3, these transparent domes immediately gain plausibility. Indeed, an eye-like design, with wide spacing between two optical sensors permitting stereoscopic 'vision', would well equip the Idaho and Vaucluse Beach devices for rapid navigation in planetary atmospheres and hydrospheres.

Strongly supporting the bot interpretation of the Idaho discs is the group behaviour evident in Buzz Montague's account. Rather than engaging in mining activities individually, as craft with humanoid pilots would, the four devices always behaved as a group, just as the anomalous objects captured by Paul Bennewitz in his 1979 Manzano images did (Chapter 10).

Interestingly, artist Brian James failed to capture this group behaviour in his illustration (Fig 91). Instead of showing the four bots working together on the tailings dump as Montague reported, he shows one device hogging the prime spot, leaving its three companions to fend for themselves. So even with efforts to be accurate, anthropomorphism creeps into depictions by human artists.

Conceding that group behaviour is what we might expect from ET bots, a sceptic might still chortle at James's depiction of the four hosepipe-like tubes the discs extended into the tailings dump. ET technology would surely be more advanced than that.

But recall electrician Max Krauss's hosepipe-like tube, writhing "like a worm". Remember engineer J.S.'s articulated arm that "moved fluidly like a snake", its head then staring at the engineers "like it was alive". It took hundreds of millions of years for worms and snakes to evolve on this planet and even in the twenty-first century our most advanced robots aren't able to replicate the fluidity of movements described by Krauss and J.S. So Buzz Montague's hose-like pipes "moving around" within the Idaho molybdenum mine tailings dump fit neatly within the picture of an ET technology involving super strong cyborg-like components that can wriggle like worms or snakes.

The tubes would need to suck powerfully as well as wriggle when in the dump, and later pump the material out into storage units in the large hovering teardrop-shaped vehicle. But with power sources of the kind large enough to drive the Los Cerrillos object's high-speed gyroscopic flywheels, that would pose no problem in the design/evolution of these bots. Indeed, if we consider the Spring Creek devices together with the Los Cerrillos device, the Vaucluse Beach device and the Moreland-type objects of Chapter 3, it's possible that all the devices feature counter rotating gyroscopic flywheels. And, instead of being windows through which aliens can peer out, any 'portholes' in this class of surveillance disc may simply be orifices allowing the devices to double up as placer mining bots.

What of the large hovering teardrop-shaped vehicle itself? Intriguingly, the shape matches that of one of the vehicles reported near Dalnegorsk on the night of 28 November 1987 (Fig 68). The teardrop shape of both is an efficient design for vehicles travelling through viscous media such as planetary atmospheres or hydrospheres.

Endnotes

1 Malthaner 1972.
2 Magor 1969.
3 Saunders 1982.
4 Howe 2013a.
5 ibid.
6 Howe 2013b.
7 Akright 1979.
8 Stride 2001.
9 Jasek 2003.
10 ibid.
11 Crowe 1965.
12 Meessen 2012a.
13 McGhee and Dickeson 1997.
14 ibid.
15 Johnson *et al*. 1998, p.18.
16 Lorenzen 1973.

19

The Collierville Bots

If ET surveillance bots, perhaps wholly or partly organically grown, von Neumann-style, from local materials have continued to operate on this planet in the twenty-first century, there should now be some excellent digital media evidence of their activities. Even if military authorities have kept their material secret, the ubiquity of digital cameras, CCTV cameras and smart phones should have led to the capture of at least one set of data providing unambiguous evidence for the activities of such anomalous devices.

There is.

On 1 February 2015 at about 0445 local time, a group of seven Fed Ex professionals were relaxing in a glass-enclosed patio surrounded by woodland in Collierville, Tennessee, lit by a wood fire. For insurance purposes the house owner, Fed Ex pilot 'Jim Brigman' (not his real name) had fitted the patio with four CCTV cameras, installed to capture nearby animal activity.

The friends, three pilots, an attorney, an engineer, an operations manager and a PR officer, were chatting about the prospects for their alma mater's baseball team, the Memphis Tigers. At 0447 they noticed the face of one of their number, engineer 'Earl Sexton', turn icy. They turned to see what had disturbed him. They were startled to see a little over a mile to the northeast a bright red-yellow object moving towards the patio. One of the CCTV camera files, viewed later, showed that the luminous output was oscillating.

As the luminous object approached the line of trees to the northeast of the property, the men could see that there were in fact three objects. Their movements were too smooth and slow to be produced by an aircraft in distress.

Then the objects silently approached the patio and their brightness engulfed it. The light and heat blinded the witnesses, forcing them to lower their heads. Jim Brigman later commented that the heat made him feel "like roast beef" and threatened the men with heat stroke. Although the light quickly diminished, the heat remained and the seven men decided to move from the patio into the house.

And so began a series of life changing, life threatening events that, through their own resourcefulness, the Fed Ex seven turned into one of most important data capture events in the history of science.

So important in fact that the digital material captured during the next hour has yet to be publicly released. Initially scheduled for Internet release on 1 October 2016, the release date was delayed for reasons linked with US government policy at that time regarding the public release of data concerning anomalous events.

Not only was the release of the digital material delayed, a key book that the friends quickly wrote soon after the events of 1 February 2015 was later withdrawn.[1]

Lee Spencer is the pseudonym of the attorney, whose real name, Andrew Lynn, can be easily established from the biographies in the book and publicly available information. Apart from Lynn I've used the book's pseudonyms for the other six friends in the account presented here. As the events are so important for all of us and the book is now difficult to obtain, the following summary is longer than I'd have otherwise considered appropriate. See also the 2016 Above Top Secret forum thread that I started on the subject, posting as 'Lowneck' (Search: www.abovetopsecret.com 'The Anomalous Events of 1 February 2015').

Back to the story of what happened on 1 February 2015. The CCTV videos show the seven men entering the house from the patio at about 0451, six minutes after the incident began. They then decided to leave the house altogether and exited by the southwestern door. They were met with a sight that they will never forget.

Andrew Lynn recalled seeing the three objects hovering in "majestic silence" about twenty feet above the ground. Although the light from the objects was now dimmed, it was still sufficient to illuminate the tree line to the northeast of the house. Knowing the distance between the trees and the house, and studying the apparent size of the objects in the CCTV footage, Lynn later estimated that the largest object was about sixty feet in diameter and the smallest about forty feet in diameter. The largest object had a dome or cupola extending about six feet above the plane of its disk.

Lynn recalled that the three objects hovered closely together with "distinct synchronism" in their motions, but never wobbled into each other. This synchronism also fascinated pilot 'James Cantrell' who recalled the dark grey objects performing a "silent dance" like "Russian ballerinas". 'Chad Davis', the PR Officer, was also struck by the three dark grey objects' dance and agreed with Lynn that the largest object appeared to have a central rise.

Fed Ex and Tennessee National Air Guard pilot 'Derrick Gibbs' recalled that the house was bathed in light as he left it and then he found himself "face to face with a scene that will never leave me as long as I live." About seventy feet away from him, and twenty feet in the air, were three hovering plates, dark grey in color. The largest had a central dome and looked as if it was "a perfect fluidic machine" that had a remarkable aerodynamic design to it. Around its outer edge were small orifices that Gibbs interpreted as possible "vortex killers". But he couldn't see how such features, normally located on wing tips, would work on a circular object.

Gibbs was fascinated by the apparent aerodynamic design of the objects and, like Lynn, was amazed at the way that such large devices could dance in the air, sometimes getting within one foot of each other, without colliding. He thought that their formation flying would make any Thunderbird pilot jealous of their skills.

Gibbs was so captivated by the dancing objects, "the design dream of an aerospace engineer," that he could have stood there looking at them for hours. But after only a few minutes, Gibbs heard 'Eric Gray', the Operations Manager, say "It must be a joke" and, for a few moments,

Gibbs went along with this idea, thinking that some clever people must have put a lot of energy and money into creating a cunning design based on balloons.

At 0456, while Gibbs was still pondering Gray's hoax theory, he and the other men saw the objects suddenly veer left, over the wooded area to the east of Brigman's house. They accelerated at a rate that ruled out not only balloons but also human devices of any kind – and the witnesses heard nothing. After disappearing for a moment, Gibbs saw red-yellowish lights come from their direction and concluded that the objects had settled in a field beyond the woods. The lights were visible because the trees had lost their leaves in the Tennessee winter.

From later study of the CCTV footage, the witnesses deduced that the three objects had completed their jump to the point behind the trees, about 700 yards away, within 1/5 of a second. Gibbs estimated that the objects' acceleration must have been over 1600 g, orders of magnitude above what humans can stand physically or generate technologically. Such acceleration would have crushed any humanoid aliens to pulp.

Coming so soon after the initial life-threatening outburst of light and heat, this astonishing display of beyond-human technology would have caused most people to panic. The men were indeed frightened – Lynn recalled "fear settled in our minds." Gibbs and the others also were scared but at the same time experienced feelings of wonder and technical curiosity.

Gibbs, the Tennessee National Air Guard pilot and staunch US patriot, recalls reasoning that either the US military knew about this technology or it didn't. If it did, nothing he could do would make any difference. But if Uncle Sam didn't know about the technology, it was Gibbs' duty, as a member of the Tennessee National Air Guard who had sworn to protect his country, to investigate and report to the authorities. This was particularly so in view of the possibility that the technology might end up in the hands of enemies of the US.

The three anomalous objects having left the immediate vicinity, the seven men went into the house. Jim Brigman and Eric Gray had left their smart phones on the kitchen table and found that they still worked. The phones of Derrick Gibbs and the others had been exposed to the patio heat and no longer functioned.

Thinking quickly, the group decided to use the two serviceable smart phones to capture further data on what they decided to call Airborne Objects (AOs), now glimmering beyond the trees. They agreed to form two science teams, each with a smart phone, which would approach the objects from different angles.

The first team, composed of Brigman, Sexton, Davis and Lynn, started walking along a track towards the objects in the east at 0501. The second team, consisting of Gray, Gibbs and Cantrell, followed at 0506. Davis recalled that the first team took about 25 minutes to reach a point close to the objects, stopping often to observe the devices, which would dim for a second or two and then brighten again.

When they reached a fork in the track, members of the first team could see the three objects in a field about 500 feet to the north. Davis recalled seeing the large object apparently resting on the ground, bathing the field in light. Jim could now hear "a low humming sound that was reminiscent of a smoothly tuned and distant fan or dishwashing machine."[2] Davis remembered that Brigman then started filming with his smart phone and all four team members started walking towards the objects.

Davis too could now hear "some sort of low buzzing noise," which he likened to the sound from "a refrigerator compressor, but a bit more refined."[3] As he watched the two smaller hovering objects, they seemed to become "clear to the point that one could see through them. It was like a sci-fi movie, only that I was there witnessing it!" he wrote.[4]

In the three-man science team, in which Eric Gray captured footage with his smart phone, Derrick Gibbs recalled that when the group reached the fork in the track, he could see the objects about 480 feet to the north. The largest object seemed to have landed, light from it illuminating the fork in the track.

As Brigman and Davis had done at this point, Gibbs could now hear some sound from the objects. As the three-man group got closer, Gibbs observed that, although still visible, the orifices around the rim of the large object were now shut. This monster now appeared "somewhat intimidating" and its light illuminated a circular area about 70 or 80 feet beyond its circumference. Gibbs tried to identify the source of the light, but couldn't. The sound was now louder, rather like "a small refrigerator during its compression cycle in the middle of the night."[5] Both smart phones recorded about 25 seconds of the sound.

With the three-man group now only about a hundred feet from the objects, and Gray continuing to capture smart phone footage, Gibbs noted that the two smaller objects were hovering about 40-50 feet above the ground, only a few feet from the large object that appeared to be resting on the ground. Once again he had the impression of coordinated movements, with no particular object in charge of the show.

Like Davis, Gibbs was perplexed by the appearance of the two smaller objects. They reflected light from the larger object but occasionally parts of their frames seemed to "disappear". It seemed like the early stage of an optical camouflage system. Later Gibbs gave much thought to the military implications of such a system.

The three men, Gray, Gibbs and Cantrell, were now standing in line about 100 feet from the objects. Like Gibbs, Cantrell thought that the large object was the main source of light, but again, like Gibbs, he could not see the source of the light. Cantrell thought that the two smaller objects were also lit, but "way too dim".

In apparent contradiction to his impression that the two smaller objects were self-illuminated, Cantrell also observed that they appeared to suck up the light, "as if the light went into them."[6] Like Gibbs and Davis, he found it difficult to describe this aspect of the two smaller objects' behaviour, writing that at times their bodies seemed to "cloak out", becoming invisible. Crucially, both smart phones captured some aspects of these effects, compared by Lynn to the scientists' concept of 'black bodies' that wholly absorb incident light.

Recall the observation of NASA's Scot Stride that ET probes might use cloaking strategies to conceal themselves optically or from radar.[7] We've already seen anecdotal reports of such apparent cloaking (Chapters 9 and 13) but Brigman's and Gray's smart phone footage evidently confirms beyond doubt that the two smaller Collierville devices did indeed display such effects.

Standoff at the OK Corral? That's the comparison that entered Gibbs' mind as the seven intrepid humans confronted the three intimidating unknowns. Looking to his right, Gibbs could see the four-man team standing about 250 feet away from him, with Brigman continuing to film the objects.

Then, although Gray, Gibbs and Cantrell were only a hundred feet from the objects, Cantrell decided to get closer. At 0538, in his own words, "I stepped forth. I walked straight to the landed AO hoping that I will be able to touch it."

What foolhardiness! Fortunately for the Fed Ex seven, the objects' response to Cantrell's provocation was measured. He had only advanced ten or fifteen feet when the light increased so much that he had to shield his eyes with his left hand. Then, within a fraction of a second, Cantrell felt a wave of unbearable heat, as if he was "next to a river of lava". Cantrell was stopped in his tracks.

The objects' outburst of light and heat, the second that morning, also temporarily blinded and immobilised the other six men. Gibbs tried to shield his face from the light and heat with his left elbow. But that wasn't enough, he felt dizzy and collapsed to the ground. Brigman was temporarily blinded and forced to cover his head again. Despite being a hundred feet or so from the objects, Brigman estimated that their heat had caused the temperature to rise by at least fifteen degrees Fahrenheit.

As before, the light quickly dimmed and, with no patio to conserve the heat, that too dissipated within a few seconds. An angry Gibbs opened his eyes "ready to let them [the objects] have a few words of my mind." But there was nothing to see, apart from an empty field. The objects had vanished, and the smart phone footage ends with the flash that temporarily blinded the witnesses and forced them to the ground.

So at 0539, about 52 minutes after the three anomalous objects had irrupted into the Fed Ex seven's lives, Cantrell's mindless bravado brought to an untimely end one of the most important captures of camera data in the history of science. As Lynn put it, "All that was left were seven grown men sitting in a field in Tennessee wondering whether they've lost their minds…"

But the seven friends were true professionals. The anomalous objects had vanished but their traces may have remained – not only in the CCTV and smart phone footage, but also in soil traces where they had hovered on the lawn next to the house and in the field. And the intense patio heat might have left traces in the patio materials, the CCTV cameras, the gutters and the electrical wiring of the house. Electromagnetic fields linked with the objects might also have left traces. To do a thorough professional job, the seven friends needed to collect and record photographically as much trace evidence as possible.

So when dawn came they used the smart phone cameras to capture still images and videos of the places on the lawn and the field where the objects had hovered. The still images showed flattening of grass in spots in the field. But they found no circular flattening beneath the spot where the large object had apparently rested, and so concluded that it had in fact hovered a few inches above the ground. They also collected grass and soil samples from the two sites.

The men also collected evidence showing how heat from the objects had caused candles in the south patio wall to melt. Davis and Sexton tested this a couple of days later by buying similar candles and heating them until they melted. Repeating the experiment twice, they found that the candles began melting at 112 degrees Fahrenheit.

Evidence of patio heating also came from the CCTV camera stands, particularly the one facing the north-northwest, which were twisted and tangled. But the cameras had nevertheless managed to capture 2.2 GB of digital video. The men quickly made backups.

Further evidence of heating in the patio lay in damage to the Samsung smart phones worn in the patio by the five of the seven men who had not left their phones in the kitchen. The men found that the SIM cards were wiped of data and kept the smart phones for future investigation.

There was also damage to the house, especially to the gutter edge. Brigman had to rip out part of the roof in order to replace wires feeding the cameras. At first he merely replaced the CCTV cameras, but electricians found the wires leading to them were faulty.

The electricians called in to replace these wires were surprised to find that although the surrounding woodwork was undamaged and lacked burn spots, the wires themselves were seared by heat and in places so burned that they had fused together. Of the seventy-five feet of wiring, about sixty feet was damaged. The aluminium gutters surprisingly were undamaged. A surge of induced current in the copper wiring caused by a magnetic pulse at 0456 could perhaps explain how the wiring was heated without affecting the woodwork.

So in their book the seven Fed Ex friends described a classic generalist surveillance bot operation, dozens of which have been described since the 1956 Castle AFB incident investigated by James McDonald (Chapter 2). Often misinterpreted by both eyewitnesses and UFOlogists as the work of humanoid aliens, the CCTV and smart phone footage of the Collierville bots clearly ruled out humanoids in this case. That supports this book's argument that all humanoid aliens are illusions conjured up by human HAD (hyperactive agent-detection) systems.

Like many such cases (for example Boianai 1959, described in Chapter 3), the putative surveillance devices appear to have been attracted to the well-lit Collierville patio by its lights. The sudden outburst of heat and light at about 0447 that left solid evidence in the melting of the patio candles, can be interpreted, like a human shining a torch, as an aid to help the bots gather more information about the patio's puzzling contents. The enigmatic light surrounding the objects throughout the incident may have come from the objects' luminous plasma coronas.

The putative bots' synchronised 'dancing' also has many precedents, including the dancing Mercury Space capsule described by Dr Wellaide Carvalho in 1977 (Chapter 7) and the synchronised disc behaviour captured in the movie frames of Paul Bennewitz at Kirtland AFB in 1979 (Chapter 10). Once again, such precise coordination rules out humanoid pilots.

The three objects' jump at 0456 of about 700 yards within 1/5 of a second, captured by the CCTV cameras, likewise has precedents. Such alien-killing accelerations, or more precisely as Lynn pointed out, jerks (jerk being the second derivative of velocity with respect to time) have, for decades, been recognised as one of the key characteristics of putative probes. Recall Claude Poher's conclusion (Chapter 5) that at Minot AFB on 28 October 1968, at about 0406 local time, an anomalous object moved 1.98 nautical miles within 1.29 seconds, for which Poher calculated an acceleration of at least 449 g.

In the light of Auguste Meessen's key presentations at the 2012 Moscow meeting of the US-based Electromagnetics Academy,[8,9,10] discussed in Chapter 8, it's reasonable to first consider whether Professor Meessen's proposed MHD-type mechanisms – a magnetic pulse plus an ionisation pulse generating an acceleration pulse through Lorentz forces – could help to explain the Collierville jump.

There is an interesting clue supporting this interpretation. As already mentioned, although the wiring leading to the CCTV cameras in Brigman's house was so severely damaged as to have fused in places, the surrounding woodwork was undamaged. A surge of induced current in the copper wiring caused by a magnetic pulse at 0456 could perhaps explain how the wiring was heated without affecting the woodwork.

What to do with all this evidence, including the important physical evidence of damage to the house and patio that Brigman documented photographically? The US government had long ceased open public investigation of UFO reports and, in 2015, the only non-government group even remotely capable of conducting a public scientific investigation of the Collierville events was the organisation MUFON (Mutual UFO Network).

But MUFON had problems that continue today. It is a commercial organisation run by UFOlogists and depends financially on selling content and organising conferences that appeal to believers in abduction-bent space aliens. Although it has some competent amateur investigators, it wasn't (and isn't) capable of fielding a high-powered multidisciplinary science team capable of investigating and interpreting the remarkable material that the seven friends had put together.

Indeed, by serendipity, the three anomalous objects had stumbled into the hands of a group of experts more competent to study them scientifically than any team that MUFON could field. Aware that involving MUFON might not advance their aim of having an authoritative scientific study of their data, the seven men decided to bypass UFOlogy and patriotically place all their evidence, digital and physical, in the hands of the US authorities. Bypassing UFOlogy also meant avoiding the ridicule-prone term 'UFO'. Having already decided to call the unknowns AOs (Airborne Objects), the group planned to always use this term in their discussions with US officials.

They decided to first approach the FAA's Memphis TRACON (Terminal Radar Approach Control, the range of which is about fifty nautical miles from the antenna, in Democrat Road, Memphis, 25 miles from Brigman's house). The group approached Memphis TRACON on 23 February 2015 and gave them copies of the first two minutes of the CCTV videos as well as videos and pictures of the damage done to Brigman's porch.

TRACON responded within three days, assigned two investigators, accompanied by two NTSB (National Transportation Safety Board) investigators, to the case and interviewed the Fed Ex seven one by one, accumulating over 42 hours of evidence, written, audio and visual, in response to their questions.

On 2 March 2015, the NTSB investigators also took possession of a large body of material evidence, including samples of damaged CCTV cameras and affected roof and gutter construction materials.

Three days later the FAA asked for one copy of all the evidence that the Fed Ex seven had, presumably including all their digital data.

The Fed Ex seven expected a follow up after submission of so much evidence, but nothing happened until 20 July 2015, on which date they were individually interviewed in the Memphis NTSB office. Each interview took about two hours, was video-recorded and conducted simultaneously by a separate investigator in a separate room.

Investigators treated Derrick Gibbs (who retired from the Tennessee National Air Guard in April 2015 to take up freelance piloting) as a special case, giving him a longer interview. He was asked three times in different forms whether he had ever experienced similar sightings as a Guard pilot and he always replied "No".

In regard to Fed Ex seven's planned release of digital data, the NTSB investigators insisted that they needed more time to come to conclusions before publicly releasing the digital data online. Both Lynn and Davis asked the interviewing NTSB investigators how much time they would need and both were given the same answer – the investigators simply didn't know.

Although they didn't exactly distrust the NTSB investigators, overall, the investigators' approach angered the seven men. Lynn felt that the investigators weren't really trying to advance the investigation but rather, "to point out to us in a subtle way that there was no point to the whole incident and that we needed to drop the whole thing." Indeed, the Fed Ex seven found the NTSB investigators' approach "sufficiently abrasive, intrusive and misguided" that, on 21 July 2015, the day after the interviews, they came together as a group to record their experiences, compare notes and plan future actions.

Since the seven friends heard no more from the NTSB investigators, they asked them at beginning of October 2015 if they could give a time frame for the completion of the investigation. The answer surprised them in two ways. First, they were asked to consider the incident "a matter of public safety" and that this aspect should take precedence over everything else, including the need to release the digital data online. Second, what startled them – but perhaps not the readers of this book – was that the NTSB was no longer in charge of the investigation. When asked who was in charge, the chief NTSB investigator refused to tell them, but added that no decisions would be made until six to nine months' time.

"Something's up," the Fed Ex seven thought. Meeting at Brigman's house in early November 2015, this little group of patriots concluded that they should give the US authorities – whoever they were – more time to come to a conclusion, but that a date of 1 October, 2016 should leave them more than enough time. If the government wanted them to change this date, the Fed Ex Seven concluded, it would have to "prove unequivocally that the release of evidence would present some clear and real danger to public safety."

The Fed Ex seven wrote open letters to both the FAA and NTSB offices in Memphis, informing them of this decision. They personally handed these letters to the officials.

As the evidence wasn't released on 1 October 2016, we are left with much to ponder.

First, if the digital evidence is as convincing as Lynn claims – and the US government response certainly supports the attorney's claim that "the quality of the evidence will be sufficient to gather the necessary momentum for its proliferation" – it might indeed pose a threat to public safety, a possibility that has been well rehearsed in the US since the 1940s. Not just through harmful beams from ET bots though, but through spreading global panic about an impending ET invasion. The 'candid camera' aspects of the CCTV footage, coupled with the obvious sincerity and professionalism of the Fed Ex seven, might not only lead to the proliferation of the digital material through social media, it might induce global panic, that would indeed pose a threat to public safety.

Of course, some might argue that people are now so used to digitally concocted 'space invaders' scenarios that such panic would not, after all, materialise. But the risk of panic would remain.

And there's another reason, not mentionable in public, why US authorities might wish to block any public release of the digital material. It was the argument put forward by Derrick Gibbs, after the anomalous objects had jumped about 700 yards in a time that the Fed Ex seven later found was less than 1/5 of a second. At all costs, Gibbs felt, such a technology must be made available to Uncle Sam and prevented from getting into the hands of enemies of the US.

If that's how Tennessee Air Guard member Derrick Gibbs felt, it's likely also to have been the way the secretive authorities reasoned when they took the Collierville case out of NTSB hands in 2015.

This argument may have been the clincher in persuading the Fed Ex seven to delay, perhaps indefinitely, the Internet release of their digital data. The threat to public safety would arise not through panic but through potential enemies of the US, including terrorist groups, using the data to attempt to copy the mind-boggling technology involved in the 0456 'jump'.

One might think that the secret US authorities that took charge of the Collierville evidence in 2015 would have found it easy to set up a high-powered technical team, including aerospace engineers and plasma physicists, competent to study the digital and physical data that the Fed Ex seven had amassed.

Not necessarily. The Collierville problem, centring on the 0456 jump of the three objects of about 700 yards within 1/5 of a second was one of the most technically challenging that scientists have ever faced. The official(s) selecting the team would have to quickly grasp the nature of the problem – not easy for ranking non-scientific government officials of any stripe. Then, they would have to identify the right experts to hire. And finally, they would have to contend with the extreme virulence of the scientists' 'UFO taboo'.

The few known experts qualified to be team members may have simply refused to link themselves with the acronym 'UFO' in any way. For although the savvy Fed Ex seven were well aware of this problem, calling the objects AOs (Airborne Objects) in their technical discussions, by titling their important book *The Memphis UFO Incident*, they themselves had made the 'UFO connection' impossible to conceal.

It's possible that the high-up officials who took the Collierville evidence out of NTSB hands in 2015 gave up trying to establish a science team good enough to interpret it. They may have had to content themselves with preventing the digital part of the evidence from being released into the public domain.

Endnotes

1 Spencer 2015.
2 ibid. p.53.
3 ibid. p.35.
4 ibid. p.36.
5 ibid. p.47.
6 ibid. p.27.
7 Stride 2001.
8 Meessen 2012a.
9 Meessen 2012b.
10 Meessen 2012c.

20

Growing Probes

UFOlogists tell us little about how Greys, Reptilians or other humanoid aliens manufacture their spaceships. Until recently probe theorists could do little better. But since remains from the Height 611 high-temperature event were displayed at the National Atomic Testing Museum in Las Vegas in 2012 that position has changed. Although not yet in the open peer-reviewed science literature, we now have provisional accounts of the Russian and Ukrainian Height 611 technical studies, which the Museum curators tried to describe in their 2012 display and which I've attempted to summarise in Chapters 15 and 16.

In the preliminary study of apparent von Neumann activity (Chapter 18) we now also have a set of technical eyewitness accounts of putative ET devices ranging from possible geochemical prospecting bots, through those that, like NASA's Mars Curiosity Rover, appear to use high-energy beams to identify elements of interest, and then to devices that may have been involved in the actual mining of gold placers, monazite-bearing minerals sands and molybdenite-bearing tailings dumps.

What's exciting is the match between the two independent sets of data. The prospecting and mining accounts feature some of the very hi-tech materials identified in the Height 611 remains. In particular, the finding of silica fibres and fine gold wires in the Height 611 mesh ties in with the evidence pointing to prospecting for gold placers at Los Cerrillos, New Mexico in 1977, in Brazil's Amazon provinces in 1977/8, near Dawson City in the Yukon in July 1996, and perhaps at Knittelfeld, Austria in 2003 and near Pucallpa, Peru in 2008.

If silica polymorphs and gold, apparently as components of simple organically grown AI systems, have a role in ET technology, then in one fell swoop we have one scientifically plausible answer as to 'why they are here'. 'They' being von Neumann machines, not humanoid aliens.

Apart from silica and gold, what other constituents would the Height 611 microcable networks have needed to grow in this way? Stable isotopes of carbon, nitrogen, oxygen, silicon, phosphorus, iron and nickel, all created by fusion from hydrogen and helium in the interiors of stars and then expelled into the interstellar medium, are widely available in the galaxy. They wouldn't require the special planetary prospecting and mining operations required for gold, lead, molybdenum, tungsten, rare earths and other heavier-than-iron elements that are scarce because they are only made in rare events such as the explosion of massive stars or the merging of neutron stars.

So, as is the case with carbon-based life on this planet, postbiological von Neumann systems will have had no problem in obtaining sufficient carbon and other lighter elements as nutrients for growing or assembling surveillance, prospecting and mining vehicles, as the giant mother probes cruise through the interstellar medium from one information-rich or hi-tech-metal-rich location to another. If we stick with the modest guessed velocity of $0.01c$, consistent with the account of the 1986 and 1987 Dalnegorsk events given in Chapter 14, there would be plenty of time for organic growth to take place during these long interstellar voyages. In the protected environments of giant mother probes, at life-friendly temperatures, supplied with nutrients, protected from damaging radiation, and with plenty of time, ET probes could grow and evolve just like organisms do on this planet.

But not all kinds of technology could grow organically. In the case of the Height 611 object, the molybdenum hull and the microcable networks – perhaps serving as a command-and-control system or even a simple brain – may have grown organically. Other components – units involved in propulsion, navigation, communications, beam-projection and so on – may have been assembled from subcomponents by robots. And those subcomponents, in turn, could have been robot-made from hi-tech metals extracted from planetary placers and derivative ceramics or cermets.

For example, the tiny part of the Height 611 object, less than one millimetre in size, composed of rare earth elements and tungsten, discussed in Chapter 15 could be a subcomponent made from monazite-derived mischmetall and tungsten from planetary sources. Such subcomponents could have been fashioned by micromachining robots, perhaps using techniques like advanced versions of our own ion beam or 3D printing technologies.

Where would such machining and micromachining robots have come from? Perhaps they descended from long lines of self-replicating robots going back to originals designed by the probes' biological precursors. There'd be plenty of space on the cruising mother probes for the robots to self-replicate and manufacture components while the probes themselves grew.

Some putative ET surveillance devices – for instance, the small machinelike device witnessed at close quarters by a scientist at Nancy in 1982 and investigated by French government authorities (Chapter 13), at first glance look as if they may have been wholly assembled from subcomponents by robots. But if the Height 611 object's molybdenum hull grew organically, metallic probe hulls generally, even the suspected beryllium hull of the Nancy device, may have grown in this way. If this seems surprising, we only need consider how shellfish in our own oceans grow their own robust tests from dissolved calcium and carbonate ions in the surrounding water. Or, in the case of one foraminifera genus, from dissolved silica.

Whether or not all metallic hulls of probes grew organically, many devices, although chiefly robot-built and machinelike in appearance, may include organically grown components. Examples may include the Moreland-type objects (Chapter 3), the Los Cerrillos machine of 1977 (Chapter 18) and the apparently molybdenum-mining bots reported in Spring Creek, Idaho in 1965 (Chapter 18).

Within the sheltered environments of giant mother probes, the growth and assembly of bots could generally have taken place somewhat along the lines suggested by Paul Davies's concept of auto-teleological super-systems, self-designing systems that combine artificial life forms with machinelike elements and that can grow, improve and adapt (Chapter 4).

To mastermind the growth of individual devices and permit the evolution of such auto-teleological super-systems over millions of years, some kind of 'ET DNA' – not necessarily like our own DNA – would be needed. The super-systems could perhaps use inherited DNA from biological precursors. Alternatively, the identification of components of DNA in carbonaceous chondrite meteorites suggests the possibility that the super-systems may have found ready-made components for their own DNA in space.[1]

As far as growth of individual bots goes, such 'ET DNA' might control development in an analagous way to that in which earthly DNA choreographs growth of organisms on this planet. But in key respects the growth of the Height 611 object and similar postbiological probes would differ from the growth of biologicals like us. The whole point of growing hulls of molybdenum or other metals resistant to high temperatures and of using silica-gold technology in command-and-control systems or even artificial brains would be to create robust devices that could work indefinitely under extreme temperatures, radiation levels and g forces outside the protection of the giant mother probes. So while we stop work before we die, probes – strictly their living parts – would die before they start work.

For example, modeling the growth of the Height 611 object, as they grew, the carbon-rich mesh organic networks may have somehow entrained particles of molybdenum in shaping the hull and fibres of silica-gold in forming the microcable networks. After the organic parts died, the more robust molybdenum hull and silica-gold microcable networks would continue to perform. Molybdenum's high melting point of 2896 degrees centigrade has already been mentioned. The silica polymorph cristobalite with a melting point of 1750 degrees centigrade is well suited to withstand extreme temperatures and, although gold melts at 1064 degrees centigrade, surrounded by the still solid silica threads, the fine gold wires may have continued to serve as electrical conductors well above that temperature.

Why grow metal hulls at all, when high-melting-point metals like molybdenum evidently require so much effort to obtain? Why not use dead carbon-rich mesh? When heated in a vacuum, the Height 611 mesh apparently withstood temperatures of 3000 degrees centigrade. If ET has a command of advanced carbon nanotube technology, as suggested in Chapter 16, then the light, strong, easily grown mesh material may indeed be widely used to form the hulls of ET probes. Perhaps carbon-rich material involving advanced carbon nanotube technology forms or coats the hulls of larger ET vehicles, such as the triangular vehicle reported by Ellen Crystall and her colleagues at Pine Bush, New York in 1980 (Chapter 12). Perhaps such technology played a part in achieving the light-absorbing effects of the three anomalous objects captured on smart phones by the Fed Ex seven at Collierville, Tennessee on 1 February 2015 (Chapter 19).

It's even possible that the hulls of some of the giant mother probes themselves are carbon-based and grown by advanced carbon nanotube technology, perhaps in the dense regions of the interstellar medium known as giant molecular clouds. There's plenty of carbon there in a variety of molecular forms, including fullerenes, and it's possible that postbiological systems involving 'radiation hardened ET DNA' may have evolved to control the growth of such carbon-hulled giants. Perhaps nanotube technology could even play a part in the apparent antiradar and LO (low observable) characteristics of such mother probes.

So much for the hypothetical role of 'ET DNA' in the growth of individual ET probes. 'ET DNA' could also permit the evolution of probe families during the aeons of time available, as the parent mother probes make their way from one object of interest to another. Although losses such as that of the Height 611 object in 1986 may be rare, over time they would add up and replacements would be needed. Rather than replace failed bots with identical von Neumann style copies, there could be some advantage to creating variation in the new probes and the 'ET DNA' could play a part in generating that variation.

This notion opens up an exciting possibility. Eyewitness accounts of single anomalous objects suggest that no two are exactly alike. Instead, witnesses have reported 'variations on a theme' (Chapter 3). But when groups of objects have been reported (recall examples discussed in Chapters 10, 12 and 18) typically either all are identical or one is larger and the others smaller but of similar shape, like, say, a mother duck with her ducklings. That assessment has been recently supported by a remarkable collection of digital images captured at high shutter speed during the period 2012-2018 by Dr Rob Hartland, a biochemist-turned schoolteacher, mostly from his home in the Perth Hills, Western Australia (Appendix 3).

So, in line with the biologists' concept of varying genotypes resulting in varying phenotypes, according to probe theory, most anomalous objects would vary to a greater or lesser degree. But those operating in 'family groups' would resemble each other more because they share the same or similar 'ET DNA'.

From the viewpoint of Steven Dick's Intelligence Principle (Chapter 4), the advantages of such a system are obvious. Surveillance and prospecting bots of various sizes and shapes, incorporating a variety of machinelike passive and beam-like sensors, would be able to operate in a wider variety of environments and yield richer harvests of information than if they were identical von Neumann-style replicators.

Finally we come to a central question of probe theory – how might the postulated powerful AI brains housing the interpretation- and decision-making units in the giant mother probes grow? These brains would be the physical substrates of the supervising postbiological minds (Chapter 4). Science fiction enthusiasts may like to compare them to the powerful AI Ship Minds of Iain Banks.

In default of any other clues, theorists can speculate that, as suggested in the case of the Height 611 object, slowly grown organic networks, in some cases resembling neural nets, form the basis of their architecture. Once again, the systems would have aeons to grow and evolve and, once again, during growth the expanding superbrains could incorporate machinelike components for communications and other specialised purposes in the way that Paul Davies has suggested with his concept of auto-teleological super-systems.

But unlike exploratory bots such as the Height 611 object, the superbrains would remain in the sheltered life-friendly environment of the mother probes throughout their long lives. Therefore, there would be no need to replace the organic networks with gold-silica and, even if their machinelike components don't yet include silicon chips – ET may be working on that now – the possibilities for physical development of the superbrains and concomitant growth of scientific understanding could be huge.

Endnotes

1 Choi 2011.

21

Science not UFOlogy

It happened just over a year later than expected. Not on 1 October 2016, but on 16 December 2017. Clips of anomalous aerial activity were referred to. But instead of showing apparent surveillance devices investigating an internally lit glass-enclosed patio, they showed them turning their attention to the US military. In 2004, a FLIR (Forward Looking Infra-Red) video clip, obtained by a Navy FA-18F fighter from the aircraft carrier USS Nimitz off the coast of Baja California, showed an unknown oval object, about the size of a commercial plane. Another FLIR video clip (date not released), from a Navy fighter F/A-18 Super Hornet, showed an aircraft surrounded by some kind of glowing aura (normal in infrared footage of this kind), traveling at high speed and rotating as it moved. "The Navy pilots can be heard trying to understand what they are seeing," reported the *New York Times*. "There's a whole fleet of them," one exclaims.

The *New York Times* piece, rather misleadingly entitled *Glowing Auras and 'Black Money': The Pentagon's Mysterious UFO Program*, sparked a media revolution. Even *The Independent* in the UK joined in, managing to keep aliens out of the story this time.

The Black Money aspect of the *New York Times* piece concerned a sum of 22 million dollars, spent between 2008 and 2011. It's a small amount, given the 600-billion-dollar US defence budget, but it is highly significant in that it represents the first officially revealed government cash for UFO research since the closure of Project Blue Book in 1969. The *New York Times* stated that the provision of funds was largely due to Harry Reid, the Nevada Democrat who was the Senate majority leader at the time. Most of the money went to an aerospace company run by a billionaire entrepreneur and longtime friend of Mr. Reid's, Robert Bigelow, who, the *New York Times* said in its 16 December 2017 piece, was currently working with NASA to produce expandable craft for humans to use in space.

At first that looks fine. Bigelow Aerospace, packed with aerospace engineers – just the people to work as a team with plasma physicists, to build on the work of the AIAA UFO subcommittee and at last face the technical challenges of anomalous incidents in the Earth's atmosphere and hydrosphere, as James McDonald and Frank Drake had advocated many decades ago.

But it soon emerged that, when it came to UFOs, Bigelow Aerospace wasn't exactly the technical paragon one might expect. First, as the *New York Times* itself reported, on CBS's *60 Minutes* in May 2017, Robert Bigelow said he was "absolutely convinced" that "aliens exist and that U.F.O.s have visited Earth."

That looks bad. Did the 22 million dollars then not go to fund Bigelow Aerospace's teams of aerospace engineers but to Robert Bigelow, former real estate agent and believer in humanoid space aliens, in other words, Robert Bigelow, billionaire UFOlogist?

So it seems. Like many other people in the Las Vegas area, the young Bigelow came to believe in space aliens as a result of a perfectly credible incident that happened to his family. In 1947 his grandparents encountered an anomalous object while driving in a canyon road. In June 2017 Bigelow told the *Tech Times*:

> "It really sped up and came right into their face and filled up the entire windshield of the car… And it took off at a right angle and shot off into the distance." (*Tech Times*, 2 June 2017)

Bigelow's description brings to mind thoughts of the 2015 incident captured by the Fed Ex seven's CCTV cameras and smart phones (Chapter 19) and evidently too convincing to be released. Or dozens of other similar incidents that intrigued Allen Hynek and James McDonald. 'Intelligent control' is the modern sophisticated description of such behaviour – recall Colonel Charles Halt's use of that phrase in his 2015 BBC interview (Chapter 11). But in 1947 actual humanoid 'space beings', possibly from Mars, were the only interpretation available, so it's easy to understand why the young Bigelow came to believe in aliens.

Back to the 2017 *New York Times* piece. If Senator Harry Reid had channelled taxpayers' money to his friend UFOlogist Robert Bigelow, who actually ran the Pentagon's secret programme? It turned out to be a military intelligence official called Luis Elizondo, with an office on the fifth floor of the Pentagon's C Ring. It was he, the *New York Times* stated, who had responsibility for investigating incidents such as the USS Nimitz encounter in 2004.

But on 4 October 2017, the paper reported, Elizondo sent a resignation letter to his boss, Secretary of State for Defense James Mattis, explaining that there was a need for more serious attention to "the many accounts from the Navy and other services of unusual aerial systems interfering with military weapon platforms and displaying beyond-next-generation capabilities."

What Elizondo didn't mention in this resignation letter or say later publicly is that in 2015 an authoritative, secret US government entity took a key set of digital and physical data, confirming the certain existence of an "unusual aerial system" displaying "beyond next generation capabilities" out of NTSB (National Transport Safety Board) hands and may have been studying, or trying to study, those data ever since. Although the three Collierville bots (Chapter 19) didn't actually interfere with military weapon platforms, their ability to jump about 700 yards within 1/5 of a second at 0456 local time on 1 February 2015 presented a potentially gigantic threat to such conventional weapons systems. The secret US government entity evidently took this threat so seriously that it intervened to prevent the planned Internet release of the digital part of the Collierville data on 1 October 2016.

Who was this secret US government entity? It seems to have been Luis Elizondo himself.

This emerged from Elizondo's presentation at a Huntsville, Alabama, meeting that took place in February 2019. At this meeting of the MUFON-friendly Scientific Coalition for UAP Studies,[1] Elizondo reiterated an idea that he's propounded since his Pentagon days of 'five observables' that distinguish UFO technology from everything else: instantaneous acceleration, hypersonic velocity, low observability or stealth, positive lift and the ability to freely navigate multiple environments, including space, the atmosphere and water.

Then Elizondo told the Huntsville audience:

"You will see that we even had people from the NTSB (National Transportation Safety Board) on camera, analysing... I've never seen anything like that in my career. For the record. On camera."[2] Two years after his resignation letter to James Mattis, Elizondo was evidently still keen to squeeze as much as he could from his Collierville-inspired relations with the NTSB.

UFO nuts the Huntsville audience may have been, but they were also technically informed and capable of asking good questions. One individual raised the key question of the reports by many military veterans of UAP (unidentified aerial phenomena) busting security around thermonuclear weapons sites.

Elizondo handled this skilfully. "Yes," he replied, "we do know for a fact that there's some strategic interest in our nuclear capabilities, albeit whether it's nuclear energy, nuclear weapons development, nuclear delivery capabilities – that's about all I can say.

"If I didn't have a security clearance, I could probably talk more about this, but I can't. I can't even speculate. The crown jewel of US defense is its nuclear capability, and the US government is very, very protective of that information."[3]

That wise response reminds us that Elizondo still enjoys high security clearances, and knows a lot that his critics don't. Indeed, his statement that "there's some strategic interest in our nuclear capabilities" is probably the most important statement ever on this crucial subject from a former Pentagon official.

So Luis Elizondo is evidently a man whom probe theorists need to take very seriously. But on leaving the Pentagon he made one huge mistake. He joined a new commercial venture called To the Stars Academy of Arts and Sciences (TTSA) led, bizarrely, by Tom DeLonge, founder of pop punk band Blink-182.

DeLonge bought the whole ludicrous space alien package. His book, *Sekret Machines*,[4] written with A.J. Hartley, includes a Betty and Barney Hill account in which not only does Barney see humanoids in the anomalous object but also the Hills are later abducted by them.

TTSA's octogenarian science star, Dr Hal Puthoff, former Scientologist and remote viewing guru, soon brought further discredit to TTSA. For example, in an 8 June 2018 address to a joint conference of the Society for Scientific Exploration and the International Remote Viewing Association,[5] he focused attention, as an example of "metamaterials for aerospace use" on a sample of multi-layered bismuth and magnesium sent anonymously many years earlier to talk show host Art Bell. This lump of dubious provenance meets none of the criteria for possible remains of an ET device and its layering may well have resulted from the use of magnesium in the Betterton-Krohl process for removing impurities such as bismuth from molten lead (see Wikipedia).

So unfortunately for Elizondo it soon became apparent that the TTSA group was even less capable of doing good science than Robert Bigelow or MUFON. In his Pentagon office, surrounded by intelligent officials and analysing reports from competent military professionals, Elizondo may have failed to gauge the extent to which amateur commercial UFOlogy groups, dependent on believers in space aliens for cash, have left science behind.

Fortunately the 16 December 2017 *New York Times* piece on the 2004 USS Nimitz encounter that had first brought Luis Elizondo out of the shadows had a broad lasting positive impact on serious discussions of anomalous activity. For example, ten months later, on 15 October 2018, Nick Pope, a former UK Ministry of Defence official charged with investigating UFO reports, reported in the science pages of the UK newspaper *The Guardian* that the Senate Armed Services Committee was interviewing Navy pilots and radar people involved in the Nimitz incident (Appendix 4).[6] Pope suggested that if these interviews evolved into Congressional hearings (a House Armed Services Committee was also involved), "they might turn out to be the most fascinating hearings in history."

But rather than analysis of the 2004 USS Nimitz events, it is, rather surprisingly, analysis of the Height 611 remains that we should thank Nick

Pope for promoting.[7] The key document here is a UK government report on UAP known as Project Condign, completed in 1999.[8] According to Pope,[9] Project Condign had its origin in 1993 discussions he had with his DIS (Defence Intelligence Staff, now Defence Intelligence) opposite number. Pope claimed that the pair was responsible for introducing the more scientific term UAP to replace Captain Ed Ruppelt's term 'UFO'. Although useful at first, by 1993 'UFO', meaning something in the sky the observer can't identify, had become, in Pope's view, as obsolete and baggage-laden as the older term 'flying saucer'. As he pointed out in his 2018 *Guardian* piece, when the question "do you believe in UFOs?" is misinterpreted as "do you think we're being visited by aliens?" we clearly have a problem.

As its title UAP in the UK Air Defence Region implies, the anonymous Condign Report does indeed generally use the term UAP. But in the key section dealing with the scientific studies of the Height 611 remains, quoted below, the author reverts to the older term. This probably reflects the fact that 'UAP' fails to capture the object-like nature of those 'UFOs' that have left behind metallic and other solid material remains.

Quotes from the Condign Report

Page 22-1

METALLIC ARTEFACTS

2 Although no such artefacts have been found in the UKADR, it is claimed in Russia and Ukraine that items have been scientifically analysed. The results are not known. The Russians, like the USA, have never produced the artefacts which are claimed by some media reports to have been found. This seems to be quite extraordinary in view of the fact that it would be resonable (sic) to expect that this might solve the extra-terrestrial hypothesis of 'UFO' origins once and for all. The Brazilian claim of 'extra-pure aluminium' artefacts was not sustainable after analysis.

SUMMARY

3 No proven tangible artefacts have been obtained by the public for display, or shown by governments to exist. The metallic materials analysed scientifically have not been shown to be of unknown elements.

Although the Condign author correctly stated that because of their extent, the scientific studies of the Height 611 remains might be expected to "solve the extra-terrestrial hypothesis of 'UFO' origins once and for all" he (or his editor) also attempted to distance himself from that assessment by denying the very existence of the remains. Presumably, that was because for political reasons the Condign Report, like its Condon predecessor, had to reach an anti-ET (adjective) conclusion.

Let's look at this carefully. Since he had written "the results [of the scientific studies of the Height 611 material] are not known", the Condign author could not honestly reach an anti-ET conclusion by showing that the multiple teams of scientists had found a prosaic explanation for the Height 611 high-temperature event and the remains it had left behind. So he, or his editor, adopted the drastic solution of denying that the Height 611 remains existed at all. After all, the 'media reports' might be false and the remains, he claimed, had never been put on public display.

A high-risk strategy as well as a dishonest one. For in 2012, as we've seen (Chapter 1), the National Atomic Testing Museum, Las Vegas, put some of these nonexistent Height 611 remains – carbon-rich meshlike (сеточка) material given by former schoolteacher Valery Dvuzhilni to journalist George Knapp in the 1990s – on very public display. Although the Museum's description of those remains was flawed, their statement that "Three Soviet academic centers and 11 research institutes analyzed the objects from this UFO crash" is correct. And, thanks to Google Translate, we now have a provisional account of that analysis (Chapters 15 and 16).

This weird cyborg-like material appears to be precisely what scientists outside UFOlogy like Paul Davies and Jim Al-Khalili, Professor of Theoretical Physics at the University of Surrey, UK, expect from

ET. Here's Al-Khalili, editor of Aliens,[10] explaining to journalist Linda Howe why, instead of humanoid aliens, scientists expect any ET devices operating here to be cyborg-like in nature.[11]

> "...it would make a lot of sense if we are to explore space to send machines, robots, cyborgs, artificial intelligence, out to do the job for us. After all, we are made of rather sensitive biological material that wouldn't survive the rigors of space, whether it's radiation, whether it's the length of the journey. So it makes much more sense for us to send robots. But then of course, the reverse is true. If there's an alien civilization out there that's advanced enough to travel the galaxy, why would they risk traveling themselves? Why would they not send their cyborgs and their robots to visit us?"

And why, Professor Al-Khalili, could the cyborg-like Height 611 mesh, as studied by those fourteen research institutes and displayed at the National Atomic Testing Museum, Las Vegas in 2012, not be a precise example of what you have in mind?

Restoration of that huge chunk of missing science – the work done at those three Soviet academic centres and 11 research institutes, as stated in the National Atomic Testing Museum's display (Chapter 1) – might be expected to be a slow, funeral-by-funeral process. The leaders of global science, in particular the crucial SETI faction, would apparently rather die than give up their UFO taboo.

But several developments are rapidly changing the situation. One is the publication in 2018 of a provocative paper in *EdgeScience* by anthropologist Eric Wargo (Appendix 5).[12] Titled *Welcome to the Noöverse: Big Data, Deep Anthropology, and Von Neumann Probes*, the paper offers an intriguing new perspective on ET probe theory that complements the ideas of better-known thinkers like Paul Davies and Steven Dick.

Another concerns the attitudes of popular science journals. For example, on 27 July 2020, *Scientific American* published an important piece by Ravi Kopperapu and Jacob Haqq-Misra (2020) *Unidentified Aerial Phenomena, Better Known as UFOs, Deserve Scientific Investigation*.[13]

Yet another concerns recent developments in space activities. As recounted in a masterly survey by Robert Zubrin,[14] in the period since Elon Musk's SpaceX Falcon 9 rocket landed safely at Cape Canaveral on 21 December 2015, there has been a cost revolution in rocketry. As a result recent years have witnessed a rush into space. Not just Musk. Amazon's Jeff Bezos and dozens of smaller entrepreneurial companies have seen opportunities to make money. But the scope of current plans is limited by the slowness of chemical rockets. So there are now staggering commercial opportunities for new advanced propulsion technologies.

For example, Zubrin[15] pointed out that a theoretical D-He3 fusion rocket could reach 10% of light speed, making human interstellar travel possible. But such fusion rockets may well remain forever theoretical and, if so, humans will need another way to reach the stars.

So what about those actual ET devices, exemplified by the three Collierville bots jumping about 700 yards within 1/5 of a second on 1 February 2015 (Chapter 19)? Although 'full ET technology' likely incorporates physical principles not yet known to humans, the advanced magnetic materials in the Height 611 remains (Chapter 15), Professor Meessen's papers presented at Moscow in 2012 (Chapter 8) and the Fed Ex seven's own technical analysis of the Collierville CCTV and smartphone digital data (Chapter 19) suggest that some aspects of ET technology, such as MHD-type propulsion systems, could be copied right now.

Might such copying provoke ET to take preemptive action against us, as suggested in Chapter 14? That's certainly a risk. But that risk has been there since the atomic bombing of Japan in 1945 (Chapter 5).

In any case, aerospace engineers alone can't carry through a successful replication of ET technology. The challenge exemplified by the 2015 Collierville jump is so great that only multidisciplinary teams of top experts, including physicists of various kinds, practical and theoretical, have a chance of making progress. Such experts are rare creatures and, to date, because of the scientists' UFO taboo, appear to have been reluctant to risk their careers by linking themselves in any way with the dreaded acronym 'UFO'. Thus, despite sufficient US government funding, Pentagon official Luis Elizondo was apparently unable to recruit a science team good enough to tackle the challenge of the Collierville jump.

Time, therefore, to deal with the absurd and dangerous taboo once and for all.

Of course only scientists themselves can dismantle their taboo. James McDonald almost did it in 1968 (Chapter 2). But then he shot himself in the head, never a good way to win a scientific argument. We need a new McDonald.

In March 2018 Silvio Colombano, of NASA's Ames Research Center, California, entered the fray. A member of the AIAA Space Architecture Technical Committee, Colombano is an acknowledged authority on 'self-sustaining robotic ecologies' and has authored or co-authored more than 80 technical publications.

So, like McDonald, Colombano is an influential figure with the aerospace engineers of the AIAA. Although he is not quite James McDonald, he is precisely the kind of rare accredited expert that could have helped Luis Elizondo put together his Collierville science team and convince Jim Al-Khalili that SETI people are at last beginning to take seriously his own suggestion that if any ET technology is active here, it would likely consist of "machines, robots, cyborgs, artificial intelligence".

In his key paper, presented as a White Paper at the SETI Institute's March 14-16 2018 Workshop *Decoding Alien Intelligence,* Colombano made several important points.[16]

First, he pointed out that the Kepler Space Telescope Project (Chapter 3) has recently identified planetary systems as old as 10.4 billion years (Kepler-10) and 11.2 billion years (Kepler-444). There could, therefore, be Earthlike planets that are more than six billion years older than our own 4.5-billion-year old Solar System. Considering that our system has seen the rise of 'scientific methodologies' only in last 500 years, we might have a problem in predicting technological evolution even for the next thousand years, let alone the next six billion years.

In the light of these numbers, Colombano suggested that "we need to re-visit even our most cherished assumptions." These include the assumption that "intelligent civilizations would be based on carbon life." While such life, based on elements common throughout the universe, might be a common starting point, it might in fact "just be a tiny first step in a continuing evolution that may well produce forms of intelligence that are far superior to ours and no longer based on carbon 'machinery'". "After a mere 50 years of computer evolution," Colombano pointed out, "we are already talking about 'super-intelligence' and we are quickly becoming symbiotic with computer power." Therefore, Colombano argued, "the intelligence we might find and that might choose to find us (if it hasn't already) might not at all be produced by carbon-based organisms like us."

Colombano concluded his 2018 SETI White Paper with four recommendations for action by SETI. First, he suggested that they "engage physicists in what might be called 'speculative physics', still grounded in our most solid theories but with some willingness to stretch possibilities as to the nature of space-time and energy." Second, he suggested they "engage technologists in futuristic exploration of how technology might evolve, especially w/r Artificial Intelligence, 'Evolvable Robotic Systems' and symbiosis of biology with machines." Third, he recommended that SETI "engage sociologists in speculation about what kinds of societies we might expect from the above developments, and whether and how they might choose to communicate."

Fourth, he suggested that SETI "consider the UFO phenomenon worthy of study in the context of a system with very low signal to noise ratio, but nevertheless with the possibility of challenging some of our assumptions and pointing to new possibilities for communication and discovery." Avoiding MUFON's UFOlogists (see Chapter 19), Colombano suggests that SETI might use Big Data Analysis to find useful data in 130,000 pages of declassified US Air Force documents, the National UFO Reporting Center Database and several other international databases.

Although Colombano wrote his White Paper before there was even a provisional account of the missing Height 611 science, in light of that account (Chapters 14, 15 and 16), Colombano's speculations "especially w/r Artificial Intelligence, 'Evolvable Robotic Systems' and symbiosis of biology with machines" seem remarkably prescient. Recall that the Height 611 mesh apparently initially grew organically in a sheltered, life-friendly environment but, that after its 'death', the organic material was supplemented by robust, non-carbon, silica-gold AI systems that could perform in a vacuum at the extreme temperatures and radiation levels characteristic of the interstellar medium.

So Silvio Colombano's groundbreaking 2018 SETI White Paper is highly compatible with the conclusions of the Height 611 analysis, and what influential scientists outside UFOlogy, like Paul Davies and Jim Al-Khalili, expect from ET. And by hastening the end of the scientists' dangerous UFO taboo, it has also breathed life into the dream, so eloquently expressed by Robert Zubrin, of humanity at last reaching the stars.

Endnotes

1 Cox 2019. Posted on April 24 2019 (http://devoid.blogs.heraldtribune.com/15808/elizondos-call-to-action/) by Billy Cox (http://devoid.blogs.heraldtribune.com/author/cox/). Downloaded 25 April 2019.

2 ibid.

3 ibid.

4 DeLonge and Hartley 2016.

5 Puthoff 2018.

6 Pope 2018.

7 Pope 2014.

8 Ministry of Defence 2006.

9 Pope 2014.

10 Al-Khalili 2017a.

11 Al-Khalili 2017b.

12 Wargo 2018.

13 Kopperapu and Haqq-Mistra 2020.

14 Zubrin 2019.

15 Zubrin 2019, p.90.

16 Colombano 2018.

Appendix 1

The 1976/77 US Navy 'fence'
Source: Vallee (2019) page 334

Gulf of Alaska Sunday 8 September 1996
First day at sea. Slowly, gradually, the mind empties itself of inconsequential worries. The ship sails up College Fjord: Glaciers reach the water line: An eerie landscape of prehistory, an ice age sea, still and dirty with melted dust, the mud of centuries. Sleep again, release of stress. We've left Prince William Sound. Nothing to see but light blue ocean, the sky vaguely brushed with elongated clouds.

Just before we left an interesting letter arrived from one of my readers, Marshall Tate of San Jose. He wrote that in 1976 and 1977 he was in charge of a military detecting installation, the US Naval Space Station at Elephant Butte, New Mexico.

"The facility was run by the Naval Weapons command in Dahlgren, Virginia; its data was also linked to Norad HQ. The system operates like this: at Lake Kickapoo, Texas, a 10-million watt RF is generated and transmitted, in an extremely narrow east-west pattern termed "the fence" covering the entire U.S. Objects that fly through this "fence" of RF energy reflect a portion of it back to the ground. Equipment determines speed by the Doppler Effect and altitude by the phase difference of the signal received at antennas separated by a known distance. Computers predict when the target will pass again if it's in orbit and looks for it. Subsequent passes permit the prediction of apogee and perigee, as well as the time of reentry. The equipment is sensitive to log mere pieces of wire from exploded rockets; the range extends tens of thousands of miles."

Marshall Tate goes on to write: "Several times per week I was noting very fast objects going through the fence. Recorded speeds of

6,000 to 20,000 miles per hour were common; one object was recorded at 55,000 miles per hour. Tests of the equipment revealed nothing unusual. Curious, I called headquarters at Dahlgren. They advised me to forget it; nothing could go that fast, it was just an anomaly of the system, yet…as I said, the equipment was working perfectly."

Appendix 2

US Secret Satellite Detection of 'Fast-Walkers', 1988
Source: Vallee (2012) Kindle location 4849

Spring Hill Sunday 13 March 1988
'On Friday I had lunch with Dick Haines. He told me about an invitation he's received to brief staffers of an Army undersecretary, describing his research on pilot sightings. Hal [Puthoff] and John Alexander had suggested this briefing to try to get a final decision. Thus, contrary to what people have been told, the Secret Onion project has not been established yet. Dick was able to attend the presentation that followed his own briefing. An intelligence officer spoke about objects detected by certain satellites, American satellites on low orbits, known as 'slow walkers' are often catching *luminous objects in groups of two or three that make right-angle turns or even reverse course.* These observations, according to Dick, stunned the Army folks, who had been unaware of these "FastWalkers".

Appendix 3

The Hartland Digital Images

During the period 2012-18, Dr Rob Hartland, a biochemist-turned-schoolteacher, captured a remarkable set of digital images, mostly from his home in the Perth Hills, Western Australia (http://www.wispyclouds.net).

He used a Sony DSC Cyber-shot DSC RX 100 compact camera with 20.1 megapixels and a Zeiss lens. He typically set it in continuous shooting mode so that it took multiple images with a delay of 0.47 seconds between frames. On fine days, Hartland pointed his camera at the edges of wispy clouds in the stratosphere, and took hundreds of high-shutter-speed (1/400 second or faster) images in each session. He transferred the images to his computer and, avoiding those that might be birds, insects or seeds, etc., enhanced those that appeared possible anomalous objects.

With this simple protocol, the industrious Hartland acquired hundreds of intriguing images. Some, for example DSC02012, acquired on 30 April 2013 (Cover) and DSC00697, acquired on 17 November 2012 (Fig 92), could be interpreted as giant high-aspect-ratio tube-like mother probes (compare Fig 38). Others, for example DSC01935, acquired on 22 May 2014 (Fig 93), may be probes releasing plasma ball microprobes, yet others, for example DSC01646, acquired on 20 May 2014 (Fig 94), could be probes surveying air traffic.

Hartland does himself no favours by coupling his images with interpretations in the 'space brothers' genre that seem ultra-loony even by UFOlogists' own loony standards. But if probe theorists discount Hartland's personal interpretations, they will see that because it can be entirely automated, his simple protocol has great potential for capturing possible mother probes, probes and microprobes on a planet-wide scale.

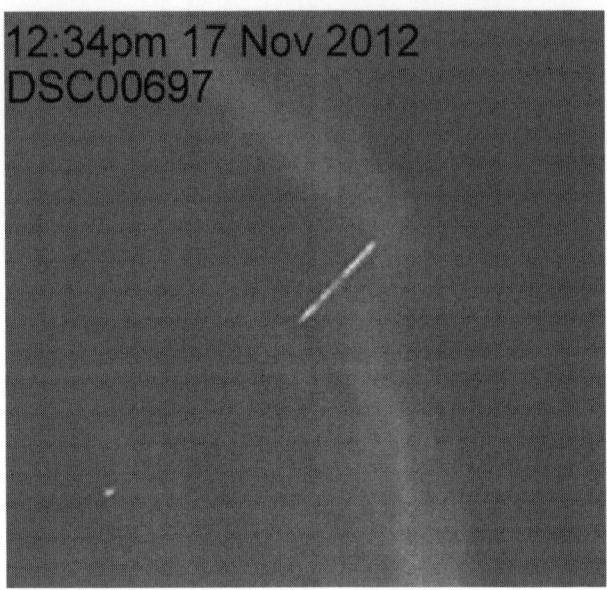

Fig 92. Enhanced digital sky image DSC00697, exposure 1/800 second, acquired at 1234 local time on 17 November 2012 by biochemist-turned-schoolteacher Dr Rob Hartland from his home in the Perth Hills, Western Australia.

This is one many images acquired using a Sony DSC Cyber-shot DSC RX 100 compact camera with 20.1 megapixels and a Zeiss lens. Hartland typically set the camera in continuous shooting mode so that it took multiple images with a delay of 0.47 seconds between frames. On fine days Hartland pointed his camera at the edges of wispy clouds in the stratosphere, and took hundreds of high-shutter-speed (1/400 second or faster) images in each session. He transferred the images to his computer and avoiding those that might be birds, insects or seeds etc, enhanced those that appeared possible anomalous objects.

One interpretation of this image would be that it represents a giant high-aspect-ratio tube-like mother probe. Courtesy: Dr Rob Hartland.

[http://www.wispyclouds.net/DSC00697]

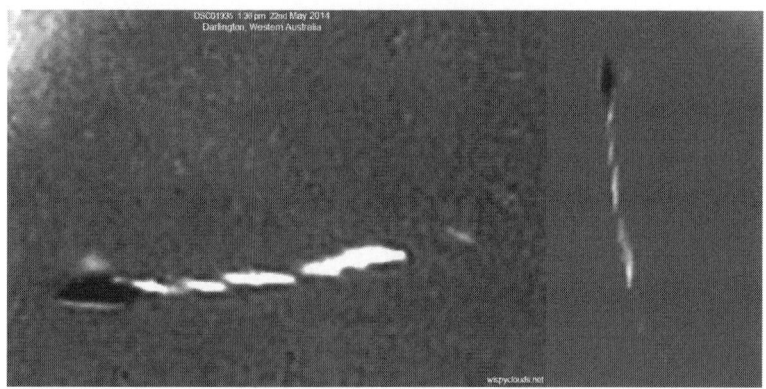

Fig 93. Enhanced digital sky image DSC01935, exposure 1/500 second, acquired at 1336 local time on 22 May 2014 by Dr Rob Hartland from his home in the Perth Hills, Western Australia with his Sony DSC Cyber-shot DSC RX 100 compact camera. One interpretation of this image would be that it represents a domed disc probe releasing a group of plasma ball microprobes. Courtesy: Dr Rob Hartland. [http://www.wispyclouds.net/DSC01935]

Fig 94. Enhanced digital sky image DSC01646, exposure time 1/400 second, acquired at 0955 local time on 20 May 2014 by Dr Rob Hartland from his home in the Perth Hills, Western Australia with his Sony DSC Cyber-shot DSC RX 100 compact camera. One interpretation of this image would be that it represents a domed disc surveillance probe investigating a Qantas airliner. Courtesy: Dr Rob Hartland. [http://www.wispyclouds.net/DSC01646]

Appendix 4

US Congress attending to UFOs
(First published in The Guardian Monday 15 October 2018)

Space
UFO sightings may be falling, but Congress is still paying attention
Nick Pope

Renewed US interest could produce some fascinating hearings, but the focus should be on the quality not just the quantity of reported sightings
Mon 15 Oct 2018 07.00 BST Last modified on Mon 15 Oct 2018 07.02 BST

There's renewed interest in the UFO phenomenon and it's coming from an unexpected source: The United States Congress.

The Senate Armed Services Committee is looking into a 2004 incident where US Navy pilots flying with the USS Nimitz strike group encountered, chased and filmed fast-moving unidentified objects. Reliable sources say at least two of the military pilots involved have already been interviewed, and a radar operator was subsequently invited to get in touch.

In parallel, the House Armed Services Committee is taking an interest. Records from April show the committee received a Defence Intelligence Agency (DIA) briefing on the Pentagon's UFO project, the cryptically-named AATIP. We know so little about AATIP that there's even dispute over whether the acronym stands for Advanced Aerospace Threat Identification Program or Advanced Aviation Threat Identification Program. The very existence of the project caused a sensation, because until the New York Times broke the story in December 2017, the US government claimed it had not investigated UFOs since the 1960s when sightings were looked at in a study called Project Blue Book. Recently, data from two civilian UFO research organisations show that the number of reported sightings has fallen in recent years. However, there's no single, global focal point for reports (the Ministry of Defence stopped investigating UFOs in 2009) and statistics will never tell the full story.

It would be better if the phenomenon were assessed and judged not on numbers alone, but by focusing on cases where we have compelling evidence: independently submitted reports from pilots on different flights; visual sightings corroborated by radar; photos and videos regarded as genuinely intriguing by intelligence community imagery analysts. Irrespective of the methodology we use to assess the phenomenon, how can we do so in an even-handed way when the subject has so much pop culture baggage?

A first step in reframing the debate might be changing the language. The term "UFO" has become as obsolete and baggage-laden as the now largely-defunct "flying saucer". Both are widely, but wrongly, regarded as being synonymous with "extraterrestrial spacecraft", when self-evidently all the phrase should mean is something in the sky that the observer cannot identify. When the question "do you believe in UFOs?" is misinterpreted as "do you think we're being visited by aliens?" then we clearly have a problem.

We addressed this in the MoD in the 1990s by replacing "UFO" with "UAP", for Unidentified Aerial Phenomena. It got us increased funding and made a few senior officials take the matter more seriously, because they felt we were looking at a science problem, not a science fiction mystery.

Years later, in 2011, I was one of the briefers at a private gathering in Washington DC, chaired by Bill Clinton's former chief of staff John Podesta, who has a longstanding interest in the issue. It was reminiscent of an episode of The X-Files and there was even a former CIA director sitting at the back, playing no part in the discussion, but silently taking notes. I briefed attendees on the MoD's use of the term "UAP" and the message clearly hit home.

During Hillary Clinton's presidential campaign, for which Podesta was the campaign chair, she occasionally discussed UAPs and in one interview on the Jimmy Kimmel show she corrected the host for using the term "UFO". We have yet to learn what Donald Trump thinks about UAPs, but his enthusiasm for a Space Force has certainly created a few conspiracy theories.

When it comes to UAPs, truth really is stranger than fiction. It turns out that AATIP was largely the brainchild of the then Senate majority leader Harry Reid, and that much of the work was contracted out to Bigelow Aerospace, run by former budget hotel magnate (and believer in extraterrestrial visitation) Robert Bigelow. A 2009 letter from Harry Reid about AATIP reads like science fiction in places.

Now, some of the people formerly involved with the project – including the DIA official who ran it, Luis Elizondo – have joined a Public Benefit Corporation called To the Stars Academy of Arts and Science, fronted by Tom DeLonge, the former vocalist/guitarist and founder of pop punk band Blink-182. Their mission statement talks about creating a consortium "to explore exotic science and technologies… that can change the world".

If current US Congressional interest evolves into formal hearings, either specifically on AATIP, or on UAPs more generally, I hope they can get past debates about terminology, and avoid getting bogged down in statistical analyses. I have made clear my willingness to testify on the basis that my experience with the MoD might be relevant.

Focusing on the quality of reports and not simply the quantity should result in a far more meaningful assessment of the phenomenon. Irrespective of the outcome, these might turn out to be the most fascinating Congressional hearings in history.

- *Nick Pope worked at the Ministry of Defence for 21 years. From 1991 to 1994 he was posted to a division where his duties included investigating UAP sightings to determine whether they had any defence significance.*

Appendix 5

The Wargo hypothesis

In March 2018 anthropologist Eric Wargo published a provocative paper in *EdgeScience* (Wargo, 2018) that presented a new version of ET probe theory. I've attempted to summarise some of his key points below.

Dr Wargo started with a critique of French scientist Jacques Vallee's decades-old critique of the ETH (extraterrestrial hypothesis). Wargo pointed out that Dr Vallee's critique was based on assumptions that are no longer valid in the light of recent scientific developments. "Even some of the strangest aspects of the UFO phenomenon would not be inconsistent with a massive, long-duration, and most importantly, automated ET program of behavioral research and surveillance," Wargo wrote. He added, "It is entirely possible we are living in a noöverse: an already densely surveilled, studied, and networked cosmos swarming with artificially intelligent and infinitely patient 'science machines'… Big Data and AI/robotics are thresholds that any spacefaring ET will long since have crossed, just as it will have mastered 3-D printing.

"The use of local resources to create copies of machines and create needed supplies by rebuilding matter at the molecular level may make human life and work on the Moon and Mars and the asteroid belt feasible by the second half of this century. And once a 3-D printer prints out another 3-D printer, the robot reproductive system is a reality. Couple a 3-D printer to a smart probe or drone and you have exactly what John Von Neumann envisioned as the tool any advanced civilization would use to explore beyond its solar system.

"Self-replicating probes can propagate from planet to planet, star system to star system (via solar sail or whatever better technology comes along), completely autonomously. Because they can perpetually repair themselves and reproduce, such probes would have limitless durability, and this would give them limitless patience. They could multiply like rabbits and conduct science tirelessly. When they encounter really interesting planets with life, or even a pre-biological soup of organic molecules, they could swarm such a world and dig in quietly for the long haul.

"These will be more than space probes as we usually think of them, but full, autonomous science platforms, sharing data among themselves and constantly or periodically relaying that information back home for storage and future use by the civilization that built them, by that civilization's robot protectors, or by its machine descendants. They may continue to do science long after their original builders are gone.

"This is where the ancientness and ubiquity of the UFO phenomenon starts to make sense in terms of what we might call 'machine ETH'. Given the likelihood that countless ET civilizations have arisen over the past few billion years that are capable of populating space with such machines, a planet like ours could potentially have been swarmed with untold millions of probes, not only quietly observing and recording but also overtly interacting with the local flora and fauna for the purposes of experimentation and hypothesis-testing over the full course of the planet's history.

"Again, Von Neumann probes would have a built-in motive for curiosity and the ability not merely to observe and record but to actually behave like experimenters: to generate their own hypotheses, design experiments to test them, and tediously replicate and re-replicate their findings alone or collaboratively, to constantly nuance and update their deepening understanding of their subject species. Such probes will not passively limit themselves to observation and sample collection but will also interact in a very precise, deliberate, controlled fashion, and repeat these interactions obsessively and tirelessly in the same and varied conditions, again and again and again, building up conclusions of high confidence…"

Wargo wrote, "One might ask why an ET civilization would want to engage in such 'deep anthropology', but there is no real mystery there. Whatever varied forms alien life might take, there is nothing anthropocentric about saying that any space-exploring ET civilization will certainly have gotten there by following the exact same path we did: through science.

"Our civilization is already built on centuries of basic science – that is, science undertaken for its own sake, often without any direct or foreseeable payoff in application. Knowing about the reproductive behavior of deep-sea sponges or plate tectonics on Pluto's moon may seem useless to most people (including some taxpayers who do not grasp the importance of this kind of science), but scientists and smart policymakers who fund the science know that every little detail is part of a vast puzzle and that any bit of information may ultimately pay off in unforeseen ways, years or decades or centuries down the long road. Thus, our basic curiosity about the universe, and our collective ability to invest resources in that curiosity, are adaptive.

"More basically, knowledge is power. It enables prediction and control. There is no limit to the degree of prediction and control over illness, for example, that medical researchers at universities and government institutions would like to attain, given unlimited scientific resources. Likewise, if money (and legality) were no object, there is certainly no limit to the degree of prediction and control an intelligence agency like our NSA would like to achieve over even the remotest long-term threats to the nation's security. We are still on the eve of such a scientific/intelligence singularity, constrained by limits on funding and resources, limits of human bias, and limited ability to use all the data we are gathering effectively. But if those limitations can be overcome through advanced artificial intelligence and robotics, and if we do not destroy ourselves in the process (a big 'if', obviously), we will be in a position to undertake knowledge acquisition of mind-boggling scope and resolution, and we will have no reason not to.

"Any advanced civilization, even if it evolved in different directions than 'outward' (i.e., colonization), would still send its eyes and ears and roving brains throughout its stellar neighborhood and beyond, if only for the sake of its own security. Everywhere, those eyes and ears would settle in for the long duration, learning all that is learnable over the whole history of every star and moon and planet, about its geology and weather and organic chemicals and primitive flora and fauna (if any) – because who knows what will happen in a million or a billion years? Who knows where life will emerge from primordial muck? Who knows what tree-dwelling shrew might become a spacefaring, militaristic species down the long road, and thus be worth learning how to predict and control should that species ever pose a threat to its security?

"By some estimates, we are latecomers to the galactic party. There could be many civilizations or 'intelligences' with the capabilities described, preceding us by millions or billions of years. Thus, roving probes and CCTV cameras having many different origins, based on different kinds and levels of technology, could be literally everywhere. Some could be organic; some could be luminous; some could be embedded in the fabric of spacetime itself."

Eric Wargo's stimulating ideas complement those of Silvio Colombano and those of other scientists presented in this book. This is just what scientists expect when an exciting new field is opening up – multiple variant hypotheses based on a common set of newly available data.

Appendix 6

War of Words

An important part of the problem in discussing reports of anomalous activity, as Nick Pope, a former UK Ministry of Defence employee, responsible for investigating UFO reports, pointed out in his 15 October 2018 Guardian piece (Appendix 4), is terminology. For example, the National Atomic Testing Museum, Las Vegas's 2012 display linked the Height 611 remains with the terms 'UFO crash', 'Roswell incident' and 'Alien artifact'. Not likely to impress influential scientists like Paul Davies and Jim Al-Khalili.

But in science and technology, careful terminology is more than presentation – it's essential. So in this book I've used "high-temperature event" rather than the Museum's "UFO crash" for the Height 611 event because it more accurately describes this above ground event. We know it took place above the ground because of the near-spherical "solidified raindrop" nature, resembling volcanic lapilli, of some of the metal-rich droplets described by the Height 611 scientists (Chapter 15).

And, although Pope didn't mention it in his 2018 Guardian piece, another key technical term due for clarification is "the extraterrestrial hypothesis". Scientists use 'extraterrestrial' as an adjective. James McDonald used it thus in his conjecture "something in the nature of extraterrestrial devices engaged in something in nature of surveillance". The Condign author also used it as an adjective when he referred to the "extraterrestrial hypothesis of 'UFO' origins" and I've used its abbreviation ET as an adjective in this book's "ET probe theory". But UFOlogists often understand 'extraterrestrial hypothesis' as a pair of nouns to mean the notion that we're being visited by humanoid aliens (extraterrestrials) perhaps from the Zeta Reticuli system. The safe way, now, when discussing anomalous activity, is not to use 'extraterrestrial hypothesis' at all. 'ET probe theory' does the job perfectly well.

Of all the technical terms now needed, however, the most useful three, perhaps, are the neuroscientists' notion of hyperactive agency detection (HAD) (Chapter 3), Paul Davies's concept of auto-teleological super-systems (ATS), self-designed systems that grow, improve and adapt through their own intellectual creativity (Chapters 4 and 16) and Steven Dick's Intelligence Principle – to the extent that intelligence can be improved it will be improved (Chapter 4). Silvio Colombano's 2018 concepts of 'Evolvable Robotic Systems' and 'symbiosis of biology with machines' (Chapter 21) seem so close to Davies's 2011 ATS that it seems unnecessary to distinguish between them here.

With these three powerful technical terms, probe theorists can now go to war. HAD will be a key weapon but a defensive one only. Sceptical scientists laugh at the notion of abduction-bent space aliens visiting Earth. HAD theory gives them a short answer – they're right. Instead of coming from the Zeta Reticuli system, humanoid aliens likely come from UFO witnesses' own minds.

So Paul Davies' ATS and Steven Dick's Intelligence Principle can be the chief attack weapons to help probe theorists win fellow scientists' minds. They can work with the exotic Height 611 mesh to convince sceptics that a probe of extraterrestrial origin indeed disintegrated above the ground near Height 611 on 29 January 1986, just as Jean-Baptiste Biot's notion of exotic stones falling from the sky worked with the exotic remains of the 1803 L'Aigle (Normandy) meteorite to convince sceptics that stones of extraterrestrial origin had indeed fallen from the sky.

Science and General References

Akright, Robert L. (1979) 'Geology and Mineralogy of the Cerrillos Copper Deposit, Santa Fe County, New Mexico' *Robert L Akright, Occidental Minerals Corporation, 777 South Wadsworth Boulevard, Lakewood, Colorado, 80226.*

Al-Khalili, Jim (2017a) Aliens: The World's Leading Scientists on the Search for Extraterrestrial Life. Kindle Edition.

Al-Khalili, Jim (2017b) Part 1 - Aliens: Scientists Search for Extraterrestrial Life

Interview with journalist Linda Howe, 26 May 2017. Downloaded from www.earthfiles.com on 29 August 2017.

Al-Khalili, Jim (2017c) Part 2 - Aliens: Scientists Search for Extraterrestrial Life

Interview with journalist Linda Howe, 26 May 2017. Downloaded from www.earthfiles.com on 29 August 2017.

Anglada-Escudé et al. (2016) 'A terrestrial planet candidate in a temperate orbit around Proxima Centauri' *Nature vol 536, p 437-440, 2016.*

Antonison, M., Smith, W. and Myrabo, L (2012) The Apollo Lightcraft Project Published Online:17 Aug 2012 https://doi.org/10.2514/6.1988-4486

Avramenko, Rimili Fedorovitch (1991, 2012) 'On the observation of a UFO cover-up materials and the Tunguska meteorite' 1991 document posted on Anomolia website, https://translate.google.co.uk/translate?hl=en&sl=ru&u=http://aeninform.org/material/2753-o-nablyudenii-nlo-sokrytii-materialov-i-tungusskom-meteorite-doklad-

rfavramenko-na-2-k&prev=search, 25 March 2012, and retrieved by author 3 March 2016.

Baker, Robert M.L (1968) Statement by Dr Robert M.L. Baker, JR., at the Symposium on Unidentified Flying Objects held before the Committee on Science and Astronautics of the US House of Representatives, Ninetieth Congress, July 29

Barrett, Clark (1999) 'Human cognitive adaptations to predators and prey' *Doctoral dissertation, Santa Barbara: University of California.*

Barrett, Justin L (2000) 'Exploring the natural foundations of religion' *Trends in Cognitive Science, 4(1), pp. 29-34.*

Baure, J-F, David Clarke, Paul Fuller and Martin Shough (2008) 'Unusual Atmospheric Phenomena Observed Near Channel Islands, UK, 23 April 2007' *Journal of Scientific Exploration. Vol. 22, No. 3, p 291-308, 2008*

Baxter, Stephen (2013) Proxima. Kindle Edition

Baxter, Stephen (2014) Ultima. Kindle Edition

Bond, A, et al (1978) 'Project Daedalus – the Final Report on the BIS Starship Study' *Journal of the British Interplanetary Society vol 31* (JBIS Interstellar Studies Supplement, 1978)

Bond, Alan (2018) 'Alien Aircraft: Have they been observed on Earth? *Journal of the British Interplanetary Society vol 71 (6) p 225-232*

Bounias, Michel (1990) 'Biochemical Traumatology as a Potent Tool for Identifying Actual Stresses Elicited by Unidentified Sources: Evidence for Plant Metabolic Disorders in Correlation with a UFO Landing' *Journal of Scientific Exploration. Vol. 4, No. I p 1 - 1 8, 1990*

Boyer, Pascal (2001) Religion Explained: The Human Instincts That Fashion Gods, Spirits and Ancestors. William Heinemann Ltd, London

Butler, Samuel (1863) 'Darwin Among the Machines' The Press newspaper, Christchurch, New Zealand, 13 June 1863. Published under name 'Cellarius'.

Centre Nationale d'Etudes Spatiales – Groupe d'Etude des Phénomènes Aérospatiaux Non-Identifiés (CNES 1983a)

Toulouse, le 1 er mars 1983 ENQUETE 81 / 01 ANALYSE D'UNE TRACE ISSN : 0750-6694 NOTE TECHNIQUE No.16 p 1-66 Centre Nationale d'Etudes Spatiales – Groupe d'Etude des Phénomènes Aérospatiaux Non-Identifiés) (CNES 1983b) Toulouse, le 1 er mars 1983 ENQUETE 86 / 06 L'AMARANTE ISSN: 0750-6694 NOTE TECHNIQUE No.17 p 1-70

Choi, Charles Q (2011) 'Building blocks of DNA found in meteorites from space' https://www.space.com 8 October 2011

Clarke, A.C. (1956) Book Review [E. Ruppelt's Report on Unidentified Flying Objects] *Journal of the British Interplanetary Society vol 15 No. 5 1956 p 289-290*

Clarke, David and Andy Roberts (2003a) UFOs in History: The Foo Fighters – The RAF Experience (originally published in UFO Magazine (UK) January 2003) Downloaded from http://www.uk-ufo.org/condign/histfoo1.htm on 6 August 2010

Clarke, David and Andy Roberts (2003b) UFOs in History: The Foo Fighters – The RAF Experience (originally published in UFO Magazine (UK) January 2003) Downloaded from http://www.uk-ufo.org/condign/histfoo2.htm on 6 August 2010

Clarke, David and Andy Roberts (2003c) UFOs in History: The Foo Fighters – The RAF Experience (originally published in UFO Magazine (UK) January 2003) Downloaded from http://www.uk-ufo.org/condign/histfoo3.htm on 6 August 2010

Clarke, David and Andy Roberts (2003d) UFOs in History: The Foo Fighters – The RAF Experience (originally published in UFO Magazine (UK) January 2003) Downloaded from http://www.uk-ufo.org/condign/histfoo4.htm on 6 August 2010

Clemence, Gerald M., H.R. Crane, D.M. Dennison, W.O. Fenn, H.K.

Hartline, E.R. Hilgard, M. Kac, F.W. Reichelderfer, W.W. Rubey, C.D. Shane and O.G Villiard, Jr. (1969) Book Review of the Condon Report *Icarus 11, 403-443, 1969*

Colombano, S.P. (2018) 'New Assumptions to Guide SETI Research'. Paper presented at the SETI Decoding Alien Intelligence Workshop; 15-16 March 2018, Mountain View, California. Published 15 March 2018.

Condon, Edward U. and Gillmor, Edward (1968) 'Final report of the Scientific Study of Unidentified Flying Objects' Bantam Books, 1968. www.avia.it.com

Cornet, Bruce (2019) 'Unconventional Aerial Phenomena: In the Hudson and Wallkill River Valley of New York' Kindle Edition Sold by Amazon Media EU S.à r.l.

Cornet, Bruce and Scot L. Stride (2003) 'Solar System SETI Using Radio Telescope Arrays' Proceedings of SETICon03: a collection of papers submitted for The SETI League's 2003 Technical Symposium, published in 2003 by the American Radio Relay League.

Cox, Billy (2019) 'Elizondo's Call to Action.' Posted on http://devoid. blogs.heraldribune. com/author/cox/ on April 24 2019 Downloaded 25 April 2019

Crowe, Denis (1965) *'The Thing on the Beach.'* Sydney Daily Telegraph 21 July 1965

Cruttwell, Rev. Norman (1960a) A report on Papuan Unidentified Flying Objects. Self-published 45-page document reproduced in part in Gross (1999).

Davies, Paul (2011) The Eerie Silence, Penguin Books, London

Dick, Steven J. (2001) Life On Other Worlds, Cambridge University Press

Dick, Steven J. (2003) 'Cultural evolution, the postbiological universe and SETI' *International Journal of Astrobiology*, 2: 65-74

Dick, Steven J and Lupisella, Mark (2009) Cosmos and Culture. Edited by Steven J Dick and Mark Lupisella, NASA SP 2009-4802.

Dickeson, F and P (1959) The Moreland Sighting 1959. Document first published in NZSSR Group Newsletter in 1959. Later published as online article by UFOCUS NZ Research Network. Downloaded from http://www.ufocusnz.org.nz on 30 August 2011

Druffel, Ann (2003) Firestorm Dr James E. McDonald's Fight for UFO Science Wildflower Press, Columbus, NC

Dunér, David (2011) 'Astrocognition: Prolegomena to a Future Cognitive History of Exploration' In: Humans in Outer Space – Interdisciplinary Perspective, eds. Ulrike Landfester, Nina-Luisa Remuss, Ka-Awe Schrogl and Jean-Claude Worms, 117-140. Wien: Springer.

Faraday, Michael (1846) Experimental Researches in Electricity. Nineteenth Series *Phil. Trans. R. Soc. Lond. 1846,136, 1-20*

FBI (1991) Foreign Press Note FB FN 91-04 10 January 199 UFO Sightings No.4 Statements by Military and Government Officials. Downloaded from http://www.openminds.tv/wp-content/uploads/FBIS-doc-1991.jpg on 25 September 2017

Freitas, Robert A. (1980) 'A Self-Reproducing Interstellar Probe' *Journal of the British Interplanetary Society vol 33 p 251-264*

Gallagher, Paul (1993) 'Russian SDI proposal points to La Rouche' *EIR (Executive Inteligence Review) International Volume 20, No. 1, April 16 1993, p 26-29*

Gross, Loren E. (1997) The Fifth Horseman of the Apocalypse UFOS: A History, 1957: November 3rd – 5th Loren E Gross, Fremont CA

Gross, Loren E. (1999) The Fifth Horseman of the Apocalypse UFOS: A History, 1959: April-June Loren E Gross, Fremont CA

Gross, Loren E. (2003a) The Fifth Horseman of the Apocalypse UFOS:

A History, 1956 September-October Supplemental Notes Loren E Gross, Fremont CA

Gross, Loren E. (2003b) The Fifth Horseman of the Apocalypse UFOS: A History, 1957 October 1st_November 2nd Supplemental Notes Loren E. Gross, Fremont CA

Hall, Richard H. (Ed.) (1997) The UFO Evidence. The National Investigations Committee on Aerial Phenomena (NICAP) (Original Edition published by NICAP in 1964), Barnes and Noble Books, New York 1997

Harder, James A. (1968) Statement by Dr James A Harder at the Symposium on Unidentified Flying Objects held before the Committee on Science and Astronautics of the US House of Representatives, Ninetieth Congress, July 29

Hastings, Robert (2008) UFOs and Nukes Extraordinary Encounters at Nuclear Weapons Sites. AuthorHouse, Bloomington, Indiana

Hesemann, Michael (1998) UFOs: the Secret History Marlowe and Company, New York.

Hill, Paul R (1995) Unconventional Flying Objects, A Scientific Analysis. Hampton Roads Publishing Company, Inc.

Hynek, J. Allen (1968) Statement by Dr J Allen Hynek at the Symposium on Unidentified Flying Objects held before the Committee on Science and Astronautics of the US House of Representatives, Ninetieth Congress, July 29

Hynek, J. Allen (1969) Preliminary Proposal for USAF contract, 1969. Document prepared by Dr J.A Hynek, Scientific Consultant to the Air Force, for the attention of Colonel George Weinbrenner, Commander FTD, Wright-Patterson AFB, Ohio 45433. project1947.com Downloaded 7 July 2017

Hynek, J. Allen (1972) The UFO Experience, Abelard-Schuman, London

Hynek, J. Allen (1978) The Hynek UFO Report, Sphere Books Ltd, London

Jasek, Martin (2003) 'Giant UFO over the Yukon Gold Fields' Posted on http://www.ufobc.ca/yukon/indian-river-ufo/irufo-page 2 by Martin Jasek on 5 January 2003. Downloaded 17 February 2012.

Johnson, Rick, Close, Terry and McHugh, Ed (1998) Mineral Resource Appraisal of the Salmon National Forest, Idaho *US Geological Survey, Open-Fie Report 98-478, 1998.*

Kean, Leslie (Ed.) (2010) UFOs Generals, Pilots and Government Officials Go on the Record, Harmony Books New York Kindle Edition

Knuth, K.H., Powell, R.M. and Reall, P.A. (2019) 'Estimating Flight Characteristics of Anomalous Unidentified Aerial Vehicles' *Entropy*, 21, 939, 1-19

Kopperapu, Ravi and Jacob Haqq-Misra (2020) 'Unidentified Aerial Phenomena,' Better Known as UFOs, Deserve Scientific Investigation' *Scientific American, July 27, 2020*

Kuettner, J.P. et al (1970) 'UFO: An Appraisal of the Problem, A Statement by the UFO Subcommittee of the AIAA' *Aeronautics and Astronautics,* vol 8, No. 11. p 49

Kurzweil, Ray (2005) The Singularity is Near Kindle Edition.

Lambright, Christian (2011) X Descending eBook Published by X Desk Publishing ISBN: 978-0-9853546-0-2

Lambright, Christian (2011) X Descending Kindle Edition ASIN: B007LSDHQ8, *Amazon Media EU S.à r.l.*

Lebelson, Harry (1980) 'Death on the Range' *Omni*, January, p 132

Lebelson, Harry (1981) 'The Pine Bush Adventure' *Omni*, September, p 34-38

Lebelson, Harry (1980s) The Hidden Harry Lebelson Files. www.pinebushufo.com/lebelsonfiles.htm Downloaded from www.pinebushufo.com/lebelsonfiles.htm, 26 August 2011

Maccabee, Bruce (1993) 'Strong Magnetic Field Detected following a Sighting of an Unidentified Flying Object.' *Bulletin of the American Physical Society*, Vol 38, p 1041, 1993

Maccabee, Bruce (2014) The FBI-CIA-UFO Connection, Richard Dolan Press, Rochester, New York, 14619 Kindle Edition

Maccone, C, (2011) 'Interstellar radio links enhanced by exploiting the Sun as a Gravitational Lens' *Acta Astronautica,* 68, 76-84.

Marler, David (2013) Triangular UFOs: An Estimate of the Situation Richard Dolan Press, Rochester, New York, 14619

McDonald, James E. (1967a) 'UFOs: Extraterrestrial Probes?' *Aeronautics and Astronautics vol. 5, 1967 p 19-20*

McDonald, James E (1967b) 'UFOs: Greatest Scientific Problem of Our Times?' Paper presented before the 1967 Annual Meeting of the American Society of Newspaper Editors, Washington D.C. April 22 1967

McDonald, James E. (1968a) 'UFOs – An International Scientific Problem' *Paper presented on March 12 1968 at the Canadian Aeronautics and Space Institute Astronautics Symposium, Montreal, Canada*

McDonald, James E. (1968b) Statement by Dr James E. McDonald at the Symposium on Unidentified Flying Objects held before the Committee on Science and Astronautics of the US House of Representatives, Ninetieth Congress, July 29.

McDonald, James E. (1969a) Book Review of the Condon Report *Icarus 11, 443-447, 1969*

McDonald, James E. (1969b) "Science in Default: 22 Years of Inadequate UFO Investigations", *American Association for the Advancement of Science, 134th Meeting, December 27* http://dewoody.net/ufo/Science_in_Default.html Downloaded 2 April 2011

McDonald, James E. (1970) 'Meteorological Factors in Unidentified Radar Returns' Paper presented at the 14th Radar Meteorology

Conference, American Meteorological Society, Tucson, Arizona, 17-20 November 1970, published by American Meteorological Society, Boston, 1970, p 456-463

McDonald, James E. (1971) 'UFO Encounter I - Air Force Observations of an Unidentified Flying Object in the South-Central U.S., July 17, 1957' *Aeronautics and Astronautics*, July, p 66-70

Meessen, Auguste (2000) 'Analyse et implications physiques de deux photos de la vague Belge' *Inforespace*, No 100, 5-40 Downloaded from http://www.meessen.net/AMeessen/Photo1/ on 3 March 2011.

Meessen, Auguste (2012a) 'Pulsed EM Propulsion of Unconventional Flying Objects' *PIERS Proceedings, Moscow, Russia, August 19, p 508-512*

Meessen, Auguste. (2012b) 'Evidence of Very Strong Low Frequency Magnetic Fields' *PIERS Proceedings, Moscow, Russia, August 19, p 524-528*

Meessen, Auguste. (2012c) 'Production of EM Surface Waves by Superconducting Spheres: A New Type of Harmonic Oscillators' *PIERS Proceedings, Moscow, Russia, August 19, p 529-533*

Ministry of Defence (2006) UAP in the UK Air Defence Region: Executive Summary (Condign Report) Internet document downloaded on 13 September 2014 from http://webarchive.nationalarchives.gov.uk/20121026065214/http://www.mod.uk/

Minucci, M.A.S., P.G.P. Toro, A.C. Oliveira, A.G. Ramos, J.B. Chanes Jr., A.L. Pereira, H.T. Nagamatsu and L.N. Myrabo (2005) 'Laser-Supported Directed-Energy "Air Spike" in Hypersonic Flow' *Journal of Spacecraft and Rockets, Vol. 42, No. 1, January–February 2005*

Moravec, H. (1988) Mind Children: The Future of Robot and Human Intelligence. Cambridge, MA: Harvard University Press

Myrabo., L.N. (1978) 'Solar-powered global aerospace transportation' *13th International Electric Propulsion Conference, San Diego CA, 25-7 April, 1978* Downloaded on 14 December 2017 from: https://doi.

org/10.2514/6.1978-689

Myrabo, L.N. and Raizer, Yu. P (1994) 'Laser Induced Air Spike for Advanced Transatmospheric Vehicles' *AIAA paper 2451, June 1994*

Page, Thornton (1969) 'Review of the Condon Report' *American Journal Of Physics Vol 3. No 10, 1071-1072, October 1969*

Parnjakov, Valerii P (1997) 'Tectono-Sedimentary Complexes of the Dalnegorsk Ore Region', In: Late Paleozoic and Early Mesozoic Circum-Pacific Events: Biostratigraphy, Tectonic and Ore Deposits of Primoryie (Far East Russia) *Volume 272 of International Geological Correlation Programme: IGCP project, Editor Aymon Baud, page 183-189, Université de Lausanne, 1997*

Petit, J. P and B. Lebrun (1986). 'Shockwave cancellation in gas by Lorentz force action'. *Proc. 9th Meeting on Magnetohydrodynamic Electrical Power Generation, Tokyo, September 1986, p 1359-1366.*

Poher, Claude and Vallee, Jacques (1975) 'Basic Patterns in UFO Observations' *AIAA Paper 75-42, AIAA 13th Aerospace Sciences Meeting, Pasadena CA, January 20-22, 1975*

Poher, Claude (2005) 'Analysis of Radar and Air-Visual UFO Observations on 24 October 1968 at Minot AFB, North Dakota, USA' minotb52ufo.com/poher/pdf/POHER_Report.pdf. Downloaded from http://minotb52ufo.com/poher/pdf/ on 16 July 2019

Pope, Nick (2014) Encounter in Rendlesham Forest: The Inside Story of the World's Best-Documented UFO Incident. Kindle Edition Amazon.co.uk

Pope, Nick (2018) 'UFO Sightings may be falling but Congress is still paying attention' *The Guardian Monday 15 October 2018*

Pratt, Bob (1996) UFO Danger Zone. Terror and Death in Brazil – Where Next? Horus House Press Inc. Madison Wisconsin

Pratt, Bob and Luce, Cynthia (1999) 'Huge UFO Awes Military Intelligence Officers' (document downloaded from http://www.mufon.

com/bob_pratt/hollanda.html 27 February 2011)

Puthoff, Hal (2018) Address to the SSE/IRVA Conference, 8 June 2018. Document downloaded from http://paradigmresearchgroup.org/wordpress/blog/ on 14 June 2018

Rempel, Alexander (2011) 'Dalnegorsk - Height 611' Economic News Agency. Scientific report translated with Google Translate. Downloaded from http://aeninform.org 15 March 2012

Rullan, Antonio F. (2006) The Southwestern UFO Wave of 1957 *International UFO Reporter vol. 31 No.3*

Ruppelt, E.J. (1956) The Report on Unidentified Flying Objects Doubleday and Co, Garden City N.Y. Available online from gutenberg.org

Rutledge, Harley D. (1974) 'Light flashes in the sky' *Physics Today vol. 27 No. 9 p 11*

Rutledge, Harley D. (1981) Project Identification The First Scientific Field Study of UFO Phenomena Prentice-Hall, Inc. Englewoood Cliffs, New Jersey

Sagan, Carl (1968) Statement by Dr Carl Sagan at the Symposium on Unidentified Flying Objects held before the Committee on Science and Astronautics of the US House of Representatives, Ninetieth Congress, July 29

Sagan, Carl and Thornton Page (Ed.) (1974) UFO's – A Scientific Debate W. W. Norton & Company Inc. New York

Saunders, C.R. (1982) 'Schemo Property, Hazelton, British Columbia NTS 93M/4' Pharaoh Exploration Inc., 15 February 1982

Scott, Irena McCammon (2017) UFOs today – 70 years of Lies, Misinformation and Government Cover-Up Kindle Edition. Amazon.co.uk

Sparks, Brad (2016) Blue Book Unknowns Catalogue Version 1.26, Jan 31 2016 Downloaded from: http://www.cisu.org/wp-content/uploads/2017/01/Sparks-CATALOG-BB-Unknowns-1.27-

Dec-20-2016.pdf

Speigel, Lee (2012) 'Russian Roswell UFO Debris is Part of Area 51 Exhibit at National Atomic Testing Museum' *Huff Post Weird News August 1*

Spencer, Lee (2015) The Memphis UFO Incident February 2015 With NTSB and FAA Handling of Video, Audio and Photo Evidence to be released in 2016 CreateSpace Independent Publishing Platform, 16 Feb 2015 – 126 pages

Stanford, Ray (2003) 'Instrumented Sensing, Recording and Documentation of Transient Phenomena in UFO Events' Internet document downloaded from: http://www.nicap.org/madar/psi-sympap80-part8.htm on 9 December 2013

Stanford, Ray, Robert Weems and Martin Lockley (2004) 'A new Dinosaur Ichnotaxon from the Lower Cretaceous Patuxent Formation of Maryland and Virginia' *Ichnos, 11, 3-4, 2004, 251-259*

Stride, Scot (2001) 'An Instrument-based Method to Search for Extraterrestrial Interstellar Robotic Probes' *Journal of the British Interplanetary Society vol. 54 2001 p 2-13*

Sturrock, Peter. A. (1974) 'UFO Reports from AIAA Members' *Aeronautics and Astronautics Vol. 12, p 60-64*

Sturrock, Peter A. (1999) The UFO Enigma Warner Books, New York

Swords, Michael (2006) Ufology: What have we learned? *Journal of Scientific Exploration Vol. 20, No. 4 p 545-589*

Swords, Michael (2009) 'Did War Attract UFOs?' *The Big Study, Sunday, August 30, 2009* thebiggeststudy.blogspot.com

Swords, Michael (2010) 'From Bill to Gill to Hill: Part Three – Hill' *The Big Study, Friday, June 11, 2010* thebiggeststudy.blogspot.com

Swords, Michael (2014) 'SETIans & UFOs: A {pathetic} Snapshot of who we are.' *The Big Study, Sunday, March 23, 2014* thebiggeststudy.blogspot.com

Swords, Michael, Robert Powell, Clas Svahn, Vicente-Juan Ballester Olmos, Bill Chalker, Barry Greenwood, Richard Thieme, Jan Aldrich and Steve Purcell (2012). UFOs and Government Anomalist Books, San Antonio, Texas

Taylor, Herbert S. (2004) 'Satellite Objects and Cloud Cigars' *International UFO Reporter, Spring 2004, Volume 29 No 1, p 1-10*

Teodorani, Massimo (2006) 'An Alternative Method for the Scientific Search for Extraterrestrial Intelligent Life: The Local SETI' *J. Seckbach (ed.) Life As We Know It, Springer (USA) Vol. 10, p 487-503*

Teodorani, Massimo (2014) 'Instrumented Monitoring of Aerial Anomalies – A Scientific Approach to the Investigation on Anomalous Atmospheric Light Phenomena'. *CAIPAN 2014 Workshop –CNES-GEIPAN Paris, France, 8-9 July, 2014, p 1-43*

Tough, Allen (1998) 'Small Smart Interstellar Probes' *Journal of the British Interplanetary Society vol. 51 No. 5 p 167-174*

Vallee, Jacques (1990) Confrontations: A Scientist's Search for Alien Contact. Anomalist Books, San Antonio Texas Kindle Edition Amazon.co.uk

Vallee, Jacques (2012) Forbidden Science Volume Three On the Trail of Hidden Truths. Kindle Edition Amazon co.uk.

Vallee, Jacques (2019) Forbidden Science Volume Four Journals 1990-1999 The Spring Hill Chronicles. Documatica Research, LLC, California

Vallee, Jacques F and Eric Davis (2005) Incommensurability, Orthodoxy and the Physics of High Strangeness: A 6-layer Model for Anomalous Phenomena *Consciência 2*

Veigia, A.T. and J.G.C. Barros (1991) 'Genetic-Exploratory Model of Alluvial Gold of the Brazilian Amazon' *Gisements alluviaux d'or, La Paz, 1-5 Juin, 1991*

Velasco, Jean-Jacques, (1990) 'Report on the Analysis of Anomalous

Physical Traces: The 1981 Trans-en-Provence UFO Case'

Journal of Scientific Exploration Vol.4 No. I p 27-48, 1990

Wargo, Eric (2018) 'Welcome to the Noöverse: Big Data, Deep Anthropology and Von Neumann Probes' *EdgeScience No 33, March 2018/3 p 3-5*

Wendt, Alexander and Duvall, Raymond. (2008) 'Sovereignty and the UFO'. *Political Theory Vol. 36 No. 4 607-633*

Williamson, Tom (1977) Exploring Our Changing Climate Science Museum, London. Her Majesty's Stationery Office

Williamson, Tom (2012) 'Hendrick de Keyser, Nicholas Stone, Inigo Jones and the founding of the modern Portland Stone industry *Proceedings of the Dorset Natural History and Archaeological Society, vol. 133 33-36*

Williamson, Tom (2012) Inigo's Stones Inigo Jones, Royal Marbles and Imperial Power Troubador Publishing Ltd, Leicester, UK

Zubrin, Robert (2019) The Case for Space Kindle Edition. Amazon.co.uk

UFOlogy References
(may include erroneous data and interpretations)

Bowen, Charles (Ed.)(1969) The Humanoids: A Survey of Worldwide Reports of Landings of Unconventional Aerial Objects and Their Occupants Henry Regnery, Chicago

Collins, Andrew (1978) 'Jelly-like Entities at Machynlleth' *Flying Saucer Review*, Vol 24, No 4, p 14-16.

Crivellen, J.P. (1986) 'Enormous UFO detected visually and also by radar over Barcelona region of N.E. Spain on night of November 29/30 1985' *Flying Saucer Review, Vol 32, No 1, p 2-5*

Cruttwell, Rev. Norman E. (1960b) 'What happened in Papua in 1959?' *Flying Saucer Review, vol 6 No 6, p 3-7*

Crystall, Ellen (1991) Silent Invasion, Paragon Books, New York

DeLonge, Tom and Hartley, A.J. (2016) Sekret Machines Kindle Edition. Amazon

Dutton, T.R, (2011) UFOs in Reality AuthorHouse UK Ltd

Fuller, John. G. (1966) The Interrupted Journey Kindle Edition, 2015, Amazon.co.uk

Giese, Daniel Rebisso, Cynthia Luce and Bob Pratt (2001) 'Ufos Filmed Entering and Leaving Bay', downloaded Weds 2 March 2011 http://www.mufon.com/bob_pratt/colares.html).

Hall, Richard H. (2001) The UFO Evidence Volume II Scarecrow Press Inc. MD.

Howe, Linda (2010) Aerial Disc Beam Interacted with Nuclear Weapons Bunkers at Whiteman AFB. Downloaded from https://www.earthfiles.com on 1 December 2013

Howe, Linda (2013a) Part 1: 60 Feet from A Landed UFO. Downloaded from https://www.earthfiles.com on 25 October 2013

Howe, Linda (2013b) Part 2: Disc Light Searches and Bleaches Sand. Downloaded from https://www.earthfiles.com on 25 October 2013

'Kandinsky' (2010) 'The Colares 1977 Case' Internet Document published 18th August 2010 by the Above Top Secret Forum's 'Kandinsky.' Downloaded from abovetopsecret.com on 2 March 2011

Keatman, Martin and Collins, Andrew (1979) 'Physical Assault by Unidentified Objects at Livingston – Part 1 *Flying Saucer Review, Volume 25, No.6, p 4*

Keatman, Martin and Collins, Andrew (1980) 'Physical Assault by Unidentified Objects at Livingston – Part 2 *Flying Saucer Review, Volume 26, No.1, p 4*

Lorenzen, Coral (1973) 'Idaho "Mining UFOs"' *A.P.R.O Bulletin Vol 22, No. 2, Sept/October 1973.*

Lorenzen, Coral (1987a) 'UFO Show over Tucson' *A.P.R.O Bulletin Vol 33. No. 3 p 1-5*

Lorenzen, Coral (1987b) 'Canyon yields info on Tucson flyover' *A.P.R.O Bulletin Vol 33. No. 5 p 1-2*

Magor, John (1969) 'Canadian UFO Report' Republished in *Flying Saucer Review Special Issue Number 2, June 1969, p 30*

Malthaner, Hubert (1972) 'Mystery Flying Object Rolls Along a German Road' *Flying Saucer Review, Volume 18, No.4, p 15-17*

McGhee, Moira and Dickeson, Bryan. (1997) 'The Gosford Files' *Mufon UFO Journal, Number 345, January 1997, p 10-14*

Pratt, Bob (2005) *Operação Prato* document downloaded 22 July 2019 from The blackvault.com/documents/MUFON/Pratt/prato.pdf.))

Pratt, Bob and Cynthia Luce (1999}, Hollanda internet doc Hollanda 'Huge UFO awes Military Intelligence Officers' Bob Pratt files MUFON site, downloaded 27 February 2011 http://www.mufon.com/bob_pratt/hollanda.html

Vallee, Jacques, (1969) Passport to Magonia: From Folklore to Flying Saucers. Henry Regnery, Chicago

Index

Numbers in bold italics refer to pages with relevant illustrations

Agnew, Vice President Spiro, 38
Akins, Alvin, *25*, 26
Albuquerque, New Mexico, 145
Al-Khalili, Jim, 302, 303, 305, 321
American Association for the Advancement of Science (AAAS), 119, 120
American Institute of Aeronautics and Astronautics (AIAA), 16, 25, 33, 38, 39, 40, 41, 65, 114, 115, 119, 169, 172, 297, 305
anthropomorphism, 11, 32, 93, 234, 272
Area 51, Nevada, 9, 10. 15
Arnold, Hap, 72, 73
Arnold, Kenneth, 74
artificial life, 68, 234, 235, 291
atomic bombs, 72, 75, 77, 205, 304
Authentic Alien Artifact display, 9, *10*, 214
auto-teleological super-systems (ATSs), 68, 234
Avramenko, Rimili Fedorovich, 129, 130, 132, 142
B-52H Stratofortress bomber, 79, 80
B-52H radarscope photographs, 79, 80, *81*
Baía do Sol, Brazil, 97, *100*, *101*, 102, *104*, 107, 115, 138
Baker, Robert, 33, 130
Baker, Sarah, 256, *257*, *258*, *259*
Banks, Iain, 294
Barnard's Star, 239
Baxter, Stephen, 69, 133

Bellingeri, Carla, 62
Bellingeri, Mauro, 62
Bellingham, Massachusetts, *50*, 51
Benford, Gregory, 69
Bennewitz, Paul, 145, 146, 147, 148, 149, 150, 151, 152, 156, 160, 161, 163, 172, 264, 272, 283
Bentwaters RAF base, Suffolk, England, UK, 40, 154, 156, 157, 160
Benz, Allen, 271
Berliozov, V.V., 193, 194, 208
Bezos, Jeff, 304
Bigelow, Robert, 297, 298, 300, 316
Biot, Jean-Baptiste, 322
bismuth, 218, 300
Black Projects, 9, 152
Blue Book, Project, 18, 19, 21, 23, 31, 34, 37, 38, 46, 78, 79, 80, 133, 145, 150, 151, 296
Boianai, New Guinea, 24, 52, *53*, 55, 56, 57, 78, 132
Bor mining laboratory, Dalnegorsk, Russia, 195, 208
Bounias, Michel, 178
Bowen, Charles, 46, 47
Bowyer, Ray, *127*, 128
Boyer, Pascal, 47, 61
Brasil, Gabriel, 102, 103
Brink, E.G, 144
Brisbane Water, New South Wales, Australia, 267, 268
British Interplanetary Society (BIS), 70, 239, 255
Brownfield, John, *28*, 29
Bussard ramjets, 140
Bystryantsev, D.I, 200
calcium, 229, 291
Carajás Metallogenic Province, *90*, 107, 115, 256
carbon, 216, 226, 228, 229, 230, 233, 237, 290, 292, 293, 302, 305, 306
carbon nanotubes, 237, 293

Carson, Charles, *20*, 21, 163
Carvalho, Wellaide, 93, *94*, 95, 96, 99, 105, 107, 113, 203, 283
cassiterite, 107
cementite, 223
Center for UFO Studies (CUFOS), 114
cerium, 222, 223, 246, 267
Chamorro, Julio, 109
Chamorro, Teresa Lucia, 109
Chernobrov, Vadim, 240, 242
chupa chupa, 88
Clarke, Arthur C., 32, 77, 133
Clarke, David, 73, 128
Clinton, President Bill, 315
Clinton, Hillary, 315, 316
cobalt, 222, 229
cobalt-60, 94
Cockroft, G.N., 74
Coffey, Bernard, *50*
Colares, Brazil. 89, *91*, 93, 94, 95, 97, 98, 99, 100, 103, 105, 109, 111, 113, 203
Collierville, Tennessee, 275, 283, 287, 298, 304
Colombano, Silvio, 305, 306, 307, 320
Comet 67P/Churyumov-Gerasimenko, 66
Condign Report, 301, 302, 321
Condon, Edward, 35, 36, 38. 40, 64, 65, 83, 214
Condon Report, 35, 36, 37, 145, 190
Conte, Silvio, 42
copper, 107, 229, 250, 255
Corpus Christi, Texas, 132, 133, 170, 171, 172
Coryton, William, 73, 204
Costa, Flavio, *92*, 96, *97*
cristobalite, 232, 233, 292
Crowe, Denis, 262, *263*, 264, 265, 272
Cruttwell, Norman, 52, *53*, 54, 55
Crystall, Ellen, 164, *165*, 166, 167. 168, 202, 293, *Colour Plate 7*
CUFOS (Center for UFO Studies), 64, 114

Curiosity Rover, 66, 105, *106*, 163, 186, 187, 250, 255, 267, 289
Dalnegorsk, Russia, 9, 11, 12, 190, *192*, 196, 200, 202, 203, 208, 209, 210, 211, 220, 273
Dalnegorsk events of 28 November 1987, 196, *197*, *198*, *19*, 242, 273
Dalnegorsk Ore Region (DOR), *210*, *211*
Dalpolimetall mining laboratory, Dalnegorsk, Russia, 195, 208
da Silva, Airton Mendes, 135
Davies, Paul, 68, 71, 234, 235, 237, 291, 302, 321
Dechmont Woods, Livingston, Scotland, UK, *181*, *182*, *185*, *186*
DeLonge, Tom, 299, 300, 316
Derrida, Jacques, 13
Dick, Steven, 34, 68, 69, 70, 107. 115, 205, 234, 235, 237, 294
Dickeson, Bryan, 58, *59*
Dickeson, Phyllis, 58
Direct smelting, 220, 221, 267
Directed-Energy Air Spike (DEAS) effect, 172, *173*
do Espirito Santo, Manoel, 91, *92*
Doppler effect, 125, 308
Doty, Richard, 151
Drake, Frank, 29, *30*, 34, 36, 37, 64, 65, 297
Drummond, Malcolm, 182, 183
Duich, Paul, 131, *139*
Dutton, Roy, 65
Duvall, Raymond, 13, 36
Dvuzhilni, Valeri (Valery), 10, 189, 191, 193, 194, 195, 196, 203, 208, 213, 214, 216, 217, 221, 222, 229, 235, 240, 302
Eggers, Al, 19, 55, 83, 88
Eldorado dos Carajás, *90*
Elizondo, Luis, 298, 299, 300, 304, 305, 316
engins, 175, *176*
E. O. Paton Electric Welding Institute,

Kiev, Ukraine, 216
ETPs (Experimental Tactical Platforms), 67
Evennett, Ernest, 55, *56*, 57
Faraday, Michael, 117
Faraday effect, *112*, 117, 118, 119, *121*
Fed Ex seven, 275, 276, 283, 285, 286, 287, 288, 293, 297
Fermi Paradox, 13, 34, 65, 138
Field, Ethel, 60, 61
Flying Saucer Review, 46
Ford, President, 18
Foucault, Michel, 13
Freitas, Robert, 240, 241
Friedman, Stanton, 52, 204
Fuller, Buckminster, 237
fullerenes, 237, 293
galena, 220, 221, 269
garimpeiros, 108
GEIPAN (*Groupe d'Études et d'Informations sur les Phénomènes Aérospatiaux Non-identifiés*), formerly GEPAN, 79, 179
geochemical prospecting, 247, *248*, 249, 250
Gernikom, V., 215
Gerstein, Michael, 193
giant tube-like mother probes, Cover picture, 4, *112*, 113, 115, 124, 125, 126, 131, 132, 133, 138, *139*, 205, 255, 311, *312*
Gill, William, 24, 52, *53*, 54, 55, 56, 57, 58, 61, 78
Giwa, New Guinea, 55, *56*, 57
gold, 107, 108, 157, 229, 233, 237, 243, 244, 246, 247, 255, 256, 257, 258, 261, 268
Google Translate, 12, 130, 137
Gorshkov, E., 215
Gosford, New South Wales, Australia, 265, *266*, 267
green fireballs, 75, 76, 77, 78

grid search, 103, 155, 157, 158, *159*, 160, 161
Griggs, David, 73, 74
Gröschel. Gerhard, 243, 244, *245*
Guseman, Mr. and Mrs. Donald, *51*
Guyorobo, Dulcie, *53*, 54, 55, 57
hafnium carbide, 223, 246
Haines, Dick, 310
Halt, Charles, 154, 156, 157, 160, 298
Hambling, John, 249
Haqq-Misra, Jacob, 303
Harder, James, 117, 118, 119
Harris, Daniel, 111, *112*, 115, 118, 119, 146
Hartland, Rob, 294, 311, *312*, *313*
Hartmann, Bill, 76
Hauge, Bjørn Gitle, 67
Height 611, 11, 12, 13, *14*, 175, 191, 190, *192*, 193, 195, 196, 200, 201, 202, 203, 205, 206, 208, 209, 212, 214, 215, 216, 217, 219, 220, 221, 222, 226, 229, 234, 237, 240, 242, 243, 246, 289, 290, 291, 300, 301, 302, 303, 304, 306, 321
Hendry, Elaine, 114
Henri, Monsieur, 175, 176, 179, 180
Herman, Benjamin, 17
Hill. Betty, *48*, 49, 51, 52, 57, 78, 299
Hill, Barney, *48*, 49, 51, 52, 57, 61, 78, 91, 299
Hill, Paul, 168
Hippler, Robert, 37
Hogan, Dale, 157, *158*, *159,* 160, 161, 162
Hollanda, Uyrange, 89, 91, *93*, 96, 97, 98, 99, *101*, 102, 103, 108, 203, 255
Hovis, Dennis, 84
Howe, Linda, 158, 160, 251, 252, 303
humanoids, 11, 32, 46. 47, 61, 150, 152, 156, 234, 289, 297, 298, 300, 321
Humphrey, Vice President Hubert, 24
Hunt, Betsy, 17, 42, 43
Hynek, Allen, 19, 23, 30, 31, 32, 35. 36,

37, 39, 41, 43, 46, 47, 49, 52, 54, 61, 64, 65, 77, 79, 83, 114, 138, 234, 261, 297
hyperactive agent-detection (HAD), 47, 51, 57, 61, 91, *92*, 283, 322
'hypnotic regression', 47, 49
Icarus, 38, 64
ICBMs (intercontinental ballistic missiles) 79, 80, 129, 130, 205
ilmenite, 261
Indian Head, New Hampshire, 47, 48, 49, 51, 78, 205
Indian River valley, Yukon, Canada, 256, *257*
Institute of Atmospheric Physics, University of Arizona, 17, 43, 143, 144
Intelligence Principle, 68, 69, 70, 72, 75, 115, 205, 294, 322
interstellar medium, 117, 133, 134, 140, 198, 239, 290, 293, 306
iron, 221, 222, 223, 229
iron carbide, 223
IZMIRAN (Institute of Terrestrial Magnetism, Ionosphere and Radiowave Propagation of the Russian Academy of Sciences), 215, 219
James, Brian, *270*, 271, 272, 273
Jammer, Don, 132, 133
Jasek, Martin, 256, 258, 259, 260
Jastrow, Robert, 166
Johnson, President, 16, 23, 24
Jones, Frederick, *50*
K2 mission, 62
Kaliba, Waltraud, 242, 243, 244, 245
Kaser, R.M., 144
Kepler Space Telescope, 62, 305
Kholodninskoye lead-zinc sulphide deposit, Russia, 219, 220, 221, 246, 269
Kincumber monazite-processing plant, New South Wales, Australia, 261, 265
Kirtland Air Force Base, New Mexico, 75, 144, 145, 149, 150, 151, 156, 160, 163
Knapp, George, 11, 129, 130, 235, 302

Knittelfeld, Austria, 242, 243, 260
Kondakov, Vladimir, 193
Kopperapu, Ravi, 303
Korytko, V.M, 191
Kotov, N., *197*, 200
Krantz, Reinhold, 27
Krauss, Max, 247, *248*, 249, 273
Krichnina, Julia, 193, 202
Kudla, Peggy, *50*
Kulikov, Alexey, 233, 235, 237
L'Aigle (Normandy) meteorite of 1803, 322
Lambert, Lee, 27
Lambright, Chris, 146, 147, 150, 152, 156, 161, *171*, 172
Langenschemmern, Germany, 247, 249
lanthanum, 219, 223, 246, 267
LaPaz, Lincoln, 75, 76
Laser Induced Breakdown Spectroscopy (LIBS), 105, *106*
lead, 201, 217, 219, 220, 221, 241, 246, 250, 261, 269
lead isotope studies, 219, 220, 241, 246
Lebelson, Harry, 164, 165, 166
Lehmann, William, 151, 152, 160
LO (low observable), 66, 255
Lorentz force, 117, 161, 167, 284
Lorenzen, Coral, 171, 271
Lorenzen, Jim, 171
Los Alamos National Laboratory, Albuquerque, New Mexico, 75, 76, 77, 169
Los Cerrillos, New Mexico, 250, *251*, *252*, 254, 255, 273, 289, 291
Losh, Hazel, 24
Low, Robert, 37
Luce, Cynthia, 105
Lynn, Andrew, 276, 277, 279, 280, 281, 283, 286
Maccone, Claudio, 206
Machynlleth, Wales, UK, *60*
magnetic anomalies near Height 611,

212, *213*
magnetite, 213, 215
magnetohydrodynamics (MHD), **112**, 116. 117. 118, 120, ***121***, 122, 149, 178, 223, 254, 260, 284, 304
Makeev, A.A., 232, 233, 234, 235
Malcolm, Sue, 256, ***257***, ***258***, ***259***
Malthaner, Hubert, 248
manganese, 229
manganese oxides, 223, 246
Manzano Weapons Storage Area, Kirtland AFB, New Mexico, 145, 146, 156, 160, 264
Markina, T.J., 198, 202
Mattis, James, 298, 299
Maxwell, James Clerk, 117
McDonald, James, 16, ***17***, 20, 23, 24, 25, 26, ***28***, 29, 30, 31, 32, 33, 34, 35, 36, 37, 38, 40, 41, 42, 43, 46, 52, 54, 58, 61, 62, 64, 65, 70, 73, 74, 77, 83, 84, 88, 89, 117, 120, 122, 133, 143, 144, 151, 163, 169, 172, 189, 190, 283, 297, 305, 321
McDonald Conjecture, 40, 65, 74, 138
Meessen, Auguste, 116,120, ***121***, 123, 150, 164, 264, 284, 304
Menzel, Donald, 21, 46, 55, 56
Mercury Space Capsule, 96, 97, 99, 113, 116
mesh (сеточка) found near Height 611, 217, ***226-31***, 233, 235, 292, 303, 322
metal droplets found near Height 611, 213, 217, ***218***, 221, 222, 228
Miller, Jerry, 150, 151
Milner, Julia, 242
Milner, Yuri, 242
Minot Air Force Base, North Dakota, 79, 80, 156, 205
mischmetall, 267, 268
Moi, Stephen Gill, ***53***, 54
molybdenite, 269, 272
molybdenum, 219, 221, 239, 240, 241, 242, 246, 250, 255, 269, ***270***, 272, 290, 291, 292
molybdenum isotope studies, 241, 242
monazite, 107, 221, 261, 262, 263, 265, 267, 268
Montague, Buzz, ***270***, 271, 272, 273
Moreland, Eileen, 58, ***59***, 60, 61, 62
Moreland-type objects, 58, ***59***. ***60***, 69, 132, 180, 254, 272, 273, 291
mother probes, 65, 66, 69, 72, 112, 113, 115. 116, 124, 126, 130, 131, 132, 133, 138, 139, 142, 161, 205, 206, 239, 255
MTI (moving target indication) radar, 125, 126, 130, 131
MUFON (Mutual Ufo Network), 169, 284, 298, 300, 306
Musk, Elon, 304
Myrabo, Leik, 169, 170, 172
NACA (National Advisory Committee for Aeronautics) duct, ***137***
Nancy, France, 175, ***176***, 179, 180, 291
National Academy of Sciences, 16, 29, 35, 37, 40
National Atomic Testing Museum, Las Vegas, 9, ***14***, 91, 189, 222, 235, 289, 302, 303, 321
National Transportation Safety Board (NTSB), 285, 286, 287, 288, 298, 299
Neff, Wilbur, ***22***
neodymium, 222, 223, 246, 261, 267, 268
New Horizons spacecraft, 71
New Scientist, 39
Newton's Third Law, 117, 167
nickel, 196, 222, 290
Nicolai, Renato, 175, ***177***
Nikolaev, N.L., 196
Nova Cygni 1975, 85
Oberg, Jim, 201, 207
Odessa, Delaware, ***51***
Offutt Air Force Base, Omaha, Nebraska, 131, ***139***
Olenick, Alois, 62

Olkhovoy, Sergei, 191, 193
Operação Prato, 89, 102
Page, Thornton, 29, 34, 36, 37, 39
Palmer, Allan, *14*. 15, 235
Passport to Magonia, 46
Pelotas, Brazil, *131*, 134, 135, 137, 138, 163
Patterson, Patrick, 127
Peruvian Air Force, 109
Petit, Jean-Pierre, *112*, 116, 178, 241
Petit, Marco, 93
Piedmont, Missouri, 83, 84
Pine Bush, Orange County, New York State, 164, 165, 202, 293
plasma, 27, 52, 67, 80, 99, 105, 106, 114, 115, 116, 117, 118, 119, 120, 124, 129, 130, 144, 146, 147, 148, 150, 156, 161, 163, 167, 168, 170, 171, 172, 174, 202, 204, 209, 215, 216, 218, 220, 221, 241, 254, 260, 264, 283, 287, 297, 311, *313*
plate tectonic theories, 209, 211
Pluto, 71, 319
plutonium-239, 157, 162
Poher, Claude, 79, 80, *81*, 283
Pope, Nick, 300, 301, 314, 315, 321
Porres, Sergio, *131*, 134, *136*, 138
Portage County, Ohio, 19, 21, *22*, 23, 24, 34, 36, 46
postbiologicals, 34, 68, 69, 70, 72, 74, 75, 78, 142, 161, 205, 294
potassium, 219, 229
Powers, William, 23
praseodymium, 219, 222, 246, 261, 267, 268
Pratt, Bob, 94, 98, 99, 101, 102, 105
Project Daedalus, 70, 239, 240
Project Identification, 86
Project Starlight International (PSI), 111, 114, 119, 150, 170, 172
Proxima b (planet), 133
'pseudostar', 66, 84
Pucallpa, Peru, 108, 109, 247, 289

Pushkarev, Yuri, 219, 220, 228, 241, 242, 246
Puthoff, Hal, 300, 310
pyrrhotite, 213, 215
quartz, 108, 115, *228*, *229*, *230*, 232, 233
Quintanilla, Hector, 23, 201
Rand, Frank, 24
Rarata, Ananias, *53*, 54, 55, 57
Rayl, A.J.S., 155
Red Bluff, California, 19, *20*, 24, 34, 36, 46, 49, 78, 118, 132, 163
Redlands, California, 27, *28*, 35, 36, 46, 51, 52
Redlands object, *28*, 51
REEs (Rare Earth Elements), 201, 219, 221, 222, 223, 229, 261, 265
Reid, Harry, 296, 297, 298, 316
Rendlesham Forest, Suffolk, England, UK, 154
Ribamar, José, 102, 103, 138
Roberts, Andy, 73, 74
Roberts, Walter Orr, 38, 39
Robertson Panel, 29
Robinett, Jerry, *25*, 26
Rockefeller, Laurence, 190, 191, 235
Rosetta ESA probe (including Philae lander), 66, 255
Roswell, New Mexico, 9, 10, 189, 321
Rudnaya Pristan (Rudnaya Havens), Russia, 196, *199*, 200, 212, 219
Ruppelt, Edward, 76, 77, 79, 301
rutile, 261
Rutledge, Harley, 83, 84, 85, *86*, 88, 96, 105
Sagan, Carl, 29, 30, 34, 39, 49, 64, 234
Sage, James, 84, 85, 86, 96, 105
Salnikov, Vladimir, 209, 212, 214, 219, 228
Sanderson, Judson, *28*
Sandia National Laboratories, Albuquerque, New Mexico, 75, 166, 167

scandium nitride, 223, 246
Schmitt, Harrison, 150, 151, 152
Schuessler, John, 86
Science Museum, London, 15, 16
Scott, Stanley, *20*
Seff, Philip, *28*
Serebrov, Eugene, 191
SETI (Search for Extraterrestrial Intelligence) 29, 40, 65, 68, 206, 246, 305, 306, 307
Sharon, Massachusetts, *50*, 51, 52
Shere, Patrick, 144
Shough, Martin, 79, 128
silica, 232, 235, 236, 237, 289
silicon, 229, 232
silver, 107, 229, 250, 255
Simon, Benjamin, 49
Siqueira, Biamir, 102, 103, 138
Skavinsky, Victor, 212, *213*, 215
Smithsonian Institution, Washington, 10
sodium, 219, 229
Soviet Union 9, 10, 13, 129, 162, 190, 220
space aliens, 37, 38, 46, 52, 64, 65, 71, 91, 93, 289. 322
Spaur, Dale, *22*
Speigel, Lee, 11, 12
Spring Creek Mine, Idaho, 242, 269, *270*, 271, 273, 291
Sputnik 1, 142, 144
Sputnik 2, 142, 144
SSTs (supersonic transports), 41, 42, 43
Stanford, Kitty-bo, 111, 113. 114, **121**
Stanford, Ray, *111*, 113, 114, 115, 116, 119, 120, *121*, 123, 128, 132, 133, 150, 168, 170, *171*, 172, 255
Stellarium, 55, 196
Strand, Erling, 67
Stride, Scot, 65, 66, 67, 68, 69, 84, 39, 129, 144, 255, 280
Sturrock, Peter, 114, 190, 191, 235
Suenaga, Claudio Tsuyoshi, 105, 107

Swords, Michael, 21, 24, 30, 36, 73
Sydow, Earl, 142, *143*, 144
Symposium on Unidentified Flying Objects, 29
tantalum carbide, 223, 246
tantalum hafnium carbide, 223
Tarrasa, Spain, 124, 125, 126, 128, 130, 138
Tate, Marshall, 308
Taylor, Robert, *180*, *181*, *182*, 183, *184*, 187
Teodorani, Massimo, 67
The Humanoids, 46
The Hynek UFO Report, 79
The Independent, 154, 156, 157
The Sun, 154
The UFO Experience, 46, 49
thermonuclear warheads, 75, 77, 78, 79, 80, 156, 157, 205, 299
thorium, 261
tin, 107, 218, 268
titanium, 239, 261
Tomsk Polytechnical University (TPU), 12, 189, 191, 208, 218, 219, 221, 226, 232, 236
Tough, Allen, 65, 66, 249
Trans-en-Provence, France, 175, *177*, *178*
tridymite, 232
Trieb, Jürgen, 242, 243, 244, 245
Tulien, Tom, 79
tungsten, 219, 221, 223, 246, 250
UFO taboo, 12, 13, 15, 31, 65, 89, 189, 190, 209, 214, 266, 288, 303, 305
UFOlogists, 11, 37, 40, 47, 65, 76, 91, 92, 93, 103, 150, 156, 214, 215, 284, 289, 297, 300
UFOs, 9, 10, 11, 13, 18, 19, 21, 29, 31, 33, 34, 35, 37, 38, 39, 40, 41, 46, 64, 77, 94, 140, 152, 154, 169, 189, 190, 224, 297, 301, 303, 314, 315
United Nations, 16, 24, 107

University of Arizona, 17, 28, 43
University of Redlands, 27, 28, 30
uranium-235, 157
USS Nimitz, 296, 298, 300
U Thant, 24, 31
Vallée. Jacques, 47, 94, 95, 107, 317
van Dyke, Paul, 166, 167
Vaucluse Beach, New South Wales, Australia, 262, **263**, 265, 272, 273
Venus, 55, 56, 58, 132
von Neumann machines, 65, 69, 70, 72, 107, 202, 203, 206, 240, 246, 256, 260, 265, 268, 269, 272, 275, 289, 290, 317, 318
Vysotki, Vladimir (В.Высоцкий), 233, 235, 236, 237
Wargo, Eric, 303, 317, 318, 320
Warren, John, 169
Webb, Walter, 75, 77
Webb, Wells Allen, 118, 119, 122
Wells, Gregory, 89
Wells, H.G., 11
Wendt, Alexander, 13, 36
Westendorff, Haroldo, **131**, 134, 135, **136**, **137**, 138, 163
Whiteman Air Force Base, Missouri, 157, **158**, **159**, 160, 162, 204
Williamson, Tom, 15, 107, 267, 276
Wood's alloy, 218
World War II, 17, 72, 142, 204, 205
X Descending, 147, 171
xenotime, 261
Yassin, Catherine, 193
yellow glassy beads found near Height 611, 217, **232**
Zeta Reticuli star system, 49, 205, 321
zinc, 221, 229, 250
zircon, 261
zirconium, 261
Zubrin, Robert, 304, 307